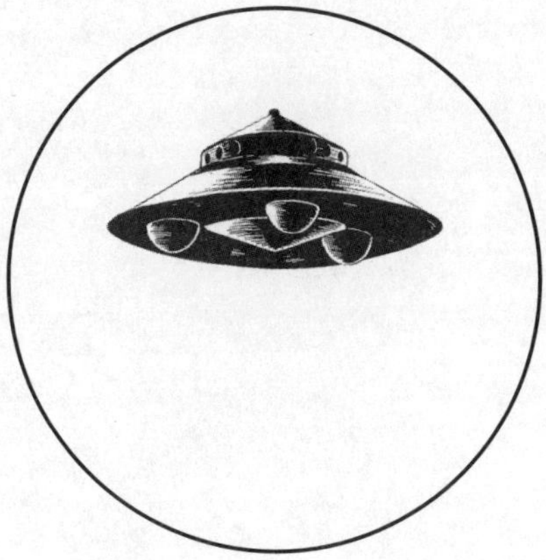

EXTRAORDINARY ENCOUNTERS

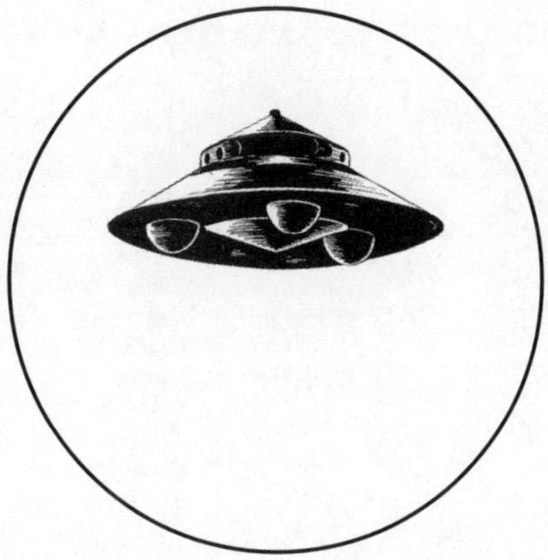

EXTRAORDINARY ENCOUNTERS

An Encyclopedia of Extraterrestrials and Otherworldly Beings

Jerome Clark

ABC-CLIO
Santa Barbara, California
Denver, Colorado
Oxford, England

Library of Congress Cataloging-in-Publication Data
Clark, Jerome.
Extraordinary encounters : an encyclopedia of extraterrestrials and otherworldly beings / Jerome Clark.
p. cm.
Includes bibliographical references and index.
ISBN 1-57607-249-5 (hardcover : alk. paper)—ISBN 1-57607-379-3 (e-book)
1. Human-alien encounters—Encyclopedias. I. Title.
BF2050.C57 2000
001.942'03—dc21 00-011350
CIP

06 05 04 03 02 01 00 10 9 8 7 6 5 4 3 2 1

ABC-CLIO, Inc.
130 Cremona Drive, P.O. Box 1911
Santa Barbara, California 93116-1911

This book is printed on acid-free paper ♾.
Manufactured in the United States of America.

To Dakota Dave Hull and John Sherman,
for the many years of friendship, laughs, and—always—good music

Contents

Introduction

Extraordinary encounters have been reported for as long as human beings have been around, and they are richly documented in the world's folklore and mythology. A full accounting of traditions of otherworldly belief would easily fill many fat volumes. This book, however, is not about traditions but about experiences, or perceived experiences, of otherworldly forces as claimed by a wide range of individuals over the past two centuries (with the rare look farther back if the occasion calls for it). In other words, it is about things that people, many of them living, say happened to them, things far outside mainstream notions about what it is possible to experience, but, at the same time, things that seem deeply real to at least the sincere experients (that is, those persons who have had the experiences). Not everyone, of course, is telling the truth, and when there is reason to be suspicious of the testimony, that consideration is noted.

Mostly, though, I let the stories tell themselves; I have left my own observations and conclusions in this introduction. Though much of the material is outlandish by any definition, I have made a conscious effort to relate it straightforwardly, and I hope readers will take it in the same spirit. No single person on this earth is guiltless of believing something that isn't so. As I wrote this book, I tried to keep in mind these wise words from scientist and author Henry H. Bauer: "Foolish ideas do not make a fool—if they did, we could all rightly be called fools."

Most of us believe in at least the hypothetical existence of other-than-human beings, whether we think of them as manifestations of the divine or as advanced extraterrestrials. At the same time most of us do not think of these beings as intelligences we are likely to encounter in quotidian reality. God and the angels are in heaven, spiritual entities who exist as objects of faith. Extraterrestrials, though not gods, "exist" in much the same way, as beings who science fiction writers and scientists such as the late Carl Sagan theorize may be out there somewhere in deep space, though so far away that no direct evidence supports the proposition. When devout individuals report feeling the "presence of God," they usually describe a subjective state that the nonbeliever does not feel compelled to take literally.

Of course we know there was a time when our ancestors were certain that otherworldly beings of all sorts walked the world. Gods communicated openly with humans. One could summon up their presence or encounter them spontaneously. Fairies and other supernatural entities haunted the landscape as things that existed not just in supernatural belief but in actual experience. We also know that our poor, benighted ancestors knew no better. Superstitious, fearful, deeply credulous, they mistook shadows and dreams for denizens of realms that had no reality beyond the one ignorance and foolishness assigned it.

Finally, most of us are aware, even if only dimly so, that a handful of people in our own enlightened time make more or less public claims that they have personally interacted with supernormal beings. Such persons are thoroughly marginalized, treated as eccentric and novel, as different from the rest of us; if they are not lying outright, we suspect, they are suffering from a mental disturbance of some kind. And we may well be right, at least in some cases. As for the rest, we could not be more mistaken.

As it happens, reports of human interaction with ostensible otherworldly beings continue pretty much unabated into the present. They are far more common than one would think. The proof is as close as an Internet search, through which the inquirer will quickly learn that material on the subject exists in staggering quantity. A considerable portion of it is about channeling (in which an individual is the passive recipient of messages from the otherworld, usually speaking in the voice of an intelligence from elsewhere) from a wide assortment of entities: nebulous energy sources, soul clusters, extraterrestrials, ascended masters, interdimensional beings, discarnate Atlanteans and Lemurians, nature spirits, even whales and dolphins. Besides these purely psychic connections with the otherworld, there are many who report direct physical meetings with beings from outer space, other dimensions, the hollow earth, and other fantastic places. Not all of these ideas are new, of course. The hollow earth and its inhabitants were a popular fringe subject in nineteenth-century America, and in the latter half of that century, spiritualist mediums sometimes communicated with Martians or even experienced out-of-body journeys to the red planet. In 1896 and 1897, during what today would be called a nationwide wave of unidentified flying object (UFO) sightings, American newspapers printed accounts of landings of strange craft occupied by nonhuman crews of giants, dwarfs, or monsters presumed to be visiting extraterrestrials.

But in the UFO age—that is, the period from 1947 to the present, when reports of anomalous aerial phenomena became widely known and their implications much discussed—a small army of "contactees," recounting physical or psychic meetings with angelic space people, has marched onto the world stage to preach a new cosmic gospel. In a secular context, UFO witnesses with no discernible occult orientation or metaphysical agenda have told fantastic tales of close encounters with incommunicative or taciturn humanoids. Some witnesses even relate, under hypnosis or through conscious "recall," traumatic episodes in which humanoids took them against their will into apparent spacecraft. The early 1970s, the period when most observers date the beginning of the New Age movement, saw a boom in channeling—again nothing new (spirits have spoken through humans forever) but jarring and shocking to rationalists and materialists. The same decade spawned such popular occult fads as the Bermuda Triangle and ancient astronauts (prehistoric or early extraterrestrial visitors), based on the notion of otherworldly influences—benign, malevolent, or indifferent—on human life.

As cable television became ubiquitous, television documentaries or pseudodocumentaries (some, such as a notorious Fox Network broadcast purporting to show an autopsy performed on a dead extraterrestrial, were thinly concealed hoaxes) served to fill programming needs and proved to be among cable's most popular offerings. Books alleging real-life encounters with aliens, such as Whitley Strieber's *Communion: A True Story* (1987), fueled interest and speculation. In the 1990s Pulitzer Prize–winning Harvard University psychiatrist John E. Mack, who had hypnotized a number of persons who thought they may have encountered UFO beings, championed the idea—which not surprisingly generated furious controversy and even a failed effort to have him removed from his job—that well-intentioned extradimensional intelligences are helping an unprepared humanity to enter a new age of spiritual wisdom and ecological stewardship. Mack, along with other prominent investigators of the abduction phenomenon such as Budd Hopkins and David M. Jacobs, pointed to the results of a 1992 Roper poll as evidence that as many as 3.7 million Americans have been abducted—a conclusion many critics, including some who are open-minded about or even sympathetic to the abduction phenomenon, would dispute. Still, there seemed no doubt, based on the experiences of investigators who have found themselves inundated with reports, that thousands of otherwise seemingly normal individuals believe themselves to be abductees.

The abduction phenomenon is undoubtedly the most recent manifestation of the otherworldly-beings tradition, but older beliefs and experiences, though eclipsed, continue. Even into the 1990s, encounters with fairies—which extraterrestrial humanoids were supposed to have supplanted in the imaginations of the superstitious and impressionable, according to any number of skeptical commentators—were noted on occasion. At least one recent book from a reputable publisher—Janet Bord's *Fairies: Real Encounters with Little People* (1997)—argued that such things are a genuine aspect of a universe "so complex that we cannot begin to understand it." The Blessed Virgin Mary appeared, as usual, all over the world, as did other sorts of divine entities.

The world, of course, goes on with its business as if none of this were true, taking serious (as opposed to tabloid) note only when belief in otherworldly beings goes horrendously wrong and thirty-nine cult members commit suicide while awaiting the arrival of a spaceship following a comet. The March 1997 mass death in San Diego of the faithful of Heaven's Gate (a contactee-oriented group that, in various incarnations, had existed since the early 1970s) sparked big headlines even in such august media as the *New York Times* and the *Washington Post*. In the wake of the tragedy came all the predictable lamentations about alienation and irrationality in a world that more and more seems to have lost its bearings. But the San Diego incident, although hardly unprecedented (history records numerous episodes of group suicides committed in the name of otherworldly powers), was anomalous in one important sense: few who hold such extraordinary beliefs, including the conviction that they personally interact with beings from other realms, harm themselves or others. In fact, most incorporate their experiences into lives so seemingly ordinary that their neighbors, unless told directly (which they usually are not), suspect nothing.

In the late 1970s, when I lived in a North Shore suburb of Chicago, I met a likable, generous-hearted family man named Keith Macdonald. Macdonald recounted a UFO sighting (also witnessed by his family) after which he felt that something had taken place that he could not consciously recall. Under hypnosis, he described what would later be judged a rather ordinary abduction experience: gray-skinned beings took him into the UFO and subjected him to a physical examination against his wishes. The experience, if that is what it was, frightened him severely. For a time I lost touch with Keith. When I next saw him, he told me he had been hearing mental voices and channeling messages from a planet called Landa, populated by wise, spiritually committed beings who looked like Greek gods and goddesses. Keith had learned that he was originally from that planet but had gone through many earthly incarnations so that he could lead the Earth as it entered a period of turmoil and destruction before the ships from Landa arrived to save the elect. Over the years I monitored Keith's emerging beliefs and sat in on a few—to me unimpressive—channeling sessions during which the all-wise David, his father on Landa, spoke on a level of verbal and intellectual sophistication that exactly matched Keith's.

Though I never for a moment believed in the literal reality of "those of Landa," as they called themselves in their characteristically stilted syntax, I was struck by a number of things. One was the almost staggering complexity of the cosmos Keith had conjured up in his imagination—the only place that I could believe such a cosmos existed, with its many worlds, peoples, religions, politics, enmities, and alliances. None of it, I should add, was anything somebody could not have made up, consciously or unconsciously. But all of it would have done credit to a gifted writer of science fiction. Though he possessed a keen native intelligence, Keith was neither a writer nor a reader. He did, however, have some previously existing interest—not profound or particularly well informed, in my observation—in UFOs, the paranormal, and the occult. As I listened to him over many hours, I began to feel as if somehow in his waking life Keith had tapped into the creative potential most of us experience in our dreams. As we doze off to sleep and dream, images begin to well up out of the unconscious; in no more than a moment we may find ourselves inundated with psychic materials sufficient to fill a fat Victorian novel. When our eyes open in the morning, all of that, alas, is gone. Keith had the capacity, it seemed to me, not only to live inside his dreams but to keep them stable and evolving.

Only once, when asked outright, did I acknowledge my skepticism. The confession was moot because Keith had inferred as much from my noncommittal responses to his typically excited revelations about the latest from the Landanians. He had no doubt—well, maybe 98 percent of the time he had no doubt—that he was in the middle of something real in the most fundamental sense of the word. He also understood that he had no proof that would satisfy those who, like me, found the Landanians' word insufficient. Therefore, he continually implored the Landanians to provide him that proof, and in turn they regaled him with a series of prophecies, often about explosive world events (bloody uprisings, devastating earthquakes), none of which came true; then, as if to add insult to injury, their rationalizations for the failure of the prophecies to be fulfilled bordered on, and sometimes surpassed, the comical. The prophecies and promises continued in a steady stream until Keith's premature death in 1999, and his closest friend told me that even at the end, Keith's faith had not faltered.

Perhaps the most amazing aspect was Keith's manifest sanity, which he never lost through the many ups and downs of his interactions with the Landanians (not to mention the literally crippling health problems he suffered at the same time). He worked—as a garage mechanic in a Waukegan, Illinois, car dealership—until he was physically incapable of doing so any longer. He was a good husband to his wife, a good father to his two boys, and a good friend to those who were lucky enough to claim him as a friend in turn. His children, in their teens at the initiation of Keith's adventures with Landa, and his wife vividly recalled the original UFO sighting they too had experienced and Keith's conviction that, after they had gone to bed and he had continued watching the object, something had happened. Still, they did not believe much in Landa, and his older son told me once of his certainty that his father's communications were psychological in origin. Yet they loved him, and only those very close to him had any idea that at any given moment a good portion of Keith's attention was focused on a world far, far away from the small suburban town where he spent much of his adult life.

In 1985, I flew in a private plane with Keith and two others (both, incidentally, convinced of the literal truth of Keith's messages) to the Rocky Mountain Conference on UFO Investigation, held every summer on the campus of the University of Wyoming in Laramie. The title is something of a misnomer; only a relative few who attend can be called "investigators." The emphasis is on experience not just with UFOs but with the space people who fly them. The bulk of the attendees—the number ranges from a few dozen to as many as two hundred from year to year—are in regular contact with benevolent extraterrestrials. The aliens communicate through channeling, automatic writing (in which information is dictated to an individual from allegedly unearthly beings), dreams, visions, or voices in the head, or they are perceived as if physical entities. (I use this last phrase deliberately; on close questioning, the individuals involved usually turn out to have a fairly elastic definition of the infinitive "to see" in all its permutations.) Few of the contactees assembled in Laramie matched the stereotype of the flamboyant charlatan or nut case. A few—such as a young Japanese woman whom space friends had guided to the United States in pursuit of her mission for them—had traveled some distance. Except for the small detail of their associations with extraterrestrials, most were decent, ordinary local folk. The majority were from the small towns, ranches, and farms of the Great Plains, the sort of people to whom the phrase "salt of the earth" is often applied.

Among his own at last, Keith could not have been happier. If he noticed that no one else spoke of Landa and its impossible-to-overlook plans for the Earth's future, or that every other contactee had his or her special space friends, all with their own individual hard-to-overlook plans for the Earth's future, he never said a word about it to me.

Of course, nothing is as simple as we would like it to be, and as I look back on the episode, I realize that I will never know *why* "those of Landa" called on Keith. Not that I had any difficulty understanding who they were. However tangled some of the details, there was no mistaking their underlying banality or their all-too-apparent shallow earthiness, with their Greek togas, pretentiously fractured English, and (yes) Roman Catholic faith. They themselves were not that interesting; what made them worthy of attention and reflection was this curious paradox: to the man who had (unwittingly) created them, they had a nearly certain independent reality; to virtually any independent observer, there could be no question of who had brought them (for whatever reason) into the world and to whom they owed what passed for an existence.

Yet Keith was not crazy. Nor, according to psychological surveys of other space communicants who attend the Laramie conferences, are his fellows. The evidence from this and other psychological inventories tells us that we can be mentally well and yet hold beliefs—and, more dramatically, have vivid experiences—that are far outside the mainstream, far outside our conventional understanding of the possible. In a book-length survey of out-of-ordinary perceptions, three well-regarded psychologists observe, "Notwithstanding the presence of anomalous experiences in case studies of disturbed individuals, surveys of nonclinical samples have found little relationship between these experiences and psychopathology" (Cardena, Lynn, and Krippner, 2000, 4). The authors stress that psychotherapists must understand the difference if they are to treat their clients effectively. Psychological research into extraordinary encounters of the sort with which this book is concerned is in its infancy.

Still, to anyone who looks carefully at the testimony regarding otherworldly contacts, it becomes apparent that such phenomena do not arise from a single cause. There is, for example, little in common between the average channeler and the average witness to a close encounter of the third kind (a UFO sighting in which, according to a classification system defined by the late astronomer and ufologist J. Allen Hynek, "the presence of animated creatures is reported" [1972, 138]). Typically, channelers have had a long history of occult interests before they begin communicating with supernatural entities holding forth on familiar metaphysical doctrines. Close-encounter witnesses, on the other hand, fit the profile of witnesses to less exotic UFO sightings; in other words, they are pretty much indistinguishable from their fellow citizens.

Consequently, channelers look more like candidates for subjective experience, and indeed to every indication channeling is just that. It is not veridical (that is, independently witnessed or otherwise shown not to be a subjective experience); no channeling entity can prove its existence, and the information provided through the channeling process is susceptible to neither verification nor falsification. The "authority" of the channeling entity rests solely on its self-identification. If you believe he, she, or it is a discarnate Atlantean, space alien, or ascended master, you will believe what he, she, or it has to say. If you choose not to believe any of that, the channeling entity will prove helpless to get you to change your mind. Experiences such as close encounters, conversely, may be veridical in the sense that on occasion they involve multiple—or, more rarely, independent—observers. In the case of multiply witnessed close encounters, subjective explanations are applied only with difficulty. An investigator in search of an explanation has limited choices, usually three: (1) the claimants made up the story; (2) they naively misperceived what were in fact conventional stimuli; or (3) they underwent an extraordinary experience that defies current understanding.

Between the extremes is a broad range of nonexperiential material, a modern folklore in which the world and the cosmos are reinvented on the basis of believed-in but undocumented (and often, to those who care about such things, certifiably false) allegations. Most persons who circulate such stuff are sincere, but some of those who feed the stuff to them are not. Hoaxers provide documents, such as the supposed diary attesting to Adm. Richard E. Byrd's voyage into the hollow earth through a hole at the North Pole, that believers cite to prove their cases. Most observers believe James Churchward's famous (or notorious) books on the alleged lost continent of Mu are literary hoaxes—Churchward was never able to produce the ancient documents on which he asserted he had based his work—but earnest occultists and New Agers cite his books as overwhelming evidence that Mu (more often called Lemuria) was a real place. Of course, embellishments grow on top of embellishments, and every legend of a place, a world, or a realm that is home to otherworldly beings evolves and has its own rich history. Atlantis, for example, began as an advanced civilization for its time, but by our time its people had come to be seen as advanced even beyond us, the creators of fantastic technologies and even the recipient of knowledge from extraterrestrial sources. The hollow earth of John Cleves Symmes (1779–1829) is not the hollow earth of Walter Siegmeister (a.k.a. Raymond W. Bernard, 1901–1965), any more than the imagination of one century is the imagination of the century that follows it. Flying saucers were not part of Symmes's world; consequently, they did not exist in his hollow earth. By the time Siegmeister wrote *The Hollow Earth* (1964), no alternative-reality book could lack flying saucers.

It is entirely likely that nothing in the book you are about to read will tell you anything about *actual* extraordinary encounters and otherworldly beings. If such exist, however, it is not beyond the range of possibility that somewhere amid the noise of folklore, belief, superstition, credulity, out-of-control thinking, and out-of-ordinary perception a signal may be sounding. If so, it is a faint one, indeed. The world has always been overrun with otherworldly experiences, some of which certainly appear to resist glib accounting; yet so far it has proved exasperatingly tricky to establish that otherworldly experiences are also otherworldly events. The otherworld, perhaps, can happen to any of us at any time, but we may not live in it—at least if we know what's good for us—in the way that we live enclosed within the four walls of the physical structure in which we read these words. It is not wise to pass through a world of physical laws while distracted by all-encompassing dreams. Even so, there is still a nobility to dreaming. There is also an undying appeal to the sort of romantic impatience that imagines new worlds bigger and more wondrous than our own, then brings these worlds and their marvelous inhabitants into our own. If extraordinary encounters are occurring only with otherwise hidden sides of ourselves, they are still—or surely all the more so—worth having.

—*Jerome Clark*

References

Cardena, Etzel, Steven Jay Lynn, and Stanley Krippner, eds., 2000. *Varieties of Anomalous Experience: Examining the Scientific Evidence.* Washington, DC: American Psychological Association.

Hynek, J. Allen, 1972. *The UFO Experience: A Scientific Inquiry,* p.138. Chicago: Henry Regnery Company.

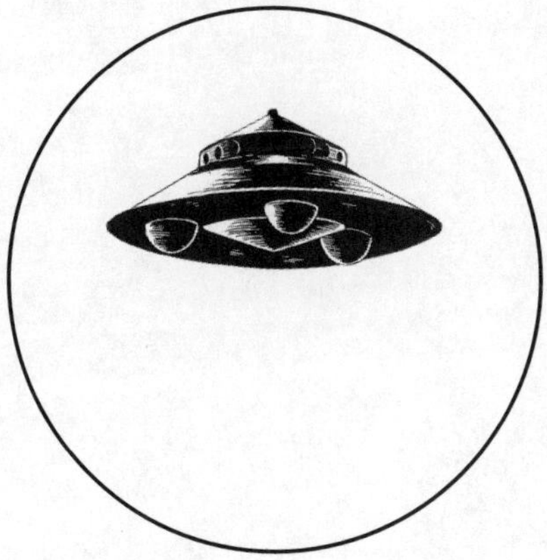

EXTRAORDINARY ENCOUNTERS

A

A

"A" is the pseudonym Ann Grevler (a writer who uses the pen name "Anchor") gives the Venusian whom she allegedly encountered while driving through South Africa's Eastern Transvaal on an unspecified day in the 1950s. Grevler, a flying-saucer enthusiast sympathetic to the contactee movement (contactees are individuals who claim to be in regular communication with kindly, advanced extraterrestrials), met A when her car inexplicably stopped on a rural highway. As she was looking under the hood, she became aware of a buzzing sound in her ears and looked up to see a smiling spaceman standing not far away. Then a spaceship flew toward her and landed, and she and A stepped into it. With A and another spaceman, B, Grevler flew into space. They approached what Grevler describes as "a positively huge Mother Ship," which tinier ships, similar to the one they were aboard, were entering.

Once inside the mother ship, Grevler and her friends went to "the Temple, visited by returning crews to thank the Creator for a safe voyage." Subsequently, either in the mother ship or in the smaller scout craft (her account is vague on this detail), she visited Venus and saw beautiful buildings and a kind of university. At the latter, students were taught universal knowledge and trained in extrasensory perception. They also learned "Cosmic Language—which is expressed simply by symbols of various forms and colors, so that meanings are the same in any language" (Anchor, 1958).

Grevler had other space adventures. One was a visit to a depopulated, destroyed planet, the dreary result of science gone amok.

See Also: Contactees

Further Reading

Anchor [pseud. of Ann Grevler], 1958. *Transvaal Episode: A UFO Lands in Africa.* Corpus Christi, TX: Essene Press.

Abductions by UFOs

Since the mid-1960s a number of individuals around the world have reported encounters in which humanoid beings took them against their will—usually from their homes or vehicles—into apparent spacecraft and subjected them to medical and other procedures. As often as not, witnesses spoke of experiencing amnesia, aware at first only of unexplained "missing time" (a much-used phrase that has become almost synonymous with abduction) consisting of a few minutes to a few hours. Later, "memory" would return, sometimes spontaneously, sometimes in dreams, and often (and most controversially) through hypnotic regression.

In the first case to come to the attention of ufologists, a Portsmouth, New Hampshire, couple, Barney and Betty Hill, experienced a close encounter with a UFO on the night of September 19–20 while traveling through the White Mountains. At one point, Barney Hill stopped the car and stepped out with a pair of binoculars; through them he saw humanlike figures inside the craft. One was staring directly at him. Terrified, the couple fled, all the while hearing beeping or buzzing sounds. Once back home, the Hills eventually realized that at least two hours seemed missing from their conscious recall. In November Betty had a series of unusually vivid dreams in which beings forced her and her husband into a UFO. She and Barney were separated, and Betty underwent a medical examination with a gray-skinned humanoid, whom she understood to be the leader. In January they sought out Boston psychiatrist Benjamin Simon in an effort to deal with the continuing anxiety they felt about the incident. Dr. Simon had them hypnotized, and under hypnosis they separately recounted an abduction episode. Subsequently, the story appeared in a Boston newspaper, and soon afterward journalist John G. Fuller wrote a best-selling book, *The Interrupted Journey*, on the case.

A generally similar incident took place in Ashland, Nebraska, in the early morning hours of December 3, 1967, when police officer Herbert Schirmer saw a hovering UFO a short distance from him. He originally believed that the sighting had lasted no more than ten minutes, but when he later realized that a half hour had passed, he got nervous, experienced sleeplessness, and heard a buzzing sound inside his head. Later under hypnosis Schirmer related an onboard experience with short, gray-skinned humanoids with catlike eyes.

During a wave of UFO sightings in October 1973, two Pascagoula, Mississippi, fishermen claimed that robotlike entities had floated them into a UFO. The story received enormous publicity, as did an even more spectacular incident in November 1975, when a forestry worker from Snowflake, Arizona, disappeared after six colleagues saw a beam of light from a UFO hit him and knock him to the ground. Travis Walton returned five days later with fragmentary memories of seeing two kinds of UFO beings, little gray men and humanlike (but not human) entities. A few other stories, now being called "abductions" as opposed to "kidnappings," saw print in the UFO literature but were little noticed elsewhere. The first book on the larger phenomenon of UFO abductions (as opposed to a single case, such as the Hills's), Jim and Coral Lorenzen's book *Abducted!* was published in 1977.

From the Hill incident on, critics focused on the use of hypnosis to elicit "recall," pointing out that confabulation under hypnosis is a well-documented psychological phenomenon, most dramatically manifesting in "memories" of past lives. As early as 1977 three California investigators attempted to demonstrate that volunteers under hypnosis, instructed to imagine UFO abductions, told stories indistinguishable from those related by "real" abductees. Other investigators and observers disputed these conclusions, pointing to methodological and logical problems in the experiment, and subsequent efforts by other researchers to replicate it failed. One later study indicated that nearly one-third of abductees consciously remembered their experiences; their testimony, folklorist Thomas E. Bullard concluded, was indistinguishable from corresponding accounts emerging under hypnotic regression. Still, hypnosis and its vagaries would play a large and continuing role in the controversy surrounding the abduction phenomenon.

In the late 1970s Budd Hopkins, a New York City artist and sculptor, working with psychologist and hypnotist Aphrodite Clamar, began to investigate the abduction reports. Through Hopkins's work new dimensions of the phenomenon emerged, including not just little gray humanoids that would come to dominate abduction reports but also experiences that began in childhood and recurred

Betty and Barney Hill, who believed they were abducted and taken aboard a UFO, New Hampshire, September 1961 (Fortean Picture Library)

throughout abductees' lifetimes. Some bore scars, the causes of which were mysterious until hypnosis revealed them to have been the result of alien medical procedures. A number claimed that their abductors had placed implants, usually through the nose or ear, inside their bodies. Hopkins and his colleagues took their cases to mental health professionals, whose tests of abductees suggested that they were psychologically normal.

In his much-read book *Missing Time* (1981) Hopkins argued for a literal interpretation of abduction stories. In other words, he held that extraterrestrials were literally taking human beings and doing things to them without their consent. Other ufologists disagreed. Ufologist Alvin H. Lawson, who had overseen the earlier "imaginary-abduction" experiment, offered his own exotic hypothesis that abductees were suffering imaginary experiences in which they relived the "trauma" associated with their births. More modestly, others proposed more conventional psychological explanations, such as hallucinations and confabulation. Few observers believed that conscious hoaxing played much of a role in abduction-reporting. Unlike contactees, abductees seldom had any background in occultism or esoteric interests, and hardly any sought profit or publicity. To every indication they believed that they had undergone frightening, bizarre experiences. Some psychological studies found that abductees often evinced all the symptoms of post-traumatic stress disorder of the sort ordinarily associated with victims of crime, personal assault, or other threatening terrors.

In 1987 Thomas E. Bullard, author of an Indiana University Ph.D. dissertation on the relationship of UFOs to folklore, released a two-volume study of all abduction accounts then known, some three hundred. Through a searching examination of the narratives, Bullard concluded that a real phenomenon of strikingly consistent features existed, that "abductions" were not simply an assortment of random fantasies. He noted patterns that had escaped even the most attentive investigators, including "doorway amnesia"—the curious failure of abductees to remember the moment of entry or departure from the UFO. Besides establishing the uniform nature of hypnotic and non-hypnotic testimony, Bullard determined that the phenomenon's features remained stable from investigator to investigator, thus casting doubt on a favorite skeptical argument concerning investigator influence on the story. Beyond that, Bullard wrote, it was difficult to say more, except that "something goes on, a marvelous phenomenon rich enough to interest a host of scholars, humanists, psychologists and sociologists alike as well as perhaps physical scientists, and to hold that interest irrespective of the actual nature of the phenomenon" (Bullard, 1987).

Hopkins's next book, *Intruders* (1987), introduced fresh features that would figure largely in all subsequent discussions. From his latest investigations he had come to suspect a reason for alien abductions: the creation of a race of hybrid beings to replenish the extraterrestrials' apparently exhausted genetic stock. Female abductees would find themselves pregnant, sometimes inexplicably; then, following subsequent abductions involving vaginal penetration by a suction device, they would discover that those pregnancies had been suddenly terminated. In later abductions they would be shown babies or small children with both human and alien features. The abductors would explain that these were the women's children. Hopkins also uncovered a pattern of cases of sexual intercourse between male abductees and more-or-less human alien women (perhaps adult hybrids).

Other investigators began finding similar cases. Hybrids were a new wrinkle, significantly augmenting the already considerable peculiarity of the abduction phenomenon. As long ago as 1975, in his book *The Mothman Prophecies,* investigator John A. Keel noted, in passing, a pattern of what he called "hysterical pregnancies" in young women who had had close encounters. Even so, the reports met with skepticism among scientifically sophisticated ufologists, for example, Michael D. Swords, who said that such hybridization is biologically impossible. Other critics argued that mass abductions for such purposes would not be necessary; once the basic reproductive materials were collected, they could easily be duplicated. Most damning of all, independent inquiries by physician-ufologists found no evidence of mysteriously ended pregnancies in colleagues' experiences or in the pediatric literature. Still the reports continue.

Another significant development in 1987 was the publication of *Communion* by Whitley Strieber, heretofore known as a novelist specializing in horror and futuristic themes, now a self-identified abductee with a series of strange adventures in his past. The gray-skinned, big-eyed alien on the best-selling book's cover triggered a flood of "memories" among many who saw it. Even ufologists who had been abduction literalists grew puzzled, then uneasy, at the apparent quantity of recovered abduction recollections. Strieber also was the first to express a kind of New Age view of the abduction phenomenon, now seen not as an entirely negative experience (as Hopkins and others held it to be) but as an initiation, however painful, into an expanded, enlightened view of large cosmic realities. What to Hopkins were "intruders" to Strieber were "visitors." *Communion* was only the first of a series of books Strieber would write recounting ever more exotic experiences with aliens possessing vast paranormal powers.

By now UFO abductions were no longer the property of abductees and ufologists. They had expanded into popular culture, and the gray alien became a staple in cartoons, advertisements, television shows, and more. Alarmed at the spread of what they regarded as a popular delusion, skeptics and debunkers sought to discredit the phenomenon. In 1988 the first book-length attack on the phenomenon, its claimants, and its advocates, Philip J. Klass's *UFO-Abductions: A Dangerous Game,* lambasted its subject as the product of delusion and deceit.

Dr. John E. Mack, Harvard University psychiatrist, 1993 (Dennis Stacy/Fortean Picture Library)

Though the phenomenon itself remained elusive, psychologists understood that at least those who claimed to have experienced it could be studied. Using standard psychological tests, they documented the essential psychological normality of the average abductee. They also found that, contrary to one popular theory, abductees were not prone to fantasy or imaginative flights so intense that they could be mistaken for reality. Little if anything seemed to distinguish abductees from their neighbors.

The phenomenon's most notable champion, Harvard University psychiatrist John E. Mack, became a lightning rod in the controversy. To his colleagues, who went so far as to try to have him removed from his professional position, he was a good scholar gone bad. To New Age–oriented saucerians on the other hand, Mack was almost something of a prophet. His controversial book *Abduction* (1994) argued for a benevolent interpretation of abducting aliens, paranormal and interdimensional intelligences who, in Mack's view, are here to teach us—particularly those of us who live in the industrial West—to embrace other realities and to take better care of each other and the world we live in. Mack wedded the contactee message to the abduction experience, to the consternation of Hopkins, Jacobs, and others who refused to draw larger metaphysical inferences from the abduction experience. Jacobs, if anything, went to the opposite extreme. A history professor at Temple University, Jacobs worked with abductees whose testimony, usually under hypnosis, led him to the radical hypothesis that the abducting extraterrestrials are creating a population of hybrids to replace the human race at some point in the not-distant future.

From their interactions with their readers and other members of the public, Hopkins and Jacobs came to suspect that the abduction experience, far from rare, was ubiquitous. Hopkins, for example, wrote as early as 1981 that there may be "tens of thousands of Americans whose encounters have never been revealed" (Hopkins, 1981). In 1991 he and Jacobs were given funding for a survey to be conducted by the Roper Organization. Using five "indicator" questions, they sought evidence for possible abduction experiences among those surveyed. Pollsters interviewed 5,947 adult Americans. In their reading of the results, Hopkins and Jacobs deduced that "the incidence of abduction experiences appears to be on the order of at least 2% of the population" (*Unusual Personal Experiences,* 1992). That comes to 3.7 million abductees. Critics rejected this assertion, arguing that the study contained too many methodological flaws to mean much. Three social scientists, all with backgrounds in ufology, examined the poll and came to a wholly different conclusion: "For the present we have no reliable and valid estimate of the prevalence of the UFO abduction phenomenon" (Hall, Rodeghier, and Johnson, 1992).

In a study of the various theories advanced to explain UFO abductions, psychologist Stuart Appelle observed that all testable, more or less conventional hypotheses (confabulation, fantasy proneness, false memory, sleep hallucination, and the like) stand on shaky empirical ground. On the other hand, literalistic interpretations suffer from an absence of anything like solid, veridical evidence. All that can be said with certainty is that abduction experiences have the feeling of reality to those who undergo them. Most do not fall into an easily identifiable psychological category. They appear to be reasonably consistent in their core features, and some cases involve multiple witnesses. These last cases, in Appelle's view, "may provide the greatest challenge to prosaic explanations" (Appelle, 1995/1996).

See Also: Alien DNA; Aliens and the dead; Cocoon people; Contactees; Dual reference; Gray Face; Hopkins, Budd; Hybrid beings; Insectoids; Keel, John A.; MU the Mantis Being; Nordics; Puddy's abduction; Reptoids; Strieber, Whitley; Walton's abduction

Further Reading

Appelle, Stuart, 1995/1996. "The Abduction Experience: A Critical Evaluation of Theory and Evidence." *Journal of UFO Studies* 6 (new series): 29–78.

Appelle, Stuart, Steven Jay Lynn, and Leonard Newman, 2000. "Alien Abduction Experiences." In Etzel Cardena, Steven Jay Lynn, and Stanley Krippner, eds. *Varieties of Anomalous Experience: Examining the Scientific Evidence,* 253–282. Washington, DC: American Psychological Association.

Bullard, Thomas E., 1987. *UFO Abductions: The Measure of a Mystery. Volume 1: Comparative Study of Abduction Reports. Volume 2: Catalogue of Cases.* Mount Rainier, MD: Fund for UFO Research.

———, 1989. "Hypnosis and UFO Abductions: A Troubled Relationship." *Journal of UFO Studies* 1 (new series): 3–40.

———, 1991. "Folkloric Dimensions of the UFO Phenomenon." *Journal of UFO Studies* 3 (new series): 1–57.

———, 2000. "Abductions under Fire: A Review of Recent Abduction Literature." *Journal of UFO Studies* 7 (new series): 81–106.

Clark, Jerome, 2000. "From Mermaids to Little Gray Men: The Prehistory of the UFO Abduction Phenomenon." *The Anomalist* 8 (Spring): 11–31.

Fuller, John G., 1966. *The Interrupted Journey: Two Lost Hours "Aboard a Flying Saucer."* New York: Dial Press.

Hall, Robert L., Mark Rodeghier, and Donald A. Johnson, 1992. "The Prevalence of Abductions: A Critical Look." *Journal of UFO Studies* 4 (new series): 131–135.

Hopkins, Budd, 1981. *Missing Time: A Documented Study of UFO Abductions.* New York: Richard Marek Publishers.

———, 1987. *Intruders: The Incredible Visitations at Copley Woods.* New York: Random House.

Jacobs, David M., 1992. *Secret Life: Firsthand Accounts of UFO Abductions.* New York: Simon and Schuster.

———, 1998. *The Threat.* New York: Simon and Schuster.

Keel, John A., 1975. *The Mothman Prophecies.* New York: Saturday Review Press/E. P. Dutton and Company.

Klass, Philip J., 1988. *UFO-Abductions: A Dangerous Game.* Buffalo, NY: Prometheus Books.

Lawson, Alvin H., 1980. "Hypnosis of Imaginary 'Abductees'." In Curtis G. Fuller, ed. *Proceedings of the First International UFO Congress,* 195–238. New York: Warner Books.

Lorenzen, Jim, and Coral Lorenzen, 1977. *Abducted! Confrontations with Beings from Outer Space.* New York: Berkley Medallion.

Mack, John E., 1994. *Abduction: Human Encounters with Aliens.* New York: Charles Scribner's Sons.

Strieber, Whitley, 1987. *Communion: A True Story.* New York: Beach Tree/William Morrow.

Swords, Michael D., 1988. "Extraterrestrial Hybridization Unlikely." *MUFON UFO Journal* 247: 6–10.

Unusual Personal Experiences: An Analysis of the Data from Three National Surveys Conducted by the Roper Organization, 1992. Las Vegas, NV: Bigelow Holding Corporation.

Abraham

Channeler Esther Hicks heard from abraham in the early 1980s. She renders the name in lowercase because abraham is not an individual but a collection of highly evolved entities speaking in one voice. In 1986 she and her husband, Jerry, confided their experiences with abraham to business associates, who soon were peppering them with financial and personal questions they wanted abraham to answer. When the Hickses saw how satisfied their friends were with the results, they decided to take abraham to a larger public. Today the couple conduct workshops, put out a newsletter, and lecture widely out of their San Antonio, Texas, headquarters.

Abraham teaches that each of us is a physical extension of an essence that begins in the spiritual realm. Each is here because he or she has chosen to be so, and we are here to exercise freedom and experience joy. The universe is benevolent, and it gives us the potential to realize all of our dreams. There is no such thing as death; all of us live forever.

Further Reading

Melton, J. Gordon, 1996. *Encyclopedia of American Religions.* Detroit, MI: Gale Research.

"A Synopsis of Abraham-Hicks's Teachings." http://www.abraham-hicks.com/bio.html.

Abram

Folklorist Peter M. Rojcewicz relates the experiences of a young university student to whom he gives the pseudonym Polly Bromberger. In the early 1980s Bromberger conjured up a spirit guide—a "personal archetype," she sometimes called it—and gave it the name Abram. With long, unkempt hair and wearing a white robe and sandals, Abram looked "biblical." He came more clearly into focus after Bromberger had undergone a period of meditation and reflection.

A student of the great psychologist and philosopher C. G. Jung, Bromberger used a process she learned from Jung's writings—"active imagination"—to bring Abram into her life. In time she came to feel that he had a kind of independent existence. She told Rojcewicz that "sometimes I feel he can be a force opening me on purpose to make me stretch myself, and work myself, and sometimes I get frustrated with it." On the whole, however, she was convinced that Abram was a positive influence in her life.

Further Reading

Rojcewicz, Peter M., 1984. *The Boundaries of Orthodoxy: A Folkloric Look at the UFO Phenomenon.* Ph.D. dissertation. University of Pennsylvania, Philadelphia.

Adama

Adama, who channels through Dianne Robbins, is an Ascended Master and High Priest of Telos, the great Lemurian city now located under Mount Shasta in northern California. Because of his pure thoughts, Adama, like the million other persons who live in the city, is able to live for hundreds of years. He is currently more than six hundred years old. He is a descendant of the Lemurians who fled inside the mountain when Lemuria and all else on Earth's surface were destroyed in a nuclear holocaust. Only twenty-five thousand Lemurians escaped in time.

Since then the Lemurians' consciousness has evolved significantly. Besides attending to their spiritual betterment, the Lemurians have fought off marauding extraterrestrials who are causing harm to surface dwellers. "We are all part of God's grand plan for the Universe," Adama says, "and WE ARE NOW MERGING OUR THOUGHTS INTO ONE THOUGHT FOR THE ENTIRE HUMAN RACE. Soon we will all be on the same wave band of consciousness, broadcasting our love and light to all in the cosmos and letting the cosmos know that we are ready to join with them in one grand FEDERATION OF PLANETS" ("Adama," 1995).

See Also: Lemuria; Mount Shasta

Further Reading

"Adama," 1995. http://www.salemctr.com/newage/center36.html.

Adamski, George (1891–1965)

Though largely forgotten today, George Adamski was once an international occult celebrity, perhaps the most famous of all flying-saucer contactees. His claimed meeting with a Venusian in the California desert in November 1952 electrified esoterically inclined saucer buffs. In three books published between 1953 and 1961 he recounted his trips into space along with extensive encounters with benevolent Venusians, Martians, and Saturnians. In 1962 he boarded a spaceship and flew to Saturn to attend an interplanetary conference. By 1965, when he died, many of his most devoted followers had broken their connection with him, convinced either that he was lying or that evil space people were misleading him.

Born in Poland, Adamski emigrated with his parents to upstate New York when he was one or two years old. In the early 1920s he moved to California, where he eventually established a role for himself on the local occult scene as head of the Royal Order of Tibet, a metaphysical school based on channeled teachings from Tibetan lamas. When flying saucers became an object of popular interest in the late 1940s, Adamski produced photographs of alleged spacecraft; some of the pictures were said to have been taken through his six-inch telescope. Published in the popular occult and paranormal digest *Fate* in 1950 and 1951, the photos along with accompanying text afforded Adamski his first wide exposure. On November 20, 1952, as six others (including contactee and fringe archaeologist George Hunt Williamson) watched from a distance, Adamski observed the landing of a saucer and the emergence of the beautiful, blond-haired Orthon, a visitor from Venus, who expressed concern about the human race's warlike ways. (In later years Adamski would tell confidants that his first contacts with extraterrestrials occurred in his childhood, but he never said as much publicly.) Three weeks later Orthon returned in his scout craft over Adamski's Palomar Gardens residence and allowed the ship to be photographed. The resulting pictures would generate enormous controversy and, for many, virtually define the image of a flying saucer as a domed disc with a three-ball landing gear.

A fifty-four-page account of Adamski's early contacts was added to an already existing manuscript (on supposed space visitations throughout history) by Irish occultist Desmond Leslie and published in 1953 as *Flying Saucers Have Landed.* Two years later, in *Inside the Space Ships,* Adamski expanded his claims to encompass further interactions with extraterrestrials, both on Earth and aboard saucers. According to Adamski, the "Space Brothers," as he called them, had come to help the human race out of its backward, violent ways, which were leading inexorably to nuclear war. They espoused a benign occult philosophy much like the one Adamski had taught for many years.

Though revered by many, Adamski also had bitter critics, none more so than conservative ufologists who dismissed his stories as absurd and feared that he was bringing ridicule to all of UFO research. Some ufologists actively investigated his claims and uncovered discrepancies and other evidence of untruthfulness. One found, for example, that the weather on a particular day on which Adamski claimed contact was not as he had described it. Most photo analysts concluded that the pictures of "spacecraft" were in fact of small models. On one occasion skeptical ufologists proved that one Adamski allegation was unambiguously false. Adamski had reported that as he was traveling to Iowa to give a lecture, the train suddenly stopped en route. When he stepped out to take a short walk, space people met him and flew him to his destination. From interviews with the train crew, investigators learned that the train had made

UFO contactee George Adamski with his six-inch telescope on Mount Palomar, California (Fortean Picture Library)

no such stop. In these circumstances Adamski tended to blame his accusers of being agents of a sinister "Silence Group" trying to destroy the space people's good works. But in later years, following his death, several individuals disclosed that Adamski had acknowledged to them that his stories were not true.

By 1959 Adamski's renown was such that he was able to embark on a worldwide tour, first to New Zealand and Australia, then to

Europe. In May of that same year, Queen Juliana of Holland received him, igniting fierce commentary in the press and a riot at the University of Zurich when Adamski attempted to give a lecture in Switzerland. Adamski charged that the students—and indeed most of his critics—were agents of a sinister Silence Group, which sought to frustrate the moral reforms and technological advances advocated by the space people and their terrestrial allies. Though the reality of Adamski's audience with Queen Juliana was never in doubt, other purported meetings with notables, including President John F. Kennedy, Pope John XXIII, and Vice President Hubert H. Humphrey, that figure in the Adamski legend almost certainly did not occur outside Adamski's imagination.

In the early 1960s, after Adamski openly embraced psychic approaches of which he had, till then, been outspokenly critical, some of his followers started to question his sincerity, especially when he began doing psychic consultations for profit. His associate C. A. Honey circulated damning evidence that Adamski was recycling his 1930s-era Tibetan-masters teachings and putting them in the mouths of space people. When Adamski claimed that he had flown to Saturn, the story only fueled growing doubts even among devoted followers.

His career in decline, his credibility never lower, Adamski went on a final lecture tour through New York and Rhode Island in March 1965. For the preceding month, his financial resources exhausted, he had been living with Nelson and Madeleine Rodeffer in Maryland. He died of a heart attack at their home on the evening of April 23.

See Also: Contactees; Orthon; Ramu; Williamson, George Hunt; Yamski

Further Reading

Adamski, George, 1955. *Inside the Space Ships.* New York: Abelard-Schuman.

———, 1961. *Flying Saucers Farewell.* New York: Abelard-Schuman.

———, 1962. *Special Report: My Trip to the Twelve Counsellors Meeting That Took Place on Saturn, March 27–30th, 1962.* Vista, CA: Science of Life.

Bennett, Colin, 2000. "Breakout of the Fictions: George Adamski's 1959 World Tour." *The Anomalist* 8 (Spring): 39–84.

Ellwood, Robert S., 1995. "Spiritualism and UFO Religion in New Zealand: The International Transmission of Modern Spiritual Movements." In James R. Lewis, ed. *The Gods Have Landed: New Religions from Other Worlds,* 167–186. Albany, NY: State University of New York Press.

Good, Timothy, 1998. *Alien Base: Earth's Encounters with Extraterrestrials.* London: Century.

Heiden, Richard W., 1984. Review of Zinsstag and Good's *George Adamski—The Untold Story. The A.P.R.O. Bulletin* 32, 5 (August): 4–5.

Leslie, Desmond, and George Adamski, 1953. *Flying Saucers Have Landed.* New York: British Book Centre.

Moseley, James W., ed., 1957. *Special Adamski Exposé Issue. Saucer News* 27 (October).

Zinsstag, Lou, 1990. *UFO . . . George Adamski: Their Man on Earth.* Tucson, AZ: UFO Photo Archives.

Zinsstag, Lou, and Timothy Good, 1983. *George Adamski—The Untold Story.* Beckenham, Kent, England: Ceti Publications.

Aenstrians

For a time in the mid to late 1960s, Warminster, Wiltshire, was the focus of a series of mysterious sightings of UFOs and hearings of apparently related sounds. The excitement produced what was called the "Warminster mystery," which was also the title of a popular book by Arthur Shuttlewood, a reporter for the *Warminster Journal.* Shuttlewood, who led sky watches and became the leading publicist of the phenomena, also reported receiving phone calls from self-identified extraterrestrials, as well as a personal visit from one. The aliens said they were from a planet named Aenstria.

The first calls came in early September 1965. The calls continued for a period of seven weeks, according to Shuttlewood. The callers were three Aenstrians: Caellsan (the senior spacecraft commander), Selorik (an interpreter), and Traellison (the queen of Aenstria). In each case they phoned from a public booth in a particular district in the city, though Shuttlewood wrote that he never heard the sound of coins dropping before the voices began to speak.

The messages were standard contactee fare. Earth is in trouble because of atomic weapons and environmental pollution. Human beings—the product of special creation, not evolutionary processes—should return to simpler, more spiritual ways. The Aenstrians lived long lives and suffered few illnesses. Traellison, for example, was 450 years old, a fairly young age on her home planet. The Aenstrians were communicating with Shuttlewood so that he could pass on their information to Earth's "councils."

On May 24, 1967, Shuttlewood's *The Warminster Mystery* was published. In it he relegated the story of the Aenstrians's phone calls to an appendix, where he suggested that they were no more than an interesting hoax. On the afternoon of the twenty-sixth, the phone rang at the Shuttlewood residence. It was an Aenstrian named Karne, expressing displeasure at what the author had said of his colleagues' trustworthiness. Shuttlewood responded that if Karne wanted to prove he was who he claimed to be, he should pay a personal visit. Karne took up the challenge and showed up at Shuttlewood's door seven seconds later.

Karne, who spent a total of nine minutes with the journalist, looked like an ordinary man in most ways, except for an apparent absence of pupils in his eyes, which were covered by thick glasses. He also had blue blotches on his cheekbones and lips. He also had a manner that unnerved Shuttlewood, who felt that the ostensible extraterrestrial had powers that, if provoked, could instantly destroy him. Karne said that Traellison, Caellsan, and Selorik had returned to their home "cantel" (planet). He spoke of an imminent war in the Middle East—the Six-Day War erupted the following June—and of further UFO appearances, this time of cross-shaped craft, in the fall. He said a Third World War was almost inevitable at some point in the not-distant future. If it was fought with nuclear weapons, he hinted, extraterrestrials would intervene in some unspecified fashion. A new order, in which earthlings would be trained to become cosmic citizens, would be put in place.

"I noticed that Karne sometimes had difficulty with his breathing," Shuttlewood wrote. "From time to time, as I shot questions at him . . . he glanced at the pale gold disc on his wrist. He replied to certain queries immediately, shaking his head in the negative over others, after looking at his 'watch'" (Shuttlewood, 1978). At one point Shuttlewood asked if George Adamski's contact claims were genuine. Karne replied sternly that he could not answer that question, though he hinted that the late California contactee was not of earthly origin. At the conclusion of the meeting, Shuttlewood gripped Karne's wrist and left thumb in what he intended as a gesture of good will, but the visitor winced in pain. Earlier, at the commencement of their meeting, Karne had not responded to Shuttlewood's outstretched hand.

Shuttlewood watched him walk, turning stiffly to wave farewell, then continue up the street. "From the waist up," Shuttlewood wrote, "his bearing was smart, military, almost arrogantly proud. From the waist down, however, his movements were slow and deliberate. His legs seemed weighted, feet slightly dragging; yet to a casual onlooker he would have been dismissed as an old gardener type or old-fashioned and hard-worked farm laborer" (Shuttlewood, 1978).

The next day Shuttlewood's sixteen-year-old son, Graham, saw a man who looked like Karne at a Warminster park. He was looking upward as military jets flew by, shaking his head in disapproval. His left hand was bandaged as if it had been recently injured. That was the last either saw of Karne.

See Also: Adamski, George; Contactees

Further Reading

Dewey, Stephen, 1997. "Arthur Shuttlewood and the Warminster Mystery." *Strange Magazine* 18 (Summer): 16–21, 56–58.

Shuttlewood, Arthur, 1967. *The Warminster Mystery.* London: Neville Spearman.

———, 1978. *UFO Prophecy.* New York: Global Communications.

Aetherius

Aetherius is one of the Cosmic Masters who preside at the Interplanetary Parliament on

Saturn. In 1954 Aetherius made his presence known psychically to George King, a London man with longstanding occult interests. Soon King was channeling other space people, including Jesus. By January he had gone public with the cosmic gospel—essentially earthbound occult doctrines ascribed to philosophical extraterrestrials—and soon was issuing a mimeographed bulletin titled *Aetherius Speaks to Earth* (later *Cosmic Voice*). In August 1956 King established the Aetherius Society, among the most successful and enduring contactee groups. King died on July 12, 1997, in Los Angeles, where he had been living for many years.

In the theology of the Aetherius Society, good and evil extraterrestrials are engaged in constant warfare. From time to time, during crisis situations, the Cosmic Brotherhood will place its spaceships above Earth and direct positive energy downward. Society members receive the energy and make sure that it reaches its targets. Over a three and a half year period, beginning in 1958, King climbed no fewer than eighteen mountains at the behest of the space people.

The society maintains headquarters in London and Los Angeles, as well as chapters all over the world.

See Also: Channeling; Contactees

Further Reading

Aetherius Society, 1995. *The Aetherius Society: A Cosmic Concept.* Hollywood, CA: Aetherius Society.

Curran, Douglas, 1985. *In Advance of the Landing: Folk Concepts of Outer Space.* New York: Abbeville Press.

Saliba, John A., 1995. "Religious Dimensions of UFO Phenomena." In James R. Lewis, ed. *The Gods Have Landed: New Religions from Other Worlds,* 15–64. Albany, NY: State University of New York Press.

Wallis, Roy, 1974. "The Aetherius Society: A Case Study of a Mystagogic Congregation." *Sociological Review* 22: 27–44.

Affa

Affa first appeared in 1952 among the extraterrestrials who communicated to a small Prescott, Arizona, occult group headed by George Hunt Williamson. Affa, identified as being from the planet Uranus, first spoke through automatic writing, then later allegedly by radio, warning of threats to Earth by evil humans and menacing aliens from the "Orion Solar Systems."

Affa later surfaced in automatic-writing communications to Frances Swan of Eliot, Maine, beginning in 1954. Mrs. Swan's Affa, like Williamson's, did his communicating from a giant Uranian spaceship. Affa urged Swan to alert the United States Navy so that it could receive his radio messages. Swan told her neighbor, retired navy Adm. Herbert B. Knowles, about Affa's request. Knowles, a UFO enthusiast, sat in on a writing session and addressed questions to Affa. Impressed by the answers, he wrote the Office of Naval Intelligence (ONI), which on June 8 sent two officers to Swan's house. They also asked questions of Affa, who promised a radio transmission at 2 P.M. on June 10. When none came, ONI lost interest and turned the letters over to the navy's Bureau of Aeronautics. John Hutson, a security officer, was curious enough to fly up to Eliot for two days in late July. On his return he spoke with an FBI agent, but the agency chose not to pursue the matter.

In the summer of 1959 navy Commander Julius Larsen, an ONI liaison officer to the CIA's Photographic Intelligence Center in Washington, DC, stumbled upon a file on the incident. Larsen, a navy pilot who harbored a private fascination with spiritualism, called on Swan and Knowles. At one point Larsen tried automatic writing and believed he had communicated with Affa, though Swan insisted he had not contacted *her* Affa.

Back in Washington Larsen talked with Center Director Arthur Lundahl and Lundahl's assistant, Lt. Cmdr. Robert Neasham, a navy officer. In their presence Larsen entered a trance state and supposedly contacted Affa while Lundahl and Neasham peppered him with questions. At one point, challenged to prove his existence, Affa replied, "Go to the window." Lundahl saw nothing but clouds, though Neasham seemed convinced that a spaceship was hiding in them. Neasham would also claim that radar operators at Washington National Airport told him that that particular portion of the sky was mysteriously "blocked out." No independent evidence supported that allegation.

Neasham notified Major Robert Friend, head of the air force's UFO-investigative agency, Project Blue Book. For Friend's benefit Larsen even related telepathic messages from Affa and other space people, but the aliens refused his request for a flyover. Friend wrote a memo on the episode and sent it to his superiors. Nothing further was done. The incident remained buried in Pentagon, FBI, and CIA files until the early 1970s, when Friend shared his notes with UFO historian David M. Jacobs. Subsequently, some exaggerated accounts of the episode were published in the UFO literature, a few even claiming that the CIA itself had communicated with extraterrestrials.

See Also: Williamson, George Hunt

Further Reading

Emenegger, Robert, 1974. *UFOs Past, Present and Future.* New York: Ballantine Books.

Fitzgerald, Randall, 1979. "Messages: The Case History of a Contactee." *Second Look* 1, 12 (October): 12–18, 28–29.

Jacobs, David M., 1975. *The UFO Controversy in America.* Bloomington: Indiana University Press.

Williamson, George Hunt, and Alfred C. Bailey, 1954. *The Saucers Speak! A Documentary Report of Interstellar Communications by Radiotelegraphy.* Los Angeles: New Age Publishing Company.

Agents

"Agents" are human beings whom extraterrestrials have contacted and who have agreed to help the space people in their benevolent mission to Earth. George Hunt Williamson wrote that agents, who come from all social and economic backgrounds, sometimes have a "strange, far-away, glassy look in their eyes." Their necks may throb or jump spasmodically, indicating that they are receiving telepathic instructions. The Agents conduct a variety of tasks. They introduce persons who are of potential use to them to each other, recommend books, ask provocative questions, and in other ways, subtle or obvious, get people thinking about space visitors and spiritual reform. They also minister to the needy and have a particular interest in orphaned children.

Extraterrestrials get in touch with Agents in assorted ways. Sometimes it is through a car or ham radio, sometimes via thought waves, on occasion by direct, physical encounter.

See Also: Williamson, George Hunt

Further Reading

Williamson, George Hunt, 1953. *Other Tongue—Other Flesh.* Amherst, WI: Amherst Press.

Agharti

Agharti is a subterranean kingdom, which allegedly exists in Tibet or Mongolia. It is, depending on whom one believes, a paradisiacal realm or a sinister lair of sorcerers and other evildoers—mostly, however, the former. The legend of Agharti seems loosely based on the Buddhist realm of Shambhala, a city of adepts and mystics said to be located in a hidden valley (called "Shangri-La" in James Hilton's popular novel *Lost Horizon* [1933] and in the movie of the same name). Shambhala first appeared in a 1922 Polish book, soon afterward translated into English as the best-seller *Beasts, Men and Gods.*

The author, Ferdinand Ossendowski (1876–1945), fled Russia in the wake of the Bolshevik revolution. An anti-Communist, Ossendowski participated in the White Russian government, that nation's short-lived experiment in democracy between the overthrow of the tsar and the triumph of the Communists. He wandered through Mongolia, itself torn by political unrest and bloody conflict. There he learned, he said, of a mysterious "King of the World." A lama in the town of Narabanchi took him into a temple in which there was a throne. Ossendowski was told that in 1890 horsemen had ridden into town and instructed all the local lamas to come to the temple. One of the horsemen sat on the throne, at which point all present "fell to their knees as they recognized the man who

The hidden world of "Shangri-La" as depicted in the film Lost Horizon, *directed by Frank Capra, 1937 (Photofest)*

had been long ago described in the sacred bulls of the Dalai Lama, Tashi Lama, and Bodgo Khan. He was the man to whom the whole world belongs and who has penetrated into all the mysteries of Nature. He pronounced a short Tibetan prayer, blessed all his hearers and afterwards made predictions for the coming half century. This was thirty years ago and in the interim all his prophecies are being fulfilled" (Ossendowski, 1922). The King of the World lived in an underground realm called Agharti.

Whether this King of the World, or even the author's supposed informant, ever existed, he and his kingdom soon entered occult lore. In *Darkness over Tibet* (1935) Theodore Illion recounted his allegedly true adventures in an underground city in a distant valley. At first he thought he had entered a utopia, but soon he realized that the inhabitants, for all their advanced spiritual knowledge and supernatural powers, were cannibals. Illion wrote that his reported experiences proved the existence of Agharti. In 1946 Vincent H. Gaddis, a regular contributor to *Amazing Stories* who later achieved a degree of fame as the inventor of the concept of the Bermuda Triangle, picked up on the theme, depicting Agharti as a city of evil that was linked to tunnels all over the world. He incorporated Agharti into the Shaver mystery, the subject of a series of tales *Amazing Stories* was running about an alleged underground realm populated by deros, demonic entities in possession of a fantastic Atlantean technology, which they used to torment surface humans.

In a variant of the legend, Robert Ernst Dickhoff's *Agharta: The Subterranean World* (1951) contended that two and a half million years ago Martians landed at Antarctica, then a tropical region, and created the first humans. Then reptoid (that is, biped reptilian) Venusians attacked, forcing the Martians and their human associates to create two huge underground cities, connected by tunnels of vast length, in order to protect themselves. One of these cities was Shambhala, under Tibet, and the other Agharta, under China's Tzangpo Valley. Eventually, the Venusians conquered Agharta, sending their evil minions into the world until 1948, when the Martian/human alliance reclaimed the city and slew its ruler, the King of the World, and many of his troops.

There is no real-life Central Asian tradition of Agharti, though Chinese and Tibetan equivalents to Western fairy lore spoke of magical caves, on the other side of which the traveler would find a beautiful land and lovely but ultimately treacherous supernatural beings.

See Also: Reptoids

Further Reading

Dickhoff, Robert Ernst, 1965. *Agharta.* New York: Fieldcrest.

Kafton-Minkel, Walter, 1989. *Subterranean Worlds: 100,000 Years of Dragons, Dwarfs, the Dead, Lost Races and UFOs from inside the Earth.* Port Townsend, WA: Loompanics Unlimited.

Ossendowski, Ferdinand, 1922. *Beasts, Men and Gods.* New York: Dutton.

Ahab

On a camping trip through eastern Oregon in the summer of 1975, a young married couple identified as Darryl and Toni M. stopped along the banks of the Owyhee River to cool their truck. They spotted an odd object parked on a nearby hillside. The next thing they knew, it was two hours later, and their truck started as if it had long since cooled off. Later, under hypnosis, they recounted the experience of wandering into the UFO in a trance state. Hairless humanoids with slits for eyes, mouth, and nose, with gray, wrinkled skin assured them via telepathy that they meant no harm. As Toni watched, the aliens, who communicated with each other with a "buzzing bee" sound, subjected Darryl to an apparent physical examination by light beam. Sometime later Toni awoke to find a figure with a skull-like face and a small mouth standing at the foot of her bed. He spoke to her, but all she could remember was that he had told her his name was Ahab.

Further Reading

Hartman, Terry A., 1979. "Another Abduction by Extraterrestrials." *MUFON UFO Journal* 141 (November): 3–4.

Akon

Akon appeared to Elizabeth Klarer on April 6, 1956, when his spaceship landed in the Drakensberg Mountains of Natal, South Africa. She was flown to a waiting mother ship, where she met other friendly space people and learned that they came from the beautiful planet Meton in the orbit of Alpha Centauri four light years away. The Metonites, she learned, are vegetarians who live in a utopian society without conflict or disease. They are also a passionate people, and in due course, as the contacts continued, Klarer and Akon became lovers. She bore him a son, Ayling, during a four-month stay on Meton.

Klarer became well known in saucer and occult circles in South Africa and Europe where she lectured from time to time. She distributed photographs of Akon's spacecraft and showed inquirers a ring she said he had given her. Though many dismissed her stories and evidence as bogus, her friend Cynthia Hind, a well-known ufologist from Zimbabwe, believed her to be sincere and has helped keep her name and story alive. On the occasion of her death in February 1994, Hind wrote, "Elizabeth Klarer died in comparative poverty. . . . Her incredible story brought her some fame (or more accurately, notoriety!) but certainly no riches" (Hind, 1994).

Further Reading

Hind, Cynthia, 1982. *UFOs—African Encounters.* Salisbury, Zimbabwe: Gemini.

———, 1994. "MUFON Forum: Contactee Klarer." *MUFON UFO Journal* 315 (July): 18.

———, 1999. "Ufology Profile: Elizabeth Klarer." *MUFON UFO Journal* 379 (November): 10–11.

Klarer, Elizabeth, 1980. *Beyond the Light Barrier.* Cape Town, South Africa: Howard Timmins.

Alien diners

An alien family ate at a restaurant and stayed overnight in a motel in suburban St. Louis in May 1970, according to ufologist John E. Schroeder, who interviewed employees and heard a strange and comic tale. Dorothy Simpson, a front desk clerk at the motel and a fellow member of the UFO Study Group of Greater St. Louis, tipped Schroeder off to the incident soon after its occurrence.

Simpson was examining billing documents at her desk at 10:30 A.M. on May 15 when a "whistling sigh" sounded. She looked up, and on the other side of the desk stood four tiny people, apparently members of a family: a couple and their two children. All looked strikingly alike. All were youthful in appearance, and the children were nearly the height of the ostensible parents. They were so short that they barely reached the level of the desk. They were all expensively dressed, the males in tailored suits, the females in pastel peach dresses. Their hair did not look real. Odd as it seemed, Simpson suspected that they were wearing wigs.

In a falsetto voice the man said, "Do you have a room to stay? Do you have a room to stay?" She told him what the charges would be, but he seemed not to understand what she had said. He turned to his female companion as if expecting her to clarify matters, but she remained silent. An uncomfortable period of silence followed, broken finally when the man reached into his pocket and pulled out a thick wad of bills, many of large denomination. The bills were so crisp and new that Simpson wondered if they were counterfeit, but some quick informal testing suggested they were not. She took two twenty-dollar bills from the stack and gave the rest back.

Because the man was too small to reach up to fill out the reservation form, Simpson said she would do it for him. He said his name was "A. Bell." As he stepped forward she got a better look at him and was able to compare his face with his companions'. According to Schroeder, whose composite description comes from his interviews with Simpson and other motel employees who saw them, they were "wide at eye level, their faces thinned abruptly to their chins. Their eyes were large, dark and slightly slanted. . . . Their noses had practically no bridges and two slits for nostrils, and their mouths were tiny and lipless—no wider than their nostrils. All look uniformly pale. (Color descriptions varied from pearl to pale pink to light grey.)"

"And where are you from?" Simpson asked. At that the man's arm shot upward as if pointing to the sky, and he said, "We come from up there. Up there." The woman pushed his arm down and spoke for the first time. She said they were from Hammond, Indiana, and she gave a street address. The man signed the register but did it so awkwardly that Simpson thought he seemed not to know how to use a pen. The woman wanted to know where they could eat. Simpson indicated the direction of the motel restaurant.

Meanwhile, the bellhop came over to store their bags while they ate. At the manager's insistence Simpson checked the Indiana address and learned that both the name and the address were bogus. The bellhop checked the parking lot for a car with an Indiana license plate but found none.

The hostess who led the strange family to a table in the restaurant noticed that the chins of even the adults barely reached the top of the table. The man read aloud from the menu and kept asking odd questions about where milk, vegetables, and other common foods come from. The woman ordered peas and milk for herself and the children, and for the man peas, a small steak, and water. Their eating was similarly peculiar. Each picked up a single pea with a knife, brought it to his or her tiny mouth, and inhaled it with a sucking sound. The father was unable to get even a small piece of steak through his slit of a mouth. They stopped eating all at the same time. The man produced a twenty-dollar bill and gave it to the waitress, who went to get change; when she returned, they were gone.

When the bellhop saw them, he retrieved their baggage and stepped into the elevator to lead them to their room. When the elevator door opened, though, the family recoiled in fright and confusion. The bellhop had to assure them that there was no danger. After letting them into the room, he turned on the lights. Suddenly the man began shouting at him that the light would hurt the children's eyes. Suddenly frightened himself, the bellhop fled without waiting—one suspects futilely, in any case—for a tip.

The bellhop, the manager, and Simpson vowed to watch for the little people's departure in the morning, but they were never seen again, though the front door was the only door they could pass through without setting off a security alarm. The alarms were checked, and nothing was amiss. Schroeder interviewed all five employees who had interacted with the family. All seemed sincerely bewildered by the curious series of events.

See Also: Extraterrestrials among us

Further Reading

Schroeder, John E., 1987. "The Strangers among Us." *The UFO Enigma* 7, 7 (June): 36.

Alien DNA

Physical evidence of abduction experiences is hard to come by, and physical evidence of actual aliens is all but nonexistent. A case from Australia may be an exception. Biochemists were able to analyze, with curious results, a strand of what was reported to be the hair of an alien woman.

The events that led to the analysis began on the night of July 12, 1988, when Peter Khoury, a Sydney resident of Lebanese background, was awakened suddenly when he sensed that something had grabbed his ankles. A numbness crept up his body from the feet, and soon his entire body except for his eyes was paralyzed. To his right he spotted three or four small hooded figures with wrinkled, shiny black faces. Through telepathy they assured him he would not be harmed. Khoury then saw two other figures on his left. "These two," he later told investigator Bill Chalker, "were thin, tall with big black eyes and a narrow chin." They were "gold-yellow in color." One of these beings shoved a needle into the left side of his forehead, and he passed out.

The next day he showed the puncture wound to his fiancée. Later he showed it to his doctor, who thought he had walked into a nail. When Khoury told him what had happened, the physician laughed at him. He found that this was a typical response and grew despondent and anxious, worried about the strange nature of the experience, about the future, about his inability to communicate with anyone who would listen to him. Eventually, his fiancée found a copy of Whitley Strieber's *Communion* (1987), detailing the author's personal abduction experiences. In time he heard about and joined a local UFO group but left it still unsatisfied. In April 1993 he founded the UFO Experience Support Association.

On July 23, 1992, Khoury had a second, even stranger encounter. He was suffering from the effects of an assault by three men at his job, and as a consequence he was on strong medication and mostly bed-ridden. On the morning in question, he managed with considerable difficulty to drive his wife—he was now married—to the train station so that she could get to work. Once home he crawled back into bed and passed out, only to awaken a few minutes later. He was sitting straight up and staring at two nude women sitting on the bed.

They were strange-looking, with a weird, glassy-eyed expression. One looked generally Asian, something like an East Indian; the other was blond, with eyes two or three times larger than normal. Their cheekbones seemed abnormally high. The dark woman was watching her companion closely, as if the blond were demonstrating something to her. The blond pulled Khoury toward her breasts, apparently initiating a sex act. He tried to resist, but she was too strong for him. As he struggled, he bit her nipple so hard that he bit it off. He could feel it in his throat. The woman only looked at him in puzzlement. She did not act as if she were in pain, and there was no blood. At that point the two vanished.

The nipple was caught in his throat, causing him to cough persistently for hours. Eventually, he was able to swallow it. In the meantime, feeling pain in his genital region, he examined his penis. There he found two hairs wrapped tightly around it. He had no idea how they had gotten there, unless they had been placed on his penis as he was sleeping. As he untangled them, he felt enormous pain. He preserved the strands—one about twelve centimeters long, the other about six—in a plastic bag.

Though many abductees have reported sexual experiences with aliens (or, as some researchers think, alien/human hybrids), none have come out of the experience with a supposed part of an alien body.

In 1999 Chalker, a chemist by profession and a well-regarded UFO investigator by avocation, brought the strands to a group of biochemists for analysis. The analysis reads in part:

> The blonde hair provides for a strange and unusual DNA sequence, showing five consistent substitutions from a human consensus . . . which could not easily have come from anyone else in the Sydney area except by the rarest of chances; is not apparently due to any sort of laboratory contamination; and is found only in a few other people throughout the whole world. . . .
>
> While it may not be impossible for him to have had sexual contact with some fair-skinned, nearly albino female from the Sydney area, such an explanation is ruled out by the DNA evidence, which fits only a Chinese Mongoloid as a donor of the hair. Furthermore, while it might be possible to find a few Chinese in Sydney with the same DNA as seen in just 4% of Taiwanese women, it would not be plausible to find a Chinese woman here with thin, almost clear hair, having the same rare DNA. Finally, that thin blonde hair could not plausibly represent a chemically-bleached Chinese (including the root) because then its DNA could not easily have been extracted.
>
> The most probable donor of the hair must therefore be as the young man claims: a tall blonde female who does not need much color in her hair or skin as a form of protection against the sun, perhaps because she does not require it. Could this young man really have provided, by chance, a hair sample which contains DNA from one of the rarest human lineages known . . . that lies further from the mainstream than any other except for African Pygmies and aboriginals? (Chalker, 1999).

See Also: Abductions by UFOs; Hybrid beings; Strieber, Whitley

Further Reading

Chalker, Bill, 1999. "Strange Evidence." *International UFO Reporter* 24, 1 (Spring): 3–16, 31.

Strieber, Whitley, 1987. *Communion: A True Story.* New York: Beach Tree/William Morrow.

Aliens and the dead

In the view of UFO-abduction investigator David M. Jacobs, aliens sometimes take on the form of deceased relatives in the interest of keeping their activities secret.

He recounts the experience of a woman to whom he gives the pseudonym Lily Martinson. Vacationing with her mother in the Virgin Islands in 1987, Martinson woke up in her hotel room to observe the apparition of her dead brother watching her from the foot of the bed. The experience comforted her. Later, however, when Jacobs put her under hypnosis, Martinson saw the individual she had thought was her brother as, in Jacobs's words, "a person without clothes, small, thin, no hair, and large eyes." He calls such individuals as Martinson "unaware abductees." Unaware abductees "explain their strange experiences in ways acceptable to society, interpreting the entities they see as ghosts, angels, demons, or even animals."

See Also: Abductions by UFOs

Further Reading

Jacobs, David M., 1998. *The Threat.* New York: Simon and Schuster.

Allingham's Martian

According to *Flying Saucer from Mars* (1954), Englishman and author Cedric Allingham witnessed the landing of an extraterrestrial spacecraft while vacationing in Scotland in February 1954. A tall man, human in all ways except for an unusually broad forehead, stepped out of the vehicle. The occupant, who indicated that he was from Mars, spoke in a friendly fashion, saying that he had earlier visited Venus and the moon. He asked if earthlings would soon visit the latter world, and when Allingham replied yes, the Martian acted concerned. He wanted to know if a war would soon erupt on Earth. After this conversation, which occurred mostly by gestures, the Martian reentered his craft and flew away, though not before Allingham had photographed him (from the back) and his ship. The book asserted that a man named James Duncan had witnessed the entire encounter.

A year earlier George Adamski had published his account of a meeting with the Venusian Orthon in the southern California desert. Allingham's tale thrilled British saucerians, who now felt they had their own contact. Waveney Girvan, who had published the British edition of Adamski and Desmond Leslie's book, wrote, "If Allingham is telling the truth, his account following so soon upon Adamski's amounts to final proof of the existence of flying saucers" (Girvan, 1956).

Allingham proved strangely elusive, however, making only one public appearance. He showed up in the company of a virulently anti-UFO science writer and media personality Patrick Moore. That, plus the failure of inquirers to find the alleged witness to Allingham's contact, should have warned British saucerians that all was not well with the story told by their native Adamski. In 1956 Allingham's publisher—also the publisher of Moore's books—released a statement asserting that the contactee had died of tuberculosis in a Swiss sanitarium.

In a book on British UFOs published thirteen years later, journalist Robert Chapman reported that he had found no evidence that a Cedric Allingham had ever existed. In his judgment, *Flying Saucer from Mars* amounted to "probably the biggest UFO leg-pull ever perpetrated in Britain" (Chapman, 1969). It was an open secret among Moore's friends that he and a friend, Peter Davies (the "Martian" in the photograph), had written the book as a spoof on those gullible enough to believe Adamski's contact tales. Moore, well known as a practical joker, once had regaled a contactee magazine with letters, written under an assortment of absurd pseudonyms (including "L. Puller"), claiming scientific confirmation of the contactee cosmos.

Eventually word of Moore and Davies's involvement trickled down to British ufologists. Two of them, Christopher Allan and Steuart Campbell, interviewed Davies who admitted the hoax and added that he had rewritten the original manuscript to disguise Moore's distinctive literary style. After the hoax was exposed for the first time in print in the London ufology journal *Magonia,* Moore professed to be outraged, threatened legal retaliation, and then retreated into telling silence.

See Also: Adamski, George; Brown's Martians; Dentons's Martians and Venusians; Hopkins's Martians; Khauga; Martian bees; Mince-Pie Martians; Monka; Muller's Martians; Orthon; Shaw's Martians; Smead's Martians; Wilcox's Martians

Further Reading

Allan, Christopher, and Steuart Campbell, 1986. "Flying Saucer from Moore's?" *Magonia* 23 (July): 15–18.

Allingham, Cedric [pseud. of Patrick Moore and Peter Davies], 1954. London: Frederick Muller.

Chapman, Robert, 1969. *Unidentified Flying Objects.* London: Arthur Barker.

Girvan, Waveney, 1956. *Flying Saucers and Common Sense.* New York: Citadel Press.

Leslie, Desmond, and George Adamski, 1953. *Flying Saucers Have Landed.* New York: British Book Centre.

"News Briefs," 1956/1957. *Saucer News* 4,1 (December/January): 12.

Tory, Peter, 1986. "I See No Hoax, Says Patrick." *The* [London] *Star* (July 28).

Alpha Zoo Loo

Trucker Harry Joe Turner allegedly met an alien named Alpha Zoo Loo during a frightening encounter on a Virginia highway. The first incident reportedly took place on the night of August 28, 1979, when a UFO hovered over his truck. Even though the truck was moving at seventy miles per hour, an alien figure opened the door, and a terrified Turner fired several pistol shots at it, without apparent effect. Turner blacked out, returning to consciousness in the Fredericksburg warehouse that had been his destination.

Turner noted other anomalies. His odometer indicated that he had traveled seventeen miles though he knew that Winchester, his starting point, and Fredericksburg were eighty miles apart. An odd, filmy substance covered the truck, and parts of his CB and AM/FM antennae were missing, as if they had been melted or cut off. He also complained of a burning sensation in his eyes. While trying to enter his truck to resume his journey, Turner passed out and was taken to a hospital. After a short stay he was released and, on returning home, suddenly "remembered" that the UFO had lifted both him and the truck inside it.

Turner also recalled that the craft carried a crew of white-clad, humanlike beings who wore caps. When they took the caps off, Turner could see a series of numbers stamped, or otherwise impressed, on their heads. They spoke in a squeaky, high-pitched tone. Only when one of them, Alpha Zoo Loo, slowed his speech could Turner understand it.

As they traveled through space, Alpha Zoo Loo asked Turner questions about his truck. Eventually they arrived at a planet two and a half light years beyond Alpha Centauri, where dome-covered cities dotted an otherwise devastated landscape. Turner had the impression that the civilization had experienced a nuclear war in its not-distant past.

Back on Earth, Turner later claimed other contacts with Alpha Zoo Loo and assorted aliens. His erratic behavior, however, undercut his credibility, leading friends, family members, and onlookers to wonder about his psychological stability. Investigators also learned of Turner's reputation for yarn-spinning.

Further Reading

Hendry, Allan, 1980. "Abducted! Four Startling Stories of 1979." *Frontiers of Science* 2, 4 (July/August): 25–31, 36.

Whiting, Fred, 1980. "The Abduction of Harry Joe Turner." *MUFON UFO Journal* 145 (March): 3–7.

Alyn

"Alyn" is the name Constance Weber, who wrote under the name Marla Baxter, gives Howard Menger in her book *My Saturnian Lover* (1958). Weber/Baxter relates that after being widowed, she devoted herself to an interest in flying saucers. In the summer of 1956, she joined a group headed by Alyn R., who "was said to have had contacts with people from other worlds." Alyn eventually reveals his secret to her: "I am not of this world! I am a volunteer to Earth from the planet Saturn." On Saturn, he tells her, he was the spiritual teacher Sol da Naro. In the meantime, on Earth, the two become lovers. She writes, "My

Howard and Connie Menger (August C. Roberts/Fortean Picutre Library)

Saturnian lover did wonderful things for me. . . . My body seemed to grow more softly contoured through this pygmalion transformation as the Saturnian sculptor, by his unique artistry, molded me by his every electric touch and caress." At the end of the book, she learns that in a previous incarnation she had been Marla, a Venusian beauty in love with Sol da Naro.

During the time period covered by the book, Howard Menger, a sort of East Coast counterpart to California's George Adamski, left his wife, Rose, for Connie Weber. At one point during their affair, but before Menger had ended his marriage, four disillusioned followers accused Weber of impersonating a spacewoman who was supposed to be granting them an audience in an unlighted room. The couple survived the scandal, however, and were married in due course. Eventually, they moved to Florida, where they live now.

See Also: Adamski, George

Further Reading

Baxter, Marla [pseud. of Constance Weber Menger], 1958. *My Saturnian Lover.* New York: Vantage Press.

"'Very Sincere Fellow' Howard Menger Returns to Long John Program," 1957. *CSI News Letter* 21 (November 1): 14–16.

Ameboids

A professional woman writing under the pseudonym Lisa Oakman claims that from childhood into her early twenties she experienced many encounters with nonhuman beings. Most were generally humanlike in appearance, but the most exotic she calls "ameboids."

The ameboids were "horrible" and "nightmarish" entities, shaped like amoebas, with the colors of bruises. They attached their wet snouts to the fleshy areas of her body, sucked, and left round, red marks in their wake. Some seemed to be taking energy, others blood. They would come into her bedroom at night, and she was too terrified to resist them. She lay paralyzed while they did their work, and she did not resume activity—in this case, screaming—until they were gone.

Further Reading

Oakman, Lisa [pseud.], 1999. "UFO Beings, Folklore, and Mythology: Personal Experiences." *International UFO Reporter* 24, 4 (Winter): 7–12.

Andolo

Andolo was a being channeled by contactee Trevor James Constable. Andolo, a member of the Council of Seven Lights, a kind of cosmic governing board consisting of wise space people, communicated from a vast extraterrestrial satellite, Shan-Chea, in orbit around Earth.

In the mid-1950s, concerned about mysterious disappearances of airplanes and their crews, Constable asked Andolo if he and his associates ever abducted or killed human beings in this way. Andolo assured him that the "Universal plan" kept them from causing "a physical death wittingly under any circumstance." He warned, however, that "dark ones" did not recognize these laws. They would steal earthly aircraft in order to learn about earthly technology, and "they may desire the entities [persons] in the airplane for purposes of their own, regarding which I shall presently tell you nothing" (James, 1958).

See Also: Contactees

Further Reading

James, Trevor [pseud. of Trevor James Constable], 1958. *They Live in the Sky.* Los Angeles: New Age Publishing Company.

Andra-o-leeka and Mondra-o-leeka

Chief Frank Buck Standing Horse, an Ottawa Indian from Oklahoma, met Andra-o-leeka and Mondra-o-leeka onboard a spaceship that took him to several planets in July 1959. The ship, called *Vea-o-mus,* landed around 10 P.M. on the evening of the twelfth. Piloted by Andra-o-leeka, the ship took off again, this time going to Mars, then to Venus. After a short stay there, a female pilot, Mondra-o-leeka, a Venusian, relieved Andra-o-leeka, and the ship went on to Clarion, a planet hidden on the other side of the sun. (Clarion first appears in contactee stories after Truman Bethurum reported meeting a "scow" [a small spacecraft] and its pilot, the beautiful Aura Rhanes, who hailed from that planet.) After a short stop on Clarion, *Vea-o-mus* took a two-hour journey to a planet called Oreon (as opposed to "Orion," a constellation). Standing Horse stayed there for two days.

Oreon, he reported, was a beautiful planet, so lovely that as a man of the gospel he wondered if he were in heaven. "Heaven is a long way from here," he was told (Dean, 1964). While there, he ate well, mostly fish as well as fresh fruit from giant plants.

Several years later on December 22, 1962, Standing Horse entered a spacecraft near Bakersfield, California, and was taken to Jupiter where he saw a magnificent building made of marble. He witnessed the dancing of "five tribes of Indians." In a Jupiter city, at the Church of the Open Door, he heard a concert in which Handel's *The Messiah* was sung. At one point he saw a screen that recorded scenes from Earth. According to Standing Horse, the people of Jupiter are better-looking versions of earthlings, with the races living together in harmony.

The chief was returned to Earth three days later, on the evening of Christmas Day. His hosts drove him back to a Hollywood bus station in a car without wheels and powered by electromagnetic energy. "Two cops were arresting two men on the corner," Standing Horse wrote to John W. Dean, "and were they dumbfounded when they saw the car come down and let me out!"

Standing Horse claimed to have met Mondra-o-leeka one more time on the streets of Cedko, California, on October 11, 1962.

See Also: Aura Rhanes; Bucky; Contactees

Further Reading

Dean, John W., 1964. *Flying Saucers and the Scriptures.* New York: Vantage Press.

Angel of the Dark

On several occasions, New Age writer Alice Bryant has encountered the Angel of the Dark, who sometimes calls herself "an Angel of the Divine Plan." The angel stands nearly three stories tall. "Large, matte-dark feathers with iridescent tips" cover her. She wraps her wings around herself like a cloak and wears a wooden bird mask from which a long, sharp beak extends.

She is here to take away all those feelings and fears that impede spiritual progress. Her bird mask symbolizes her connection with the vulture, which removes carrion, and the eagle, which soars toward the light. "I cleanse the shadow side into perfection," she says.

Further Reading

Bryant, Alice, and Linda Seebach, 1997. *Opening to the Infinite: Human Multidimensional Potential.* Mill Spring, NC: Wild Flower Press.

Angelucci, Orfeo (1912–1993)

Orfeo Angelucci was among the most interesting of the early contactees. Unlike many of his contemporaries, he was generally deemed

UFO contactee Orfeo Angelucci (Fortean Picture Library)

sincere, even by skeptics who tended to see him as something of a religious visionary in a flying-saucer context rather than as a cynical exploiter of the credulous. Angelucci's initial contact allegedly occurred on May 24, 1952, in Burbank, California. Driving home from work at an aircraft factory, he saw a saucer, which emitted two small globes. The globes approached him, and a masculine voice assured him that he had nothing to fear. Angelucci saw a crystal cup materialize, and he drank a delicious, healing liquid from it. A screen appeared before him, showing a striking-looking man and woman who seemed to read his mind. Another visionary experience, initiated like the first time by a "dulling of consciousness" (Angelucci, 1955), occurred two months later. On August 2, he had a physical encounter with space people for the first time.

Angelucci soon went public with his experiences, warning that a world war was imminent. From the ruins of the world, a "New Age of Earth" would arise. He also related that after six months of unusual psychological symptoms, as well as "vivid dreams of a hauntingly beautiful, half-familiar world," he was transported to a beautiful otherworld. He learned that he had lived there in another life, when he was known as "Neptune." Angelucci wrote two books on his experiences and became a prominent figure on the contactee circuit. With the passing of the initial wave of enthusiasm about contactees, Angelucci became little more than a distant memory of saucerdom's heady early days. His death in Los Angeles on July 24, 1993, was little noted.

In his time, however, his claims attracted the attention of the celebrated psychologist and philosopher C. G. Jung, who wrote about them in one of his last books. Jung observed, "The individuation process, the central problem of modern psychology, is plainly depicted . . . in an unconscious, symbolic form . . . although the author with his somewhat primitive mentality has taken it quite literally as a concrete happening" (Jung, 1959).

The cover of The Secret of the Saucers *by Orfeo Angelucci (Fortean Picture Library)*

See Also: Contactees

Further Reading

Angelucci, Orfeo, 1955. *The Secret of the Saucers.* Amherst, WI: Amherst Press.

———, 1959. *Son of the Sun.* Los Angeles: DeVorss and Company.

Jung, C. G., 1959. *Flying Saucers: A Modern Myth of Things Seen in the Skies.* New York: Harcourt, Brace and Company.

Anoah

Anoah, associated with the Melchizedek Order of the White Brotherhood, consisting of wise extraterrestrial and spiritual entities, channeled through Austin, Texas, psychic medium Jann Weiss in the 1980s. The Planetary Light Association, which at its peak had some 3,200 members around the world, distributed books and tapes of these channeling sessions. It also held workshops at which enthusiasts listened to Anoah discuss the transition from an old age to a new age of expanded consciousness and cosmic awareness.

See Also: Channeling

Further Reading

Ached, Fretter, 1963. *Melchizedek: Truth Principles.* Phoenix, AZ: Lockhart Research Foundation.

Weiss, Jann, 1986. *Reflections by Anoah.* Austin, TX: Planetary Light Association.

Anthon

At the contactee-oriented Rocky Mountain Conference on UFO Investigation held in Laramie, Wyoming, in May 1982, Ken McLean read a statement from "a Mr. Watanabe," who claimed to be an extraterrestrial living in a human body. His true name was Anthon, and he was in his third earthly incarnation. The first was during the Revolutionary War, he said. He was one of 150,000 "incarnate beings" living on our planet and observing our activities. These beings telepathically communicated their findings to space people both on the surface of our planet and in our upper atmosphere.

According to Anthon, we are now entering the end of an age that began with Jesus' appearance, though Anthon believes Jesus was not the Son of God but "the only human being to have incarnated through enough lifetimes and enough karmic experiences to transcend death. . . . He is in charge of the transition into a 'New Age' which will occur sometime in the near future."

Anthon claimed that many incarnate beings do not know their true identity; thus they have to be awakened to it.

See Also: Contactees

Further Reading

Sprinkle, R. Leo, ed., 1982. *Proceedings: Rocky Mountain Conference on UFO Investigation.* Laramie: School of Extended Studies, University of Wyoming.

Antron

Driving along a section of highway between Jacksonville and Callahan, Florida, one August night in 1974, businesswoman Lydia Stalnaker saw a bright, flashing light just above some nearby treetops. A suffocating sensation enfolded her, and she lost consciousness. When she awoke, she was still behind the wheel, but on a different road. Soon she learned that three hours, for which she could not account, had passed. Under hypnosis in May 1975, she "recalled" being taken into a spacecraft, where aliens told her that another woman would be placed inside her body. She saw the woman sitting on the other side of a table from her. Stalnaker's head was placed inside some kind of mechanical device, and she passed out. When she revived, a spaceman told her she was now one of them. He escorted her out of the ship, and she returned to her car.

Subsequently, Stalnaker claimed, she found that she had extraordinary psychic gifts that allowed her to read other people's minds and to practice paranormal healing. Before long Stalnaker was channeling the alien woman, who called herself Antron. Antron reported that she was from a "star galaxy." She had come to prepare earthlings for a great cataclysm. "We want to take the good people with us to recolonize elsewhere," she said (Beckley, 1989).

See Also: Channeling

Further Reading

Beckley, Timothy Green, 1989. *Psychic and UFO Revelations in the Last Days.* New Brunswick, NJ: Inner Light Publications.

Gansberg, Judith M., and Alan L. Gansberg, 1980. *Direct Encounters: The Personal Histories of UFO Abductees.* New York: Walker and Company.

Anunnaki

Ancient-astronaut theorist Zecharia Sitchin, author of a series of books under the rubric *The Earth Chronicles,* argues that a race of humanlike beings, the Anunnaki, live on the planet Nibiru (also known as Maldek), the alleged twelfth planet of our solar system. Though unknown to astronomers, Nibiru, on an elliptical orbit, circles our sun every 3,600 years. According to Sitchin, Nibiru will be in our immediate planetary space in the near future and will be detected between Mars and Jupiter. When that happens, the Anunnaki will make their presence known by appearing on Earth.

Sitchin's ideas are based on his reading of ancient Sumerian documents. In his view they confirm that the Anunnaki—a Sumerian term—created humans in their image, via genetic engineering with the DNA of native anthropoids, after their arrival some four-hundred thousand five-hundred years ago. These original earthlings were created so that they could work as slaves in the Anunnaki's terrestrial gold mines; the extraterrestrials needed the gold to preserve the atmosphere of their home world. Many thousands of years later, they returned to give the Sumerians and Egyptians their respective civilizations and actually lived among these people for a thousand years. One visitor from Nibiru, Enki, reportedly saved the human race. When a hostile alien, Enlil, tried to keep the Anunnaki from warning humans that the passing near Earth of Nibiru would cause an immense tidal wave, which would sweep over Earth and destroy its inhabitants, Enki resisted. He told Noah, of biblical fame, about the coming deluge, and Noah set to work on his ark, thus ensuring the survival of earthly life.

The Anunnaki supposedly live a very long time because one year to them is the number of earthly years it takes their planet to go around the sun. Their technology is so advanced that they developed space flight half a million years ago. They are also able to revive the dead.

One critic has written, "Clearly, Sitchin is a smart man. He weaves a complicated tale from the bits and pieces of evidence that survive from ancient Sumeria to the present day. Just as clearly, Sitchin is capable of academic transgressions (fracturing quotes, ignoring dissenting facts) . . . and flights of intellectual fancy. . . . Worst of all, he is almost utterly innocent of astronomy and other assorted fields of modern science" (Hafernik, 1996).

See Also: Greater Nibiruan Council

Further Reading

Hafernik, Rob, 1996. "Sitchin's Twelfth Planet." http://www.geocities.com/Area51/Corridor/8148/hafernik.html

Schultz, Dave. "The Earth Chronicles: Time Chart." http://www.geocities.com/Area51/Corridor/8148/zchron.html

Sitchin, Zecharia, 1976. *The Twelfth Planet.* New York: Stein and Day.

———, 1980. *The Stairway to Heaven.* New York: St. Martin's Press.

———, 1985. *The Wars of Gods and Men.* New York: Avon Books.

Apol, Mr.

In the mid to late 1960s, while researching material for a series of books, occult journalist John A. Keel allegedly received a series of phone calls from "Mr. Apol," a badly confused, interdimensional entity. Apol did not know where he was in time, often confusing past and future, and traveling through both involuntarily. According to Keel, "he and all his fellow entities . . . [played] out their little games because they were programmed to do so" (Keel, 1975). In the fashion of psychic vampires, they lived off the energies of contactees and other experients of the paranormal. Keel believed Apol to be an ultraterrestrial as opposed to an extraterrestrial, because in Keel's view such entities come from other realities rather than other planets.

Though Keel did not meet Apol himself, a Long Island woman saw him pull up to her house in a black Cadillac, a vehicle favored by the enigmatic men in black, earthly agents for unearthly intelligences. Keel reported that the woman thought Apol looked "Hawaiian." When he introduced himself, he shook her hand. His own hand was "as cold as ice."

Keel dedicated his book *Our Haunted Planet* (1971) to "Mr. Apol, wherever you are."

See Also: Contactees; Keel, John Alva; Time travelers; Ultraterrestrials

Further Reading

Keel, John A., 1975. *The Mothman Prophecies.* New York: Saturday Review Press/E. P. Dutton and Company.

Arna and Parz

Between 1976 and 1980 a family at Oakenholt in northern Wales underwent a complex series of extraordinary experiences. Perhaps the first event involved six-year-old Gaynor Sunderland, who, while playing in a field one summer afternoon, spotted a cigar-shaped craft resting on the ground. She saw a man in a spacesuit walking in front of the object, using a gunlike device to burn holes into the ground. Apparently caught by surprise, the being stared at her, and Gaynor had the impression that he was probing her mind. An angry-looking woman appeared alongside him, and Gaynor felt the same sensation of mind-intrusion. Hearing noises from within the craft, the woman returned to the spacecraft, and the young girl took the opportunity to flee. Many other bizarre UFO incidents involving all five Sunderland children as well as their parents took place subsequently.

In February 1979 Gaynor glimpsed two smiling beings who had appeared in some nearby bushes and then vanished when she turned away. On June 24 she encountered the same alien couple in a sort of out-of-body experience. Lying in bed at 11 P.M., she saw the ceiling open into a tunnel, sucking her in toward a distant light. Once she reached the end of the journey, the couple—now accompanied by a small boy—greeted her. The woman was named Arna, the man Parz. They gave her a tour of their world, showing her a stream as well as some vegetation unlike anything on Earth. Their manner was courteous but not particularly warm. When Arna touched Gaynor's hand, the visitor witnessed a great city under a red sun and unclouded blue sky. All of the people in the city looked young. After the vision faded, Arna said good-bye via telepathy and promised another meeting. Gaynor returned to the tunnel and ended up in her bed.

A few weeks later, in August, Arna reappeared to display images of a destroyed Earth. She asked Gaynor for her assistance in directing an energy being back to its proper residence. Gaynor, her brother Darren, and her parents walked to a field and meditated until they sensed that the intruder was gone.

On the night of September 14, Arna and Parz appeared and took Gaynor into their spacecraft. Besides the couple she knew, there were three others. One looked so close to being purely human that Gaynor wondered if the young woman, who looked to be about nineteen years of age, was some kind of hybrid. Gaynor noticed a picture on the wall of a male being like Parz, only older. He was standing by a globe of a planet that clearly was not Earth. The ship flew into space. Half an hour later Arna and Parz told her that it had reached its destination, which turned out to be a kind of zoo full of bizarre creatures, all of them in twos. The animals were not in cages and had a great deal of space in which to wander. Finally, the sights were too unsettling for Gaynor, and her hosts permitted her to return to the ship. Before they parted, however, Gaynor learned that Arna and Parz were "about 3500 of your years old" (Randles and Whetnall, 1981).

Gaynor sensed somehow that she had not really been in space. What she had experienced were vivid mental images that the aliens had beamed into her brain. At the same time, she was certain that she had not dreamed any of this; it was much too real and had none of the distinguishing characteristics of dreams.

See Also: Hybrid beings

Further Reading

Randles, Jenny, and Paul Whetnall, 1981. *Alien Contact: Window on Another World.* London: Neville Spearman.

Artemis

Artemis hails from the planet Miranda, located in an uncharted region of the Milky Way galaxy. He and the thirteen thousand beings on his team orbit Earth in a giant space platform, focusing their attention on most of the North American continent. Other spaceships from other places attend to the rest of Earth. Artemis, who channeled through Anthony and Lynn Volpe in 1981, said that he seeks to raise humanity's collective vibration. Coming cataclysms will radically alter the population and surface of the planet. Certain chosen earthlings who are advanced spiritually will be taken up just before the disasters. Others will be left on the surface for a time as they help suffering Earth people. Eventually, spiritually unenlightened but otherwise harmless persons will be taken up and resettled on uninhabited planets, while the truly evil will be left on Earth. Most, though not all, will perish. All of this, Artemis said in 1981, will happen "sooner than most people think" (Beckley, 1989).

Further Reading

Beckley, Timothy Green, 1989. *Psychic and UFO Revelations in the Last Days.* New Brunswick, NJ: Inner Light Publications.

Ascended Masters

Ascended Masters are human beings who achieved pure spiritual enlightenment before their deaths. Along with that enlightenment, they attained mystical powers that set them apart from their fellows. When their physical bodies died ("ascended"), they continued to oversee the affairs of humanity. They channel wisdom to those who will listen to them.

One source observes, "It is important for students and people to come to realize that all Ascended Beings are Real, Tangible Beings. Their Bodies are not physical but They can make them as tangible as our physical bodies are" ("Ascended Masters"). The Great White Brotherhood, a spiritual council that exists in the supernatural realm, consists of Ascended Masters.

Further Reading

"Ascended Masters." http://www.ascension-research.org/masters.html.

Ashtar

Ashtar is among the most popular and most powerfully positioned of all channeling entities. As (according to most contactees who have dealings with him) head of the Ashtar Command he is, in the words of his sponsor Lord Michael, "Supreme Director in charge of all of the Spiritual program" for Earth. From his giant starship in Earth's general vicinity he gives orders to millions of extraterrestrial and inter-dimensional beings who are trying to reform and enlighten earthlings. His home is in the etheric realm, which means that to visit our physical universe he must descend the vibratory scale, or we would not be able to hear or perceive him at all. He explains his mission thus:

"*We have come to fulfill the destiny of this planet,* which is to experience a short period of 'cleansing' and then to usher in a *NEW GOLDEN AGE OF LIGHT.* We are here to lift off the *surface,* . . . during this period of cleansing, those *souls who are walking in the Light on the Earth.* . . . The *souls of Light* are you people of Earth who have lived according to universal truths and have put the concerns of others before your own. . . . The short period of cleansing the planet is *IMMINENT—EVEN THE MIDNIGHT HOUR!*" (Tuella, 1989).

Officially, Ashtar came into the world on July 18, 1952, when George W. Van Tassel, an early and influential contactee from southern California, took a telepathic message from "Portla, 712th projection, 16th wave, realms of Schare" (pronounced Share-ee). Portla pronounced, "Approaching your solar system is a ventla [spaceship] with our chief aboard, commander of the station Schare in charge of the first four sectors. . . . We are waiting here at 72,000 miles above you to welcome our chief, who will be entering this solar system for the first time." Soon the chief spoke, introducing himself with—"Ashtar, commandant quadra sector, patrol section Schare, all projections, all waves." He addressed an emerging concern among occultists of the period: that the hydrogen bomb, then in development, would set off a chain reaction that would destroy the planet. Ashtar warned that if scientists did not stop their work on the device immediately, "we shall eliminate all projects connected with such" (Van Tassel, 1952).

Though Van Tassel would claim contacts with many other curiously named otherworldly entities, only Ashtar would make a wider mark in the contactee subculture. Before long other channelers were receiving material from Ashtar as well as his associates, such as Sananda (Jesus), Korton, Soltec, Athena, Monka, and others. So many Ashtar channelings occurred that soon Ashtar was warning some communicants that evil astral entities were impersonating him. He was also forced to deny allegations that he was "some form of giant mechanical brain" (Constable, 1958). In the 1970s and beyond, as fundamental Christians began writing books on UFOs, Ashtar was represented as a servant of Satan.

Though to nearly all who experienced him, Ashtar existed only as a disembodied voice, a very few claimed to have seen him. One woman, Adele Darrah, even alleged that she saw him before she had ever heard of an Ashtar. One night in the early 1960s, after she had gone to bed, Darrah found herself suddenly awake and in her downstairs living room, where a striking-looking stranger stood in front of the fireplace. He was tall, slim, and erect and was wearing a uniform with a high collar. "His eyebrows were slim and delicate, the nose was thin, the mouth was rather straight, the lips thin," she reported. "His eyes were brilliant and penetrating, almond-shaped with a slight oriental appearance." When she introduced herself, he smiled and indicated that he already knew her name. Then he squared his shoulders and announced, "I am Ashtar." Everything that followed faded from her memory, and only a few years later, Darrah claimed, would she learn that others knew such an entity.

Typically, however, contactees and channelers report seeing Ashtar in psychic perception or in out-of-body journeys to his starship. Perhaps not surprisingly, descriptions vary, some calling him dark, others fair, some estimating his height at less than six feet, others at more than seven.

In the 1980s and 1990s, more and more of the messages from Ashtar and his associates focused on the "Ascension," the removal of "Lightworkers"—those doing the Command's work on Earth, many if not all of them extraterrestrials in earlier incarnations—from Earth just prior to the Cleansing (the natural and other catastrophes that will afflict Earth, killing millions, before the space people land). The failure of either the Ascension or the Cleansing to take place discouraged many followers. In a channeling in the 1990s, Ashtar explained that, in fact, the Lightworkers had effected huge changes, which, though now invisible, will become apparent in due course. In the meantime, according to Ashtar associate Soltec, the human race will continue to be educated subtly through dreams, popular culture, and growing numbers of spacecraft sightings. Unfortunately, "there will be many ones who will confuse us with negative ET encounters. Indeed, the greys will take advantage of the opportunity to confuse the populace and attempt to tarnish our image. Ones must be made aware of the distinction between the ships of Light and the ships of abduction" (Soltec, n.d.).

In 2000, Brianna Wettlaufer of Van Tassel's organization, the Ministry of Universal Wisdom (Van Tassel himself died in 1978), put out a statement that sought to separate Ashtar from the Ashtar Command. Van Tassel, it was said, communicated only with Ashtar; the Ashtar Command, on the other hand, was a concept promulgated by another early contactee, Robert Short. He and Van Tassel had been friends but parted company when Short decided to make Ashtar's communications "commercial and mainstream, in order for personal notoriety, not for a truth to the public." Wettlaufer insisted that "Ashtar is not a metaphysical philosopher or rambler" and moreover, he cannot be reached via channeling (though Van Tassel's own method of communication seemed indistinguishable from channeling to most observers). The statement goes on, "The Ashtar of Ashtar Command is a real personality . . . a clone of the original Ashtar, and is dangerous . . . a disobedient angel" (Wettlaufer, 2000).

The name "Ashtar" may owe its inspiration to a nineteenth-century work, *Oahspe,* the product of alleged angelic dictation to New York occultist John Ballou Newbrough. In this complex alternative history of Earth and the universe, "ashars" are guardian angels who sail the cosmos in etheric ships. *Oahspe* had a wide readership among devotees of the early contactee movement.

See Also: Athena; Contactees; Korton; Monka; Portla; Sananda; Van Tassel, George W.

Further Reading

Alnor, William M., 1992. *UFOs in the New Age: Extraterrestrial Messages and the Truth of Scripture.* Grand Rapids, MI: Baker Book House.

James, Trevor [pseud. of Trevor James Constable], 1958. *They Live in the Sky.* Los Angeles: New Age Publishing Company.

King, Beti, 1976. *Diary from Outer Space.* Mojave, CA: self-published.

———, 1976. *A Psychic's True Story.* Mojave, CA: self-published.

Soltec, n.d. "Ashtar Command and Popular Culture." http://www.eagleswings.com/au/soltec1.html

Tuella [pseud. of Thelma B. Turrell], ed., 1989. *Ashtar: A Tribute.* Third edition. Salt Lake City, UT: Guardian Action Publications.

Van Tassel, George W., 1952. *I Rode a Flying Saucer! The Mystery of Flying Saucers Revealed.* Los Angeles: New Age Publishing Company.

Wettlaufer, Brianna, 2000. "A Brief Background between Ashtar and Ashtar Command." http://www.georgevantassel.com/Pages/005.1ashtar.html

Asmitor

In *Revelation: The Divine Fire* (1973) Brad Steiger reports a story related to him by Robert Shell of Roanoke, Virginia, concerning a malevolent entity that attached itself to a young man experimenting with psychedelic drugs. The being called itself "Asmitor" even as it explained that this was not precisely its name, but the closest approximation that the human voice could manage to pronounce.

Shell said that he met Mark while both were living in an apartment building in Richmond, Virginia, in 1969. Shell and a friend were pursuing an interest in ritual magic. Mark, then eighteen years old, expressed no interest in such things; his interests were in electronics and occasional use of hallucinogens. Thus, Shell was surprised and skeptical when Mark began speaking of contact he was beginning to experience with what he called an "entity" that gave him certain things in exchange for periodic occupation of his physical body. Around this time Shell and his wife observed poltergeistlike manifestations in their apartment.

These experiences led Shell to be more open-minded about Mark's claims. Mark confided that the entity was a multidimensional energy being. It extended across the entire universe, though by force of will it could focus on a particular place for purposes of communication. It never explained why it sought such contacts, but Mark came to sense that it had a deep interest—again for reasons it would not clearly divulge—in this level of reality. As time went by, Mark came to see the entity, now calling itself Asmitor, as evil and deceitful. It also would not let him alone and more or less possessed him.

Before that happened, however, Shell accepted Mark's endorsement of Asmitor's essentially benign intentions and asked for a personal contact. One night he underwent a frightening experience in which he awoke with a crushing sensation on his chest, which he interpreted as a visitation from Asmitor, though the sensations he describes are classic characteristics of sleep paralysis. The next day Mark, passing on Asmitor's words, told Shell that Asmitor had found him—Shell—unfit for contact.

Asmitor claimed to be in conflict with another entity, with the climactic battle imminent. The other entity was just as malevolent as Asmitor, but the two were deadly enemies, their conflict having been set up, for inscrutable reasons, by a "higher ruling force." Mark was to create a "landmark"—a "specific, easily accessible point for it to hold onto"—consisting of a pentagram with symbols drawn around it.

Though Asmitor had promised Mark complete physical protection, the young man learned otherwise when he was arrested for possession of LSD and marijuana and sentenced to jail. After serving three months, he was released. By this time Shell had moved to another city and out of direct contact with Mark, though the two exchanged some letters and talked on the phone on occasion. Mark expressed growing desperation about his plight. He was certain now that he could escape Asmitor's grip only by destroying himself. Thus, Shell said, "It came as a shock, but not really a surprise, to hear from a mutual friend . . . that on April 1, 1970, Mark had committed suicide."

Shell noted that not long afterward, while perusing a book of medieval magic, he came upon the name Asmitor, though he could not tell Steiger exactly where. "I am convinced that Mark had never read this book," he remarked, "and I am also convinced that Mark did not simply make up this name." Steiger, on the other hand, suspected that the tragic episode came out of "paranoid schizophrenia, or some other illness."

Further Reading

Steiger, Brad, 1973. *Revelation: The Divine Fire.* Englewood Cliffs, NJ: Prentice-Hall.

Maren Jensen as space commander Athena in the 1978–1979 ABC TV series Battlestar Galactica *(Photofest)*

Athena

In *Project Alert,* a self-published monograph, an Indiana contactee known as Tuieta provides a transcript of a three-day conference held at "the Tectonic base that is on planet Earth." The gathering brought together "specific commanders . . . under the immediate supervision, guidance, and counsel of Commander Ashtar." Among the speakers, who included such familiar figures in the Ashtar Command as Korton, Monka, and Soltec, was the heretofore obscure Commander Athena. Athena spoke of the role of Earth women in the coming "period of great tribulation." During this crisis many people would not survive. The woman most likely to get through the catastrophic Earth changes, according to Athena, was one who recognized "the importance of providing for loved ones and providing for those that need nurturing and counsel."

Athena is described as a small, reddish-gold-haired, beautiful woman with deep blue eyes. She exudes "great love and great compassion and tremendous strength." Her name, coincidentally or otherwise, is the same as that of the Greek goddess of wisdom, the arts, and warfare. Athena was also the name of a space commander in the television series *Battlestar Galactica,* which aired on ABC in 1978 and 1979.

According to the late Thelma B. Turrell (who was also known as Tuella, a name given her by the Ashtar Command), "Athena is the twin flame of Ashtar. He has said to me that he could turn over the whole command to her and no one would even miss him" (Beckley, 1989).

See Also: Ashtar; Contactees; Korton; Monka

Further Reading

Beckley, Timothy Green, 1989. *Psychic and UFO Revelations in the Last Days.* New Brunswick, NJ: Inner Light Publications.

Tuieta, 1986. *Project Alert.* Fort Wayne, IN: Portals of Light.

Atlantis

Atlantis, the fabled lost continent, almost certainly never existed in the real world, but it has long captured the imaginations of human beings. A vast literature—scholars estimate conservatively that more than two thousand books address the subject—has tackled Atlantis from a wide range of perspectives. Some writers have sought to establish, with what most scholars hold to be inconclusive results, that the legend arose from the mythologizing of a real event, though almost every theorist has proposed a different one. Most writing, however, has taken an alternative-history approach, paying little heed to mainstream archaeology, history, and science, while taking Atlantis into the realm of unfettered speculation.

The legend of Atlantis begins in two works, *Timaeus* and *Critias* (written circa 355 B.C.), by the great Greek philosopher Plato. As in his earlier work *The Republic,* Plato wrote these works as dialogues among four wise men, including Plato's teacher Socrates. In the course of a long discourse on philosophical issues of various kinds, Critias, a historian and Plato's great-grandfather, tells of a story that he ascribes to his grandfather, who heard it from his father. Around 600 B.C., while traveling in Europe, Solon (a historical figure remembered for his legal and poetic genius) learned of a great civilization that existed nine thousand years earlier. It was located in the Atlantic Ocean beyond the Pillars of Hercules (the present-day Straits of Gibraltar) on an island larger than North Africa and Asia combined. According to Solon's informant, an Egyptian priest, Atlantis had grown arrogant and warlike. It ruled many other islands and parts of what is now Europe. But when it attacked Athens and other Greek city-states, those communities joined forces to repel the invaders and drive them back to Atlantis, freeing other islands from Atlantis's tyranny in the process. But when the battle was brought to Atlantis's own shores, cataclysmic earthquakes and floods destroyed the island continent over a single night and day. The Greek soldiers died along with the Atlanteans, and Atlantis sank to the bottom of the ocean, to rise no more.

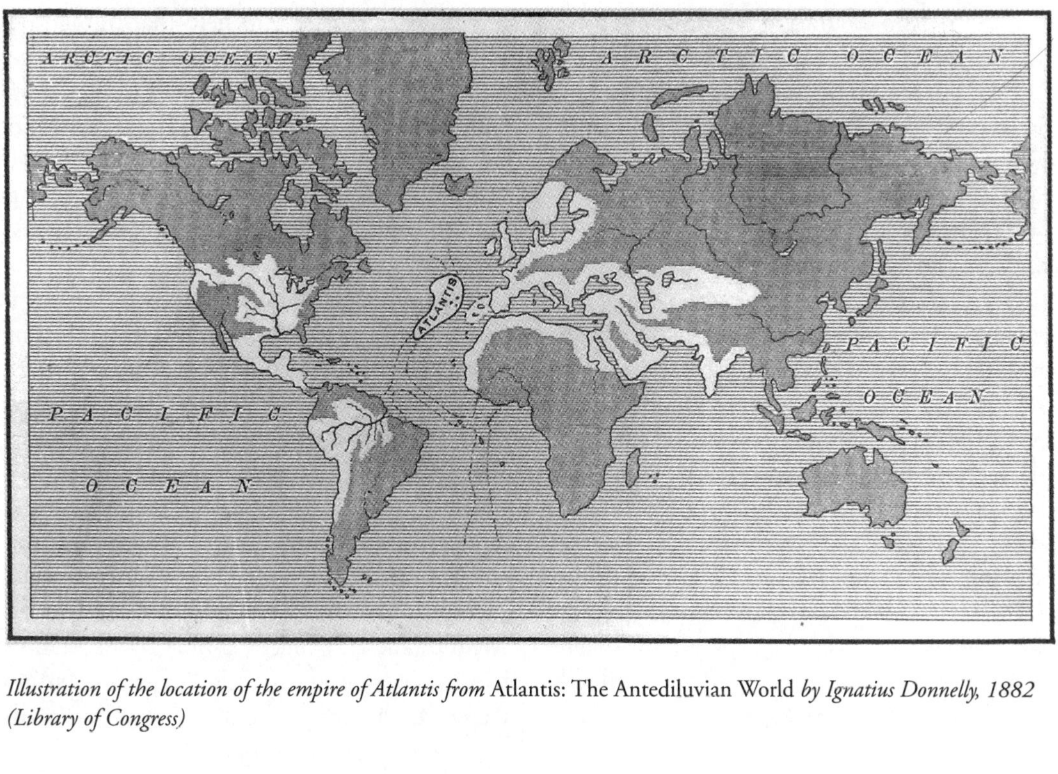

Illustration of the location of the empire of Atlantis from Atlantis: The Antediluvian World *by Ignatius Donnelly, 1882 (Library of Congress)*

That is not all the dialogues have to say, however. Most of the discussion, much of it intricately detailed, describes a civilization that was nearly perfect before pride corrupted it. Atlantis is supposed to be the place of model governance. In its prime it operated by the principles set forth in *The Republic.*

No other ancient document contains an independent treatment of Atlantis. All references to the lost continent cite Plato as the source. Some accept Plato's account as historical, while others see it as an allegory never meant to be taken literally. Plato's own student Aristotle took the latter view.

During the sixteenth and seventeenth centuries, as European explorers found their way to the Americas, several writers, most prominently Sir Francis Bacon (1551–1626), revived the myth of Atlantis and theorized that its remains could be found in the New World. That would be only the beginning of a new round of speculation. "At one time or another," a modern chronicler of the legend observes, "Atlantis has been located in the Arctic, Nigeria, the Caucasus, the Crimea, North Africa, the Sahara, Malta, Spain, central France, Belgium, the Netherlands, the North Sea, the Bahamas, and various other locations in North and South America" (Ellis, 1998).

Among the most influential books ever written on the subject, *Atlantis: The Antediluvian World* (1882) was the creation of a former Minnesota congressman named Ignatius Donnelly (1831–1901). Donnelly surveyed what he presented as evidence from such disciplines as archaeology, geology, biology, linguistics, history, and folklore to argue vigorously for the proposition that Atlantis not only existed but was the place where human beings became civilized. Atlantis sent its people all over the world and seeded the earth. The great gods and goddesses of the ancient world were based on the leaders and heroes of Atlantis; worldwide legends of a mighty deluge owe their origins to dim memories of the catastrophe that overwhelmed Atlantis. The historical civilization influenced most directly by Atlantis was ancient Egypt.

These revelations sparked international interest, and Donnelly's book went through many printings. For a time even some reputable scientists were willing to consider the possibility that the legend was true, after all. Indeed, Donnelly was elected to the American Association for the Advancement of Science. Before long, however, as critics exposed the book's errors, exaggerations, and assorted scholarly shortcomings, belief in Atlantis moved to the occult fringes, to be championed by the likes of Theosophy founder Helena Petrovna Blavatsky and other philosophers of the esoteric. Before the end of the nineteenth century, a growing body of occult literature attested that Atlantis was advanced, not just by the standards of their time, but by modern times as well; it possessed a super science that, among other marvelous accomplishments, had invented airplanes and television.

The Scottish folklorist and occultist Lewis Spence, who took a relatively more conservative approach, wrote five books on Atlantis between 1924 and 1943, citing Donnelly and his methodology as his principal inspiration. Bowing to the consensus view of historians and archaeologists, who held that human beings were living in caves nine thousand years before Plato's time, Spence held that Atlantis had existed nine hundred years before Plato. Meanwhile, allegations, rumors, and outright hoaxes of archaeological "discoveries" of Atlantean artifacts filled the popular press and kept the "mystery" alive.

The much-circulated channelings of Edgar Cayce (1877–1945), called the "sleeping prophet" because of the state of consciousness in which he vocalized his psychic readings, often concerned Atlantis. Many who came to him for psychic guidance learned that they had been Atlanteans in previous lives. In Cayce's comprehensive re-envisioning of the lost continent, Atlantis was essentially where Plato had placed it: between the Gulf of Mexico and the Mediterranean. Unlike Plato's, Cayce's Atlantis was as advanced as mid-twentieth-century America, and in a number of ways more advanced. The Atlanteans, according to Cayce, at first were spiritual beings. They eventually evolved into flesh-and-blood ones. Their society came undone when civil war erupted. A combination of natural disasters and the misuse of Atlantean technology caused the continent to break apart and sink under the ocean waters. But by the late 1960s, Cayce predicted, the western part of Atlantis would reemerge in the vicinity of Bimini, in the Bahamas. When the time came, more than two decades after Cayce's death, several expeditions searched for Atlantean ruins in the area, at one point trumpeting what proved to be natural undersea rock formations as roadways and architectural artifacts.

Atlantis has been thoroughly absorbed into fringe belief, theory, and practice. In the age of flying saucers, some writers tied UFOs to an extraterrestrial technology that the Atlanteans knew because of their frequent interactions with friendly space people. Hollow-earth enthusiasts believed that Atlantean machinery and even Atlanteans themselves could be found inside certain cavern entrances around the world. New Age channelers communicated with hundreds, perhaps thousands, of disembodied Atlanteans. A century of occult lore holds that Atlanteans and Lemurians (from Lemuria, the Pacific equivalent of Atlantis) maintain colonies inside Mount Shasta on the California-Oregon border.

With the rise of the Internet, web sites devoted to Atlantis and related materials have proliferated. One such site, run by the Hawaii-based Department of Interplanetary Affairs, provides a densely detailed overview of the Atlantis myth as it had evolved by the end of the twentieth century. In this version, Atlantis was literally a golden civilization in which gold was so plentiful that it was as common as steel is today in construction and infrastructure. The Atlanteans traveled around the globe in fantastic flying ships. These same ships took them to other planets, including Mars, where they left evidence of their presence in a gigantic structure (the "Mars face") and a number of pyramids on the Martian surface. The moon was also a colony of Atlantis. Modern-day astronauts found ruins of walls and roads there but were silenced by a government determined to keep the truth about Atlantis from the public.

The Department of Interplanetary Affairs describes Atlanteans as living lives of leisure and prosperity, while a "national work force of robots, androids, and humanoids from genetic engineering" did the empire's heavy lifting. "Atlantean science then fostered some bizarre genetic creations—they discovered ways to cross-breed species to create mermaids and mermen, Cyclops, unicorns and other creatures." That same genetic engineering gave Atlanteans huge size and great strength.

It all came crashing down, in both a literal and figurative sense, when the population surrendered itself to the pursuit of hedonistic pleasures; in the meantime, evil Atlantean scientists cracked the secret of mind control and tried to dominate the world and even the solar system. In due course the abuse of both psychic and material technology led to the geophysical cataclysms that destroyed the continent.

But that was not all. According to the Department of Interplanetary Affairs, Atlantis's problems generated a world war that spread into space. Atomic blasts decimated the moon colony. Antimatter rays vaporized nearly all of Atlantis's buildings and cities. "It is said," the department reports, "that one of these antimatter rays is still operating in the Bermuda Triangle and has been causing planes and ships to disappear. Today that ray is out of control" (Omar, 1996).

For all the allure of the Atlantis legend, nothing of substance has come to light in the nearly twenty-five centuries that separate us from Plato's account to lead reasonable people to conclude that such a lost continent ever graced the Atlantic Ocean. In *Imagining Atlantis* (1998) Richard Ellis writes, "Plato's description of Atlantis was of a rich and powerful society that was swallowed up by the sea in a great cataclysm, and every remnant of it destroyed. Like the *Iliad* and the *Odyssey,* it has managed to survive for more than two millennia. But unlike Homer's epic poems, Plato's tale—rarely considered an important part of his voluminous output—has not only survived as a demonstration of the storyteller's art, but also has become a part of our own mythology."

See Also: Bermuda Triangle; Channelings; Hollow earth; Lemuria; Mount Shasta; Shaver mystery

Further Reading

Cayce, Edgar, 1968. *Edgar Cayce on Atlantis.* New York: Paperback Library.

De Camp, L. Sprague, 1970. *Lost Continents: The Atlantis Theme in History, Science, and Literature.* New York: Dover Publications.

Donnelly, Ignatius, 1882. *Atlantis: The Antediluvian World.* New York: Harper.

Ellis, Richard, 1998. *Imagining Atlantis.* New York: Alfred A. Knopf.

Omar, Steve, 1996. "History of the Golden Ages, Volume I." http://www.nii.net/~obie/history-gold.htm

Spence, Lewis, 1924. *The Problem of Atlantis.* London: Rider.

Steiner, Rudolf, 1968. *Cosmic Memory: Prehistory of Earth and Man.* West Nyack, NY: Paperback Library.

Aura Rhanes

Heavy-equipment operator Truman Bethurum encountered the beautiful Aura Rhanes, captain of a "scow" (spaceship) from the idyllic planet Clarion, on the other side of the moon, in the early morning hours of July 28, 1952, in the Nevada desert. When male crew members ushered him inside the craft, parked in an area known locally as Mormon Mesa, Bethurum saw Aura Rhanes for the first time. She was small, had an olive complexion, and wore a black and red beret. The two engaged in an extended conversation, during which they asked each other about their respective worlds. The spacewoman spoke, Bethurum would write, "in a swinging, rhythmic tone of voice" (Bethurum, 1954). When daylight came, Bethurum was asked to leave, but they were to meet again. There were eleven meetings between July and November alone. Only on the occasion of the third meeting, on August 18, did she reveal her name. Once he spotted her walking down a street in Las Vegas, but she refused to speak with him, apparently not wanting to be recognized.

Bethurum participated actively in the 1950s contact movement. Most outside observers believed him to be a hoaxer. His wife, Mary, apparently felt otherwise. She divorced him in 1956 on the grounds that he was having sexual relations with Aura Rhanes. As with many other contactees from that period, it is impossible to judge just what Bethurum believed or did not believe about his reported interactions with extraterrestrials. A privately kept scrapbook published after his death carried a poem titled "Third Visit to Mormon Mesa Aug 18 1952" commemorating the meeting in which Aura Rhanes let him touch her to convince him of her physical reality. Other items in the scrapbook consist of clippings about himself and of materials lending support to his story. Though a skeptic of contact claims, British writer Hilary Evans remarks that "we still have no yardstick whereby we can separate contactees into 'genuine' and 'fake', and until we can establish some such criteria, we must provisionally extend the benefit of the doubt even to poor old Truman Bethurum and cute little Aura Rhanes from the far side of the Sun" (Evans, 1987).

See Also: Bethurum, Truman; Contactees

Further Reading

Bethurum, Truman, 1954. *Aboard a Flying Saucer.* Los Angeles: DeVorss and Company.

———, 1982. *Personal Scrapbook.* Scotia, NY: Arcturus Book Service.

Evans, Hilary, 1987. *Gods, Spirits, Cosmic Guardians.* Wellingborough, Northamptonshire, England: Aquarian Press.

Aurora Martian

An article in the April 19, 1897, edition of the *Dallas Morning News* told an extraordinary story in a very few words. Datelined Aurora, forty-five miles northwest of Dallas, it related that a mysterious "airship" had crashed into a local windmill at 6 A.M. two days earlier. On colliding, "it went to pieces with a terrific explosion, scattering debris over several acres of ground, wrecking the windmill and tower and destroying [windmill owner Judge J. S. Proctor's] flower garden," correspondent S. E. Haydon wrote. Haydon went on to report that citizens who rushed to the scene found the body of a "badly disfigured" being whom one observer identified as a Martian. The story concluded with the news that the funeral would occur the next day.

The story appeared in the midst of a wave of what today would be called UFO sightings, which had begun in northern California in November 1896 and moved eastward by the following spring, when newspapers all over America were full of strange and often fanciful stories. The *Morning News* carried no follow-up, suggesting it did not take the tale seriously enough to dispatch one of its own reporters to the site. In any event, it wasn't the only wild airship yarn the paper was carrying. The day before it printed the Aurora story, it recounted a Kaufman County sighting of a "Chinese flying dragon. . . . The legs were the propellers." At Farmersville, the paper stated, the occupants of an airship sang "Nearer My God to Thee" and distributed temperance tracts.

The episode of the Aurora Martian was forgotten until the 1960s, when public fascination with UFOs led to research into the phenomenon's early history. In 1966 a *Houston Post* writer revived the Aurora story, which he apparently took at face value. Investigators went to the tiny town and spoke with elderly residents. Most, if they remembered the episode at all, dismissed it as a joke. One said that Haydon had concocted the tale to draw attention to the town, which in the 1890s was suffering a serious decline in its fortunes.

Still, rumors persisted that a grave in the Aurora cemetery housed an unknown occupant, perhaps the Martian. As late as 1973, ufologist Hayden Hewes was trying to persuade local people to let him exhume the grave, a notion that Aurora's residents vehemently rejected. Confusing matters further, two elderly residents were now claiming that they had known persons who saw the wreckage. Analysis of metal samples allegedly of the airship, however, proved it was an aluminum alloy of fairly recent vintage.

There is no reason to believe that a Martian died in Aurora, Texas, late in the nineteenth century. Still, the legend inspired the 1985 film *Aurora Encounter,* a low-budget *ET* set in the Old West, and it remains one of Texas's more exotic folktales.

See Also: Allingham's Martian; Brown's Martians; Dead extraterrestrials; Dentons's Martians and Venusians; Hopkins's Martians; Khauga; Martian bees; Mince-Pie Martians; Monka; Muller's Martians; Shaw's Martians; Smead's Martians; Wilcox's Martians

Further Reading

Chariton, Wallace O., 1991. *The Great Texas Airship Mystery.* Plano, TX: Wordware Publishing.

Cohen, Daniel, 1981. *The Great Airship Mystery: A UFO of the 1890s.* New York: Dodd, Mead and Company.

Masquelette, Frank, 1966. "Claims Made of UFO Evidence." *Houston Post* (June 13).

Randle, Kevin D., 1995. *A History of UFO Crashes.* New York: Avon Books.

Simmons, H. Michael, 1985. "Once upon a Time in the West." *Magonia* 43 (July): 3–11.

Ausso

Ausso is an extraterrestrial allegedly encountered by Wyoming elk hunter E. Carl Higdon, Jr., on October 25, 1974. Five hours after he called for help, authorities found Higdon inside his pickup in an area inaccessible to all but four-wheel-drive vehicles. Taken to a nearby hospital, the shaken and disoriented Higdon claimed to have encountered a strange being named Ausso who flew him in a spaceship to another world where he was taken to a mushroom-shaped tower. While inside the tower, Higdon saw what looked like normal human beings, who paid no attention to him. Ausso explained that he was a hunter/explorer, and he and his people were visiting Earth to collect animals for breeding purposes and for food. Soon Higdon was flown back to Earth and put back in his truck.

Polygraph tests given Higdon in 1975 and 1976 produced ambiguous results, but psychological inventories suggested that he did not suffer from mental illness. Higdon did not seek to exploit his alleged experience and soon returned to private life. University of Wyoming psychologist and ufologist R. Leo Sprinkle, who investigated the incident, judged Higdon sincere, even if it had proved impossible to establish the "validity of the UFO experience" (Sprinkle, 1979).

Further Reading

Gansberg, Judith M., and Alan L. Gansberg, 1980. *Direct Encounters: The Personal Histories of UFO Abductees.* New York: Walker and Company.

Sprinkle, R. Leo, 1979. "Investigation of the Alleged UFO Experience of Carl Higdon." In Richard F. Haines, ed. *UFO Phenomena and the Behavioral Scientist,* 225–357. Metuchen, NJ: Scarecrow Press.

occupied them, the humans would take on their names. Other members who later came into the group, now calling itself Extraterrestrial Earth Mission, experienced the same (to outsiders) bewildering change of names and identities.

Extraterrestrial Earth Mission became an international movement. Outside the United States, it was particularly successful in Australia. The organization's headquarters are now in Hawaii.

See Also: Walk-ins

Further Reading

Melton, J. Gordon, 1996. *Encyclopedia of American Religions.* Fifth edition. Detroit, MI: Gale Research.

Avinash

On March 3, 1986, an extraterrestrial spirit entered the body of a man identified only as John. Till then, John, a channeler from Bellevue, Washington, had been communicating with another entity, Elihu. However, on this date the space being Avinash took control of John's consciousness. Soon thereafter, Avinash moved to Hawaii with another walk-in (a person under the control of a spirit or other-intelligence that has claimed his or her body), a woman named Alezsha. In due course, a third walk-in, Ashtridia, joined them. Avinash, however, did the channeling, teaching a doctrine that said essentially that conscious could affect reality; thus, both personal and societal reality can be altered if one rearranges one's perceptions.

Overseen by an immense extradimensional spaceship, the three moved to the popular New Age community, Sedona, Arizona, where Avinash met Arthea, and the two became a couple. They were brought together, they believed, by divine guidance. The walk-in group expanded to a dozen members in 1987, but as most members eventually moved away, only three remained by the end of the year. Those three, Avinash, Arthea, and Alana, began to host new occupying entities that would manifest for a time, then depart. While the entities

Ayala

Ayala is a deva, a divine energy, who claims to represent the animal kingdom and, beyond that, "All That Is." She appeared first on February 2, 1994, to two Sedona, Arizona, New Age women, both of them channelers. Subsequently, she directed other devas, including Shiva and Gaia, who communicated psychically on the subject of human-animal relations.

Ayala made her presence known when two psychics, Toraya (Carly) Ayres and a woman identified only as Sarafina, happened to be engaged in a discussion of nature spirits. Suddenly, Sarafina started shivering and breathing oddly. Then she lapsed into a trance, during which she voiced animal-like sounds. Soon Ayala was speaking through her, proposing that she and the two women work together on a project. The project required Ayres to be at her computer at three o'clock each afternoon to write down the messages as they came forth. When Ayres protested that this was not a good time for her in terms of her job responsibilities, Ayala insisted that that was the only time the communication could be effected, owing to the vagaries of planetary vibrations. She said, "We will meet you in your dreamtime, and you will be more aware of what your role is in the inter-planetary connection with All That Is. . . . There is an energy that needs to form. We have to contact all the devas, and it is not always up to us just which time we can do this."

For the next two days Ayala communicated with Ayres before relinquishing her spot to another entity, Shiva, "the blood, the muscle, fur, bone, and spirit of animals." Ayala told Ayres that animals are evolving spirits just as human beings are. Once love and trust had existed between people and animals. Then the ice ages came, and animals became wild, and humans began using them for food. Then humans started mistreating animals in all kinds of other ways, and they also abused nature generally. Even so, after enduring thousands of years of cruelty, animals continue to love humans, "whether in this dimension or any other." Humans and animals will be reconciled during this time of transition, when people are beginning the process that will take them out of the third—physical—dimension into higher dimensions.

In the meantime, Ayala urged human beings to communicate through meditation with animal devas. For example, someone having trouble with ants should visualize the ant deva and express a polite request, first stressing reverence for ants and all they do for the world, then asking the ants to leave the building. If human beings interact with animals in this fashion, there will be no need for environment-damaging poisons or needless slaughter of wild creatures.

See Also: Shiva

Further Reading

Ayres, Toraya, 1997. "Messages from the Animal Kingdom." http://www.spiritweb.org/Spirit/animal-kingdom-ayres.html

Azelia

Azelia is allegedly the half-extraterrestrial offspring of a Brazilian man and an alien being with whom he was forced to undergo sexual intercourse.

Just after returning home from work around 3 A.M. on June 18, 1979, night watchman Antonio Carlos Ferreira of Mirasol, Sao Paulo, was startled to see a UFO land outside his house. Three humanoids entered and paralyzed him with red lights that emanated from boxes they carried on their chests. They and he floated into the craft, which eventually took off. Ferreira passed out. Later he vaguely recalled a mother ship. Under hypnosis his "memories" grew sharper, and he saw himself inside a mother ship, looking at the distant Earth through a porthole. Approximately twelve different aliens, of two different but seemingly related types, occupied the same room. One group consisted of green-skinned humanoids with smooth dark hair, thin lips and noses, big eyes, and pointed ears. The others looked somewhat similar except they had brown skin, thick lips, and red, crinkly hair. All stood four feet tall and were clad in white uniforms and gloves. A green being seemed to be in charge.

Ferreira was taken into another room, which was dimly lit, and made to lie on a couch. A naked female walked in and approached him as the other beings tried to remove his clothing over the abductee's resistance. The woman, about a foot taller than the others, was essentially human, with a larger than usual head, thin lips, chocolate skin, and narrow nose. Her breath was foul. Ferreira inferred that the beings wanted him to engage in sex with the woman, a notion he found repellent. Only after the humanoids subdued him with a sharp-smelling chemical were they able to disrobe him. Even then, he continued to fight, until one of his arms was placed in a device and the other numbed with an injection. The beings spread an oily liquid all over him, and intercourse followed. At the conclusion of the act, oil was spread over him again, and they removed him from the apparatus and redressed him.

The beings, who addressed him via telepathy but spoke an "incomprehensible" language to each other, explained that they had conducted an experiment. He would father a male child. At some point, after three unspecified signals had been given, they would return to show him his offspring. After giving him an unpleasant-tasting liquid to quell his appetite, they took him to the disc that had brought him to the mother ship and flew him home. Ferreira suffered from a variety of small punctures and wounds, and for the next twenty days he had a burning sensation in his eyes.

There were other incidents. In one he was shown the child. In another, on board a UFO, he saw the child with its mother. On March 30, 1983, one being came to his workplace to inform him—notwithstanding what they had told him earlier—that the child was a girl. Her name was Azelia.

Further Reading

Granchi, Irene, 1984. "Abduction at Mirasol." *Flying Saucer Review* 30, 1 (October): 14–22.

Marsland. Robert, 1983. "Two Claimed Abductions in Brazil." *The APRO Bulletin* (November): 1–2.

B

Back

In the 1970s, a middle-aged Italian woman, Germana Grosso, told a Turin newspaper about her two decades of contact with an alien race that calls itself Back. She became aware of its existence twenty years earlier, when a Tibetan lama's telepathic messages explained to her how she could communicate with extraterrestrials. Soon the Back were showing her scenes of themselves and their lovely home planet, Lioaki. Grosso "saw" them as images on a sort of mental television screen. They also informed her that they have bases on Earth: under the Atlantic Ocean, in the Gobi Desert, and in a valley in northern Italy. Earth is nearing disaster, and the Back are here not to interfere but to warn those who will listen.

Further Reading

Beckley, Timothy Green, 1989. *Psychic and UFO Revelations in the Last Days.* New Brunswick, NJ: Inner Light Publications.

Bartholomew

The channeling entity Bartholomew first spoke through Mary-Margaret Moore in the mid-1970s. She was visiting friends in Socorro, New Mexico, and undergoing hypnosis in an effort to relieve back pain. Suddenly, somebody was speaking through her. For the first year of their association, Moore feared that Bartholomew was a dramatic delusion. But over time she became convinced of his wisdom and prophetic talents. She came to think of him as "the energy vortex" or "the higher and wiser level of energy" (Moore, 1984).

During the New Age boom of the 1980s, Bartholomew—known for his gentle, kind manner—was something of a channeling superstar; his messages of comfort and self-love were taken to heart. He addressed a wide range of subjects, from sex and AIDS to prayer and ego surrender. Before his popularity waned, he was the subject of two books by Moore.

See Also: Channeling

Further Reading

Moore, Mary-Margaret, 1984. *I Come as a Brother: A Remembrance of Illusions.* Taos, NM: High Mesa Press.

———, 1987. *From the Heart of a Gentle Brother.* Taos, NM: High Mesa Press.

Bashar

After two close encounters with large, triangle-shaped UFOs over the course of one week in 1973, Californian Darryl Anka—the brother of singer and composer Paul Anka—began reading UFO literature in search of answers. Through his reading about UFOs, he was led to paranormal subjects such as psychic phenomena, channeling, and spirit communication. In 1983, Anka sat in with a channeler and spent several months absorbing information from discarnate sources. The entity offered to teach whoever might be interested in learning how to channel, and Anka decided to take a course from the channeler. Midway through the course, Anka first heard from "Bashar," who said he was the pilot of the spaceship Anka had seen a decade earlier.

Bashar claimed to have come from a planet where all communication is done through telepathy. The people there do not have names as such. He called himself Bashar—Arabic for "commander"—for Anka's convenience.

After a period of telepathic communication with Bashar, Anka started to channel—in other words, to speak with his (or Bashar's) voice so that others could hear. In due course, Anka has become an internationally known channeler who has taken Bashar (as well as another entity, Anima) to a variety of nations on several continents. Bashar has told Anka that he and his people live on the planet Essassani, five hundred light years from Earth but in a different dimension. Bashar was speaking not just for himself but collectively expressing his society's sentiments.

"I have no way of proving 'Bashar's' existence to anyone," Anka concedes. "The most important thing is that the information, wherever it's coming from, had made a difference in many people's lives, including my own" (Anka, n.d.). Anka's organization, Interplanetary Connections, coordinates the channeling efforts and circulates tapes of their recordings.

See Also: Channeling

Further Reading

Anka, Darryl, 1990. *Bashar: Blue Print for Change, A Message for Our Future.* Simi Valley, CA: New Solutions Publishing.

"A Message from Darryl Anka," n.d. http://www.bashartapes.com/about/message2.html

Being of Light

In his best-selling *Life after Life* (1976) Raymond A. Moody writes of near-death experiences in which persons undergo visionary encounters of what seems to be a kind of heavenly realm. In out-of-body states, according to testimony Moody collected, percipients observe a brilliant light at the end of a tunnel-like passage. A telepathic message from the light asks the observer something like, "Are you prepared to die?" or "What have you done with your life?" Immediately afterward, the dying person experiences a "life review" in which significant events are rapidly played out either in order of their occurrence or all at once in, as Moody puts it, "a display of visual imagery . . . incredibly vivid and real."

The percipient feels great love and warmth emanating from this being, who is usually interpreted as a divine figure from the individual's own religious tradition. Some see it as God or Christ, others as an angel. All, however, feel that the being is "an emissary, or a guide."

Moody characterized the meeting with the being of light as "perhaps the most incredible common element in the accounts." Other researchers who followed in Moody's wake, however, only ambiguously replicated this particular finding. Kenneth Ring, Margot Grey, and others found fewer such encounters in their own samples of people who had undergone near-death experiences. Many near-death accounts described the observation of an overwhelmingly loving, beautiful light surrounding them and suffusing the landscape, but only a small minority of reports had that light as a "being." A typical expression of the light was more like one offered by an Englishwoman who encountered it while her heart stopped as she was anesthetized during dental surgery: "The light is brighter than anything possible to imagine. There are no words to describe it, it's a heavenly light" (Grey, 1985). Frequently, percipients encounter recognizable figures, usually either Christ or deceased friends and relatives.

Further Reading

Grey, Margot, 1985. *Return from Death: An Exploration of the Near-Death Experience.* Boston, MA: Arkana.

Moody, Raymond A., Jr., 1976. *Life after Life: The Investigation of a Phenomenon—Survival of Bodily Death.* Harrisburg, PA: Stackpole Books.

Ring, Kenneth, 1980. *Life at Death: A Scientific Investigation of the Near-Death Experience.* New York: Coward, McCann and Geoghegan.

Rogo, D. Scott, 1989. *The Return from Silence: A Study of Near-Death Experiences.* Wellingborough, Northamptonshire, England: Aquarian Press.

Bermuda Triangle

The three points of the "Bermuda Triangle" are Florida, Bermuda, and Puerto Rico. In modern legend, the Triangle is more than an arbitrary geometric shape; its three points comprise the boundaries of a passage into a mysterious otherworld. In the Bermuda Triangle, the laws of nature are suspended, and ships, planes, and people disappear without a trace.

A key event in the genesis of the legend was a real-life tragedy off the coast of Florida on December 5, 1945. That afternoon, five Avenger torpedo bombers flew out of the Naval Air Station at Fort Lauderdale. Flight 19, consisting of fourteen men (thirteen of them students in the last stage of training), headed on an eastern course toward the Bahamas, intending to participate in a practice bombing at Hens and Chickens Shoals, fifty-six miles away. After completing that part of the mission, the aircraft were to proceed to the east for another sixty-seven miles, turn north for seventy-three miles, then head west-southwest for the remaining one hundred twenty miles back to their home base. Heading the mission—the only nonstudent—was the relatively inexperienced Lt. Charles Taylor, who did not know the area well.

By late afternoon, the planes were lost. Taylor thought they were flying over the Keys off Florida's south coast, and he made a fatal misjudgment: he flew north. If he and his men had been over the Keys, of course, they would

A reward poster at a marina for the yacht Saba Bank, *which went missing in the Bermuda Triangle March 10, 1974 (Bettmann/Corbis)*

have arrived over land and to safety. Because they were over the Bahamas, however, flying northward only put them over the ocean. With weather conditions deteriorating rapidly, their radio contact with land, already sporadic, grew ever more difficult. Meanwhile, amid growing alarm about the planes' situation, a Dumbo flying boat—a large rescue aircraft built for flight over large bodies of water—was dispatched from a seaplane base in Miami and sent on a blind search. Soon other planes joined it and flew through the ever more turbulent weather. One of them, a Martin Mariner, also disappeared.

None of the missing craft were ever found. The navy's investigation determined that Taylor's confusion about his location, coupled with dangerous air and sea conditions, caused the planes under his command to run out of gas, crash, and get chewed up by the immense waves the storm had summoned. At 7:50 that evening, a ship's crew saw a plane explode. A search for survivors and bodies was unsuccessful, though the vessel passed through a large oil slick from the craft. The navy believed that the Mariner, a notoriously dangerous aircraft that was sometimes called a "flying gas bomb," had blown up.

If the facts seemed relatively straightforward, the legend that would grow in the wake of Flight 19's disappearance would be far more convoluted and fantastic. Flight 19's transformation from aviation tragedy to paranormal mystery would begin in September 1950, when Associated Press writer E.V.W. Jones wrote a story about what he called the "limbo of the lost," an area bordered by Florida, Bermuda, and Puerto Rico, where strange things happened. None, he wrote, was stranger than the unexplained fate of five Avengers and one Mariner on the evening of December 5, 1945.

Soon books and magazines dealing with UFOs and other anomalous phenomena—and even mainstream publications such as *The American Legion Magazine*—were picking up the stories, which grew in the telling. The term "Bermuda Triangle" was the invention of longtime Fortean and paranormal writer Vincent H. Gaddis; his article on the subject in the February 1964 issue of *Argosy* was titled "The Deadly Bermuda Triangle." The next year he incorporated it into a popular book, *Invisible Horizons,* on "true mysteries" of the seas. In *Invisible Residents* (1970) Ivan T. Sanderson pointed to the Bermuda Triangle and comparable places on Earth as evidence that "OINTS"—Other Intelligences—live under the oceans, sometimes snatching planes, ships, and their unlucky crews.

By the 1970s, the groundwork had been laid for a popular craze. The 1970 release of a low-budget documentary, *The Devil's Triangle,* stirred interest outside the core audience of paranormal enthusiasts. Four years later, Charles Berlitz's *The Bermuda Triangle,* a compilation of lore that had already quietly circulated for years, became a major bestseller. That same year two paperbacks, *The Devil's Triangle* by Richard Winer and *Limbo of the Lost* by John Wallace Spencer, fueled public fascination and speculation. But the next year, in 1975, Larry Kusche's in-depth inquiry into the incidents that underlay the legend, *The Bermuda Triangle Mystery—Solved,* undercut the myth-making by documenting the prosaic explanations that would have been apparent if the pro-Triangle writers had done original research and not simply rewritten each other's books. The silence of the writers whom Kusche criticized effectively ended the discussion.

See Also: OINTS

Further Reading

Begg, Paul, 1979. *Into Thin Air: People Who Disappear.* North Pomfret, VT: David and Charles.

Berlitz, Charles, with J. Manson Valentine, 1974. *The Bermuda Triangle.* Garden City, NY: Doubleday and Company.

Eckert, Allan W., 1962. "The Mystery of the Lost Patrol." *The American Legion Magazine* (April): 12–23, 39–41.

Gaddis, Vincent H., 1965. *Invisible Horizons: True Mysteries of the Sea.* Philadelphia, PA: Chilton Books.

Kusche, Larry, 1975. *The Bermuda Triangle Mystery—Solved.* New York: Harper and Row, Publishers.

———, 1980. *The Disappearance of Flight 19.* New York: Harper and Row, Publishers.
Sand, George X., 1952. "Sea Mystery at Our Back Door." *Fate* 5, 7 (October): 11–17.
Sanderson, Ivan T., 1970. *Invisible Residents: A Disquisition upon Certain Matters Maritime, and the Possibility of Intelligent Life under the Waters of This Earth.* New York: World Publishing Company.

Bethurum, Truman (1898–1969)

Truman Bethurum was one of the stars of the 1950s contactee movement. In a 1953 issue of *Saucers* magazine, Bethurum reported that in the early morning hours of July 28, 1952, he met eight little men of "Latin" appearance and was led to a nearby flying saucer. There he met the captain, a beautiful woman named Aura Rhanes from Clarion, a planet never visible to humans because it is always on the other side of the moon. Clarion, Bethurum was informed, is a peaceful, utopian world; fear of nuclear war on Earth had led the Clarionites to visit and observe earthlings at first hand. Bethurum claimed further contacts. In the mid-1950s, Bethurum established a communelike "Sanctuary of Thought" in Prescott, Arizona. He was a regular at the Giant Rock Interplanetary Spacecraft Convention and other contactee venues. He remained active on the circuit until his death in Landers, California, on May 21, 1969.

Cover of Aboard a Flying Saucer *by Truman Bethurum (Fortean Picture Library)*

UFO contactee Truman Bethurum (Fortean Picture Library)

Two early chroniclers of the contactee subculture found themselves "favorably and very deeply impressed with Mr. Bethurum's unimaginative sincerity" (Reeve and Reeve, 1957). Another apparent believer was Mary Bethurum, his first wife, who divorced him on the grounds that he was engaged in a sexual relationship with Aura Rhanes. More cynical observers, such as *Saucer News* editor James W. Moseley, judged Bethurum to be a liar, motivated by a desire to enrich himself at believers' expense. Bethurum refused to undergo polygraph examination to verify his story, and when asked to submit, for scientific analysis, a letter said to have been composed by Aura Rhanes, he declined, explaining that "paper on Clarion is made out of just the same kind of trees we have on earth" (Davis, 1957).

See Also: Aura Rhanes; Contactees

Further Reading

Beckley, Timothy Green, ed., 1970. *The People of the Planet Clarion.* Clarksburg, WV: Saucerian Books.

Bethurum, Truman, 1954. *Aboard a Flying Saucer.* Los Angeles: DeVorss and Company.

———, 1953. "I Was Inside a Flying Saucer." *Saucers* 1, 2: 4–5.

Davis, Isabel L., 1957. "Meet the Extraterrestrial." *Fantastic Universe* 8, 5 (November): 31–59.

Moseley, James W., 1961. "Recent News Stories: 1961 Giant Rock Convention Is Disappointing." *Saucer News* 8, 4 (December): 12–13.

Reeve, Bryant, and Helen Reeve, 1957. *Flying Saucer Pilgrimage.* Amherst, WI: Amherst Press.

Bird aliens

A French businessman who insisted on anonymity confided a strange tale to ufologist Lyonel Trigano about a decidedly unsettling encounter on a rural road in Var one dark, rainy night in November 1962. As he rounded a curve, he saw, some fifty to sixty feet ahead of him, a group of figures standing close to one another in the middle of the highway. He slowed down, and as he did so, the group "jerkily" broke into two parts.

"My window was down," he related, "and I leaned my head out slightly to see what was the matter; it was then that I saw beasts, some kind of bizarre animals, with the heads of birds, and covered in some sort of plumage, which were hurling themselves from two sides toward my car."

Shocked and frightened, he quickly rolled up the window and accelerated. After moving a few hundred feet to what he thought was a safe distance, he looked back to see these "nightmarish beings" flapping what looked to be wings and heading toward a glowing, dark-blue object hovering over a field on the other side of the road. The UFO looked like two upside-down plates placed over each other.

When the creatures or beings reached the UFO, they "were literally sucked into the underpart of the machine as if by a whirlwind." A dull thudding sound followed, and the UFO streaked away.

The witness told Trigano that he had said little to others about the experience for fear of being thought mad.

See Also: Close encounters of the third kind; Mothman

Further Reading

Trigano, Lyonel, 1968. "Strange Encounter in Var." *Flying Saucer Review* 14, 6 (November/December): 18.

Birmingham's ark

A bizarre experience is recorded in a fifteen-page document left by a nineteenth-century Australian, Frederick William Birmingham, who lived in Parramatta, New South Wales. Birmingham was an engineer, surveyor, and alderman for the city, today a suburb of Sydney. His tale is reminiscent in some ways of the flying-saucer contactee tales that would circulate decades later.

The document came into the hands of a well-known Australian ufologist, Bill Chalker, in 1975. Investigating its background, he traced it to a teacher named Haywood, who lived at the location where Birmingham (whose existence and occupation Chalker was able to verify) was dwelling when his encounter occurred. Haywood, apparently, later gave it to another family, which had had the manuscript in its possession since at least the early 1940s and showed it to Chalker. Chalker could find no evidence that it was a recent literary or historical hoax.

Birmingham wrote that on the evening of July 25, 1868, "I had a wonderful dream, a vision," while standing under the verandah of the cottage he rented. Looking up into the sky, he saw "the Lord Bishop of Sydney's head in the air looking intently upon me in a frowning half laughing mood." As it passed in an easterly direction, it faded out, then reappeared briefly twice more. "I retraced the course the head had taken and just in the spot where I first saw the head I saw an 'Ark,'" he wrote. As he stood and studied it, he said aloud to himself, "Well, that is a beautiful vessel."

At that moment he heard a voice to his right and just a little behind him. It said, "That's a machine to go through the air." The speaker was someone Birmingham thought of as a "spirit," looking like a "neutral shade and the shape of a man." The ark was brown in color "with faint, flitting shades of steel blue . . . like . . . magnified scales on a large fish." After a while Birmingham replied to the spirit. He remarked that the ark looked more like a ship meant for sailing on water; in any event, he had never seen anything so beautiful.

He accepted an invitation to board the vehicle. He found himself floating through the air in the spirit's company. When they reached the upper part of the ark, they entered the "pilot house" by walking down three steep steps. Inside the barely furnished room was a table situated two feet from the wall. Something like an oilskin covered the table. Birmingham stood at the rear end, and, not far away, the spirit held papers in its hand. One paper was covered with "figures and formulae." After Birmingham asked if the papers were for him, the spirit replied slowly and emphatically, "It is absolutely necessary that you should know these things, but you can study them as you go on."

Birmingham, apparently not knowing what to say, looked down at his hands. When he raised his head, the spirit was gone. He stood alone inside the strange ship. In his manuscript he recorded this ambiguous conclusion to the encounter: "So I fell, I suppose, into my usual sleeping state, and waking next morning deeply impressed with that vision of the night."

The following January, at work on an engineering problem, Birmingham was surprised to see a formula that he had first seen on the paper the spirit had shown him. It had to do with centrifugal pumps.

One day in 1873, at sunset, Birmingham saw three small "clouds" suddenly appear. Two "screws" extended from one. Between them, a shape "like two flat necks on a turtle-shaped body" came into view, then disappeared, only to reappear soon afterward. Finally, "the two big . . . screws folded up like the arms of a bear and lost their shape in the middle cloud" (Chalker, 1996).

The manuscript indicates that Birmingham had become obsessed with the ark and its secrets. He died in 1893, however, without ever being able to unlock them.

See Also: Contactees

Further Reading

Chalker, Bill, 1996. *The Oz Files: The Australian UFO Story.* Potts Point, New South Wales, Australia: Duffy and Snellgrove.

———, 1992. "UFOs in Australia and New Zealand through 1959." In Jerome Clark. *The Emergence of a Phenomenon: UFOs from the Beginning Through 1959—The UFO Encyclopedia, Volume Two,* 333–356. Detroit, MI: Omnigraphics.

Blowing Cave

One of the odder stories related to hollow earth lore is set in Blowing Cave, near Cushman, Arkansas, where a man named George D. Wight is said to have found a subterranean civilization and proven the Shaver Mystery. Though Wight disappeared, his story survives in a diary he allegedly wrote.

In the 1950s, Wight was a UFO buff from Michigan. Wight knew of Richard Shaver's claims, published in the 1940s in the Ziff-Davis science-fiction magazines *Amazing Stories* and *Fantastic Adventures,* that the remnants of two advanced races, tero and dero (good and evil respectively), lived in vast caverns under Earth's surface. Though Wight was skeptical of these claims, he had an interest in cave-exploring that he indulged with David L., for whose mimeographed saucer newsletter Wight contributed a regular column. They did their spelunking with three other men. All of them were acquainted with Charles A. Marcoux, another columnist for the magazine. Unlike the others, Marcoux was an obsessed believer in Shaverian concepts, to the extent that he gave occasional public lectures on the subject. The spelunkers sometimes attended those lectures but considered his beliefs absurd.

In 1966, the group, now consisting of twelve persons, went down to Arkansas to explore Blowing Cave on a week-long expedition. On their return, members wrote letters to Ray Palmer, once editor of *Amazing Stories* and Shaver's principal promoter, claiming that they had encountered intelligent beings—Shaver's teros—deep inside the cavern. Palmer did not reply. Apparently a few months later, Wight went back and chose to stay with the underearth people. He returned in 1967 to give a written account to David L., who by this time had left the UFO field and no longer wanted to be publicly associated with it. Wight asked L. to pass on the diary to Charles Marcoux. Wight felt that in ridiculing his beliefs he had wronged him and wanted to provide him with the proof that Shaver was right. He then returned to his tero friends and has not been seen since.

David L., however, had long since lost track of Marcoux, and it was not until thirteen years later that he came upon his name. He tracked him down and handed him the manuscript. Its effect on Marcoux was electrifying, and it set in motion the events that would eventually lead to his premature death.

The manuscript related that while exploring Blowing Cave, the group spotted a light at the end of a tunnel. As the spelunkers approached it, Wight noticed a narrow crevice, just big enough for him to squeeze inside it. There he found clearly artificial steps. He called to his friends, and they climbed through the opening. On the other side of it, the opening expanded, and they were able to walk upright. "Suddenly," Wight wrote, "we came into a large tunnel/corridor, about twenty feet wide and just as high. All the walls and the floor were smooth, and the ceiling had a curved dome shape. We know that this was not a freak of nature, but manmade. We had accidentally stumbled into the secret cavern world" (Toronto, n.d.).

Soon they encountered blue-skinned but otherwise humanlike individuals. The strangers said that they had permitted the crew to find the tunnel and enter it because they had instruments that measured people's emotions; the explorers were determined to have good intentions. They learned that the tunnels went on for hundreds of miles and led to underearth cities populated by entities that included serpentlike creatures and Sasquatchlike hairy bipeds. Soon after their initial conversation, Wight and his companions were taken to a kind of elevator that led them to the underearthers' place of residence, a city made of glass. It turned out that their guides were Noah's direct descendants, who had found their way underground in the wake of the flood. There they found supertechnology and the remains of an advanced civilization, along with teros. Apparently at some point, Wight's group met the teros who had been there all along.

This was not the only trip the group took to Blowing Cave. Unable to get anybody on the surface to believe their story, Wight and his friends vowed to return with conclusive proof. During one expedition, they captured a giant cave moth, preserved it in a bag, and brought it up with them. When they opened the bag, however, the sunlight disintegrated the insect into a fine dust.

Not long afterward, Wight decided to stay with the underearth people. According to one source, "all evidence of [his] ever existing began to mysteriously disappear from the surface. Birth certificates, school records, computer records, bank records, etc., all seemed to vanish, apparently the work of someone in a very influential position" (Untitled, n.d.). Other members of the group made another trip into the cave, where they saw their friend for the last time. Wight returned once to the surface to meet David L.

In 1980, Marcoux saw the manuscript and read Wight's words addressed to him: "Yes, Charles, all that you told us is true. . . . I owe you a debt of gratitude, because the Teros healed my crippled leg, instantly. I am grateful for more than just that, and I have left these notes and somewhere a map so that you, too, can . . . visit with these people. . . . Maybe we will meet here some day" (Toronto, n.d.). Marcoux set about organizing an expedition, soliciting members in such small-circulation hollow-earth publications as *Shavertron* and *The Hollow Hassle.*

Marcoux and his wife moved to Cushman in 1983. There, in November, as he was visiting the land around the cave, a swarm of bees descended on him. The resulting shock and trauma precipitated a heart attack, and he died on the spot.

Some hollow-earth enthusiasts speculated that sinister forces that wanted to keep the caves a secret had caused the attack. Others saw it as just a tragic accident. In any case, Marcoux's death ended efforts to explore Blowing Cave in search of underearthers.

See Also: Hollow earth; Shaver mystery

Further Reading

Toronto, Richard, n.d. "The Shaver Mystery." http://www.parascope.com/nb/articles/shaver/Mystery.htm.

Untitled, n.d. http://www.rcbbs.com/docs/empire7.txt.

Bonnie

In 1977, William Hamilton, a California man interested in UFOs, met "a young, very pretty blond girl with almond-shaped eyes and perfect small teeth." Bonnie, whom Hamilton judged sincere and sane, told him she was born in 1951 in the Lemurian city of Telos, located inside an artificial domelike cavern a mile beneath Mount Shasta on California's northern border.

Bonnie told him that she, her parents, her two sisters, and her two cousins move freely back and forth between our society and their native city. They also travel to other subterranean Lemurian and Atlantean cities, via a tube transit train system that travels as fast as 2,500 miles per hour. The Lemurians are also able to fly into outer space in saucerlike vehicles, and they interact with visiting extraterrestrials. Telos has a population of one and a half million who live a communal existence without money. She warned Hamilton that by the end of the century, Earth's axis will shift. The result will be massive devastation and huge loss of life. On the other side of this terrible event, human beings would come together as one and fashion a utopian society "on a higher plane of vibrations" (Beckley, 1993).

In Bonnie's account the Lemurians came to Earth two hundred thousand years ago from the planet Aurora. Atlantis (in the Atlantic) and Lemuria (in the Pacific) fought a war against each other twenty-five thousand years ago, but it was a natural catastrophe that brought Lemuria to the ocean bottom ten thousand years later. Atlantis was destroyed a few centuries later when Atlantean scientists conducted irresponsible experiments with cosmic, energy-generating "fire crystals."

See Also: Atlantis; Lemuria; Mount Shasta

Further Reading

Beckley, Timothy Green, ed., 1993. *The Smoky God and Other Inner Earth Mysteries.* New Brunswick, NJ: Inner Light Publications.

Boys from Topside

Wilbert B. Smith (1910–1962), an engineer who worked for Canada's Department of Transport (DOT), believed himself to be in contact with philosophically and scientifically inclined extraterrestrials. He called them the "Boys from Topside."

It is unclear when these psychic messages began, but it could have been as early as 1950. Smith was at first circumspect about them, though he was willing to acknowledge an interest in UFO investigation. In late 1950, he secured access to use DOT laboratory and field facilities during off-hours in an effort to gather technical data about UFO sightings. (According to one source, Smith was acting under the guidance of space people all the while, though he said nothing about them to his superiors.) Smith hoped for a breakthrough sufficient to overthrow conventional technology and put in its place a wholly new one. He called his work "Project Magnet," reflecting his conviction that flying saucers flew along magnetic fields. In 1952 Smith participated in a small UFO study group put together by the Canadian government's Defense Research Board. The following year, Smith released Project Magnet's findings, which were—perhaps not surprisingly—that UFOs performed in ways that are "difficult to reconcile . . . with the capabilities of our technology"; thus, "we are forced to the conclusion that the vehicles are probably extra-terrestrial" (Smith, 1953).

He urged his superiors to set up a monitoring station that would check for UFO activity over a twenty-four-hour period. They agreed to the proposal and provided a DOT-owned hut on Shirley's Bay, some ten miles west of Ottawa. The installation contained an ionospheric reactor, an electronic sound-measurement device, a gamma-ray detector, a gravimeter, a magnetometer, and a radio. If a passing UFO set off any of these, an alarm would sound. Two government scientists and two civilian astronomers worked with Smith. This work was done on their own time, but the "flying saucer observatory" garnered much embarrassing publicity for the Canadian government. It was closed at the end of August 1954. Even so, Smith was privately assured that he could continue UFO research so long as it was not at the taxpayer's expense; he was also welcome to use government equipment.

Because of his credentials and his employer, conservative ufologists who otherwise avoided persons associated with contact claims welcomed Smith into their ranks, ignoring, as much as possible, his private assertions about the Boys from Topside. Through his own and others' psychic contacts, he conversed with extraterrestrials and attempted to learn from them. In a letter to the prominent (and outspokenly anticontactee) ufologist Donald E. Keyhoe on December 11, 1955, Smith wrote, "I have learned a great deal, but I am a small child attempting to assimilate a college course. Believe me, I have been shown glimpses of a philosophy and technology almost beyond comprehension."

By now, Smith had largely abandoned more conventional techniques of UFO investigating, and he was entirely focused on contactees, whom he quizzed intensely and whose stories he compared before deciding on their validity. At least some of them, he thought, were telling the truth. He was gratified that the space people were patient enough to put up with his methods. In an article in England's *Flying Saucer Review,* after he went public with his extraterrestrial connections, he declared, "I began for the first time in my life to realize the basic 'Oneness' of the Universe and all that is in it" (Smith, 1958).

In 1956, Smith formed the contactee-oriented Ottawa Flying Saucer Club. When not grilling contactees or taking direct messages himself, he occupied himself with sky watches in parks and rural areas with like-minded friends. He lectured and wrote about his beliefs in saucer magazines, and he even spoke openly with reporters. He died of intestinal cancer on December 27, 1962.

See Also: Contactees

Further Reading

Beckley, Timothy Green, and Ottawa New Sciences Club, eds., n.d. *The Boys from Topside.* New York: UFO Review.

Cooper, Philip, 1959. "Men from Mars among Us—He's Talked to Them!" *Ottawa Citizen* (April 14).

"Flying Saucers Project Denied," 1953. *New York Times* (November 14).

Gross, Loren E., 1982. *UFOs: A History—1950: August–December.* Fremont, CA: self-published.

Nixon, Stuart, 1973. "W. B. Smith—The Man behind Project Magnet." *UFO Quarterly Review* 1, 1 (January/March): 2–11.

Smith, Wilbert B., 1953. *Project Magnet Report.* Ottawa, Ontario: Department of Transport.

———, 1954. *Project Magnet, the Canadian Flying Saucer Study.* Ottawa, Ontario: self-published.

———, 1958. "The Philosophy of the Saucers." *Flying Saucer Review* 4, 3 (May/June): 10–11.

Brodie's deros

In the mythology of the Shaver mystery, the creation of Richard Sharpe Shaver, deros are cannibalistic, sadistic idiots who live in caves underneath the earth. As the degenerated descendants of an advanced race of extraterrestrials that thousands of years ago colonized our planet, they have access to the elders' advanced technology. They use it, however, for destructive and even perverted purposes on each other and, most of all, on surface humans, whom they sometimes kidnap for torture and other unpleasant purposes. The bulk of the Shaver mystery material was published, mostly as true, in two science-fiction magazines, *Amazing Stories* and *Fantastic Adventures,* in the mid- to late 1940s.

Few other people claim to have encountered deros. The late John J. Robinson, a New Jersey man with a longstanding interest in UFOs and the paranormal, often told the story of Steve Brodie, who had his own horrifying, and possibly ultimately fatal, dealings with the deros.

According to Robinson, in 1944 he was living on the third floor of a Jersey City house. Directly beneath him on the second floor was a reclusive individual, Steve Brodie, who claimed to be an artist. Over time, Robinson won his trust, and the two often spoke. Among Brodie's quirks was his aversion to meat; and more unusual, as Robinson recalled, "he seemed to be afraid that someone might be attempting to sneak up behind him." When he walked on the street, he walked in the middle of the street, apparently out of fear that someone might jump out of an alley or a doorway. On several occasions, Robinson watched Brodie paint. Sometimes the artist would enter a trancelike state and create weird, otherworldly landscapes that looked nothing like the paintings he did in ordinary consciousness. Asked where these images came from, Brodie replied, "I don't know. I feel as if I paint these pictures from memory. It's like I can close my eyes and let it."

Once Brodie seemed startled when he saw Robinson with an issue of *Amazing Stories* in his coat pocket. Robinson, who was closely following the Shaver mystery tales the magazine was running, launched into an explanation of Shaver's claims. When he heard the word "dero," Brodie blanched. "He writes of the dero!" he exclaimed. Robinson persuaded Brodie to explain his remark. Reluctantly, after securing assurances that Robinson would not ridicule him, he related something that had happened to him and a friend seven years before.

The two had gone to a western state in search of semiprecious stones. Local people warned them to stay away from a certain desert mesa because several individuals who had gone there were never seen again. Disregarding these words of caution, the young men repaired to the site and spent the next few days energetically stone-hunting. Finally, one day, hearing his companion shout, Brodie looked up to see a figure in a black cowl standing at the base of the mesa. Another figure joined the first. The first of them pointed a rodlike device at Brodie, who abruptly felt himself paralyzed. His friend began to run, and the other figure pointed a rod at him. To his horror the smell of burning human flesh rose up in Brodie's nostrils. He never saw his friend again.

A third figure, holding what looked like earphones, approached Brodie and then walked past him. He felt something being placed just beneath his ears just before he lost consciousness. "At this point in his narrative," Robinson said, "Steve showed me why he wore his hair long at the back of his head. Behind each ear at the base of the parietal bones of his skull were bare, seared, scarred patches of skin upon which no hair could grow. Both of these areas behind the ears were a little smaller than the size of a silver dollar and were perfectly circular. Steve said they were the marks of a dero slave!"

In the ordeal that followed, Brodie was only intermittently conscious. On three or four occasions, he awoke to find himself in a cage with other human beings. They told him that he was "in the caves," and they were under the control of the "deros," who could snatch any human being off the face of the earth if they so chose. Each time it became evident that he was conscious, a black-cowled figure would zap him back into oblivion.

Then one day he found himself walking down a street in New York City with no idea how he had gotten there. He was dressed in his prospecting clothes. His personal items were still in his pockets, including a hundred dollars in bills. Though to his awareness only a day had passed, he soon learned that it was two years later.

Brodie said that ever since he could not eat meat. The very scent of it nearly made him ill.

Robinson had observed that Brodie was not a reader, and he was certain that he had not concocted a tale from reading the Shaver series.

Not long afterward, business concerns forced Robinson to move from his Jersey City apartment. He fell out of contact with Brodie for six months. When he came back for a visit, Brodie was gone. Robinson talked with a mutual acquaintance who had his own strange story. He said he had seen Brodie on a train in Arizona. When he had spoken to Brodie, he had not responded or even acknowledged his presence. He seemed to be in a "stupor," the man thought, though Robinson knew Brodie was not a drinker. The train stopped at a small town, and when the train resumed its journey, Brodie was no longer on it. Robinson saw this as evidence that the deros had reclaimed their victim.

After relating this anecdote on Long John Nebel's popular radio talk show on New York's WOR one night in March 1957, Robinson went to work the next day and was surprised when a business associate confided his own experience. He said that maybe Brodie's experience explained something that had happened to him in 1942, when he was seventeen years old. He had been visiting his friend Fred when they decided to go to a "haunted mine" nearby. Supposedly, it had a long history of accidents, disasters, and unexplained disappearances of miners. Undeterred, the two climbed over a pile of debris to get to one side of the entrance. There they were shocked to observe a grotesque entity, four and a half feet tall, with a bulky body. It let out a soul-chilling scream and chased the boys back to town. They took refuge in a movie theater. Even so, they swore they could see dark forms moving up and down the aisles as if looking for them. That night they thought they saw the figure sitting in a tree near the house.

Later, Fred vanished without a trace. Searchers came upon his bicycle near the haunted mine, and nothing further was learned of his fate. "To this day," the man told Robinson, "I am afraid that whoever or whatever it was that got Fred will find me."

See Also: Shaver mystery

Further Reading

Steiger, Brad, and Joan Whritenour, 1968. *New UFO Breakthrough.* New York: Award Books.

Brown's Martians

Clairvoyant Courtney Brown reports that his psychic probing of Mars has uncovered the startling truth that Mars was, and is, inhabited. Brown came to this conclusion while using psychic talents to explore the Cydonia region of the planet's surface, where some have felt that enigmatic artifacts, including the so-called Martian Face—an alleged structure said to depict human features—are situated.

The Martians now live underground. Millions of years ago, they lived on the surface but were nearly driven to extinction when an immense asteroid passed through the atmosphere and severely damaged it. The atmosphere continued to deteriorate until what little was left of it was sucked into space. Many Martians died, but their race was preserved when Grays—the gray-skinned humanoid reported in UFO abduction cases—intervened. They collected the Martian DNA and stored it and genetically altered the surviving inhabitants of the Red Planet. They put them into underground cities, where they live now.

The Martians' problems are far from over, however. The genetic alterations have not entirely worked, and their own technology has not been able to overcome the existing shortcomings. More and more Martians are looking to Earth as their potential home. According to Brown, the Martians are much like human beings in appearance but different enough so that humans and Martians would never be confused. They have light skin, eyes bigger than humans' and no hair.

See Also: Abductions by UFOs; Allingham's Martian; Aurora Martian; Dentons's Martians and Venusians; Hopkins's Martians; Khauga; Martian bees; Mince-Pie Martians; Monka; Shaw's Martians; Smead's Martians; Wilcox's Martians

Further Reading

Brown, Courtney, 1996. *Cosmic Voyage: Scientific Remote Viewing, Extraterrestrials, and a Message for Mankind.* New York: Dutton Books.

Bucky

Buck Nelson, a sixty-five-year-old bachelor who lived on a remote farm in the Ozark Mountains of Missouri, met Bucky of Venus on March 5, 1955. But his first sighting of spaceships took place when three of them hovered over his farm on July 3, 1954, and one shot a beam of light at him, healing his lumbago and restoring his eyesight to the degree that he no longer needed glasses. The following year on February 1, a saucer returned. This time a voice, speaking in clear English, came through a loudspeaker to ask if Nelson were friendly. The voice went on to explain that the saucer's crew was from Venus. Nelson glimpsed three human-looking, muscular men inside the craft. Around midnight on March 5, the three men, with their dog, 385-pound Big Bo, entered Nelson's house and conversed with him. All three men were nude, carrying their clothes on their shoulders; before putting their uniforms back on, they explained that they wanted to assure Nelson that except for their place of origin they were normal men. One of them said his name was Bucky.

Bucky—sometimes referred to in subsequent accounts as "Little Bucky" to distinguish him from the much older Buck—said he had been born nineteen years earlier on a Colorado farm. In 1940, a Venusian spaceship landed on the family property, and members of the crew offered to fly the whole family to their home planet for a visit. Only Bucky, then four years old, wanted to go. The Venusians agreed to return one day when he was old enough to make a mature decision on the matter. They came back in 1953, and Bucky accompanied them to Venus, where he had resided for two years before Buck Nelson met him. Besides Bucky, Nelson's visitors included Bob Solomon, a two-hundred-year-old Venusian, and an old man who, his age notwithstanding, was a trainee learning how to fly a spacecraft. After an hour the visitors left, but not before telling Nelson that they would fly him to other planets, Nelson wrote later, "if I would tell about it to the world" (Nelson, 1956).

Around midnight on April 24, Bucky and his friends arrived to take Nelson into space. He and his dog, Teddy, went to Mars. There Nelson ate a delicious meal and talked with the friendly human inhabitants, and then the ship went on to the Moon for another meal and a good rest. He, Teddy, and Big Bo went for a short walk before embarking for Venus. During one brief stop they saw the "ruler" of the region engaged in painting. He was clad, like Nelson himself, in bib overalls. Venus, like Mars and the Moon, turned out to be a pleasant place without war or conflict, where people lived in harmony under the Twelve Laws of God (essentially the Ten Commandments and a couple of verses from the New Testament). On Venus, the races were strictly segregated. Nelson also was told that his own parents were Venusians.

Bucky became a regular visitor at Nelson's house. They spent Christmas 1956 together. On another occasion, he brought a fully cooked Venusian turkey with him. On yet another Christmas, Bucky took Nelson to his home on Venus.

In the late 1950s and early 1960s, Nelson was a minor celebrity on the contactee scene. At one point, he sold packets of hair reported to be from Big Bo, who, he said, had been left in his custody for a time. New York City radio personality Long John Nebel, who met Nelson at the Fourth Interplanetary Spacecraft Convention at Giant Rock, California, in 1957, said: "It is my impression that Buck Nelson has made very little money out of his wild, if somewhat crude, stories, but there are those who believe in him, many for just that reason. Frankly, I suspect that he would change this aspect of his activities if he could" (Nebel, 1961).

See Also: Contactees

Further Reading

Dean, John W., 1964. *Flying Saucers and the Scriptures.* New York: Vantage Press.

Nebel, Long John, 1961. *The Way Out World.* Englewood Cliffs, NJ: Prentice-Hall.

Nelson, Buck, 1956. *My Trip to Mars, the Moon, and Venus.* Mountain View, MO: self-published.

———, 1955. "A Strange Tale from Missouri." *Flying Saucer Review* 1, 2 (May/June): 4–5.

Buff Ledge abduction

The UFO abduction that reportedly occurred at Buff Ledge, north of Burlington, Vermont, is unusual in that it involved two persons who, though separated by years and distance, provided strikingly similar accounts to an investigator.

The incident took place at Buff Ledge Camp, a since-closed girls' camp. The two witnesses have never been publicly identified, but astronomer and ufologist Walter N. Webb, who spent years probing the episode, gives them the pseudonyms Michael Lapp and Janet Cornell. On the evening of August 7, 1968, Lapp and Cornell, who worked as counselors, were relaxing on an L-shaped dock that jutted one hundred feet out into Lake Champlain and which was largely concealed by the bluff from the view of others. The camp was nearly deserted; most campers and counselors were off on a trip elsewhere.

Lapp and Cornell witnessed the approach of a bright light that soon resolved into a white, glowing, cigar-shaped object. Soon three smaller white lights emerged from the bottom right side. As the last light came into view, the cigar-shaped object sailed away. The small UFOs executed various maneuvers through the sky, moving close enough so that the observers could see that they were domed and disc-shaped. After five minutes, two of them departed in opposite directions, to the north and south, emitting sounds like "thousands of tuning forks," as Lapp would put it. The remaining UFO flew toward them, and now it looked the size of a small house. Abruptly it streaked upward, vanished, then reappeared to plummet into the water about a mile away.

Soon the UFO came back to the surface and flew, at an altitude of fifteen feet above the water, toward the witnesses again. It stopped some sixty feet from them, and now it was so near that Lapp could see right into its transparent dome, where he was shocked to observe two large-headed figures, short in stature with big eyes and small mouths, who were clad in gray or silver uniforms.

Turning to his companion, Lapp saw a woman in an apparent trance. She did not act as if she had heard him when he spoke to her. At that point Lapp decided to try an experiment, and he addressed the entities. Who were they, he asked, and why were they here? To his surprise a voice with a "feminine quality" spoke inside his head to assure him they meant no harm. Over the next few minutes, as Lapp spoke his questions aloud, and the alien woman replied telepathically, he was told that the aliens had "returned after the first atomic bomb exploded" and that they were seeking some form of energy about which the voice provided no details. They were also engaged in war with others of their race, characterizing these enemies as "evil." When Lapp asked where they came from, he heard a name he could not pronounce or subsequently remember.

Finally, with the two beings disappearing below the deck, the UFO positioned itself ten feet above the witnesses' heads. A beam shone down on them, a kind of "liquid light" that felt weirdly as if it were shining inside Lapp's head. He and Cornell fell down on the deck as voices and machine sounds echoed.

The next thing they knew, it was dark. They were lying on the deck as two girls atop the bluff were shouting about a UFO. The object was ascending and shooting beams of light toward the girls.

The following evening Lapp drove home to tell his parents, who responded with skepticism, about his sighting. He also informed his girlfriend, who was similarly unreceptive. He did not discuss the incident with Cornell and soon lost contact with her. In the years ahead, he had dreams about being onboard the UFO and developed an interest in mysticism and religion. In 1978 he discussed his experience with Webb, then an astronomer employed by Boston's Hayden Planetarium.

Subsequently, Webb traced Cornell to Atlanta. She confirmed the sighting though all she could recall of it was that a "big light" had approached them, they had fallen down, and some sort of mental block had ensued. Webb had refrained from sharing the details Lapp provided him; still, Cornell's account matched Lapp's to the extent that her memory allowed.

Separately placed under hypnosis, the two recounted an abduction experience. Lapp "remembered" standing on the deck with one of the humanoids looking into space and observing Earth, Moon, stars, and the cigar-shaped craft. Cornell was stretched on a table in the lower level as two aliens conducted what seemed to be a physical examination on her. Lapp was put on a table next to hers and lost consciousness. On recovering, he found that the ship had entered a hangar that was inside yet a larger one. He and an alien companion sailed on a beam of light through a wall. An elevator took them to an enormous domed room occupied by many humanoids, who were watching something out of Lapp's line of vision. Taken into another room, he had a vision of an unknown landscape occupied by distraught, weeping human beings. He passed out. When he awoke, he seemed to be falling through space, while a globe full of television screens with his picture on each appeared in front of him. He stepped through one of the screens, and on the other side of it, he and Cornell were back on the dock.

Cornell's story was less detailed than Lapp's. She remembered being suddenly aboard the UFO and described the entities nearly exactly as her companion had. Her "recall" of the vehicle's interior matched Lapp's.

Webb devoted five years to the investigation in an effort to substantiate anything that could be substantiated. To his disappointment, he found no one, who had been at the camp in August 1968, who could corroborate the UFO sighting. Background checks and psychological tests attested to Lapp's and Cornell's sincerity and honesty.

See Also: Abductions by UFOs

Further Reading

Webb, Walter N., 1994. *Encounter at Buff Ledge: A UFO Case History.* Chicago: J. Allen Hynek Center for UFO Studies.

Bunians

Ahmad Jamaludin, a ufologist and veterinary surgeon who lives in Malaysia, says that nothing precisely like the abduction phenomenon known to his Western colleagues seems to be occurring in his country, but there are traditions of kidnappings by what are called the "Bunian people." The Bunians are the Malaysian version of fairies. Like fairies elsewhere, the Bunians exist not only in oral tradition, but also in what are alleged to be actual experiences.

One such incident is said to have taken place in June 1982. A twelve-year-old girl, Maswati Pilus, had gone one morning to the river behind her house, intending to wash clothes there. She encountered a small female being whose sudden appearance had a strange effect on the girl's consciousness. She felt as if only she and the being existed. There were no other sounds or sights. The being offered to take her to another land, and Maswati, who felt no fear, found herself looking at a bright, beautiful landscape. She sensed that time was passing, but the events that occurred during her experience were blurred and vague in her memory.

Meanwhile, her relatives were looking frantically for her. Two days later, they came upon her in a location near her house where they had already searched more than once. She was unconscious but soon recovered.

See Also: Abductions by UFOs; Fairies encountered

Further Reading

Randles, Jenny, 1988. *Abduction: Over 200 Documented UFO Kidnappings Investigated.* London: Robert Hale.

C

Calf-rustling aliens

On April 23, 1897, a Kansas newspaper, the *Yates Center Farmers Advocate,* printed an affidavit attesting to an instance of interplanetary calf-rustling. There were three witnesses, the most prominent of whom was Alex Hamilton, a rancher from LeRoy, who soberly related the following:

> We were awakened by a noise among the cattle. . . . Upon going to the door I saw to my utter amazement that an airship was slowly descending upon my cow lot about forty rods [six hundred feet] from the house. Calling my tenant, Gid Heslip, and my son Wall, we seized some axes and ran to the corral. Meanwhile the ship had been gently descending until it was not more than thirty feet above the ground and we came within fifty yards of it. It consisted of a great cigar-shaped portion, possibly three hundred feet long, with a carriage underneath. The carriage was made of glass or some other transparent material. It was brightly lighted within and everything was plainly visible—it was occupied by some of the strangest beings I ever saw. There were two men, a woman, and three children. They were jabbering together but we could not understand a syllable they said.

The occupants suddenly turned a searchlight on the trio, and the ship got closer to them. The witnesses then noticed a calf caught in the fence, with "a cable . . . fastened in a slip knot around her neck one end passing up to the vessel and tangled in wire." They tried to cut the cable, but when they failed, they watched as it and the ship sailed away. The following day a neighbor found the calf's butchered remains in a field where there was, Hamilton said, no "track of any kind on the soft ground."

Appended to the published account was a statement by some of the county's leading citizens who attested to Hamilton's truthfulness and good character. The story was published during a nationwide wave of sightings of mysterious "airships" (UFOs). Some newspapers had speculated, seriously or otherwise, that extraterrestrial visitors were flying the ships. When Hamilton's story was rediscovered decades later, after UFOs had entered popular consciousness, it was widely published in the UFO literature, which cited it as an example of an early close encounter of the third kind.

In 1976, however, writer Jerome Clark collected testimony from an elderly woman who had known the Hamilton family. She recalled hearing the elder Hamilton tell his wife that he and his friends from a local liars' club, one of them the newspaper editor, had made up the story. Several years later UFO historian

An example of cattle mutilation at Morrill Farm, Piermont, New Hampshire, September 27, 1978 (Loren Coleman/Fortean Picture Library)

Thomas E. Bullard came upon a letter Hamilton had written to a Missouri paper, the *Atchison County Mail* (May 7, 1897), cheerfully confessing that there was no truth to the story.

Many years later, psychologist Susan Marie Powers studied the claims of a woman who claimed to have been abducted by extraterrestrials on a number of occasions. Once, while aboard a UFO, the occupants would lasso a cow, take it inside the craft, and extract blood from it. "I watched [as] the blood went into a tube and then into a big tank," the woman reported. "The cow's eyes would glaze over. Then I knew she was dead. We would fly back and drop her in the pasture with the other cows. The little people do not eat meat. They take the blood home with them" (Powers, 1994).

Another abductee, a Texas woman named Judy Doraty, related under hypnosis her alleged observation of a levitation of a calf into a UFO one night in 1973. The gray-skinned humanoid crew cut up the animal while still alive, apparently as part of its study of the effects of pollution on earthly creatures. Myrna Hansen told a similar story under hypnosis, of an abduction in New Mexico in 1980, during which a calf was brought into a UFO and mutilated while still alive.

According to ufologist Linda Moulton Howe, a rancher near Waco, Texas, came upon two greenish humanoids with almond eyes and big, egg-shaped heads as they were carting away one of his calves. Terrified, he fled the scene. When he had recovered his nerve a couple of days later, he, his wife, and his son went to the scene. There they found, in Howe's words, "the calf's hide pulled back over the skull and folded inside out on the ground. . . . About a foot from the empty hide was a complete calf backbone without ribs" (Howe, 1989).

In July 1983, Ron and Paula Watson, a Missouri farm couple, spotted a landed UFO in a pasture. A bipedal "lizard-type creature"—known to ufologists as a reptoid—stood nearby. Through binoculars the Watsons watched as two other beings, white-skinned humanoids in silver suits, ran their fingers over a black cow, which, though alive, was immobile as if paralyzed. Suddenly the cow floated up the ramp into the UFO, which then, weirdly, seemed to fade into the hill, along with the three aliens.

See Also: Aurora Martian; Close encounters of the third kind; Hopkins's Martians; Michigan giant; Reptoids; Shaw's Martians

Further Reading

Bullard, Thomas E., ed., 1982. *The Airship File: A Collection of Texts Concerning Phantom Airships and Other UFOs, Gathered from Newspapers and Periodicals Mostly during the Hundred Years Prior to Kenneth Arnold's Sighting.* Bloomington, IN: self-published.

Clark, Jerome, 1977. "The Great Airship Hoax." *Fate* 30, 2 (February): 94–97.

Howe, Linda Moulton, 1989. *An Alien Harvest: Further Evidence Linking Animal Mutilations and Human Abductions to Alien Life Forms.* Littleton, CO: Linda Moulton Howe Publications.

Powers, Susan Marie, 1994. "Thematic Content Analyses of the Reports of UFO Abductees and Close Encounter Witnesses: Indications of Repressed Sexual Abuse." *Journal of UFO Studies* 5 (n.s.): 35–54.

Captive extraterrestrials

Along with rumors of dead extraterrestrials supposedly found in or near crashed spacecraft, there is a persistent lore of aliens who are held in captivity.

Ufologist William L. Moore claims to have heard one such account from anonymous military and official sources said to be privy to highly classified UFO secrets. In 1949, the sources asserted, a male humanoid was discovered alive in the southwestern desert, the survivor of the crash of an extraterrestrial spacecraft. Authorities housed the being, called EBE (ee-buh, after extraterrestrial biological entity), at the atomic installation at Los Alamos, New Mexico. An air force captain was assigned the job of watching over the being. Communication with the alien proved impossible until a speech device was invented and implanted into his throat, enabling him to speak a kind of broken but understandable English. EBE said he had been the equivalent of a mechanic on the crashed craft. EBE died of unknown causes in 1952.

Moore's sources alleged that EBE later was called EBE-1, because two other aliens—EBE-2 and EBE-3—later fell into U.S. government hands. The three captives revealed that nine alien races were visiting Earth. One in particular, the little gray-skinned beings, had been especially active. This group had been monitoring human activities for twenty-five thousand years and had manipulated our religious beliefs.

In his book *UFO Crash at Aztec* (1986), William S. Steinman reports another alleged 1948 incident, this one involving a physician from Bishop, California, named Claude E. Steen, Sr. (Elsewhere in his book Steinman gives the year as 1949 and spells the last name "Steene.") A "member of a special military unit" contacted Steen and led him and his nurse to a location where an alien was being kept alive. It was in a chamber with a controlled environment. The being appeared to be some kind of reptile. Its appearance so upset the nurse that she said it looked like something "from the pits of hell."

On July 23, 1952, a Colorado newspaper, the *Pueblo Chieftain,* related a peculiar story. Speaking to the local Chamber of Commerce, Joseph Rohrer, president of Pikes Peak Broadcasting, said he knew of three saucer crashes in Montana. One of the occupants that had survived, a three-foot-tall humanoid, was still being kept alive in an incubator in California, where efforts were being made to communicate with him. In April 2000, ufologist Kenny Young conducted inquiries into these curious claims, eventually learning that Rohrer was a prankster with a sense of humor. Even though the paper had treated his story seriously, its audience understood that he was speaking tongue in cheek.

See Also: Dead extraterrestrials; Extraterrestrial Biological Entities

Further Reading

Moore, William L., 1987. Personal communication to Jerome Clark.

Steinman, William S., with Wendelle C. Stevens, 1986. *UFO Crash at Aztec: A Well Kept Secret.* Tucson, AZ: UFO Photo Archives.

Young, Kenny, 2000. "'Talk Startles Crowd': Investigation of Strange 1952 Newspaper Article." http://home.fuse.net/ufo/rohrer.html

Cetaceans

The Cetaceans are a "One Group Mind" consisting of the world's whales and dolphins. They channel through Rochester, New York, psychic Dianne Robbins, who also receives messages from Adama, a resident of the Lemurian city Telos under California's Mount Shasta. The Cetaceans monitor events on Earth—in the ocean, on the land, and in the skies—and keep human beings from harmful extraterrestrials. They also seek to protect the earth from pollution and other destructive forces because human beings have neglected their responsibilities as "the Guardians of Love that Earth needs as she floats along her path through space" ("We Are," n.d.). The human race, like the Cetaceans themselves, came to Earth long ago from other star systems with the specific task of taking care of this planet. Unfortunately, memories of that distant event have faded among humans, and the Cetaceans are working with space intelligences to reawaken humanity's sleeping consciousness.

If intruders enter Earth's atmosphere and violate cosmic ethical standards, the Cetaceans telepathically notify the Galactic Command, with which they are in constant contact. Often the Cetaceans will project their consciousness into the command's spacecraft.

Earth will soon enter the Photon Belt, which will have the effect of bringing humans out of the darkness and into the light, restoring them to their cosmic destiny. "We came here especially for this time when the Earth would be transiting into a higher dimensions," the Cetaceans say.

Channeling through a California-based metaphysical group, the Council of Nine from the planet Sirius B, this area's branch of the Galactic Federation, put it this way: "Guardianship by the Cetaceans can best be described by observing the use of their energies. Through the use of their rituals, their sonar songs and their ocean travels, they vivify the biosphere. Whale song has been found throughout all the oceans of the world. It is also found in, and resonates throughout, the skies of the Earth. It exists even in the deepest parts of Africa, the Americas, Asia, and Europe. Because the energies of the Cetaceans can be found both in the sky and in the water, those great energies they bring forth in their song create the resonance that sustains life" (Nidle and Essene, 1994).

See Also: Adama; Channeling

Further Reading

Nidle, Sheldon, and Virginia Essene, 1994. *You Are Becoming a Galactic Human.* Santa Clara, CA: Spiritual Education Endeavors Publishing Company.

"We Are the Cetaceans," n.d. http://onelight.com/ceta/cetabook/cetmonitor.htm

Chaneques

Traditional belief holds that little people known as Chaneques live in the forests and jungles of Mexico and Central America, guarding the spirits of wild animals and sometimes causing harm to unlucky human beings. The Chaneques are one variant of the beings known under many names, including fairies and elves. As with these traditions, Chaneque lore consists not just of distant legends and rumors but of claims of firsthand experiences.

Two English teachers from Mexico City investigated some of these claims in the early 1970s. In the state of Veracruz, they interviewed sixteen persons who had alleged encounters, either direct or through family members (usually children), with these beings. One woman, for example, told them that one day in March 1973, her son Ramiro, three and a half years old, wandered from his home in the village of La Tinaja. Searches went on for six days without success. Finally, the Chaneques informed a six-year-old neighbor that Ramiro was safe in a cave ten miles away. When rescued at the designated place, the boy was in excellent health, neither hungry nor thirsty. Though the entrance to the cave was accessible only with difficulty, and the searchers were scratched and bruised by the time they got to him, the barefoot Ramiro had no marks on him. He explained that while playing by the river, he got lost. Five little men found him and fed him "sweet food" and milk. He then fell asleep and woke up in the cave, with one of the men still with him. He and his companions, who came to the cave on occasion, played together until the rescue was accomplished.

Ricardo Gutierrez related that while walking through a forest one day in June 1970, his six-year-old nephew, Arturo, who had been accompanying him, abruptly vanished. When the boy failed to reappear, the local authorities arrested Gutierrez for murder. Thirty-three days later, as the man awaited trial, a healthy-looking, unconcerned Arturo entered his house. Asked where he had been, he said he had been living with the little men. They fed him food and honey-flavored milk and played games with him. The investigators interviewed local police, who confirmed the mysterious disappearance and the equally enigmatic reappearance.

Driving a six-ton truck between La Tinaja and Tierra Blanca at 8 A.M. on May 22, 1973, Manuel Angel Gonzalez suddenly saw five small figures standing in the road in front of him, holding their arms up in the air. He slammed on the brakes barely in time to keep from running into what he assumed were small children. As he sat in his cab trying to recover his wits, he had a chance to look more closely at the figures. Now they looked like adults, only two feet tall, perfectly proportioned, with light brown complexions and black hair. He also realized that they had not stepped out onto the road, but had materialized there.

After a time he stepped out of the truck and approached the figures. His action apparently frightened them because they scattered into the dense undergrowth and fled in the direction of a nearby mountain. When Gonzalez turned around to return to his vehicle, he was dismayed to see blue flames consuming it. Within half an hour it and its cargo—asbestos sheeting, sacked cement, and reinforcing steel—had been reduced to fused metal and ash.

The story made the Mexican newspapers. Soon afterward, the two investigators interviewed Gonzalez and his boss, who confirmed the truck's destruction, which neither could explain; neither could the police officer who was on the scene within an hour. Gonzalez thought that the little men were not Chaneques but "space travelers from some other planet," since Chaneques were not known to cause pointless destruction.

See Also: Close encounters of the third kind; Fairies encountered

Further Reading

Pantoja Lopez, Ramon A., and Robert Freeman Bound, 1974. "Chaneques: Mexican Gnomes or Interplanetary Visitors?" *Fate* 27, 11 (November): 51–57.

Channeling

Channeling is new in name only. It refers to the process whereby disembodied entities communicate ideas and information through human beings who are either in full waking consciousness or in an altered state. The communicating entities may be deceased persons, gods, angels, extraterrestrials, extradimensional intelligences, "ascended masters" (mystical adepts who have transcended physical existence), nature spirits, and more. In earlier times, channeling was called "revelation," or "mediumship." Whatever the name, it is often accompanied by visions of otherworldly entities or unearthly realms. Some channelers believe that through their consciousness alone, they can travel through the universe and into other dimensions.

In ancient times oracles and priests communicated with the gods. The resulting divine messages formed the basis of religious and mystical faiths. Such communications often involved prophecies as well. In the Judeo-Christian tradition, the Bible documents visions and messages recognizably related to the

Gerry Bowman channeling the spirit of John the Baptist, August 15, 1987, Shasta National Forest, California (Roger Ressmeyer/Corbis)

phenomenon of channeling. Channeling seems ubiquitous in human experience. Historically prominent practitioners include Nostradamus, Emanuel Swedenborg, Helena Petrovna Blavatsky (founder of the theosophical movement), and Anna Lee (founder of the Quaker sect known as the Shakers). In the latter half of the nineteenth century, spiritualism became the rage, and hundreds of mediums claimed to be in contact with dead people who, through the mediums, spoke with the living. The communicators were not always the deceased, however; in some cases space people and other nonhuman intelligences came through. Some mediums spoke of otherworldly journeys in their astral bodies.

After World War II, when flying saucers entered the popular imagination, benevolent extraterrestrial entities such as Ashtar and Monka—starship commanders who came here to oversee the transformation of the human race into cosmic citizenship—channeled through individuals who became known as contactees. As the channeling movement grew, reaching its peak in the 1970s and 1980s during the height of the New Age movement, channelers created a vast alternative-reality literature, fusing traditional occultism with modern science and pseudoscience. Some channeling entities made predictions, often of some cataclysmic or otherwise seminal events, which inevitably went unfulfilled. More typically, however, channeling consists of spiritual platitudes, self-help suggestions, and unverifiable pronouncements about the nature of spirit and cosmos.

To its critics, it is nothing more than a form of automatism, "automatic behavior over which an individual denies any personal control" (Alcock, 1996). Its sources are within, not outside, the channeler's psyche. Parapsychologist Rodger I. Anderson writes, "It has been increasingly evident to researchers that automatism of whatever kind is neither a psychic ability nor a pathway to higher knowledge. Appearances notwithstanding, it is only too clear in most cases that all the various elements that go to make up the act of automatism are owed solely to the automatist and his or her experience in . . . life" (Anderson, 1988). On the other hand, a skeptical but sympathetic observer, Brown University anthropologist Michael F. Brown, defends channeling as, at its best, "a lively arena for the free play of the religious imagination. . . . It is likely to remain a site of emotional and spiritual renewal in a culture that, perhaps more than any in human history, promotes the continuous reinvention of the self" (Brown, 1997).

See Also: Ascended Masters; Ashtar; Contactees; Monka

Further Reading

Alcock, James E., 1996. "Channeling." In Gordon Stein, ed. *The Encyclopedia of the Paranormal,* 153–160. Amherst, NY: Prometheus Books.

Anderson, Rodger I., 1988. "Channeling." *Parapsychology Review* 19, 5 (1988): 6–9.

Brown, Michael F., 1997. *The Channeling Zone: American Spirituality in an Anxious Age.* Cambridge, MA: Harvard University Press.

Klimo, Jon, 1987. *Channeling: Investigations on Receiving Information from Paranormal Sources.* Los Angeles: Jeremy P. Tarcher.

Riordan, Suzanne, 1990. "Channeling." In J. Gordon Melton, Jerome Clark, and Aidan A. Kelly, eds. *New Age Encyclopedia,* 97–104. Detroit, MI: Gale Research.

Chief Joseph

In life, Chief Joseph (1840–1894) led a group of Nez Perce Indians and was admired in his time by his people and whites, alike, for his wisdom and courage. According to a Reston, Virginia, channeler named John Cali, Joseph has been communicating from beyond the grave since 1992. Joseph delivers the familiar message that Earth is going through physical and spiritual changes. Each individual must find the God in him- or herself. Through Cali, Joseph gives personal psychic readings to those seeking guidance in their personal lives or metaphysical odysseys. Joseph's current messages are recorded in an occasional e-newsletter, *Sentinels of the Sky.*

Further Reading

"Who Are Chief Joseph and John Cali?" http://www.claimyourpower.com/sentinels/thechief.htm

Christopher

Jackie Altisi, also known as Jackie White Star, channels messages from a variety of otherworldly entities, including the spirit of martyred contactee Gloria Lee, who died in 1962 while fasting under the direction of space people. A principal communicator is Christopher, an aide to the King of the Moon and spokesman for the lunarian station of United Cosmic Planets. According to Christopher, the moon is a "complete authority in itself, but working with an interplanetary confederation." These messages are circulated through the Star Light Fellowship, established in 1962.

See Also: J.W.

Further Reading

Melton, J. Gordon, 1996. *Encyclopedia of American Religions.* Fifth edition. Detroit, MI: Gale Research.

Chung Fu

Sometime in the 1960s, Marshall Lever, then a student at a Presbyterian seminary, began ex-

Photograph of Chief Joseph by Edward Curtis (Corbis)

perimenting with trance mediumship. In this state he heard from Chung Fu, a spirit guide who in his last physical incarnation was a student of Lao-Tzu in China. In 1970, Lever and his wife, Quinta, established the Circle of Inner Truth to facilitate Chung Fu's teachings, which focused on spiritual development as the way to break out of the reincarnation cycle. These efforts included such quotidian matters as diet, health care, and psychological wellbeing, on which Chung Fu would offer guidance in sittings with individuals.

The Levers traveled widely, abandoning any permanent residence, to work for Chung Fu. Inner Circles took roots in several American cities, and one operated out of London. Finally, Chung Fu was heard from no more, and by the latter 1980s, the movement no longer existed.

Further Reading

Melton, J. Gordon, 1996. *Encyclopedia of American Religions.* Fifth edition. Detroit, MI: Gale Research.

Close encounters of the third kind

In *The UFO Experience* (1972), J. Allen Hynek, a Northwestern University astronomer and former scientific consultant to the U.S. Air Force's Project Blue Book, proposed a classification system for UFO sightings, including three varieties of close encounters. He defined "close encounters of the third kind" as those "in which the presence of animated creatures is reported." Prior to the coining of the phrase (shortened to "CE3"), ufologists had called these "occupant reports."

The modern UFO phenomenon is two centuries old. In the early nineteenth century the first reports of arguably UFO-like phenomena were recorded in scientific journals, newspaper accounts, and other sources, though such stories were relatively rare until late in the century, when alleged sightings of mysterious "airships" filled American newspapers between November 1896 and May 1897. Many were hoaxes, some concocted by the press itself. Among them were claims that the airships had landed. Reflecting a widely held belief that an ingenious American inventor had built the ships and that the occupants were human, some reports even gave the inventor a name, Wilson. Other accounts, however, described grotesque aliens, sometimes thought to be from Mars. "Hoax" probably is too strong a word to characterize these tall tales, which were apparently meant as jokes to amuse a readership that was not fooled.

After 1947—the year "flying saucers" and "unidentified flying objects" entered popular consciousness—a number of seemingly sincere individuals came forward to speak of encounters they had experienced in earlier years, some reaching as far back as 1893, when a man in the Australian state of New South Wales told a newspaper that he had seen a saucer-shaped structure land on his farm. When he went to investigate, an oddly dressed man stepped out of the craft holding a device that resembled a "torch" (flashlight). He aimed the device at the witness, who saw a light shoot out from it and hit his hand. He was knocked unconscious. When he awoke, the object and occupant were gone. For the rest of his life, he claimed, his hand was paralyzed.

New Zealand newspapers of 1909 recorded a local airship-sighting wave, including an incident in which a witness saw three figures in a craft passing overhead. One shouted at him in an unfamiliar language. In the United States, early on the morning of February 29, 1916, according to a report in the *Superior Telegram* that same day, workers along the Lake Superior dock in Wisconsin saw a "big machine . . . 50 feet wide and 100 feet long" fly by at a high rate of speed about six hundred feet in the air. Workers said they had seen three "men" inside the craft. This is the first known, seemingly credible, CE3 to be published at the time of its occurrence.

A newspaper referred to these mysterious craft by the name "flying saucers" for the first time on June 26, 1947, two days after private pilot Kenneth Arnold saw nine discs maneuvering over the Cascade Mountains. This reported account ushered in the UFO age. The same afternoon as Arnold's sighting, Oregon farmer Bill Schuening claimed to have seen a spherical object hovering five or six feet above a field. Just beneath it were "two little guys in green suits with white helmets" (McCune, 1987). They were no more than three feet tall. A few seconds later they vanished. Schuening did not see them enter the craft, which then flew off toward the Cascades.

In the early UFO era, however, such reports, relatively rare but hardly nonexistent, received little attention. In 1950, when the first book with "flying saucers" in its title, Donald E. Keyhoe's paperback *The Flying Saucers Are Real,* saw print, the occupants of the vehicles—Keyhoe believed them to be peaceable extraterrestrials who deliberately refrained from contact—could only be speculated about. Another book published that same year, Frank Scully's *Behind the Flying Saucers,* asserted that the U.S. government had recovered crashed spacecraft, containing the bodies of little men "dressed in the style of the 1890s" and believed to be from Venus. (Subsequent investigations determined that two veteran confidence artists had concocted these tales in order to peddle bogus oil-detection devices tied to advanced extraterrestrial technology.) Scully's notorious book had the effect of leading some early ufologists—as opposed to the saucerians who embraced the contactee movement—to shy away from *any* reports of humanoids, whatever the source.

A significant proportion of the reports described the occupants as humanoids. The specific descriptions may have varied, but witnesses mostly testified that UFO occupants had two arms, two legs, and generally humanlike head and facial features. Usually the beings were small. Sometimes they were grotesque-looking. Sometimes they looked like small humans. A minority were of normal human height, and a few were said to be more than that, seven or eight feet tall. Such reports came from all over the world, including remote Third World locations where UFOs were little known and the occupants were sometimes taken to be American or Russian pilots. A wave of humanoid and other encounters in France in the fall of 1954 received international attention and caused even the most cautious UFO researchers to reconsider their bias against CE3 reports. In the summer of 1955, the air force's Project Blue Book investigated a bizarre episode in which members of a rural Kentucky family claimed to have spent a night besieged by floating, big-eared humanoid entities from a UFO.

CE3s were different from the contact claims of George Adamski, Howard Menger, George Van Tassel, and other 1950s contactees in some important ways. For one, the beings seldom looked much like the golden-haired, angelic spacemen and spacewomen who figured in the contactees' tales. For another, they had little if anything to say. Communication, if any (and there seldom was), was brief, sometimes enigmatic, and always devoid of inspirational content. Unlike contactees, CE3 witnesses fit the profile of witnesses to less exotic UFO phenomena; in other words, they were ordinary citizens without a background in occultism and other esoteric pursuits, as contactees tended to be. They also did not embark on lecture tours or write books, as the more flamboyant contactees did.

A spectacular CE3 took place over Boianai, Papua New Guinea, in late June 1959. The best-known witness, the Rev. William Booth Gill, was an Anglican missionary from Australia. On the evening of June 26, thirty-eight persons observed a large, disc-shaped craft with four legs hovering in the northwestern sky. Gill estimated its apparent size to be that of five full moons lined up end to end. At the top of the UFO, behind a glass-covered cockpit, four humanlike figures, surrounded by illumination, moved back and forth, apparently working at an unknown task. The object and its crew ascended into gathering clouds after forty-five minutes. Other UFOs, though not their occupants, were intermittently visible over the next three and a half hours. Twenty five of the witnesses signed a statement attesting to what they had seen that night. At 6 P.M. the next day, the original UFO and its crew returned. At one point during the observation, Gill and others waved to the occupants, who waved back. The objects showed up for the last time the next night, though no beings were visible.

Interviewed in 1973 by J. Allen Hynek, native witnesses stuck by the story. Gill, who left the country in September 1959, stands by the report even today. It remains among the most impressive and puzzling of CE3s.

Far stranger and much harder to believe was the testimony of a young Brazilian, Antonio Villas-Boas. Villas-Boas came to the attention of ufologists in November 1957, when he wrote a letter to a journalist who had written about UFOs. Soon afterward, the journalist, Joao Martins, brought Villas-Boas to Rio de Janeiro, where he and physician/ufologist Olavo T. Fontes, of the National School of Medicine of Brazil, interviewed and examined him. The young man claimed that in the early morning hours of October 16, occupants of a UFO took him into the ship and left him alone in a room. A naked, essentially human-looking young woman soon joined him there, eventually engaging with him in two sex acts. Before leaving, she made a gesture that led Villas-Boas to believe she would bear his child on another world.

Martins and Fontes judged Villas-Boas to be sane and sincere. His intelligence and refusal to speculate on the incident made a positive impression. "In spite of this," Fontes wrote, "the very substance of his story becomes the heaviest argument against it" (Lorenzen and Lorenzen, 1967). In 1962 two representatives of a Brazilian UFO group went to Villas-Boas's village to speak with him. Though desiring no publicity, he spoke, if reluctantly, about the experience. The investigators published an account of the interview in an English-language version of their bulletin, but it attracted little notice. Fontes's 1958 report circulated privately among a few English-speaking ufologists, but because of its sexual nature no one would publish it. For

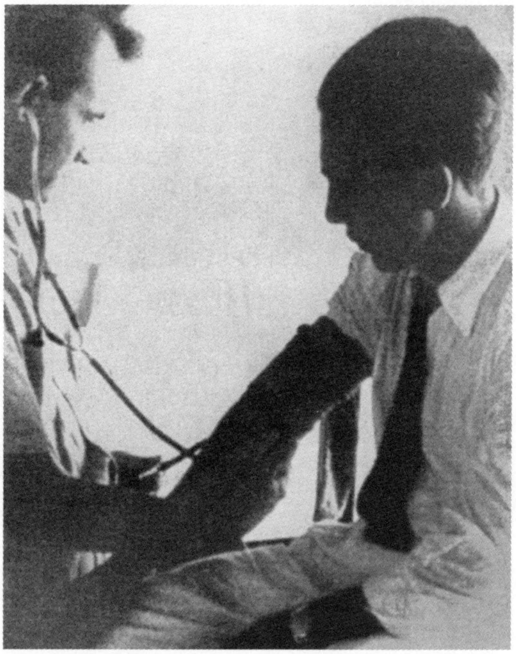

Antonio Villas-Boas being medically examined following his abduction by a UFO in Brazil, October 15, 1957 (Fortean Picture Library)

most ufologists, the Villas-Boas episode was only a vague rumor, if that, until England's widely read *Flying Saucer Review* carried a series of articles on it, beginning in its January/February 1965 issue.

The Villas-Boas case anticipated an escalation of the strangeness quotient of the CE3 phenomenon. On April 18, 1961, Joe Simonton of rural Eagle River, Wisconsin, was eating lunch when, so he would assert, a flying saucer landed on his driveway. He went outside just as a hatchway opened. A short, dark-featured man, dressed in a black, two-piece suit and wearing a tight-fitting cap on his head, held a jug. From his gestures Simonton inferred that he wanted the jug to be filled with water. He complied. As he handed the filled jug back to the man, he glanced inside the ship and saw two other men. One was sitting in front of a flameless grill, cooking something. When Simonton asked if they were eating, the man with the jug handed him four fresh "pancakes," and then the flying saucer departed. Simonton took a bite of one of the pancakes. It tasted like cardboard, he thought.

The story of the Eagle River pancakes attracted national attention and a torrent of ridicule. Even UFO groups disagreed on its significance, some championing Simonton as a naïve, sincere witness to an extraordinary event, while the conservative National Investigations Committee on Aerial Phenomena (NICAP) sneeringly dismissed the story as an absurd contact claim. Even Project Blue Book got drawn into the case, sending Dr. Hynek to the site to interview Simonton and local people. Few of Simonton's friends and acquaintances deemed him a hoaxer or even a man with sufficient imagination to make up such an outlandish tale. Still, laboratory analysis found nothing out of the ordinary in the pancake sample it examined. In common with just about everybody else who looked closely at the claim, the air force ended up confused, stating at one point that Simonton was a "balanced person of good mental health," and, at another, that he had suffered "an hallucination followed with delusion" (Mallan, 1967). Separately, a lone witness and a nearby farm family reported seeing a UFO over Simonton's residence, in the first case, at the time of the supposed landing; in the second, the next evening.

Cases such as Villas-Boas's and Simonton's suggested a degree of communication between witnesses and UFO beings. To some ufologists, many never very enthusiastic about CE3s to start with, that suggested the despised contactees, even if neither man acted much like one. These ufologists were more comfortable with a CE3 report from Socorro, New Mexico, on April 24, 1964, from Lonnie Zamora, a police officer of undisputed reliability. Around 6 P.M. Zamora spotted a small, egg-shaped UFO resting in an isolated area on the city's outskirts. Close to the object were two small figures dressed in white coveralls, apparently examining the craft. On seeing Zamora, they ran behind the craft and disappeared. The flame-spewing UFO departed with a roar. Police, Project Blue Book, and civilian investigators found burn marks and impressions at the site. Despite its hostility to UFOs and its tendency to reach for sometimes far-fetched "conventional" explanations for reports, Project Blue Book declared the case an "unknown." It has since become a classic UFO incident, often cited by those who argue for the anomalous nature of the phenomenon.

If Zamora's experience seemed relatively straightforward, Gary Wilcox's claimed encounter of the same day and a few hours earlier appeared as bizarre as Villas-Boas's and Simonton's, though not much like either in any other context. Wilcox, a young Newark Valley, New York, dairy farmer, asserted that he had spoken with two short, spacesuit-clad UFO occupants for two hours. They said that they were part of a Martian expedition, Wilcox said, engaged in Earth exploration. Wilcox's story did not come to light until a

Police Officer Lonnie Zamora, who saw a UFO land near Socorro, New Mexico, April 24, 1964 (Fortean Picture Library)

few days later, since he had sought no publicity and discussed it only with friends and family members, who eventually leaked it to the local press. Like Simonton, Wilcox had an unimpeachable reputation among locals, and psychological testing revealed no abnormalities. Wilcox made no subsequent attempt to exploit his story. Though his testimony made no sense—even in 1964 scientists had abandoned the hope of an inhabited Mars—Wilcox seemed neither crazy nor dishonest.

As comparable claims came to the fore, some ufologists speculated that UFO occupants were lying to hide their true identity and purpose. At the extreme this led theorists such as John A. Keel and Jacques Vallee to move beyond ufology's venerable extraterrestrial hypothesis (ETH) and into quasi-demonological speculation about earthbound elementals and other occult entities.

As if to compound the confusion, by the mid-1960s ufologists were confronting a new level of confrontation and contact between humans and UFO beings. In 1965, under hypnosis conducted by a Boston psychiatrist, a New Hampshire couple, Barney and Betty Hill, turned a consciously recalled CE3 (an observation of figures aboard a hovering UFO one night in September 1961) into an on-board experience, including medical examination by gray-skinned aliens and conversation with the ship's captain. All of this took place during a two-hour period of which the Hills had no conscious memory and for which they had never been able to account; to them it had always been a puzzling period of seemingly inexplicable amnesia. "Missing time," hypnotic regressions, gray aliens, and medical examinations would play large roles in the emerging abduction phenomenon.

A drawing by a pupil at Ariel Primary School in Ruwa, Zimbabwe, where a group of children saw a UFO and aliens land on September 16, 1994 (Fortean Picture Library)

In time, such abduction reports—the subject of a separate entry—would overwhelm CE3s as historically understood. Nonabduction CE3s would diminish in number and, in time, slow to a trickle, though they would not entirely disappear.

One particularly well-documented incident reportedly occurred in the early morning hours of January 12, 1975, when seventy-two-year-old George O'Barski was driving home past New York City's North Hudson Park. He observed a glowing pancake-shaped object hovering above the park ground. A door opened, a ladder emerged, and about ten small figures, dressed in one-piece suits and helmets, climbed down to collect soil and grass samples, which they scooped up with "little shovels" (Hopkins, 1981). An extensive investigation by three New York–based ufologists uncovered a body of apparent confirming testimony from an assortment of witnesses.

In the most remarkable CE3 of the 1990s, a large group of children at Ariel School, Ruwa, Zimbabwe, while on recess on the morning of September 16, 1994, reportedly observed the landing of a UFO just beyond the playground. They also saw one or two occupants, small figures (slightly more than three feet tall) with large, slanted eyes and long black hair. They were wearing tight black suits. Though teachers were alerted while the incident was in progress, none believed the children and refused to go outside. Later, they changed their minds as the children produced remarkably uniform accounts and drawings. A British Broadcasting Corporation journalist, accompanied by Zimbabwe ufologist Cynthia Hind, interviewed the witnesses within a few days of the incident.

See Also: Abductions by UFOs; Adamski, George; Contactees; Keel, John Alva; Menger, Howard; Van Tassel, George W.; Wilcox's Martians

Further Reading

Basterfield, Keith, 1997. *UFOs: A Report on Australian Encounters.* Kew, Victoria, Australia: Reed Books.

Bowen, Charles, ed., 1974. *The Humanoids.* London: Futura Publications.

Clark, Jerome, 1998. "Close Encounters of the Third Kind." In Jerome Clark. *The UFO Encyclopedia: The Phenomenon from the Beginning,* 207–239. Detroit, MI: Omnigraphics.

———, 2000. "The Extraterrestrial Hypothesis in the Early UFO Age." In David M. Jacobs, ed., *UFOs and Abductions: Challenging the Borders of Knowledge,* 122–140. Lawrence: University Press of Kansas.

Fuller, John G., 1966. *The Interrupted Journey: Two Lost Hours "Aboard a Flying Saucer."* New York: Dial Press.

Hind, Cynthia, 1996. *UFOs over Africa.* Madison, WI: Horus House Press.

Hopkins, Budd, 1981. *Missing Time: A Documented Study of UFO Abductions.* New York: Richard Marek Publishers.

Hynek, J. Allen, 1972. *The UFO Experience: A Scientific Inquiry.* Chicago: Henry Regnery Company.

Hynek, J. Allen, and Jacques Vallee, 1975. *The Edge of Reality: A Progress Report on Unidentified Flying Objects.* Chicago: Henry Regnery Company.

Keyhoe, Donald E., 1950. *The Flying Saucers Are Real.* New York: Fawcett Publishers.

Lorenzen, Coral, and Jim Lorenzen, 1967. *Flying Saucer Occupants.* New York: Signet.

McCune, Hal, 1987. "Man Sticks to His Report." *Pendleton East Oregonian* (June 24).

Mallan, Lloyd, 1967. "UFO Hoaxes and Hallucinations." *Science and Mechanics* 38, 3 (March): 48–52, 82–85.

Scully, Frank, 1950. *Behind the Flying Saucers.* New York: Henry Holt and Company.

Cocoon people

In her book *Taken* (1994), the late psychologist and abductee Karla Turner recounts the experiences of a woman identified only as Pat, at the time a fifty-year-old divorcee living in Florida. Her abduction experiences began in 1954 on the family farm near Floyd's Knob, Indiana. Over the years other experiences occurred. All of these were repressed in conscious memory until 1986, when they came flooding into her thoughts. One memory—Pat could not put a specific time frame on it—concerned "cocoon people."

She found herself inside a large room with soft white lighting. A gray-skinned humanoid stood near her. "I vaguely recall seeing a human male there," she would tell Turner, "but not what he was doing." The room contained a number of boxes that looked like sarcophagi (stone coffins). Inside them she could see what looked like human forms, alive but not moving, covered with "white misty stuff," which somehow she knew kept them alive. In a telepathic communication, the being asked if she wanted to see "yours." When she said yes, the being showed her a container with a human female inside.

"Don't ask how I knew it was female," she said. "I just felt it. I saw a little bit of human face through the mist, like a nose, mouth, eyes, definitely human. I knew this was connected with the 1954 visit, because I remembered they told me they were making a 'new me.'" When she and the others were resurrected or reanimated, she thought, "we will all be able to see and talk with them here in the body. . . . If I were to die now, I believe that my 'other body' will house my soul when Jesus says it is time, and I, too, will come back."

See Also: Abductions by UFOs

Further Reading

Turner, Karla, 1994. *Taken: Inside the Alien-Human Abduction Agenda.* Roland, AR: Kelt Works.

Contactees

Contactees are people who claim a regular, ongoing relationship with benevolent extraterrestrials, sometimes called Space Brothers. These aliens—essentially angels in spacesuits—are nearly always human in appearance, except better looking than humans are. They espouse an occult philosophy with recognizably terrestrial origins, notably in Theosophy. Contact occurs in a variety of fashions. Much, perhaps most, of it is through channeling. Other psychic communications are effected through automatic writing, dreams, visions, or astral (out-of-body) travel. A third group, the most controversial, alleges physical contacts, including trips in flying saucers to other worlds. Physical contactees frequently offer "evidence" of their experiences in the form of artifacts or photographs. Persons who follow contactees and embrace their message are sometimes called "saucerians."

The contactee movement overlaps to a degree with the UFO movement—ufology—but the two differ in fundamental ways. To saucerians, there are no *unidentified* flying objects. Flying saucers' nature, origin, and purpose are known; they are here to educate humans to their larger cosmic destiny, to prepare them for the coming Earth changes generated by nuclear war, geological upheavals, polar shifts, or combinations thereof. To ufologists, UFOs are unknowns, probably of extraordinary origin, but fundamentally a phenomenon that will eventually yield its secrets to science via conventional investigative and analytic procedures. Another way to express the difference is to see saucerianism as a kind of popular religious movement, ufology as a popular (if often naïve) attempt at scientific inquiry. Traditionally, ufologists have functioned as the contactee movement's fiercest critics.

The contactee movement envisions a densely populated cosmos with hosts of advanced, wise space people linked in a kind of celestial United Nations, usually called the Galactic Federation or something like it. A minority of evil extraterrestrials opposes the Federation's benevolent mission. Both sides have representatives on Earth, individuals who pass as normal earthlings but who are in fact aliens. Many were placed here generations ago and have lived on this planet through many incarnations, patiently waiting to be activated when the time of transition—which will include mass landings of spaceships—comes.

There were contactees before there were flying saucers. Perhaps the first of them was the Swedish scientist and mystic Emanuel Swedenborg (1688–1772). In *Earths in the Solar World* (1758), Swedenborg wrote of his astral travels to the moon and other planets. Each of these worlds, Swedenborg asserted, is inhabited, and he described, at length, the people and civilizations there. In the nineteenth century, with the rise of the spiritualist movement, psychic communications with extraterrestrials, most often Martians, were recorded on occasion. The most famous such case became the subject of a pioneering book in the emerging discipline of abnormal psychology, Theodore Flournoy's *From India to the Planet Mars* (1899). In various states of altered consciousness, a woman given the pseudonym Helene Smith (Catherine Elise Muller) interacted with persons from the Red Planet, which she also visited astrally. She produced a Martian language that Flournoy identified as an "infantile travesty of French" (Flournoy, 1963).

Reflecting a belief popularized by American astronomer Percival Lowell, Smith/Muller "saw" canals on the Martian surface. Her story, like those of Swedenborg and the contactees of the saucer era, mirrored astronomical and other scientific theories of the period. Within a few years, the notion of a Martian canal system would be thoroughly debunked. In the late 1940s and into the 1950s, it was still vaguely possible, some astronomers thought, that some neighboring planets (most likely Mars and Venus) could harbor intelligent life. Perhaps not surprisingly, the aliens in contact lore often hailed from our immediate vicinity. After space probes in the 1960s established, beyond further rational discussion, that beyond Earth there are no planets hospitable to life in this system, the extraterrestrials in contact claims were placed farther out in the cosmos. Either that, or the Venus, Mars, Saturn, and other solar planets said to harbor advanced civilizations became etheric counterparts, existing on a higher vibratory rate and distinct from the lifeless worlds we know.

Another influential early book was *Oahspe* (1882), the product of automatic writing at the guidance of angels, or so New York occultist John Ballou Newbrough asserted. Written between January and December 1881, the book is a mystical account of the cosmos, its history, and its inhabitants. The book stayed in print for decades and was widely read in contactee circles, where *ashars*—guardian angels who fly spirit ships—became extraterrestrials in spacecraft. Indeed, the ubiquitous starship commander and channeling entity Ashtar may owe his name and occupation to Newbrough's creation.

Helena Petrovna Blavatsky (1831–1891), who founded Theosophy, wrote of a hierarchy of "ascended masters," including the Venus-based "Lords of the Flame." In the 1930s the flamboyant, fascist-oriented Guy Warren Ballard marketed a simplified, popular version of Blavatsky's doctrine. He spoke of his own meeting with twelve Venusian "masters" in the Teton mountains in Wyoming. Religious studies scholar J. Gordon Melton identifies Ballard (who died in 1939) and his I AM movement as crucial to the development of the later contactee movement. "Not only did Ballard become the first to actually build a religion on contact with extraterrestrials," he writes, "but his emphasis was placed upon frequent contact with the masters from whom he received regular messages to the followers of the world contactee movement. The movement took over the I AM [spiritual] hierarchy and changed it into a space command hierarchy" (Melton, 1995).

In *The Book of the Damned* (1919), the first volume ever written on the subject that would eventually be called ufology, Charles Fort (1874–1932) speculated that strange lights and constructions observed in the sky and space during the previous century could be evidence of visitation from other worlds. He also advanced the possibly tongue-in-cheek speculation that, perhaps, some human beings were secretly in contact with the occupants of such vehicles.

The first explicit contact in the context of a UFO sighting occurred on the evening of October 9, 1946, over San Diego. Many residents had gone outside in anticipation of a predicted meteor shower. Among them was medium Mark Probert, who channeled cosmic philosophy from a group of discarnates, including a 500,000-year-old Tibetan named the Yada Di' Shi'ite. He worked with occult theorist N. Meade Layne, who the year before had founded Borderland Sciences Research Associates. Probert and many others witnessed something that, whatever else it may or may not have been, was not a meteor. Observers would describe it as resembling a huge bullet-shaped object with batlike wings and a searchlight that it occasionally swept over the ground. Dark, except for two red lights along its side, it stayed in view for an hour and a half, moving at both slow and fast speeds.

During the sighting, Probert phoned Layne, who urged him to see if the craft's occupants were interested in a telepathic exchange. According to Probert, the experiment succeeded. The crew members revealed themselves as peaceful people with lightweight, illuminated bodies. They had been trying to contact earthlings for many years. Though they were afraid to land openly, they would meet with scientists in some isolated area or on a mountaintop. They had mastered antigravity, and their ship was called the Kareeta. The *San Diego Union* carried a humorous piece on the sighting, including Probert's assertions, in its October 18 issue.

The UFO age began the next year with private pilot Kenneth Arnold's June 24 sighting of nine shiny objects that the press would soon call "flying saucers." In the wake of Arnold's report, many other people came forward to recount their own encounters with unknown aerial phenomena. Among the most outlandish claims to see print was one told by Ole J. Sneide. In a letter to the *San Francisco Chronicle* appearing in the July 3 issue, Sneide stated that the flying discs, also known as flying saucers, were spaceships from other planets. (This is one of the very earliest public attempts to link the new public sensation with extraterrestrial visitors. Nearly all other speculation held the saucers to be natural phenomena or advanced terrestrial aircraft. The association of flying saucers as spaceships did not take widespread hold until the early to mid-1950s.) Sneide also said the saucers had a base on the dark side of the moon. He knew as much because he regularly teleported himself around the galaxy. A follow-up article in the *Chronicle* determined that Sneide, a student of occultism, was serious. Though nothing more is known about Sneide, he may have been something of a contactee before the word and concept had come into currency.

The contact movement, however, did not emerge into cultural visibility until January 1952, when aircraft mechanic George W. Van Tassel began holding open weekly meetings in the high-desert country of southern California. At these gatherings Van Tassel would channel messages from starship ("ventla") commanders, introducing, among others, the destined-to-be ubiquitous Ashtar. That same year, Van Tassel published *I Rode a Flying Saucer!*, the first modern contactee book (albeit with a misleading title; it would not be until the next year that Van Tassel would claim his first physical contact and spaceship-boarding). The year 1952 saw a flurry of contact activity. In Prescott, Arizona, George Hunt Williamson, his wife, Betty, and companions were communicating with Martians, Uranians, and other extraterrestrials from the solar system via ouija board, radio, and mental telepathy. In July, in the Nevada desert, Truman Bethurum met the crew of a "scow" from the planet Clarion, invisible to earthly eyes because it is always on the opposite side of the sun from Earth.

Though arguably Van Tassel was the most influential of the first generation of contactees, the most famous was George Adamski. Adamski had a long history in California—going back to the 1930s—as a kind of minor guru. When flying saucers rose to prominence in the late 1940s, Adamski produced photographs of spaceships in the atmosphere and near the moon. On November 20, 1952, accompanied by six associates, including George Hunt Williamson, he went out into the desert to meet a landed saucer and its pilot, a blond-haired, angelic figure whom Adamski would call Orthon. Adamski went on to write books, lecture all over the world, and become the single most controversial saucer personality of the 1950s. Though despised by conservative ufologists, who charged that his accounts of meetings with Venusians, Martians, and Satur-

UFO contactee George Adamski (left) being interviewed on television by Long John Nebel (Fortean Picture Library)

nians amounted to bad science fiction, he was also widely revered.

In August 1953, more than ten thousand persons attended the Interplanetary Spacecraft Convention at Van Tassel's residence in Giant Rock, California. The speakers were mostly the new contactee stars. The movement was growing rapidly, becoming a worldwide phenomenon. It also produced a small library of books and newsletters. Over the course of the next few years, other contactees rose to occult celebrity. Many were physical contactees, but, in time, channelers and automatic writers—most of whom did not seek publicity or profit—dominated the ranks.

Not everyone was willing to take the space people at their word. Channeling contactee Trevor James Constable warned that some of them were demons in disguise. Some years later, occult-oriented ufologist John A. Keel wrote, "The demons, devils, and false angels were recognized as liars and plunderers by early man. These same impostors now appear as long-haired Venusians" (Keel, 1970). Christian fundamentalist authors of UFO books expressed similar suspicions.

Adamski's death in April 1965 marked the passing of the era of the physical contactees. Even so, the most successful contactee of later years was himself a physical contactee, Eduard "Billy" Meier, a rural Swiss man with a background in the esoteric. Like Adamski and his first-generation counterparts, Meier put forth photographs, artifacts, and allegedly confirmatory testimony to back up his stories of in-the-flesh meetings with space people and of rides in their spacecraft. Meier's extraterrestrials are from the Pleiades star system. But like Adamski's Venusians, they are handsome and beautiful, with blond hair and a generally northern European appearance. Unlike Adamski's and just about everybody else's space people, Meier's have a specifically antireligious message; the Pleiadeans, according to Meier, believe only in the laws of nature. It is also safe to say that unlike other contactees, Meier—a keen businessman—has reaped a significant, and continuing, financial reward from his supposed experiences. He has also been at the receiving end of criticism and debunking efforts. After divorcing him, his ex-wife told investigators that his claims are without factual basis.

In the United States, a major force in the movement has been the annual Rocky Mountain Conference on UFO Investigation, which has taken up where the Giant Rock conventions (the last held in 1977) left off. Started in 1980 by R. Leo Sprinkle, a psychologist and counselor at the University of Wyoming, it meets once a year, usually in the summer, and attracts contactees from all over, though most are from ranches, farms, and small towns of the Great Plains, underscoring the folk or ground-level nature of the movement.

Contactees are different from abductees—whose experiences became known only in the 1960s and did not become a major part of the UFO controversy until the 1980s—in several ways. A principal difference is that abductees tend to fit the profile of ordinary citizens, in other words, people without a background in occultism; in that way, they are also like most witnesses to UFOs. Abductees also report being taken against their will, and many consider the experience traumatic. Most do not claim to have attained superior wisdom from the experience, and most assert that their communications with their captors were devoid of messages of cosmic uplift. Yet in time contactee-oriented writers and investigators began to see abductions as contacts by other means. Some abductees come to accept their experiences as painful but necessary learning experiences. Harvard University psychiatrist John E. Mack, whose study of abduction reports has convinced him that the aliens have benevolent intentions, has stated, "If, in fact, the alien beings are closer to the divine source or *anima mundi* than human beings generally seem to be . . . their presence among us, however cruel and traumatic in some instances, may be part of a larger process that is bringing us back to God" (Mack, 1994).

See Also: Abductions by UFOs; Adamski, George; Ascended Masters; Ashtar; Bethurum, Truman; Channeling; Keel, John Alva; Meier, Eduard "Billy"; Orthon; Sprinkle, Ronald Leo; Van Tassel, George W.; Williamson, George Hunt

Further Reading

Adamski, George, 1955. *Inside the Space Ships.* New York: Abelard-Schuman.

Bartholomew, Robert E., and George S. Howard, 1998. *UFOs and Alien Contact: Two Centuries of Mystery.* Amherst, NY: Prometheus Books.

Bord, Janet, and Colin Bord, 1991. *Life beyond Planet Earth? Man's Contacts with Space People.* London: GraftonBooks.

Curran, Douglas, 1985. *In Advance of the Landing: Folk Concepts of Outer Space.* New York: Abbeville Press.

Flournoy, Theodore, 1963. *From India to the Planet Mars: A Study of a Case of Somnambulism.* Translated reprint of 1899 edition. New Hyde Park, NY: University Books.

Keel, John A., 1970. *UFOs: Operation Trojan Horse.* New York: G. P. Putnam's Sons.

Mack, John E., 1994. *Abduction: Human Encounters with Aliens.* New York: Charles Scribner's Sons.

Melton, J. Gordon, 1995. "The Contactees: A Survey." In James R. Lewis, ed. *The Gods Have Landed: New Religions from Other Worlds,* 1–13. Albany, NY: State University of New York Press.

Reeve, Bryant, and Helen Reeve, 1957. *Flying Saucer Pilgrimage.* Amherst, WI: Amherst Press.

Stupple, David W., 1994. "Historical Links Between the Occult and Flying Saucers." *Journal of UFO Studies* 5 (new series): 93–108.

Cosmic Awareness

"Cosmic Awareness" first spoke in 1962 through a retired army officer, William Durby, who harbored metaphysical interests. When asked who or what it was, Cosmic Awareness said it was a "total mind that is not any unity other than that of universality" (Melton, 1996). The following year an organization was formed around the communications in response to specific instructions from Awareness to that effect.

After Duby died in 1967, the organization split into seven factions, all at odds over which heretofore-secret teachings should be made public and which should be kept only among members. Out of the strife Cosmic Awareness Communications, which had the strongest links to the earliest group, emerged the strongest. Based in Olympia, Washington, it survives today and maintains a sometimes controversial presence on the New Age scene.

Its head, Paul Shockley, continues to channel teachings from Awareness. His organization characterizes Awareness as "the Force that expressed Itself through Jesus of Nazareth, the Buddha, Krishna, Mohammed and other great avatars who served as 'Channels' for what is commonly known as 'God,' and which expresses Itself once again as the world begins to enter the New Age of spiritual consciousness and awareness" ("Cosmic Awareness Communications," 1994).

Awareness teaches that the United States of America came into being through intervention with the Founding Fathers. The motive was to allow personal freedom, which would accelerate the process of change through which human beings must go to be reunited with Awareness. The result will be a "United States of Awareness, where entities no longer feel trapped by the physical plane, but may realize their true identity as being cosmic beings of life, light and energy" ("Cosmic Awareness Introduces Itself," n.d.).

Further Reading

"Cosmic Awareness Communications," 1994. http://net.info.nl/cosmic.html

"Cosmic Awareness Introduces Itself to the World," n.d. http://www.transactual.com/cac/intro.html

Melton, J. Gordon, 1996. *Encyclopedia of American Religions.* Fifth edition. Detroit, MI: Gale Research.

Cottingley fairies

The Cottingley fairies came into being in 1917 as images on photographs produced by two Yorkshire girls, Frances Griffiths, ten, and her cousin Elsie Wright, thirteen. The incident began as a childish trick to settle a score with adult authority figures but ended as one of the more bizarre episodes in the history of both photography and occultism. It would take six decades for the truth to emerge.

Frances and her mother and Elsie and her parents shared a house in Cottingley, near Bradford, Yorkshire, while Frances's father served in World War I. When Frances fell into a brook, one day, and came home soaking wet, she explained that the mishap had occurred while she was playing with the fairies who lived there. She was punished anyway. Offended at her friend's treatment, Elsie suggested that they borrow her father's camera, take pictures of fairies, persuade their parents of the fairies' authenticity, then later announce that they were fake. They would then clinch their case by reminding their parents that the adults had lied to them about Father Christmas.

Knowing nothing of the scheme, of course, Arthur Wright loaned his daughter his camera and provided her with a single plate. An hour later the girls returned from the brook and told Wright that they had photographed a fairy. He did not believe them, but when he developed the picture, he saw four tiny, winged women in front of Frances. The figures looked like paper cutouts, but the skeptical elders could not extract an admission from the children. A month later, a reluctant Wright gave Elsie access to the camera once more. The result was a second picture, this one of a gnome whom Elsie appeared to be inviting to jump into her lap. Annoyed at what he took to be a continuing joke, Wright kept the camera out of his daughter's hands thereafter.

That would have been that; however, in 1920, Polly Wright, Elsie's mother, attended a lecture on fairy lore. Afterward, she brought up the photographs to the speaker, who immediately asked if he could see prints. These prints soon found their way into the hands of Theosophist Edward Gardner, a believer in fairies. The Wrights provided him with copies of the originals, which Gardner showed to an acquaintance knowledgeable in photography. The expert stated, guardedly, that he could see no evidence of fraud. Excited, Gardner discussed the pictures in a lecture that May, and soon Sir Arthur Conan Doyle, the revered au-

Frances Griffiths with "fairies," photographed at Cottingley, West Yorkshire, July 1917 (Fortean Picture Library)

thor of the Sherlock Holmes stories and then an avid spiritualist, heard about the matter. Doyle had Gardner take the pictures to the Kodak laboratory in London, where two experts neither endorsed nor repudiated them. In the summer, when Gardner met the Wrights for the first time, he provided Elsie with a modern camera. In short order, she and Frances had three new fairy photographs.

Doyle wrote two articles for the popular magazine *The Strand* (December 1920 and March 1921 issues), declaring the pictures as proof of the existence of fairies. Doyle endured a great deal of ridicule for his advocacy of what many saw as a transparent hoax, but that did not stop him from elaborating on the matter in a revealingly titled book, *The Coming of the Fairies* (1922). The year before, in 1921, a self-described clairvoyant named Geoffrey Hodson, also a Theosophist, had accompanied the girls to the beck where the fairies lived. He claimed to have observed many of them, though the girls saw nothing and attempts to photograph the entities came to naught.

Two and a half decades later, Gardner wrote a memoir of the episode. He was still convinced of the authenticity of the Cottingley fairies. Occultists who championed the pictures noted that the two girls, now grown women, had never admitted to hoaxing, even when prompted to do so. Still, their answers tended to be more equivocal than their advocates seemed to understand; when they said, for example, that these were photographs of "figments of our imaginations," the occultists assumed they were talking about "thought forms"—paranormal projections from the mind to photographic film. But in a 1975 interview for *Woman* magazine, the two old women appeared to respond more positively to the inevitable questions. The following year, when asked by Yorkshire Television if the photos were fakes, Frances's response was simple—"Of course not"—spoken as if the question were a foolish and impertinent one.

That, however, was the last time the women would maintain the pretense. In 1982, *The Unexplained,* a British magazine, revealed that the two had confessed. In early 1983, they provided a signed statement to *British Journal of Photography* editor Geoffrey Crawley, who then wrote a long, definitive account of the curious episode. The women did not tell Crawley quite everything; they said they wanted to keep some of the details to themselves for a book they intended to write. Neither lived long enough, however, to produce the proposed volume. In a final, curious footnote, Frances insisted to her death that though the pictures did not show real fairies, she had seen real fairies in the beck when she and Elsie were friends and playmates.

A well-reviewed 1997 film, *Fairy Tale: A True Story,* dramatized the story, with Peter O'Toole playing Doyle.

See Also: Fairies encountered

Further Reading

Clapham, Walter, 1975. "There *Were* Fairies at the Bottom of the Garden." *Woman* (October): 42–43, 45.

Cooper, Joe, 1982. "Cottingley: At Last the Truth." *The Unexplained* 117: 2238–2340.

Crawley, Geoffrey, 1982, 1983. "That Astonishing Affair of the Cottingley Fairies." *British Journal of Photography* Pt. I (December 14): 1375–1380; Pt. II (December 31): 1406–1411, 1413–1414; Pt. III (January 7): 9–15; Pt. IV (January 21): 66–71; Pt. V (January 28): 91–96; Pt. VI (February 4): 117–121; Pt. VII (February 11): 142–145, 153, 159; Pt. VIII (February 18): 170–171; Pt. IX (April 1): 332–338; Pt. X (April 8): 362–366.

Doyle, Sir Arthur Conan, 1922. *The Coming of the Fairies.* New York: George H. Doran Company.

Gardner, Edward L., 1945. *Fairies: The Cottingley Photographs and Their Sequel.* London: Theosophical Publishing House.

Hitchens, Christopher, 1997. "Fairy Tales Can Come True. . . ." *Vanity Fair* 446 (October): 204, 206, 208, 210.

Hodson, Geoffrey, 1925. *Fairies at Work and at Play.* London: Theosophical Publishing House.

Sanderson, S. F., 1973. "The Cottingley Fairy Photographs: A Re-Appraisal of the Evidence." *Folklore* 84 (Summer): 89–103.

Smith, Paul, 1991. "The Cottingley Fairies: The End of a Legend." In Peter Narvaez, ed. *The Good People: New Fairylore Essays,* 371–405. Lexington: University Press of Kentucky.

The Council

William LePar of North Canton, Ohio, channels the Council, a single voice speaking for twelve souls communicating from the Celestial Level of the God-Made Heavenly Realms. This, the Council says, is the only time in all of history that human beings have been contacted in this way. Since the original, involuntary contact in the early 1970s, the Council has generated hundreds of thousands of words of discourse.

LePar heads the SOL Association for Research, a nonprofit, tax-exempt organization. It publishes a newsletter, tapes, videos, and books and sponsors lectures and a lending library.

Further Reading

"Biographical Sketch of William Allen LePar," n.d. http://www.solarpress.com/about/BIO-BILL.HTM

Curry

In a published letter to author and UFO abductee Whitley Strieber, an anonymous man recounts an otherworldly encounter he experienced at the age of eight, while living on an Indian reservation in South Dakota. The correspondent said he found himself inexplicably outside the house in the middle of the night, where he saw a smiling man who was somehow "different," with larger than normal eyes and a small amount of hair on his head. Instinctively, the boy knew the stranger's name was Curry, though later in life he learned that curry is "actually a sort of spice from India."

The stranger led the boy to an odd-looking black car. Inside it was a man who looked to be twenty years old or so. The man resembled Curry, and somehow the boy understood that he was to comfort him because the man was frightened. The "car" ascended and flew rapidly to a remote location where there was a crossroads. A "ship or shuttle" then took the boy and his charge apparently into space, but Strieber's correspondent had no memory of anything except being dropped off and seeing Curry again. Now Curry was wearing a hood that covered everything but his eyes.

This was only the first of a number of paranormal encounters the correspondent would have over the years, though this one, apparently, was his last with Curry. He refers to them as "dreams, or experiences, depending on how you want to look at it."

See Also: Abductions by UFOs; Strieber, Whitley

Further Reading

Strieber, Whitley, and Anne Strieber, eds., 1997. *The Communion Letters.* New York: HarperPrism.

Cyclopeans

Argentine ufologist Fabio Picasso coined the term "Cyclopeans" to characterize one-eyed aliens whose alleged presence is the subject of a handful of South American press accounts. Picasso acknowledges that some accounts are certain or likely hoaxes, and others have not been well investigated. Nonetheless, as of 1992, he had found eleven such reports.

One such case is said to have occurred on August 28, 1963, at Sagrada Familia, Brazil. Three boys witnessed the sudden appearance of a beam of light in their backyard. Inside the light, a transparent, ball-shaped object hovered. Inside it, four one-eyed entities, three males and one female, clad in tight coveralls, were visible. One stepped out of the UFO and floated in the air, communicating first by gestures, then by telepathy, to the children (the content of the message is not specified). The being returned to the craft, which then departed.

At Torrent, Argentina, in February 1965, farm laborers, returning home late at night from hunting, noticed five small figures. When one of the hunters acted in a threatening matter, the shapes suddenly grew larger until they were around eight feet tall. The beings chased the hunters to a house. Later, one man escaped from the house with the one-eyed entities in hot pursuit. One managed to grab him with its hairy hands, but the man broke loose and got away. Subsequently, the others effected an escape by van.

"Cyclopean beings can be classified into two subtypes," Picasso writes. "There are short Cyclopeans . . . and tall ones. . . . The latter beings often behave aggressively" (Picasso, 1992).

Further Reading

Picasso, Fabio, 1992. "Infrequent Types of South American Humanoids." *Strange Magazine* 9 (Spring/Summer): 34–35, 55.

Cymatrili

Enid Brady was a spiritualist medium who led a small church in Holly Hill, Florida. In the early 1950s, she began to experience telepathic communications from the "master teachers of Venus." One of them was Cymatrili. He and his companions were based in a giant ship in orbit above the southeastern United States. Venusians look much like humans but are finer featured. Their civilization is advanced, peaceful, and free of disease, poverty, and conflict. Venusians live to be several hundred years old.

Brady was little noted outside contactee circles until the summer of 1957, when a retired army major, Wayne S. Aho, took tape recordings to Washington, DC, of Brady's communications from Cymatrili, Huma Matra, Mandall, and John (the latter two "ventla"—saucer—pilots). Aho visited the Pentagon. He persuaded Defense Department personnel to listen to an hour and a half's worth of the tapes. A spokesman pronounced the messages "unimpressive and unconvincing" ("Pentagon," 1957). Aho later played the tape for a United Press International reporter, who wrote a tongue-in-cheek piece on the experience.

In other channelings, Brady's Venusians related that in 1955, Martians had landed at Edwards Air Force Base in southern California and were taken into custody. Engineers from the air force learned a great deal about extraterrestrial technology from studying the saucer the Martians had arrived in, and that technology was incorporated into later, flying-wing, experimental aircraft.

Brady's space informants also told her that landings would begin in November 1957, and that in 1962, Earth would enter a New Age under the guidance of friendly extraterrestrials.

See Also: Channeling; Contactees

Further Reading

Bryant, Larry W., 1983. "Enid Brady's E-T Contact Legacy." *MUFON UFO Journal* 179 (January): 12–13.

"Pentagon Hears 'Voices from Venus' but Fails to Be Excited about Them," 1957. *The Saucers Report* 2, 3 (October/November): 8–9.

D

David of Landa

David of the planet Landa, a distant world not recognized by conventional astronomy, channeled through Keith Macdonald (d. 1999), a Grayslake, Illinois, car mechanic who lived a quiet life outside the public spotlight. Macdonald is typical of the sorts of persons ufologist/occultist John A. Keel has called "silent contactees." Unlike the flamboyant figures who seek attention and audiences, Macdonald confided his experiences only with family and trusted friends.

Macdonald became aware of David while undergoing hypnotic regression directed by his close friend Ron Owen. In 1974, Macdonald, his wife, and two sons saw what they believed to be a UFO hovering over a field across the street from their townhouse. Four years later, reliving the experience through hypnosis, he "recalled" being taken into the object and undergoing a terrifying abduction at the hands of gray-skinned humanoids. Macdonald pursued recalling the experience through further hypnosis sessions until one session suddenly ended with his declaring that they could go no further because "they're here—right in the room with us!" (Clark, 1986). Then an entity who identified himself as "David" began speaking through Macdonald.

From then on David appeared in regular channelings. During these channelings, Macdonald would lapse into a trance state and speak in David's voice. Afterward he could not recall any of the content and would depend on Owen to explain what words had passed through his mouth. When David wished to communicate only with Macdonald, however, no trance was necessary. A "voice" inside his head would speak, and sometimes Macdonald would psychically perceive David and other people of Landa. Macdonald described the men as strikingly handsome, the women beautiful. All wore robes and reminded Macdonald of Greek gods and goddesses. Sometimes David came through spontaneously when Macdonald was speaking with Owen over the phone. At first, the channelings—a word Macdonald and Owen had not heard until they attended a Wyoming contactee conference sponsored by psychologist/contactee R. Leo Sprinkle—were relatively infrequent. With the passing of time, they occurred more often, on occasion, as many as three or four times a week.

Other extraterrestrials soon were speaking through Macdonald. There was Corinthian, David's wife. Others were Pauline, Lenoir, Chieftain, and Isaiah. Some would not give their names, insisting names were unimportant. David, however, did most of the communicating. Whenever a particular question was asked, he would excuse himself and say he had to clear the answer with higher authority. After a pause, from a few seconds to a few minutes, he would return either to answer the question or to announce he was not permitted to answer it. Other times, though rarely, the entity with whom David had conferred, the Master, would speak, always briefly. The Master's voice had an odd, eerie quality and a tone of absolute authority.

Over many dozens of hours of channeling, this story emerged:

Just before Moses was given the Ten Commandments, seven citizens of Landa were elected by the Masters for a mission on Earth. The leader of the Seven Select, also called the Habanas or the Warriors of God, was Daniel (pronounced Dan-*yell*), the son of David and Corinthian. Once on Earth, the Habanas's souls occupied human bodies. With the passing of centuries, during which the Habanas reincarnated repeatedly, other Habanas arrived, filling Earth with extraterrestrial agents who with each life gained new knowledge that would be useful when the day of reckoning—the cleansing of the human race and the final showdown with the evil forces of the universe—came. This climax would occur within the lifetimes of most living people. In this life, Daniel was Keith Macdonald.

David said, "Keith has now graduated and become a prophet. He is a prophet of Christ. He is a prophet of God." The people of Landa, devout Christians, practice a form of Roman Catholicism. Raised a Protestant, Macdonald knew little of Catholicism until the Landanians contacted him.

According to a channeling from the Master in 1985, "soon there will be forty craft of Landa truly visible to the eyes of all humans. Three more craft shall come down to receive Keith. This will be done to gain the attention of the many, for Keith has a job. His first job will be to be received by us of Landa, to be taken there for forty days and nights. During that time forty craft of Landa will travel to every nation to show Keith has been received. When the meeting is over, Keith will return to meet with the leaders of the churches and the nations. He will demand the release of the Scrolls for all human beings to see and understand." The Master explained that earthlings cannot now tell the difference between good and evil because the Scrolls—suppressed ancient religious documents—have not been available to them.

The Scrolls contain the hidden history of humanity, revealing all the truths that God, Jesus, and Mary wanted humans to know but were concealed because they did not suit the purposes of earthly political leaders and church authorities. Keith himself, the Master asserted, had this knowledge within himself, though it had not yet been released into his conscious mind.

At the time of the Lifting—which is what the Landanians called the occasion that Macdonald would be taken aboard a spacecraft (one of three that would appear in the same empty field where evil aliens had kidnapped him in 1974) and flown home to Landa—there would be thousands of witnesses. On September 22, 1985, Macdonald encountered the apparitional forms of David and Corinthian, who informed him that an earthquake would devastate San Francisco soon. Upset, he pleaded for the innocent lives that would be lost, but his space friends/parents soberly replied, "It is inevitable. You must pray for the souls of those who will be lost and for those who will miss them."

Convinced that the earthquake would occur any day, Macdonald waited gloomily and anxiously. Nothing happened. But then on the morning of October 7, as Macdonald was letting the dog out, a blinding light shot out of the sky and struck him in the face. He took this to mean that the first of the three Landanian craft that would carry him away was in place.

The following day, while talking with Owen on the phone, David took over. He said that a physical, in-the-flesh meeting between Keith and David would occur in two days in

Keith's house. David and Corinthian did not keep their appointment.

In the days and weeks that followed, Macdonald experienced a series of unusually vivid dreams. One night he dreamed that he had been accepted back into the military. To him this symbolized his role as a Warrior of God about to "fight." Another night he dreamed that he was on a college campus, knowing where every building, every door, every room was. He heard professors lecturing and knew every word they were saying. He understood that he had "graduated" to a level more advanced than college. In yet another dream, he was gazing over a crowd of hundreds of people, seeing deep inside each and recognizing each one as a fellow Warrior of God, brother and sister Habanas who would be coming together in the great events yet to occur as Earth met its cosmic destiny. A voice inside the dream told him that this was a "reunion." A blinding light cut through the dream, and when Macdonald sat bolt upright in bed, it continued to shine. It was so bright that he had to put his arm over his face.

Strange, ominous events seemed to point to the imminent Lifting. Twice on the evening of October 23, as Macdonald and Owen were talking, the phone suddenly disconnected, each time with a peculiar squealing sound. It happened just as they were discussing key points about Landanian objectives. Macdonald saw odd lights both inside the house and in the sky. Landanians appeared with increasing frequency, but only Macdonald could see them. They were invisible to his wife. Macdonald tried to capture them on film, but all that the resulting photographs showed was the interior of the house, nothing more.

Early in December, the date of the San Francisco earthquake that was to prefigure the Lifting appeared before his eyes in brilliant light: DECEMBER 22. He could not only see the date but also experience the sensations of being in the quake. As the days passed, the vision of the date recurred along with scenes of devastation. When December 22 came and went with no earthquake, David told Keith that the real date was January 3; the twenty-second was the date on which the craft would begin to show themselves. David said that Macdonald should always remember, "There is more than one meaning to a sentence."

The failure of assorted prophecies never entirely diminished Keith Macdonald's belief—a palpably sincere one—that people from Landa were communicating with him. He learned, however, to be cautious about their predictions, including promises of in-the-flesh meetings prior to the Lifting. In the years that followed, growing health problems forced Macdonald into retirement. In his last years, he spent considerable time in the hospital. During that period contacts occurred more often in unusually lucid dreams than they did via channeling.

See Also: Abductions by UFOs; Channeling; Contactees; Keel, John Alva; Sprinkle, Ronald Leo

Further Reading

Clark, Jerome, 1986. "Waiting for the Space Brothers." *Fate* Pt. I. 39, 3 (March): 47–54; Pt. II. 39, 4 (April): 81–87; Pt. III. 39, 5 (May): 68–76.

Owen, Ron, 2000. Private communication to Jerome Clark (January 6).

Dead extraterrestrials

Claims that the bodies of extraterrestrials have been found in the wreckage of spacecraft are older than the post–World War II UFO age. As long ago as 1864, a French newspaper (*La Pays,* June 17) reported the discovery, by two American geologists, of a hollow, egg-shaped rock. Inside it were various odd artifacts. They also found the mummified remains of a tiny humanoid—about three feet tall—with a bald head and an elephantlike trunk growing out of its forehead. On October 13, 1877, a provincial paper in Argentina set the identical tall tale in that country, adding the detail that the discoverers had taken the body and artifacts to a local saloon to put on display.

In 1897, during a wave of UFO (or, in the terminology of the time, "airship") sightings, ships crashed and Martians died in Illinois and Texas. In the latter instance, the pilot was reportedly buried in a cemetery in a small north Texas town. When the latter tale was revived in the late 1960s and early 1970s, hopeful investigators rushed to the scene, only to learn eventually that no such corpse or grave had ever existed outside the imagination of a turn-of-the-century prankster.

Though it did not come to wider attention until many years later, a killing of a tiny humanoid reportedly took place in 1913 near Farmersville, Texas. Three young brothers were chopping cotton on their farm when they heard the family dogs barking and then howling. On investigating, the boys saw the dogs attacking a strange little man "no more than eighteen inches high and kind of a dark green color," one witness, an old man, recalled in a 1978 interview. "His arms were hanging down just beside him, like they was growed down the side of him. He had on a kind of hat that reminded me of a Mexican hat. . . . Everything looked like a rubber suit including the hat." The dogs tore him to pieces, leaving human-looking organs and blood on the ground. The peculiar tale was known within the family for decades. Though he had a hard time believing the story, the investigator thought there was no question of the old man's sincerity.

Rumors of dead aliens, however, did not enter popular culture in any significant way until 1947, after Kenneth Arnold's June 24 observation of nine discs over Mount Rainier, Washington, brought "flying saucers" into common currency. After initial theories that tied the sightings to secret aviation experiments proved groundless, those who continued to take the reports seriously slowly began to wonder if visitors from other planets were responsible for the phenomenon. By 1949, rumors of recovered extraterrestrial bodies began to see print, notably in the entertainment industry newspaper *Variety.* Columnist Frank Scully wrote that on three occasions the previous year, beginning with an incident in Aztec, New Mexico, in March, U.S. Air Force personnel had recovered, at various desert sites, the remains of crashed spacecraft and bodies. He expanded these allegations into a book destined for lasting notoriety, *Behind the Flying Saucers* (1950). In it, he identified his source as the pseudonymous "Dr. Gee," said to be a leading scientific expert on magnetism (brought into the investigation of the recovery because it was believed that the ships "probably flew on magnetic lines of force"). The dead crews, human in every respect except for their perfect teeth and unfashionable 1890s-style clothes, were surmised to be of Venusian origin. A subsequent exposé in *True* magazine revealed that "Dr. Gee" was veteran confidence artist Leo GeBauer. With his longtime partner-in-crime, Silas Newton, GeBauer had concocted the tale to sell bogus oil-detection devices allegedly tied to advanced interplanetary technology.

As a result of the episode, even persons otherwise sympathetically disposed to the idea of space visitation were deeply skeptical of crash/retrieval claims. Still, the claims circulated in a significant body of saucer folklore, only a little of which surfaced in the UFO literature. In 1952, Jim and Coral Lorenzen of the newly formed Aerial Phenomena Research Organization (APRO)—which would prove among the most influential and durable of all UFO groups—spoke with an airman who swore that four years earlier he and others from a military-scientific team had been dispatched to a New Mexico crash site. There he had seen a disc and learned that dead, little men had been taken from its cabin. Not long afterward, a "young meteorologist" told the Lorenzens that in 1948, while visiting Wright Air Development Center (soon to be renamed Wright-Patterson Air Force Base) in Dayton, Ohio, he had spoken with an old friend, an air force man. The friend, in Coral Lorenzen's words, showed him "space suits ranging from three to about five and a half feet in height and diagrams of a circular ship that bore a strong resemblance to a 'flying saucer.' He said that people who laughed about flying saucers were going to get a big jolt some day—these suits had been taken off the bodies of men who had apparently perished in the crash of their saucer-shaped ships" (Lorenzen, 1962).

On May 7, 1955, a Caracas, Venezuela, newspaper, *El Universal,* carried a sensational story of an incident supposed to have taken place almost exactly five years earlier. A man claimed that while driving down a rural highway in Argentina, he spotted a flying saucer that had landed on the side of the road. Curious, he stopped his car, approached the craft, and eventually boarded it. Inside, he found the bodies of three little men lying near an instrument panel. After touching one, he panicked and fled, to return the next day to see UFOs hovering over the site. Where the original craft had been there was only a pile of warm, gray ashes. Years later, a retrospective investigation by Argentine ufologists determined that the "witness" had made up the story.

More intriguing was an account given in confidence to Isabel L. Davis, one of the most intelligent, hard-headed, first-generation ufologists and a fierce critic of the more outlandish saucer tales. Davis never published the account in her lifetime, but she found it intriguing, given that the informant, a medical scientist, seemed serious and credible. Even so, the scientist's claim was a fantastic one. In the late 1950s, she told Davis, she was directed to a secure, government-run facility and ordered to examine body parts that she quickly recognized as humanlike but not human. Her superiors provided no explanations or further details, and when her work was completed, they instructed her to tell nobody. As she remarked to Davis, she would not have done so anyway, since no one would have believed her.

Another tale—this one circulated by saucer personality and publisher Gray Barker—concerned Nicholas von Poppen, an Estonian refugee who had fled his native country when Soviet troops overran it and slaughtered his family. That much of the story seems true (the real Von Poppen died in Los Angeles in 1976). Beyond that, however, Barker and truth parted company. He took an unpublished science-fiction manuscript written by a subscriber to his magazine *The Saucerian* and transformed it into a "true" story. In the original, the writer/subscriber had taken a colorful, real acquaintance, Von Poppen, and placed him inside a fantasy in which Von Poppen took photographs in New Mexico of a crashed UFO and its occupants. Barker took this story and embellished it further, then marketed it as an account of an authentic incident—not the only hoax Barker would perpetrate on his impressionable readers.

In the 1970s, ufologist Leonard H. Stringfield, in the face of criticism and skepticism from some colleagues, began collecting crash/retrieval claims and rumors and publishing them in a series of monographs. None amounted to much as evidence, though some were undeniably interesting, such as the testimony of a Presbyterian pastor. This man—Stringfield protected the names of his informants—alleged that when he was a boy, he and his father (also a clergyman) visited the Museum of Science and Industry in Chicago. During one visit, they got lost. In their search for an exit, they accidentally entered a room where a number of humanoid beings lay preserved under a glass-covered case. Before they could fully grasp what they were seeing, they were discovered. The father was pressured to sign papers swearing him to silence.

In another alleged instance, said to have taken place at a New Jersey air force base in January 1978, a sergeant—who insisted on anonymity—told Stringfield that in the early morning hours a military policeman had shot and killed a humanoid being that he had encountered while chasing a UFO in his car. The body was then shipped off to Wright-Patterson Air Force Base. The sergeant eventually provided an official-looking "incident report," with the names of witnesses and investigators inked out. Stringfield's informant talked and acted in a manner that he and fellow ufologist Richard Hall, who interviewed the man in person on two occasions, deemed sincere, but, despite a serious effort, they uncovered nothing that conclusively verified the claim.

Perhaps the most interesting of Stringfield's informants were several "medical people" who had performed autopsies on alien corpses. One, a physician who "served on the staff of a major hospital" (Stringfield, 1980), provided a detailed account of an autopsy, in the early 1950s, of a humanoid reminiscent of the gray-skinned, big-eyed entities that would figure in abduction lore in later years. Stringfield, who died in December 1994, never revealed the names of these individuals, so independent investigation of their stories and status proved impossible. Nor would his family provide investigators with Stringfield's files. None disputed Stringfield's integrity, though some questioned his judgment in taking such extraordinary testimony at face value.

Lecturing in London on April 14, 1979, American occultist and channeler James Hurtak declared that a flying saucer had crashed as early as 1946. His source, he said, was a colleague who had participated in the retrieval. The crash occurred near Great Falls, Montana. "The bodies were shipped to the Edwards Air Force Base facility in California," Hurtak claimed. "It was determined that the green hue on the bodies was due to the nature of the chemistry of the fuel system. After extensive studies the bodies were put on ice and sealed in aluminum canisters" (Hurtak, 1979).

In the late 1970s, a Minnesota schoolteacher, William L. Moore, and a nuclear scientist and UFO lecturer, Stanton T. Friedman, got interested in an incident that to most was an obscure footnote: a brief flurry of excitement in early July 1947 over the supposed recovery of a "flying disc" near Roswell, New Mexico. The story had hit the presses only to be contradicted in a matter of a few hours, when the U.S. Army Air Force announced that it had all risen out of an absurd

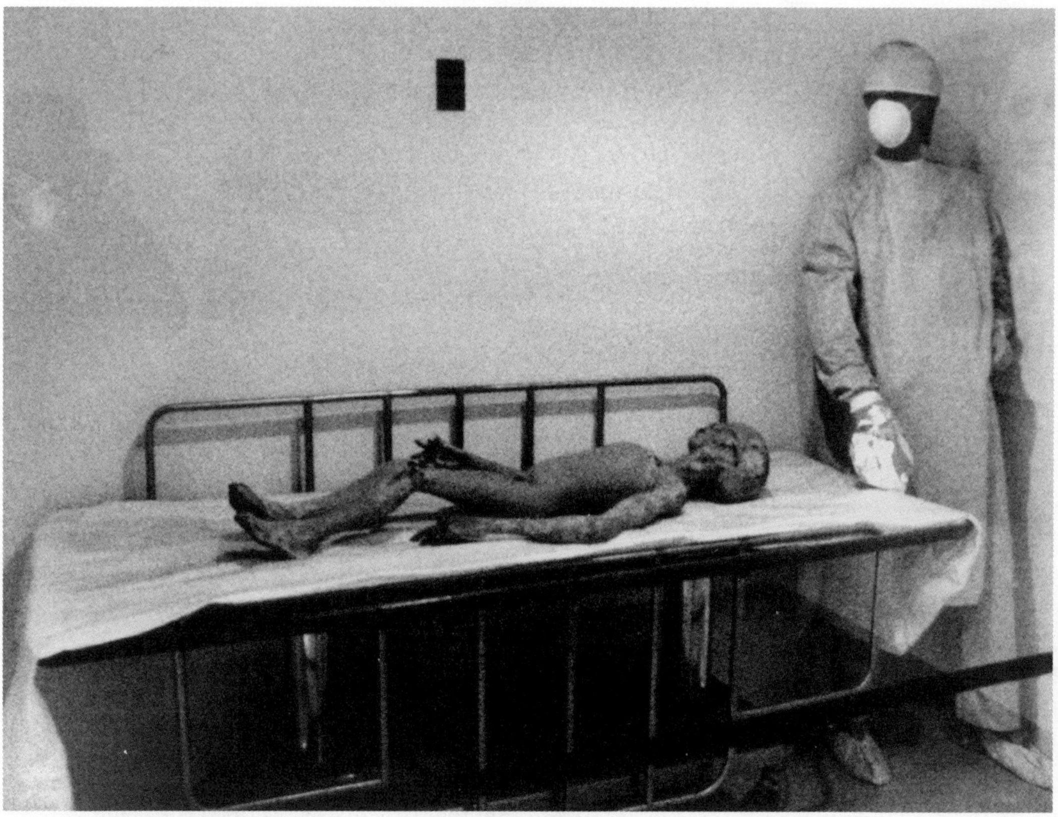

Display showing a dead alien autopsy (with models) at the UFO Museum in Roswell, New Mexico (Peregrine Mendoza/Fortean Picture Library)

misunderstanding about a downed weather balloon. During his travels, Friedman met a retired air force officer who, at the time, had been stationed at Roswell Army Air Field; the officer, Major Jesse A. Marcel, had been the first uniformed officer on the site, and his observation and experience over the next few days put into question the long-accepted balloon explanation. Friedman also interviewed a woman who had worked at an Albuquerque radio station. She vividly remembered how the U.S. Air Force had squelched coverage of the story. Both she and Marcel believed that some kind of extraordinary event that had badly rattled the military had happened.

Moore's *The Roswell Incident* (1980), written with Bermuda Triangle popularizer Charles Berlitz, would be only the first of many books to address the subject. As investigators spoke with a growing number of informants, military and civilian, they established that a cover-up, maintained in part by the threatening of witnesses, had been put into place and that the official story was not the real story. Some witnesses even asserted that the military had recovered bodies of little men at either the original crash site or another, related one some miles away. In time, the Roswell incident, as everyone called it, was no longer an arcane fascination of ufologists but a much-discussed item of pop culture, influencing any number of television shows, documentaries, movies, jokes, and more.

After years of denying that the air force had covered up the Roswell incident, the General Accounting Office, at the behest of New Mexico Congressman Steven Schiff, searched official archives for relevant documents, uncovering little of interest. Around the same time, in 1994, the U.S. Air Force declared that there had indeed been a cover-up; it had been of Project Mogul, a highly classified project in which balloons were sent aloft to monitor possible Soviet atomic tests over the horizon. A Mogul balloon had come down near Roswell, and the military's effort to keep it a secret sparked the legend of a UFO crash. In the face of press and popular skepticism (much of it focused on the explanation's failure to account for reports of bodies) the U.S. Air Force renewed its inquiries. On June 24, 1997, it contended that the supposedly alien bodies were in fact "anthropomorphic test dummies that were carried aloft by U.S. Air Force high altitude balloons for scientific research" (*The Roswell Report,* 1997). The problem with this theory was that tests involving such dummies did not occur until 1953, leaving the air force with the rationalization—unpersuasive to many—that the informants simply had their time mixed up.

Still, many ufologists, as much out of frustration as firm intellectual conviction, accepted the Mogul explanation, whatever its imperfections. The Roswell incident had spawned an industry and generated a huge body of often confusing, contradictory (and sometimes demonstrably false) testimony. It even generated documents (most notably the notorious and deeply suspect "MJ-12" papers, purportedly from the supersecret project overseeing the UFO cover-up). On the whole, it did not accomplish a great deal except to line the pockets of opportunists who didn't much care about the truth—which, in any event, seemed irrecoverable so many years past the original event. Roswell also inspired one of the most brazen hoaxes in UFO history, the so-called alien autopsy film that aired on the Fox Network in the mid-1990s, purporting to show the dismemberment of an extraterrestrial body by government scientists in 1947.

The failure of the Roswell story to come to firm resolution after two decades of furious controversy sobered many once-enthusiastic or hopeful ufologists. But as long as questions remain, the mystery will stay open to those who are sufficiently determined to keep thinking—or, perhaps, thinking wishfully—about it. And Roswell or no, rumors, tall tales, and—on rare occasion—genuinely intriguing reports of dead extraterrestrials in our midst are likely to entertain live humans for some time to come.

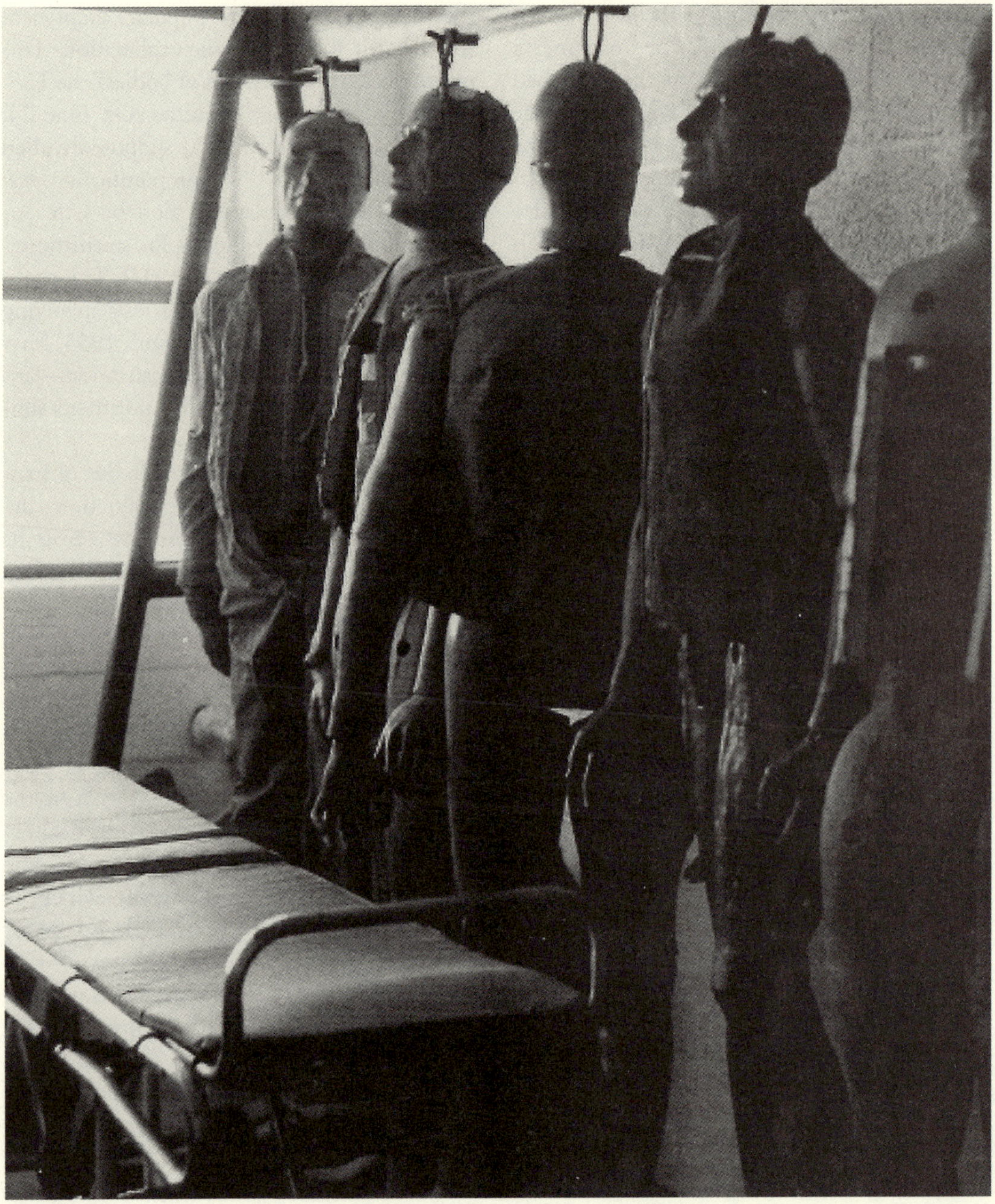

A photo from the U.S. Air Force's Roswell Report *about the 1947 UFO incident at Roswell, New Mexico, released June 24, 1997, and intended to eliminate long-standing rumors. Air force personnel supposedly used stretchers and gurneys to pick up these 200-pound dummies in the field and move them to the laboratory. (Associated Press/Air Force)*

See Also: Abductions by UFOs; Aurora Martian; Fossilized aliens; Oleson's giants

Further Reading

Barker, Gray, 1960. "Chasing the Flying Saucers." *Flying Saucers* (November): 22–28.

Berlitz, Charles, and William L. Moore, 1980. *The Roswell Incident.* New York: Grosset and Dunlap.

Cahn, J. P., 1952. "The Flying Saucers and the Mysterious Little Men." *True* (September): 17–19, 102–112.

Carey, Thomas J., and Donald R. Schmitt, 1999. "Mack Brazel Reconsidered." *International UFO Reporter* 24, 4 (Winter): 12–19.

Evans, Alex, 1978. "Encounters with Little Men." *Fate* 31, 11 (November): 83–86.

General Accounting Office, 1995. *Report to the Honorable Steven H. Schiff, House of Representatives: Results of a Search for Records Concerning the 1947 Crash Near Roswell, New Mexico.* Washington, DC: General Accounting Office.

Hurtak, James J., 1979. "The Occupants of Crashed 'Saucers'." *The UFO Register* 10, 1 (December): 2–3.

Lorenzen, Coral E., 1962. *The Great Flying Saucer Hoax: The UFO Facts and Their Interpretation.* New York: William-Frederick Press.

Pflock, Karl T., 1994. *Roswell in Perspective.* Mount Rainier, MD: Fund for UFO Research.

———, 2000. "What's Really Behind the Flying Saucers? A New Twist on Aztec." *The Anomalist* 8 (Spring): 137–161.

Randle, Kevin D., 1995. *A History of UFO Crashes.* New York: Avon Books.

Randle, Kevin D., and Donald R. Schmitt, 1991. *UFO Crash at Roswell.* New York: Avon Books.

———, 1994. *The Truth about the UFO Crash at Roswell.* New York: Avon Books.

The Roswell Report: Case Closed, 1997. Washington, DC: Defense Department, Air Force, Headquarters.

The Roswell Report: Fact versus Fiction in the New Mexico Desert, 1995. Washington, DC: Headquarters, United States Air Force.

Scully, Frank, 1950. *Behind the Flying Saucers.* New York: Henry Holt and Company.

Stringfield, Leonard H., 1980. *The UFO Crash/Retrieval Syndrome. Status Report II: New Sources, New Data.* Seguin, TX: Mutual UFO Network.

———, 1987. "The Chase for Proof in a Squirrel's Cage." In Hilary Evans with John Spencer, eds. *UFOs 1947–1987: The 40-Year Search for an Explanation,* 145–155. London: Fortean Tomes.

Swords, Michael D., 1997. "Roswell: Clashing Visions of the Possible." *International UFO Reporter* 22, 3 (Fall): 11–13, 33–35.

Dentons's Martians and Venusians

In America during the nineteenth century, spiritualists and other psychics proliferated. Among the most prominent were William Denton and his son Sherman. They called themselves "psychometers," which meant that they could discern any truth, however distant in time and space, by touching a physical object or, if it were out of reach, at least focusing on it. In this way they learned that Mars and Venus were inhabited.

As the elder Denton put it, "A telescope only enables us to see; but the spiritual faculties enable their possessors to hear, smell, taste, and feel, and become for the time being, almost inhabitants of the planet they are examining."

In 1866, as the two men were standing out in a field watching Venus rise in the evening sky, the father asked the son to study the planet and tell him what he saw. After a few minutes, Sherman described trees, water that was heavy but not wet, and animals that had the features of both fish and muskrats.

Other experiments soon followed. Sherman left his body and traveled to Mars, where he saw a thriving civilization consisting of a race that looked much like humans. "They soar above traffic on their individual flycycles," he reported. "They seem particularly fond of air travel. As many as thirty people occupy some of the large flying conveyances." The Martians also had a particular fondness for aluminum, which they employed in building houses and machines.

See Also: Allingham's Martian; Aurora Martian; Brown's Martians; Hopkins's Martians; Khauga; Martian bees; Mince-Pie Martians; Monka; Muller's Martians; Shaw's Martians; Smead's Martians; Thompson's Venusians; Wilcox's Martians

Further Reading

Steiger, Brad, 1966. *Strangers from the Skies.* New York: Award Books.

Diane

According to contactee Dana Howard, Diane was a Venusian who began appearing to humans in 1939. She returned in 1955 and was seen many times after that. "Diane came in the same miraculous manner as the Lady of The Lourdes and Our Lady of Fatima," Howard wrote. "To all appearances She is a physical being like ourselves, yet She is obviously created of *substances not of this earth*" (Howard, 1958).

Howard, who claimed to have visited Venus, reported that on October 3, 1957, as she was lecturing at the Women's Clubhouse in Fontana, California, she felt a strange warmth come over her. After the meeting, several audience members rushed up to her to say that they had seen an apparition of a young woman transposed over Howard's body. One audience member, Eleanor Warner, described "the figure of a beautiful woman, *very* young, with long golden hair, a very slim body, and small waistline. She seemed to glow in the golden light." Another witness, Trudy Allen, was "overcome by the transcendent beauty that was shining forth."

In Howard's account, Diane appeared to her, in full view of twenty-seven witnesses, for the first time on April 29, 1955, and identified herself as a Venusian. That same week UFOs appeared on four occasions over Palm Springs, California, Howard's hometown.

See Also: Contactees

Further Reading

Howard, Dana, 1958. "The Drama behind the Space Ships." *Flying Saucer Review* 4, 3 (May/June): 21–23.

Divine Fire

In a book that would prove influential in 1970s New Age circles, Brad Steiger wrote of what he called the "Divine Fire." He believed that a dramatic rise was occurring in visionary experience, channeling, and other contact with ostensible higher intelligences. "Clergymen, clerks, professors, public relations executives, housewives, students, servicemen, and factory workers have been demonstrating that Pentecost was not just a one-shot special designed to excite the Apostles and their kibitzers in Jerusalem of A.D. 30," he said (Steiger, 1973).

According to Steiger, these extraordinary experiences and communications were taking a variety of forms, but the message was the same in its essence as those given to prophets five thousand years ago. He suggested that "the very repetition of a basic message may be evidence of the vital relevancy and universality of a cosmic truth." The messages came from ostensible angels, extraterrestrials, divinities, and the like, but all spoke of a "Higher Being" from whom each individual could draw inspiration and wisdom. These messages stated that all humans have the power within themselves to contact this Higher Being. All things were one; everything and everybody was at once individual and universal. And finally, humans were entering, in Steiger's summary, "a New Age, another progression in our evolution as spiritual beings. . . . We are moving toward a state of mystical consciousness wherein every man shall be priest."

See Also: Channeling

Further Reading

Steiger, Brad, 1973. *Revelation: The Divine Fire.* Englewood Cliffs, NJ: Prentice-Hall.

Dual reference

"Dual reference" is a term coined by Massachusetts ufologist Joseph Nyman. His hypnotic investigations of abductees have led him to the discovery that many believe themselves to be of alien origin. They have no conscious memories of such a personal extraterrestrial link, but under hypnosis they gradually come to understand that the aliens who are abducting them are actually their own associates and colleagues. They eventually grasp that before their human selves were born, their alien selves made the decision to send their consciousnesses into human fetal bodies. In the very first years of their human lives, memories of their homes on other worlds are lost, but over the years, as they undergo abduction experiences, they learn—through hypnotic "recall" of these experiences—of their true past and their mission in this life and on this planet. Sometimes, while the session is going on, the hypnotist is able to speak directly with the alien intelligence in the subject's body.

Similar notions are not uncommon among contactees, many of whom are convinced that they were extraterrestrials in an earlier lives and are now here to help prepare humans for the great geophysical and spiritual changes that will be coming soon. Dual reference also is somewhat comparable to the notion of Walk-ins, popularized by occult writer Ruth Montgomery, except that Walk-ins are not always (though they are sometimes) extraterrestrials. Moreover, they are so intellectually and spiritually advanced that they only take up occupancy of the bodies of grown adults, so as not to waste valuable time.

Nyman writes, "We strongly suspect that the feeling of dual reference . . . is unconsciously present in all [abduction] experiencers" (Nyman, 1989). Most investigators of the abduction phenomenon disagree, and indeed when Nyman presented his ideas at a 1992 conference held at the Massachusetts Institute of Technology, some questioners accused him of leading his subjects into confabulation. They were particularly critical of his practice of asking the subjects to recall "memories" of their lives in the womb. Among Nyman's defenders was Harvard University psychologist John E. Mack, who was also engaged in extensive hypnotic probing of ostensible abductees.

In a book published two years later, Mack told the story of a young man he identifies only as Paul, "one of an increasing group of abductees . . . who have discovered that they have a dual identity of an alien (they do not use that word) and a human being." Paul was convinced that he was on Earth to show people how to love and accept love—this even before he found his alien identity under hypnosis.

Paul had gone to another psychologist to examine some of his life's problems, including a conviction that he had seen a weird humanoid creature. Hypnotized, he spoke of other encounters with other strange beings, including one when he was two or three years old. The psychologist did not know what to make of these stories, and he and Paul parted company; Paul eventually found his way to Mack.

With Mack, Paul explored an apparent memory of a further encounter, this one when he was six and a half. He spoke of seeing a being inside his house and of sensing that the two of them were "linked in a way." They went outside together, where they met two groups—four or five each—of humanoids. Though they did not look human, Paul felt comfortable, even joyful, to be in their company. They apparently felt the same; they hugged him and gave every indication of feeling great affection for him. The whole experience felt "like home." Subsequently he was taken aboard a ship, an experience he sensed he had undergone in other lives. One of the beings told him that he was from their planet. The alien spoke of human beings' inability to "truly open up to another" and of their hostility to the visiting extraterrestrials.

During the session Paul alternated between his human and alien selves. In the latter, he spoke of the nature of higher consciousness and of humans' destructive ways. He also expressed homesickness for the ship and the planet from which he had come. He "remembered" earlier visits to Earth, including interactions—apparently tens of millions of years ago—with intelligent, gentle dinosaurs. In another instance, the ship on which he was traveling—in earthling guise—with extraterrestrial companions rescued the surviving occupants of a crashed craft that went down in the desert after being shot down by "men in uniforms." Two of the crew died and had to be abandoned in the face of advancing soldiers. Paul felt, in this instance, ashamed to be human; yet, in a broader context, he felt certain that "peace and love" were slowly spreading over the Earth and that he had a role to play in opening up human beings to larger, benevolent cosmic truths.

According to Mack, Paul has learned powerful psychic healing powers from his ongoing interactions with his extraterrestrial friends. He has been given a great deal of information on their "unbelievable" technology but has been forbidden to share it (Mack, 1994a).

Mack rejects the theory that such attachments of abductee to abductor are analogous to the so-called Stockholm Syndrome, in which a hostage comes to identify with his or her captor. There is, he says, "little sense that the alien identity is primarily a product of 'identification with the aggressor.' . . . Rather, the dual identity appears to be a fundamental dimension of the consciousness expansion or opening that is an intrinsic aspect of the abduction phenomenon itself" (Mack, 1994b).

See Also: Abductions by UFOs; Contactees; Walk-ins

Further Reading

Mack, John E., 1994a. *Abduction: Human Encounters with Aliens.* New York: Charles Scribner's Sons.

———, 1994b. "Post Conference Note." In Andrea Pritchard, David E. Pritchard, John E. Mack, Pam Kasey, and Claudia Yapp, eds. *Alien Discussions: Proceedings of the Abduction Study Conference,* 146. Cambridge, MA: North Cambridge Press.

Nyman, Joseph, 1988. "The Latent Encounter Experience—A Composite Model." *MUFON UFO Journal* 242 (June): 10–12.

———, 1989. "The Familiar Entity and Dual Reference in the Latent Encounter." *MUFON UFO Journal* 251 (March): 10–12.

———, 1994. "Dual Reference in the UFO Encounter." In Andrea Pritchard, David E. Pritchard, John E. Mack, Pam Kasey, and Claudia Yapp, eds. *Alien Discussions: Proceedings of the Abduction Study Conference,* 142–148. Cambridge, MA: North Cambridge Press.

Dugja

According to members of a small group called Elan Vital (Vital Essence), the last queen of the lost continent of Lemuria, Dugja (pronounced doo-ja), reigns as "Spirit of the Mountain." The mountain is Shasta, in far northern California, the focus of many occult beliefs and legends. Dugja materializes whenever her mood or the situation, calls for it.

One member claimed that in 1963, while meditating on Mount Shasta's Grey Butte, he sensed an "astral man," with thin hair, white beard, and pink skin, warning him telepathically to turn back. When he ignored the threats and entreaties, other astral entities joined with the first one. Nonetheless, undaunted, the man ended his meditation and continued his trek up the mountain. Soon he encountered Dugja, who greeted him warmly and invited him to stay for a time. He returned to Shasta three years later. Since then, he told reporter Emilie A. Frank in the 1970s, he had visited the queen on many occasions in both physical and out-of-body states. "I am also responsible for cleaning negative light forces around Mount Shasta and elsewhere in the world," he said. "These light forces affect the population, and in order to make the world a better place . . . I polarize their negative influences. Eventually they will all be pure. In the meantime, I make many astral trips to Mount Shasta in order to purify the lights" (Frank, 1998).

See Also: Lemuria; Mount Shasta

Further Reading

Frank, Emilie A., 1998. *Mt. Shasta: California's Mystic Mountain.* Hilt, CA: Photografix Publishing.

E

Earth Coincidence Control Office

Scientist John Lilly, best known for his pioneering researches into dolphins and into altered states of consciousness, was on an airliner approaching Los Angeles when he had his first communication from an intelligence he would come to call Earth Coincidence Control Office. He received a psychic message that said, "We will now make a demonstration of our power over the solid-state control systems upon the planet Earth. In thirty seconds, we will shut off all electronic equipment in the Los Angeles airport. Your airplane will be unable to land there and will have to be shunted to another airport" (Lilly, 1978). Sure enough, the power blackout occurred, forcing Lilly's plane to land at Burbank; another plane crashed.

In a visionary experience not long afterward, Lilly witnessed the future of the human race. A solid-state intelligence, consisting of all computers and electronic systems, will assume control of everything and become too powerful for human beings to do anything about. By the 2500s this intelligence will be in communication with its counterparts elsewhere in the Milky Way.

Lilly believed himself to be in contact with the water-based—as opposed to solid-state—entities in the universe. The two intelligences, the latter always the creation of the former, are in conflict all through the universe. Water-based beings from elsewhere are paying close attention to developments on Earth and sending humans constant telepathic messages that usually register, at least where humans are concerned, only on a subliminal level. These beings (the Earth Coincidence Control Office, in Lilly's phrasing) seek to influence human evolution in such a way that humans do not become enslaved to their technology. The other intelligences that share our planet—dolphins and whales—are more psychically attuned to these messages and receive them clearly. Lilly holds that "whales and dolphins quite naturally go in the direction we call spiritual, in that they get into meditative states quite simply and easily. . . . Dolphins have a highly developed consciousness, and a powerful connection to higher realities" (Lilly, 1972).

Beginning in the 1950s, Lilly had experimented with sensory deprivation. He would place himself in a tank of water in a totally dark, silent room. In due course he would undergo vivid hallucinations. To him these hallucinations became more real than reality. He came to believe that through them he entered other dimensions of existence and grew aware that this dimension and others harbor innumerable varieties of intelligent entities.

Further Reading

Lilly, John C., 1972. *The Center of the Cyclone: An Autobiography of Inner Space.* New York: Julian Press.

———, 1978. *The Scientist: A Novel Autobiography.* New York: J. B. Lippincott.

Elder Race

The Elder Race, also known as Els, was the first extraterrestrial group ever to arrive on Earth. They showed up one billion years ago after already having colonized a considerable portion of the galaxy. But on Earth, these beings—originally twelve feet tall, male and female (though "not as we think of sex differentiation today" [Williamson, 1959]), and many one-eyed—radically changed. Earth would be the last planet in which they existed in physical bodies. During their stay on Earth, they conquered matter, energy, space, and time, becoming "the legendary 'gods'" able to project via mental powers "any amount of matter in any degree of density or intensity to any place on Earth at any time." In their underground city near Lake Titicaca, along what is now the Peru-Bolivia border, they built a vast control room, a kind of "Earth Center."

In this and other underground realms, they left vast libraries on which the history of the universe is recorded on crystal devices encased in magnetic fields. On occasion, a psychically sensitive individual is able to tap into these records.

Further Reading

Williamson, George Hunt, 1959. *Road in the Sky.* London: Neville Spearman.

Elvis as Jesus

In a book published in 2000, Cinda Godfrey concludes that Elvis Presley was the Messiah—the returned Jesus Christ. She writes that she began her research in 1992, determined to disprove any connection between the two, only to find "mind-boggling evidence

Stephanie G. Pierce, Celebrity Spokesminister for the 24 Hour Church of Elvis, stands inside the church's inner sanctum. (Macduff Everton/CORBIS)

that the prophecies throughout the [Bible] fit both Elvis and Jesus like a glove."

Among the similarities: Both Jesus and Elvis are called The King. Jesus was the Rock; Elvis (at least according to Godfrey) invented rock. Jesus was the Son, and Elvis began his recording career on the Sun label. "The name numbers for Jesus and Elvis both equal nine," she says. "In fact, their name-numbers match exactly, letter for letter and number for number: Jesus = 15363, Elvis = 53613." Their followers worshipped and adored them. Both could heal and read minds, and both had powerful enemies who sought to stop them. Godfrey claims that like Jesus, Elvis was Jewish.

She also notes that the Bible frequently refers to the Voice of God on many occasions. "Is there any voice more spectacular than Elvis Presley's?" she asks. The Psalms even predict that Presley one day would disappear: "I am shut up and I cannot come forth" (Psalms 88:8) and "How long, Lord? Wilt thou hide thyself forever?" (Psalms 89:46). Isaiah 4:2 states that when the Messiah comes, "In that day shall the branch [Messiah] of the Lord be beautiful and glorious." Godfrey remarks, "Now, picture Elvis at his *Aloha from Hawaii* concert, resplendent in his jeweled American Eagle jumpsuit. Curiously enough, the eagle is also a symbol for Christ" (Godfrey, 2000).

According to Godfrey (as well as more mainstream Presley biographers such as Peter Guralnick), Presley had a religious vision in the Arizona desert in March 1965. Just outside Flagstaff, as Presley was driving his bus with his spiritual advisor Larry Geller sitting next to him, he saw a cloud in a clear sky and swore that he could see the face of the late Soviet dictator Josef Stalin in it. The image faded as the cloud's shape changed, so Presley imagined, into the face of Jesus. He pulled the bus over to the side of the road and ran into the desert, feeling a sense of deep spiritual transformation. Geller would claim that Presley later wondered if maybe he was indeed Christ.

Godfrey contends that Elvis Aron Presley's own name proves his godhood. "El" means God, "vis" from power—thus "God Power." "Presley" derives from "priestly." She goes on, "In fact, all three of Elvis' major residences contain the prophetic 'EL': Grac*el*and, Tup*el*o and B*el* Air. Furthermore, according to the Bible, since Jesus' crucifixion, we are living in the Dispensation of 'Grace'—that 2,000 year period of time when sins are pardoned by the sacrificial death of Christ. The name of Elvis Presley's mansion: 'GRACE-LAND'!" And, she adds, did not Jesus say, "I am Alpha and Omega, the beginning and the ending," just as Elvis said, "I am and I was"?

Godfrey goes outside Scripture to delve into esoteric literature for further evidence, citing among other sources the prophecies of Nostradamus and Edgar Cayce. Noting one occultist interpretation of the Great Pyramid (not shared by Egyptologists), she writes that the Great Pyramid was a monument to Christ, allegedly known to the Egyptians as "Orion." The pyramid's structure, read properly, foretells the return of Christ sometime around 2000. "Elvis Presley has been mentioned in connection with the name Orion on many occasions," she observes, "including Gail Giorgio's 1978 bestseller, *Orion,* about a godlike singer who faked his death and disappeared" (Godfrey, 2000).

Further Reading

Godfrey, Cinda, 2000. *The Elvis-Jesus Mystery—The Shocking Scriptural and Scientific Evidence That Elvis Presley Could Be the Messiah Anticipated throughout History.* New Philadelphia, OH: Revelation Press.

Guralnick, Peter, 1999. *Careless Love: The Unmaking of Elvis Presley.* Boston, MA: Back Bay Books.

Emmanuel

First seen clairvoyantly as a "being of golden light" (Rodegast and Stanton, 1985), Emmanuel was a popular channeling entity during the New Age boom of the 1980s. Emmanuel, who spoke through Pat Rodegast, did not ever explain exactly who or what he was, insisting only that he was physically real but hinting that he had a body that human beings might not be comfortable seeing. He made a particular impression on psychologist and guru Baba Ram Dass (the former Richard Alpert, who worked with Timothy Leary on early LSD research and advocacy).

Emmanuel taught that "the separation" of human beings from God was only temporary, and it served a larger purpose. Through it, human beings have gained the knowledge they need to reunite with the divine and become cocreators with God.

See Also: Channeling

Further Reading

Rodegast, Pat, and Judith Stanton, eds., 1985. *Emmanuel's Book: A Manual for Living Comfortably in the Cosmos.* New York: Some Friends of Emmanuel.

Eunethia

Eunethia, who channels through Yvonne Cole, commands the starship Venusia, serving the Ashtar Command. She and her crew originally came from Venus but now live in a large ship that orbits Earth. Their purpose is to observe and to teach humans. They are also here to prepare humans for the great upheavals that will soon occur in response to their long abuse of the Earth.

According to Eunethia, more than fourteen planetary species are involved in the Earth project. "When the call went out for volunteers to assist planet Earth," she says, "the response came from all areas of the Universe. Most interaction is in the form of telepathic contact" (Bryant and Seebach, 1991), though relatively few humans are sufficiently developed in their psychic powers to communicate.

See Also: Ashtar

Further Reading

Bryant, Alice, and Linda Seebach, 1991. *Healing Shattered Reality: Understanding Contactee Trauma.* Tigard, OR: Wildflower Press.

Extraterrestrial biological entities

According to a body of modern folklore, the United States government has established secret contact with space people, whom it calls "extraterrestrial biological entities," or EBEs (ee-buhs). It also has retrieved the bodies of dead EBEs from crashed UFOs such as the one that came down near Roswell, New Mexico, in early July 1947.

Such rumors have been in circulation since the earliest days of the UFO controversy, which began with a sighting by private pilot Kenneth Arnold of nine "flying saucers" over Mount Rainier, Washington, on June 24, 1947. One of the first rumors alleged that a giant spacecraft landed not far from Juneau, Alaska, in mid-1948, and in the first interplanetary conference, President Harry Truman, along with his top aides and high-ranking military officers, met with its occupants, who were friendly and humble. In the 1950s, George Hunt Williamson, a contactee and popular author of saucerian books, wrote that "a highly secret operation known as Project NQ-707," headquartered at Edwards Air Force Base in the California desert, had established radio contact with flying saucers and was trying to get them to "land at a rendezvous point near Salton Sea in Southern California" (Williamson, 1953). Williamson's friend George Adamski insisted that the U.S. government and space people regularly spoke with one another. He would even claim that in 1962 he boarded an alien spaceship at an air force base on his way to a conference on Saturn.

In 1956, England's *Flying Saucer Review* published startling revelations by a contributor identified only as a "special correspondent." The correspondent asserted that a highly placed American official had confided to him that UFOs were known to contain friendly space visitors who were trying to find a way to breathe Earth's atmosphere before landing and declaring themselves. The magazine revealed nine years later that its unnamed informant was one "Rolf Alexander, M.D.," and that the official was the late general and diplomat George C. Marshall. It did not mention that "Alexander" was in fact an ex-convict whose real name was Allan Alexander Stirling. "Alexander" claimed vast psychokinetic powers that allowed him to break up clouds.

A related rumor held that the government did not dare to release its knowledge of extraterrestrial visitation for fear of panic. Therefore, it had embarked on an indoctrination program through which, by judicious leaks and UFO-themed movies and television shows, the public would get used to the notion and therefore be able to handle the news when it was time to deliver it.

In the early 1980s, a darker version of the legend came to the fore. This time it was tied to nightmarish conspiracy theories, in which a malevolent "secret government" worked with hostile aliens to enslave the world's population. Via abductions the aliens received certain biological materials they needed to survive, and the secret government, in turn, got access to advanced extraterrestrial technology. These speculations were tied to traditional conspiracy theories, sometimes with barely concealed anti-Semitic overtones. One of the movement's critics, Jerome Clark, coined the phrase "Dark Side" to characterize it. One principal Dark Sider, Milton William Cooper, claimed to have read highly classified documents that reported that alien technology made time travel possible. Both the space people and the secret government had learned that World War III would erupt in 1995 and escalate into nuclear conflict in 1999, preparing Earth for the Second Coming of Christ in 2011.

See Also: Abductions by UFOs; Adamski, George; Contactees; Holloman aliens; Williamson, George Hunt

Further Reading

Andrews, George C., 1986. *Extra-Terrestrials Among Us.* St. Paul, MN: Llewellyn Publications.

Clark, Jerome, 1998. "Dark Side." In *The UFO Encyclopedia, Second Edition: The Phenomenon from the Beginning,* 301–319. Detroit, MI: Omnigraphics.

Cooper, Milton William, 1991. *Behold a Pale Horse.* Sedona, AZ: Light Technology Publishing.

Ellis, Bill, 1991. "Cattle Mutilation: Contemporary Legends and Contemporary Mythologies." *Contemporary Legend* 1: 39–80.

"Let's Talk Space: 'Flying Saucers Are Real,'" 1956. *Flying Saucer Review* 2, 1 (January): 2–5.

"Report Tells of 'Top Brass' Attending Saucer Landing," 1955. *Flying Saucer News-Service Research Bulletin* 1, 9 (August 20): 3.

"Rolf Alexander, M.D.," and "Thoughts on UFOs by Dr. Rolf Alexander," 1965. *Flying Saucer Review* (March/April): 9.

Williamson, George Hunt, 1953. *Other Tongues—Other Flesh.* Amherst, WI: Amherst Press.

Extraterrestrials among us

According to flying-saucer contactees, humanlike beings from other planets walk the streets of the Earth, undetected and unsuspected by oblivious earthlings.

George Hunt Williamson, for example, declared that the program to infiltrate Earth began in the late nineteenth century. "Space visitors were actually deposited and left on our world to mix, mate, and marry with us," he wrote. "The new ideas and theories first came out in book form [in various scientific and occult texts], and this was the prelude to the appearance of spacecraft in the skies of Earth" (Williamson, 1953). In our time, the extraterrestrial agents, whom Williamson called the Wanderers, have helped turn our attention to science fiction and space travel, among other things. In a subsequent book, Williamson would argue that the Hopi and Navajo tribes long ago came to Earth from Mars and Lucifer-Maldek (a destroyed planet whose remains comprise what we now call the asteroid belt).

In February 1953 Williamson's friend George Adamski met a Martian on the streets of Los Angeles. The Martian told him, "At our work and in our leisure time, we mingle with people here on Earth, never betraying the secret that we are inhabitants of other worlds" (Adamski, 1955). Those who knew Adamski took his claims of Earthbound extraterrestrials seriously because they believed that on occasion they had seen these beings. Lou Zinsstag was Adamski's most energetic European supporter, and she accompanied him during much of a lecture tour he conducted on the continent in 1959. Adamski confided to her that Venusian men—he called them "boys"—regularly had been meeting with him in his hotel rooms on mornings. One afternoon, Zinsstag recalled, she was sitting in a sidewalk café outside Adamski's hotel when she happened to notice a handsome young man wearing sun glasses. She was unable to place his nationality. Shortly thereafter, Adamski, who had been resting in his room, came outside, smiling broadly, "his eyes sparkling with pleasure." He was also smiling at the young man, who smiled back. Adamski was unable to keep his eyes off the man, who eventually departed, "greeting George and me with a most friendly and prolonged smile" (Zinsstag, 1990). When Zinsstag asked Adamski if this were one of the Venusian "boys," he said yes.

Another account comes from Adamski associate C. A. Honey, who recalled, "I was with Adamski in 1958 during a meeting with three little people who he claimed had come to Earth from Venus. I saw them and talked with one of them but I don't know if they were anything other than what I saw—little people" (Honey, 1979). In an earlier version of the story, Honey told of seeing a small, blond woman in a roadside café while he and Adamski were on a trip to Oregon. Noticing that Adamski appeared "shocked," Honey studied her carefully. From a distance, he said, she looked to be no more than twelve years old, but up close she appeared middle-aged. She "let me know she was reading my thoughts" (Honey, 1959). The next day, when Honey told Adamski he thought she was a spacewoman, Adamski agreed and later asserted that space people had informed him that she was the sister of Kalna, a Venusian spacewoman friend of Adamski's.

Another prominent 1950s contactee, Truman Bethurum, claimed to have encountered his spacewoman friend Aura Rhanes on a sidewalk in Las Vegas. When he greeted her, she "turned around but did not seem to want to be recognized, for she shook her head and just walked across the street and joined a crowd waiting for a bus," according to Bethurum (Bethurum, 1954).

Much contactee doctrine concerning earthbound extraterrestrials focuses more on the souls of these beings than on the particular bodies they happen to inhabit. Within the contactee underground, many people believe they themselves were space people in previous incarnations; a lifetime or lifetimes ago they made the decision to be born as earthlings so to work toward the changes that will prepare humankind for membership in the Galactic Federation. In the 1970s and 1980s, the concept of "Star People," championed by writer Brad Steiger, gained popularity in New Age circles. Steiger wrote that Star People were ostensible humans but in fact reincarnated extraterrestrials; Star People shared certain physical and psychological features with each other, and they also had experienced otherworldly realities all their lives, even if consciously they did not recognize their significance. Less benignly, some writers have suggested that the menacing men in black who threaten investigators and witnesses are evil aliens.

In the era of UFO abductions some researchers reported that their female subjects had undergone mysteriously terminated pregnancies, only to be abducted at a later date to be shown an alien-human hybrid child who, they were led to believe, was their own. These hybrids had both human and alien features in varying proportions. On occasion, abductees would encounter the more human-looking hybrids in real-life situations. David M. Jacobs, in *The Threat* (1998), proposed the alarming theory that hybrids are being bred to replace the human race at some point in the not-distant future.

The abduction era also produced a story told by a man whose credentials seem impeccable, a New York book editor and former Washington correspondent for *Newsweek*. There was also a confirmatory witness, the man's wife. In January 1987, the publishing house William Morrow had just released the destined-to-be bestseller *Communion*, Whitley Strieber's account of his personal abduction experiences. The editor, Bruce Lee, claimed that just as the book was starting to show up on the stalls, he and his wife ventured into Womrath's bookstore on Manhattan's Lexington Avenue. As he related to *New York* writer Tracy Cochran, the two noticed a very short couple, bundled up in winter clothes, looking over a copy of *Communion* and complaining about how Strieber had gotten things wrong. They spoke "rapidly in what sounded like educated Upper East Side Jewish accents." When Lee introduced himself as a William Morrow employee and asked politely what it was they did not like about the book, the man ignored him, but the woman communicated such "complete loathing, hatred" that the Lees retreated in shock (Conroy, 1989). They noticed that the strange couple were wearing large tinted glasses that did not entirely hide large "dark, almond-shaped eyes." Lee later took—and passed—a polygraph test.

See Also: Abductions by UFOs; Adamski, George; Alien diners; Aura Rhanes; Bethurum, Truman; Contactees; Hybrid beings; Men in black; Star People; Strieber, Whitley; Wanderers; Williamson, George Hunt

Further Reading

Adamski, George, 1955. *Inside the Space Ships.* New York: Abelard-Schuman.

Bethurum, Truman, 1954. *Aboard a Flying Saucer.* Los Angeles: DeVorss and Company.

Cochran, Tracy, 1987. "Invasion of the Strieber Snatchers." *New York* (March 30): 26.

Conroy, Ed, 1989. *Report on "Communion": An Independent Investigation of and Commentary on Whitley Strieber's "Communion."* New York: William Morrow.

Honey, C. A., 1959. "Mail Bag: Belief Confirmed." *Flying Saucer Review* 5, 2 (March/April): 32–33.

———, 1979. "Report from the Readers." *Fate* 32, 5 (May): 113–115.

Jacobs, David M., 1998. *The Threat.* New York: Simon and Schuster.

Keel, John A., 1970. *UFOs: Operation Trojan Horse.* New York: G. P. Putnam's Sons.

Steiger, Brad, 1976. *Gods of Aquarius: UFOs and the Transformation of Man.* New York: Harcourt Brace Jovanovich.

Williamson, George Hunt, 1959. *Road in the Sky.* London: Neville Spearman.

Zinsstag, Lou, 1990. *UFO . . . George Adamski: Their Man on Earth.* Tucson, AZ: UFO Photo Archives.

F

Fairies encountered

Traditions of fairy folk can be found anywhere in the world, but they are usually spoken of in the past tense. What is less well known is that such beliefs derive not just from distant folklore but from perceived experiences of a sort that are still reported from time to time even today. British anomalist Janet Bord writes, "Today the knowledge of and belief in fairies has all but died out among country people. . . . However[,] the changes that have occurred this century have not resulted in the complete extinction of the fairies: they have survived, because people still see them" (Bord, 1997). Though Victorian popular culture perpetrated the notion that fairies are gauzy-winged creatures, the fairies of tradition have no wings. Beyond that, they vary in appearance from region to region, though most are small and humanlike, sometimes with brown or green skin. They are of uncertain temperament and, thus, best avoided.

Collectors of folklore—a notion and discipline that came into existence around 1800—came upon many firsthand accounts. These can be found in any number of scholarly texts on fairy lore. Though sometimes puzzled by the apparent sincerity of their informants, few folklorists were willing to take the leap of faith required to embrace actual belief in fairies. One who did, however, was the well-regarded W. Y. Evans-Wentz, an anthropologist of religion who had a Ph.D. from Oxford University. In the first decade of the twentieth century, Evans-Wentz traveled through the Celtic regions of the British Isles as well as Brittany (on France's northwest coast). The result was a folklore classic, *The Fairy Faith in Celtic Countries* (originally published in 1911). Aside from its worth as a record of surviving fairy beliefs and associated superstitions, it is unique in its championing of an underlying reality behind the tradition. Like the pioneering Rev. Robert Kirk, a Scottish clergyman whose *The Secret Common-Wealth* (1691) preserved fairy lore in the Highlands, Evans-Wentz deduced that fairies live in an otherworld that overlaps with the human world. He went so far as to claim that "we can postulate scientifically, on the showing of the data of psychical research, the existence of such invisible intelligences as gods, genii, daemons, all kinds of true fairies, and disembodied men."

Not all purported witnesses were the uneducated rural folk stereotypically associated with fairy beliefs and encounters. A seventeenth-century Swedish clergyman, Peter Rahm, gave this sworn statement to legal authorities:

A man is pulled back before he enters a fairy circle. (Fortean Picture Library)

> In the year 1660, when I and my wife had gone to my farm, which is three quarters of a mile from Ragunda parsonage, and we were sitting there and talking awhile, late in the evening, there came a little man in at the door, who begged of my wife to go and aid his wife, who was just in the pains of labor. The fellow was of small size, of a dark complexion, and dressed in old gray clothes. My wife and I sat awhile, and wondered at the man; for we were aware that he was a Troll, and we had heard tell that such like, called by the peasantry Vettar [spirits], always used to keep in the farm-houses, when people left them in harvest-time. But when he had urged his request four or five times, and we thought on what evil the country folk say that they have at times suffered from the Vettar, when they have chance to swear at them, or with uncivil words bid them to go to hell, I took the resolution to read some prayers over my wife, and to bless her, and bid her in God's name go with him. She took in haste some old linen with her, and went along in the wind, and so she came to a room, on one side of which was a little dark chamber, in which his wife lay in bed in great agony. My wife went up to her, and, after a little while, aided her till she brought forth the child after the same manner as other human beings. The man then offered her food, and when she refused it, he thanked her, and accompanied her out, and then she was carried along, in the same way in the wind, and after a while came again to the gate, just at 10 o'clock. Meanwhile, a quantity of old pieces and clippings of silver were laid on a shelf, in the sitting-room, and my wife found them next day, when she was putting the room in order. It is supposed that they were laid there by the Vettar. That it in truth so happened, I witness, by inscribing my name. Ragunda, the 12th of April, 1671 (Keightley, 1878).

Another cleric, Edward Williams, a British man from the next century, recalled a strange experience from his youth. In 1757, he and his fellow schoolchildren, playing in a field in Wales, happened to notice seven or eight tiny couples. Each was dressed in red, and each held a white kerchief. They were about a hundred yards away. One of the figures suddenly took after a child and nearly caught him. Up close, the children got, in Williams's words, a "full and clear view of his ancient, swarthy, grim complexion." During the chase another of the male figures shouted at the pursuer in an unknown language (Jones, 1979). Williams, who went on to become a prominent man of the cloth, never forgot the incident but was never able to explain it. "I am forced to classify it among my unknowables," he wrote (Jones, 1979).

The inherent implausibility of fairies notwithstanding, "sightings" have been recorded even in recent years. On August 10, 1977, while patrolling in the early morning hours, a Hull, England, police constable came upon a fog bank in a nearby field. When the fog lifted, he saw three small figures dancing: a man dressed in a "sleeveless jerkin, with tight-fitting trousers" and two women clad in "bonnets, shawls and white dresses"—hardly late twentieth-century clothing. Assuming they were drunks, the officer got out of his car and walked toward them, only to see them vanish in front of his eyes. Many fairy accounts describe the beings' love of dancing. During World War II, for example, W. E. Thorner, making his way with great difficulty through a furious storm along a clifftop on Hoy in the Orkney Islands, was startled to come upon small creatures "with long, dark, bedraggled hair." They were dancing wildly, "seeming to throw themselves over the cliff edge" (Marwick, 1975).

An incident in County Carlow, Ireland, in November 1959 claimed four witnesses. In Dunroe, a man named John Byrne was using a bulldozer to move a large bush when a man no more than three feet tall abruptly dashed out from underneath it. He fled across a field and was lost to view after he jumped over a fence. Three other men observed the peculiar occurrence. As late as the early 1990s, fifteen-year-old Brian Collins, vacationing with his parents in the Aran Islands off west Donegal, was taking an early morning walk when he spotted two men fishing in the sea from an overlooking bank. Three and a half feet tall, dressed in green, and wearing brown boots, they were engaged in a laugh-punctuated conversation in Gaelic. Apparently aware of his presence, they jumped off the bank and were gone. As he looked for them, the youth found a pipe that he thought was one of theirs. He put it in a locked drawer, from which it subsequently disappeared. He saw the beings again, and this time he tried to photograph and tape-record them, but nothing of them developed on either film or tape.

A series of "sightings" in 1938, in West Limerick, began when schoolboy John Keely met a two-foot-tall man, dressed in red, on a road. When Keely asked him where he was from, the strange man snapped, "I'm from the mountains, and it's all equal to you what my business is." The next day Keely and friends returned to the scene. The friends hid in the bushes while Keely approached a group of fairies. One took his hand, and they walked together for a short distance. The fairies ran away, however, when they saw the boys in the bushes. Other men and boys reported their own encounters in the same area at the same time, and the Dublin-based *Irish Press* carried stories. The men had chased the fairies, but as one witness put it, "they jumped the ditches as fast as a greyhound. . . . Though they passed through hedges, ditches, and marshes, they appeared neat and clean all the time." Witnesses said the beings had "hard, hairy faces like men, and no ears" (Barry, 1938).

On a casual walk along the shore of a peninsula in Scotland's Western Highlands one day in 1972, Artie Traum, an American folk singer, heard unusual sounds. As he listened more carefully, he realized they were voices, though he could see no one around. They were singing "run, man, run" in a weird harmony while fiddles and pipes played behind them. As the sounds grew ever louder, Traum panicked and fled into a nearby woods. Though he still saw nothing, he heard crackling sounds and "great motion" as if he were being pursued. As all this was happening, "my head was swarming with thousands of voices, thousands of words making no sense." He found his way back to open air, and the voices and the music ceased (Traum, 1972). Traum's experience is like many recounted in the tradition. Fairies are reputed to drive trespassers off their home turf and, also, to love music. Both folk fiddlers and at least one classical composer (Thomas Wood) claim to have heard fairy music; a nineteenth-century Manx fiddler, William Cain, was not alone in learning such a melody and incorporating it into his repertoire.

The American Indian tribes had their own versions of fairy traditions, but the Europeans who settled the North American continent—except for places where Celtic customs took firm root, such as Newfoundland—fairly quickly discarded their own. Nonetheless, occasional incidents in which fairylike figures appeared, even if not identified by the witness as such, have allegedly occurred. All of his life, Harry Anderson remembered something that had happened to him one summer night in 1919, when he was walking alone down a rural road near Barron, Wisconsin. To his considerable surprise, his solitary stroll was interrupted by the approach of twenty little men trooping in single file under the bright moonlight. They were heading in his direction. Everything about them was odd: they were shirtless, bald, pale-faced, and dressed in leather knee pants. "Mumbling" sounds came out of their mouths; yet they did not seem to be talking with each other. As they passed the young man, they seemed oblivious of or indifferent to his presence. By now Anderson was so unnerved that he continued on his way without ever looking back.

In Canby, Oregon, one day in April 1950, Ellen Jonerson was working on her lawn when she happened to glance over at her neighbor's yard and saw a bizarre sight: a twelve-inch little man of stocky build with a tanned face; he was clad in overalls and plaid shirt. He had what looked like a skullcap on his head. Jonerson ran inside to make a quick call about it to a friend. When she returned, the figure was walking away with a "waddling" motion. He passed under a parked car and was seen no more. At no time did the idea that she was seeing what some would call a "fairy" enter Jonerson's mind, and her report is generally thought of as a UFO-related close encounter of the third kind, though no UFO was seen.

Inevitably, some have called UFO encounters a modern form of fairy belief. Among the first to do so was Jacques Vallee, author of *Passport to Magonia* (1969).Vallee offered an occult-oriented interpretation that speculated that an incomprehensible otherworld has interacted with humankind for thousands of years, producing manifestations that are filtered through human consciousness and expectation, thus changing to reflect different times and cultures. (Kirk had concluded as much in the late seventeenth century. Fairies, of a "middle nature between man and angel," dress and speak "like the people and country under which they live" [Sanderson, 1976].) Vallee went so far as to declare flatly—if, as critics charged, hyperbolically—that "the modern, global belief in flying saucers and their occupants is identical to an earlier belief in the fairy-faith. The entities described as the pilots of the craft are indistinguishable from the elves, sylphs, and *lutins.*" Debunkers such as Robert Sheaffer have employed a different sort of argument to the effect that flying saucers and their occupants are as much a delusion as fairies and fairyland. Neither approach, however, seems a wholly adequate way of explaining the mysteries inherent in such encounters, which paradoxically offer up "real"-seeming encounters with things that almost certainly do not exist in the conventional understanding of the verb.

Fairies have found new life among New Age visionaries and channelers and other explorers of the far edges of consciousness. One writer remarks, "There are two major differences between the old oral traditional or ancestral faery contacts and those of contemporary humanity removed from oral tradition. . . . The first is that while our ancestors often sought to break away from the faery realm, many modern contacts are intentional. They are induced or encouraged by various means, ranging from naïve New Age nuttiness to expansions and willed changes of awareness involving techniques handed down within the old traditions, but developed and applied in a modern way" (Stewart, 1995). New Age fairies are a gentler lot than their harsh counterparts in tradition. Fairies are now incorporated into such concerns as healing, gardening, Earth awareness, ritual magic, and personal transformation—matters far removed from the often ill-tempered, impatient, anthrophobic concerns of traditional fairies.

See Also: Chaneques; Close encounters of the third kind; Cottingley fairies; Fairy captures; Magonia; White's little people

Further Reading

Barry, John, 1938. "Fairies in Eire." *The Living Age* 355 (November): 265–266.

Bord, Janet, 1997. *Fairies: Real Encounters with Little People.* New York: Carroll and Graf Publishers.

Briggs, Katharine, 1976. *An Encyclopedia of Fairies: Hobgoblins, Brownies, Bogies, and Other Supernatural Creatures.* New York: Pantheon Books.

Davis, Isabel L., 1970. Review of Vallee's *Passport to Magonia. UFO Investigator* (June): 3.

Evans, Alex, 1978. "Encounters with Little Men." *Fate* 31, 11 (November): 83–86.

Evans-Wentz, W. Y., 1966. *The Fairy-Faith in Celtic Countries.* New York: University Books.

Galde, Phyllis, 1993. "I See by the Papers: More Fairies Seen." *Fate* 46, 4 (April): 14–15.

Jones, T. Gwynn, 1979. *Welsh Folklore and Folk-Custom.* Totowa, NJ: Rowman and Littlefield.

Keightley, Thomas, 1878. *The Fairy Mythology.* London: G. Bell.

MacManus, D. A., 1959. *The Middle Kingdom: The Faerie World of Ireland.* London: Max Parrish.

Marwick, Ernest W., 1975. *The Folklore of Orkney and Shetland.* London: B. T. Batsford.

Narvaez, Peter, ed., 1997. *The Good People: New Fairylore Essays.* Lexington: University Press of Kentucky.

Rojcewicz, Peter M., 1984. *The Boundaries of Orthodoxy: A Folkloric Look at the UFO Phenomenon.* Ph.D. dissertation, University of Pennsylvania.

Sanderson, Stewart, ed., 1976. *The Secret Common-Wealth and A Short Treatise of Charms and Spels by Robert Kirk.* Totowa, NJ: Rowman and Littlefield.

Sheaffer, Robert, 1981. *The UFO Verdict: Examining the Evidence.* Buffalo, NY: Prometheus Books.

Stewart, R. J., 1995. *The Living World of Faery.* Glastonbury, Somerset, England: Gothic Image Publications.

Traum, Artie, 1972. "Rollin' and Tumblin': The Cambridge Festival." *Crawdaddy* (November): 20–22.

Vallee, Jacques, 1969. *Passport to Magonia: From Folklore to Flying Saucers.* Chicago: Henry Regnery.

Wilkins, Harold T., 1952. "Pixie-Haunted Moor." *Fate* 5, 5 (July/August): 110–116.

Fairy captures

In 1907, Lady Archibald Campbell, a collector of traditional lore, interviewed a blind man and his wife who lived in conditions of great poverty in an Irish glen. The man told her, in all apparent seriousness, that once he had captured a small being he called a leprechaun. It was two feet tall, with dark but clear skin and red hair. He was dressed in a red cap, green clothes, and boots.

"I gripped him close in my arms and took him home," the old man related. "I called to the woman [his wife] to look at what I had got. 'What doll is it that you have there?' she cried. 'A living one,' I said, and put it on the dresser. We feared to lose it; we kept the door locked. It talked and muttered to itself queer words. . . . It might have been near on a fortnight since we had the fairy, when I said to the woman, 'Sure, if we show it in the great city we will be made up [rich]. So we put it in a cage. At night we would leave the cage door open, and we would hear it stirring through the house. . . . We fed it on bread and rice and milk out of a cup at the end of a spoon."

At last the little being escaped, and after that the family's fortunes, never much to begin with, declined even further. The man lost his sight, and the couple sank ever deeper into poverty and despair.

A happier story recounts not so much the capture of a fairy as the domestication of one. Lady Gregory and W. B. Yeats heard it from an old couple, the Kellehers, who lived in the Wickland Mountains of Ireland. The Kellehers said the events had taken place years before, when they were newly married.

One winter day, Mr. Kelleher encountered a fairy and, in some unspecified fashion, got him to stay in the house for the next week or two. Dressed in a red cap and red clothes, the fairy was about fifteen inches tall and seemed friendly, though he kept silent. At night he slept on the dresser. The Kellers told others of their unusual guest, and sometimes "when the boys at the public-house were full of porter, they used to come to the house to look at him, and they would laugh to see him, but I never let them hurt him." Kelleher fed him bread and milk with a spoon. As the days passed, the couple noticed, he seemed to age, taking on "a sort of wrinkled look."

The fairy left them one evening after another of its kind had appeared near the property. Mr. Kelleher thought it was a fairy woman, dressed in gray. "And that evening," he related, "when I was sitting beside the fire with the Missus I told her about it, and the little lad that was sitting on the dresser called out, 'That's Geoffrey-a-wee that's coming for me,' and he jumped down and went out of the door and I never saw him. I thought it was a girl I saw, but Geoffrey wouldn't be the name of a girl, would it? He had never spoken before that time."

See Also: Fairies encountered

Further Reading

Gregory, Lady, 1920. *Visions and Beliefs in the West of Ireland.* New York: G. P. Putnam's Sons.

Fossilized aliens

Writing in *Flying Saucers* magazine in 1970, Buffard Ratliff, the head of a Kentucky UFO group, reported the discovery of an extraterrestrial artifact: a fossilized spacecraft and its tiny crew.

According to Ratliff, two years earlier Melvin Gray of Louisville had been mowing his lawn when he came upon an unusual stone. He kept it and studied it for months, eventually concluding that it was living proof of a prehistoric space visit. Gray handed it over to ufologist Ratliff, who also examined it at length. From this examination he was able to determine what the stone contained and what events had precipitated its creation. It was, as he would write, a fossilized craft containing

> seven very small creatures. . . . Three . . . are ape-like in appearance. The other four are humanoid. . . . All creatures are approximately three inches in height, are vertebrates, and have a physical build that indicates they were very strong for their size. . . .
>
> The [ape] creatures died in motion as if they were frozen in their last physical action as they met instant death. One . . . had obviously been critically injured and two of his companions are trying to rescue him. . . . Two of [the humanoids] are in a position for a crash landing. . . . The third humanoid is sitting in what looks like a bucket seat with one of his arms extended slightly forward and upward as though he was operating a control lever or device to try to bring the spaceship under control.

Ratliff contended that the crash had taken place some four hundred million years ago. The fossil survived and is a "permanent record to all mankind . . . that we had tiny alien space visitors from out there long, long ago."

Further Reading

Ratliff, Buffard, 1970. "A Fossilized Alien Spaceship and Its Occupants." *Flying Saucers* (March): 6–7.

Fourth dimension

In occult speculation the "fourth dimension" is a parallel universe that occupies the same space as ours but at a different "vibrational" level. Though its existence has never been demonstrated scientifically, it has been used to explain a variety of ostensibly mysterious phenomena, including disappearances in the Bermuda Triangle, teleportation, clairvoyance, ghosts, monsters, UFOs, and more.

The concept came into the vocabulary of occultism through Leipzig astronomer Johann F. C. Zollner, a student of Theosophy. In the 1870s, Zollner worked with American medium Henry Slade, who claimed the ability to materialize or teleport objects during seances. As Zollner saw it, such talents indicated that mediums can move things out of our dimension into the fourth and back again. Unfortunately for Zellner's theory, Slade later confessed that he produced the effects fraudulently. Later psychical researchers, however, used variants of the fourth-dimensional idea to explain the fate of the soul after death.

See Also: Bermuda Triangle

Further Reading

De Camp, L. Sprague, 1980. *The Ragged Edge of Science.* Philadelphia, PA: Owlswick Press.

Layne, N. Meade, 1950. *The Ether Ship and Its Solution.* Vista, CA: Borderland Sciences Research Associates.

Frank and Frances

Strolling through his rural property near Quebec City, Quebec, one night in 1941, inventor Arthur Henry Matthews encountered two men, each six feet tall, blue-eyed, and golden-haired. After introducing themselves as Venusians, they expressed interest in Matthews's work with electrical genius Nikola Tesla. Matthews was taken to a waiting spacecraft, a giant saucer-shaped structure called "Mother Ship X-12," which housed twenty-four smaller craft as well as living quarters for crew members. At one point, the visitors showed Matthews the control room. Contrary to his expectations, it was bare except for a circular table in the middle and four "pilots," two men and two women, each facing one of the four directions. The Venusians explained that the craft flew on mental power alone. In subsequent contacts, Matthews learned that one of his hosts was the captain, who called himself Frank. He also met Frank's "life companion," introduced as Frances. Frank said the names stood for "Truth."

Further Reading

Bord, Janet, and Colin Bord, 1991. *Life beyond Planet Earth? Man's Contacts with Space People.* London: GraftonBooks.

Fry, Daniel William (1908–1922)

Daniel Fry was among the leaders of the early contactee movement. He claimed to have had his first contact with a flying saucer—a "remote controlled cargo carrier"—in the New Mexico desert on July 4, 1950, and to have

Daniel William Fry (Fortean Picture Library)

boarded it for half an hour. In that time he was whisked to and from New York, all the while conversing with the voice of Alan, a spaceman communicating from a mother ship nine hundred miles from Earth. When Fry met Alan in the flesh eleven years later, the extraterrestrial turned out to have a purely human appearance. Intelligent and articulate, Fry was often described by his followers as a "scientist," though in fact he had been no more than a missile mechanic and technician at the White Sands Proving Ground prior to his contactee career. He founded Understanding, Inc., a forum for the space people's metaphysical and scientific teachings. After the 1950s, when the initial excitement generated by the first contactees had waned, Fry became less visible, though he remained quietly active until his death in Alamogordo, New Mexico, in 1992.

Fry recounted his early saucer adventures in the widely read *The White Sands Incident* and *Alan's Message: To Men of Earth,* both published in 1954. That same year, he spoke at

A UFO supposedly photographed by Daniel Fry at Merlin, Oregon, May 1964 (Fortean Picture Library)

the First Annual Flying Saucer Convention in Los Angeles. At a press conference, a reporter asked him if he would take a lie-detector test to verify his claims. When Fry agreed, a local television station arranged a polygraph examination. The examiner concluded that Fry was being deceptive in his answers. Forever after, Fry's critics cited the allegedly failed test, as well as a dubious Ph.D. from a London-based diploma mill, to argue that he was no more than a hoaxer. Still, Fry seemed to many to be sincere about his metaphysical beliefs, perhaps using fanciful saucer yarns as a way of attracting an audience.

See Also: Contactees

Further Reading

Fry, Daniel W., 1954. *Alan's Message: To Men of Earth.* Los Angeles: New Age Publishing Company.

———. 1954. *The White Sands Incident.* Los Angeles: New Age Publishing Company.

———. 1954. "My Experience with the Lie Detector." *Saucers* 2, 3 (September): 6–8.

National Investigations Committee on Aerial Phenomena, 1967. *Information Sheet on Daniel Fry.* Washington, DC, August.

Reeve, Bryant, and Helen Reeve, 1957. *Flying Saucer Pilgrimage.* Amherst, WI: Amherst Press.

G

Gabriel

In Christian and Islamic tradition, Gabriel is one of the two mightiest angels. He is the only angel mentioned in the Old Testament, as the destroyer of Sodom and Gomorrah. He is said to sit on God's left hand and to preside over Paradise. Mohammed credits Gabriel with dictating the Koran to him. In more recent times, an entity named Gabriel, identifying himself as an archangel, channels through a New York City man named Robert Baker.

Gabriel has spoken through Baker since 1990. His principal platform is the weekly meeting of the Communion of Souls meditation group. Baker has a cable-access show, *Gabriel Speaks,* on a New York television station every Monday afternoon. Gabriel, who speaks of himself in the plural, says, "We come to you at this most important time in the evolution of your planet, a time of unity of Soul and Spirit in the physical body through the Light and Power of your being. We encourage you to stand in the Power of One, as the individual Light that you are, to create a new vision for your world, a new Heaven on Earth through your individual expression of unconditional love for yourselves and one another. We challenge you to act upon life as creators rather than having life act upon you" ("Gabriel Speaks," n.d.).

Further Reading

Davidson, Gustav, 1967. *A Dictionary of Angels Including the Fallen Angels.* New York: Free Press.

"Gabriel Speaks," n.d. http://childrenoflight.com/gabriel.htm

Gef

Gef is the central character in an episode that psychical researcher Hereward Carrington called "preposterous"—a "palpable absurdity"—even while conceding that it baffled him. According to one of the most peculiar stories ever told as true, Gef was a talking animal—a self-identified mongoose—who plagued a family on the Isle of Man between 1931 and 1938. Numerous investigators came to the site and, despite suspicions of trickery, left empty-handed. Thirty years later, when located and interviewed, the one surviving member of the family swore to Gef's authenticity.

In 1931, the Irving family—father James, mother Margaret, and twelve-year-old daughter Viorrey—lived on a small farm known as Doarlish Cashen (Cashen's Gap in English) on the Isle of Man on the Irish Sea to the northwest of England. Facing the sea and 750 feet above it, sat their two-story stone house. Inside, the walls were lined with dark matchwood paneling set a few inches from the

Archangel Gabriel painted by Pietro Vannucci (Arte & Immagini srl/Corbis)

stone. This particular construction detail would be crucial to what would follow.

One evening in September of that year, so he would assert, James Irving heard a tapping noise from the boarded-up attic. The next morning, when he went into the attic, he found a wood carving that he recognized as his own. He had no idea how it got there, but when he dropped it, he heard the same noise that had sounded earlier. That evening there were more sounds, only louder, followed by apparent running. As Irving would tell researcher Nandor Fodor, "We heard animal sounds: barking, growling, hissing, spitting and blowing" (Carrington and Fodor, 1951). Suddenly a crack shook the building so hard that the pictures on the wall moved. Puzzled and frightened, the family listened to gurgling sounds that they presumed came from the unknown animal but which could as easily have come from a baby learning to speak. A bark "with a pleading note in it" came next. When Irving made barking and meowing sounds himself, apparently in an effort to determine whether the animal was a dog or cat, the creature imitated him.

The sounds were high-pitched and appeared to be emanating from a very small throat.

The knockings continued for the next few weeks. Then one day, Irving asked his wife, "What in the name of God can he be?" From the walls a squeaky voice echoed, "What in the name of God can he be?" These were the first recognizable words from Gef, as the animal said it wanted to be called. As time passed, Gef, whose voice was said to be two octaves above a normal woman's, appeared to learn more and more words, accumulating a vocabulary from listening to the family. He also claimed to travel widely throughout the island, overhearing others and learning from them. He also brought news and gossip and regaled family members with information they otherwise would not have known and sometimes did not want to know.

For his part, Gef would assert that for a long time he had understood what people were saying, but it was not until he took up residence with the Irvings that he learned how to speak words himself. When he was there, he knew everything that went on in the house. His favorite place, however, was in the walls of Viorrey's room.

Irving's first impulse was to kill Gef, who frightened the family with his temper and his penchant for throwing things such as stones. First, he tried to poison him, then to shoot him, but, in response, Gef caused property damage and screeched out threats. According to Irving, Gef said, "If you are kind to me, I will bring you good luck. If you are not kind, I shall kill all your poultry. I can get them wherever you put them." The family decided to do its best to get along with its strange guest.

Asked who he was, Gef first identified himself as a "ghost in the form of a weasel" but later denied that he was a ghost or a poltergeist. He was highly temperamental, his behavior unpredictable, his speech often profane. The family left food out for him. He ate the same food as the daughter, a detail that skeptics would later remark on. In return, he would provide the Irvings with dead rabbits that would show up on the doorstep. The rabbits appeared to have been strangled rather than bitten to death.

As Gef became known and feared throughout the island, someone suggested that he might be a mongoose, though at that point no one had ever seen him. Mongooses (mammals ordinarily found in India) are not native to the isle, but in 1914 a local farmer had imported them to kill rabbits. When asked if he was a mongoose, Gef said he was. At other times, though, he boasted, "Thou wilt never know who I am. I am a freak. I have hands, and I have feet." On another occasion he said, "I am the fifth dimension. I am the eighth wonder of the world. I can split the atom." Still, the idea took hold that Gef was a mongoose, and he took to calling himself one.

But if eyewitness testimony is to be believed, he could not have been a mongoose. Those who saw him, according to investigator Walter McGraw, "said he had a bushy tail like a squirrel's, yellow to brownish fur, small ears and a pushed-in face. His most-often described features were his front paws, which according to Irving were handlike with three fingers and a thumb" (McGraw, 1970). McGraw adds, "he fitted the description of a mongoose about as well as he did that of 'part of the fifth dimension'." Irving estimated that he was no more than five or six inches long and weighed no more than a pound to a pound and a half. Sightings of him were always fleeting, and on rare occasion the Irvings saw him in silhouette as a shadow in the wall. Gef said he did not want to be seen because he was terrified of being captured or killed. A photograph Viorrey took of him at a distance of five hundred feet showed little except a furry blur.

By early 1932, news of Gef's doings had spread past the isle. In a dispatch dated January 10, a *Manchester Daily Dispatch* reporter wrote that on a visit to Doarlish Cashen he had heard "a voice I never imagined could issue from a human throat," leaving him in "a state of considerable perplexity . . . The people here at the farm . . . seem sane, honest and responsible folk. . . . I find that others, too, have had my strange experience" (Wilkins, 1952). As the publicity spread, an American promoter offered the family fifty thousand dollars for the right to exhibit Gef commercially. He was refused. Other investigators heard Gef's voice and witnessed apparent evidence of his activities, including stone-throwing and knowledge of events at a distance, but none saw him. Others, such as psychical researcher Nandor Fodor, who spent some days with the Irvings, could only collect testimony. Gef tended to go into hiding when investigators showed up. In an amusing sidelight, after one investigator, BBC journalist R. S. Lambert, declared that Gef might well exist, a critic called him "crazy." Lambert took him to court and presented a sufficiently persuasive case that he was awarded seven thousand pounds in damages.

Beyond anecdotal testimony, evidence of Gef's physical existence was slight. Harry Price, the famous "ghost hunter" who later wrote a book on the case, saw liquid dripping from the wall and was told that this was Gef urinating. Hair said to be from Gef turned out to be from a dog curiously like the Irvings' sheepdog, Mona. The prints he allegedly allowed the Irvings to preserve in clay were not at all like a mongoose's or, for that matter, any known animal's.

Over time, so the Irvings related, Gef's visitations became rarer and rarer. By 1938 or so he was heard from for the last time. By then the whole outlandish affair had fallen into obscurity. It was too much even for the most sensationalistic newspapers; and parapsychologists, who first took it to be an exotic poltergeist case, did not know what to make of it. The only precedent for something like Gef was a witch's familiar (an animal form in which witches are sometimes said to appear), and on the Isle of Man in the 1930s, belief in witchcraft had largely passed.

Though investigators looked carefully for it, only one caught the Irvings in anything that looked like suspect activity. From the beginning, skeptics wondered if "Gef" weren't a fiction created by skilled ventriloquism. Early in the course of the episode, a reporter for the *Isle of Man Examiner* thought he caught Viorrey making a squeaking sound, though her father insisted the sound was coming from the other side of the room. Aside from this ambiguous episode, investigators on site expressed doubts that so complex a hoax could be accomplished so simply, even if it were physically possible, which struck them as almost out of the question. Locally, the Irvings were regarded as reliable, honest people. If they were hoaxers, their motives were clearly not financial. They made practically no money from their participation in the matter.

The Irvings eventually moved away from Doarlish Cashen and dropped into obscurity.

Skeptical theories have focused on Viorrey's role. In 1983, Melvin Harris speculated that she had first tricked her parents with ventriloquism. Later, even after they realized that they had been fooled, her parents got caught up in the hoax and played along with it. Harris writes, "Gef never had a personality or existence independent of Viorrey. He brought home rabbits, as did Viorrey. His favorite foods were also Viorrey's favorites. He shared her strong interests in mechanical things."

In the late 1960s, after thirty years of silence, Viorrey was located and interviewed somewhere in England (she insisted that her place of residence be kept confidential). She told Walter McGraw that she despised Gef, who she thought had ruined her life. She said that he had caused her pain and embarrassment, and, even at the time, she and her mother had hated the publicity. "It was not a hoax," she said, "and I wish it had never happened. . . . We were snubbed. . . . I had to leave the Isle of Man, and I hope that no one where I work now ever knows the story. Gef has even kept me from getting married. How could I ever tell a man's family about what happened?" She complained bitterly that Gef "made me meet people I didn't want to meet. Then they said I was 'mental' or a ventriloquist. Believe me, if I was that good I would jolly well be making money from it now!" (McGraw, 1970).

Further Reading

Carrington, Hereward, and Nandor Fodor, 1951. *Haunted People: Story of the Poltergeist down the Centuries.* New York: E. P. Dutton and Company.

Harris, Melvin, 1983. "The Mongoose That Talked and Lost for Words." In Peter Brookesmith, ed. *Open Files,* 19–27. London: Orbis Publishing.

McGraw, Walter, 1970. "Gef—The Talking Mongoose . . . 30 Years Later." *Fate* 23, 7 (July): 74–82.

Wilkins, Harold T., 1952. "History of the Talking Mongoose." *Fate* 5, 4 (June): 58–69.

Germane

Germane channels through Lyssa Royal. "He" is neither male nor female, and he does not have a name; Germane is simply an identification of convenience. He is from "a realm of integration that does not have a clear-cut density/dimensional level." He is not even an entity as such but a kind of personification of a group-consciousness energy. In the distant future, once human beings have been fully integrated spiritually, physically, emotionally, and mentally, they will be like him.

See Also: Channeling

Further Reading

"ET Civilizations—Germane," 1994. http://www.lemuria.net/article-et-civilizations.html

Goblin Universe

Goblin Universe is a kind of catchall phrase some people use to characterize the realm of fantastic but, according to some, real entities and creatures that seem out of place in our ordinary understanding of reality. The Goblin Universe is said to house everything from demons and fairies to ghosts, humanoids, and monstrous beasts. It is an explicitly paranormal or occult concept, rejected by some anomalists who insist that the objects of their investigations—whether UFOs or unknown animals such as Sasquatch or the Loch Ness monster—are simply so far undocumented aspects of this universe or planet.

To its proponents, however, the Goblin Universe is a deeply mysterious, elusive place. The late F. W. Holiday called it "a hall of distorting mirrors. . . . It will *not* be ignored. Poltergeists often throw objects at utter skeptics. Members of the Phantom Menagerie appear in front of bored cops who want only to scribble their daily reports and go home. UFOs swoop over cities like Washington, Rome and London to thumb their noses at bureaucrats. . . . Like it or lump it, we are all in that damned Hall of Mirrors" (Holiday, 1986).

See Also: Fairies encountered

Further Reading

Holiday, F. W., 1986. *The Goblin Universe.* St. Paul, MN: Llewellyn Publications.

Gordon

"Gordon" is the name of an ostensible extraterrestrial whom two Alaska women claim to have encountered while traveling through western Canada in October 1974. Their story amounts to a UFO-age variant of the venerable legend of the "vanishing hitchhiker."

Edmoana Toews of Anchorage and her friend Nuria Hanson were returning from a convention of the Coptic Christian Fellowship of America in Kalamazoo, Michigan. On October 18, they were driving on the summit of Steamboat Mountain in British Columbia when they spotted two lights. One, three times the apparent size of the moon, approached them, then shot away to hover in the sky. The other light resting on the mountainside, looked, on closer examination, like a derby hat with portholes. The two women pulled into an abandoned driveway and watched the two objects for forty-five minutes. At one point, the landed UFO rose and flew one hundred to one hundred fifty feet before resettling on the ground. During the sighting, a truck stopped, and the driver emerged to look at the UFOs, but the women would not approach—one of a number of actions (or inactions) they were later unable to understand.

When they resumed their journey along an icy, fog-covered highway, something seemed to take control of the car, even managing curves perfectly. But no matter what Toews did, the vehicle traveled at no more than twenty-five miles per hour. She and her friend also became aware of a bright light shining through the mist. It was coming from a white cloud twenty to thirty feet above them. As their trip went on, Toews was shocked to see that no matter how far they went, the gas gauge did not move.

Late that night, they stopped at a lodge at Muncho Lake. It was closed, but they got out of their car to stretch their legs. A young man, dark-haired and bearded, stepped out of the darkness. Though the temperature was barely above zero, the man was dressed only in shirt, pants, and shoes. The car was packed, and the women insisted there was no room for him, but he still persuaded them to drive him to the next lodge, some eighty miles away, where he said he worked. The space was so cramped that he had to sit on Hanson's lap. Strangely, she could feel no weight. When she remarked on it, he responded humorously but vaguely.

Toews asked his name. He leaned toward her and stared into her eyes before saying, "Gordon." Both women thought he looked familiar, but neither could place him. He was pleasant and friendly in his manner. After the UFO reappeared above trees along the highway, Gordon inquired about their views of life in the universe and of angels. In time, Toews understood why Gordon didn't seem to weigh anything: he was hovering about two inches in the air. She even covertly ran her hand under him to make sure.

When they stopped for the night at an inn in northern British Columbia, Gordon suddenly was no longer there. The women looked and called for him, but he had not even left tracks in the snow. They were sure that he had stepped out of the car with them and that he couldn't have been out of their sight for more than a few seconds.

The inn was closed, so they stayed in the lounge with a truck driver, who refused to believe that they could have come all the way from Steamboat Mountain—one hundred sixty-five miles away—under existing road and weather conditions. The strangeness of their situation did not hit them until the next night, when they were staying at another lodge. Toews suddenly realized that Gordon reminded her of her husband, Jim, who had the same hair color, eyes, mannerism, body shape. And her husband's middle name was Gordon.

The following morning they set off. At first conditions were good, but soon a storm came down. Weirdly, though, the road ahead of them remained dry, even as snow fell and swirled on either side. They looked up to see the mysterious cloud they had observed earlier. Later, their car engine failed, and two mysterious men who seemed to know things about the women that strangers could not have known helped them restart it. The cloud left only as Toews's car got to Anchorage and four blocks away from her house.

The women came to believe that Gordon was either a spaceman or an angel. Eventually, Joseph J. Brewer, Judge of the District Court in Anchorage, heard of their experience and interviewed them. He and Toews wrote an account of it in *Fate,* a popular magazine on the paranormal and occult.

Further Reading

Toews, Edmoana, with Joseph J. Brewer, 1977. "The UFOs That Led Us Home." *Fate* Pt. I. 30, 6 (June): 38–45; Pt. II. 30, 7 (July): 63–65, 68–69.

Gray Face

"Gray Face" was the name Clyde Preston, a North Carolina truck driver, gave to one of a number of extraterrestrials who visited him over a nearly two-decade-long period. In 1993, under hypnosis, Preston recalled being abducted into a UFO in the course of a (consciously remembered) close encounter with a UFO while he was on a run to South Dakota. While aboard the UFO, he encountered a humanoid being he calls "Gray Face."

Even before the abduction memories surfaced, however, Preston underwent a series of strange experiences that he believed were tied to his close encounter. He suffered serious migraine headaches in the wake of that sighting. They left only after he discussed his encounter with a ufologist. Soon afterward, he developed psychic abilities that would come and go erratically. They so disrupted his life that his wife, fearing he had lost his sanity, left him. He underwent out-of-body episodes and found himself doing automatic writing at a furious pace. These writings covered many subjects, from Earth's ancient history to future geological cataclysms. Much of the material had to do with the Bible. The writing claimed that the Ten Commandments were a kind of universal code that must be deciphered, then obeyed.

One night in 1993, Preston awoke and spotted a beam of light going through his chest. He felt intense pain, then had the sensation that he was being pulled out of his body. Two shadowy beings, reeking of evil and menace, had him by the arms and were forcing him to a black abyss. This abyss, he thought, was the entrance to hell. He began to pray, and the next thing he knew, a beautiful blue sky surrounded him. A soothing light, emanating apparently from God, gave him a feeling of peace and ecstasy. Though he did not wish to return to his body, something told him that he must do so, and he did. He lay awake the rest of the night reflecting on all that had happened to him, and in the morning he vowed to find a hypnotist who could help him fill in the gaps in his memory.

While hypnotized, he recounted the 1977 abduction as well as others. These abductions occurred in a foggy, dreamlike environment. Besides Gray Face, there was White Face, which looked like a carving of an Egyptian deity. Another entity, this one especially frightening, wore a mask with a face like a Mayan or Aztec god. A week after the hypnosis session, this being appeared in Preston's bedroom and removed the mask. Preston was somewhat relieved to see that it resembled Gray Face with slightly heavier features.

In each case, telepathic contact occurred, but it was always one-sided, coming from the aliens to Preston.

He also had two encounters, only an hour apart, with Mr. Brown Robe, as he called a figure clad in such a garment. It had no facial features, but it was able to communicate mentally. It stressed the importance of Matthew 24 in the New Testament, the chapter in which Jesus discusses the events that will take place just prior to the Second Coming. Preston noticed that Mr. Brown Robe, Gray Face, and the others never used the word "God" but did talk of a "universal intelligence." Still, he linked his visitors with Bible figures. He believed Brown Robe, for example, to be a kind of angel, Gray Face a "Watcher" from the Old Testament's Daniel 4.

Preston's last abduction occurred one night in 1995 when a group of gray-skinned, large-eyed humanoids—the classic "grays" of abduction lore—took him into a UFO, where he was subjected to an apparent medical examination. On his return at 2:50 A.M., he heard a mechanical voice speaking to him. It said that the world's governments not only knew about the presence of extraterrestrials but also had contact with them. The aliens warned the governments about the dangers of nuclear testing and environmental destruction. By their blundering, humans had unknowingly caused trouble with forces beyond their comprehension. One consequence was that Earth's magnetism had been altered.

Preston's contacts ended with that experience. In retrospect, he concluded that the aliens had not always told him the straight truth, that much of what they told him was not strictly accurate. He thought that some had been agents of Satan, while others, such as Gray Face and Mr. Brown Robe, had benign intentions.

See Also: Abductions by UFOs

Further Reading

Davis, Carolyn, 1998. "The UFO Messenger." *Fate* 51, 11 (November): 22–24.

Great Mother

In *Escape from Destruction* (1955), which was later reprinted as *Escape to the Inner Earth,*

Raymond Bernard—the pseudonym of Walter Siegmeister—wrote of his association with a Puerto Rican psychic known as Mayita, "whose body functions as an interplanetary radio." From extraterrestrial sources, Mayita learned that an atomic war would erupt on Earth between 1965 and 1970 and that by 2000, the planet's surface would be devoid of any kind of life. Those few humans of sufficiently pure body and spirit would be lifted from Earth and flown by flying saucers to a safe haven on Mars. Mayita's principal contact was the Great Mother, who lived on the sun—not, she informed the psychic, the unendurably hot star we believe it to be. The Great Mother, described as having a beautiful face, long golden hair, and deep blue eyes, related to her the story of humankind's secret past.

One hundred fifty thousand years ago, the Great Mother, then living on Uranus, gave birth, via parthenogenesis (self-fertilization), to the first members of a race of superwomen. For the next fifty thousand years they lived in a utopian society. That ended when a mutant named Lucifer came into the world. Lucifer was a "defective . . . sterile female"—a man, in other words. Filled with resentment, he eventually convinced himself of his superiority. Using electromagnetic waves (sexual intercourse did not yet exist), he persuaded some of his sisters to let him impregnate them so that they would give birth to males as well as females. Outraged that more mutants were being brought into the world, the Great Mother exiled Lucifer, his wives, and their children to Saturn. On that planet, Lucifer changed his name to Satan and used his male aggressiveness and propensity for anger and violence to institute harsh rule. His children thrived, however. After another fifty thousand years Lucifer/Satan turned his eyes on the one planet the Great Mother's daughters had yet to colonize: the Earth.

A fleet of spaceships landed on Earth, and Satan's reign began. Many of the immigrants from Saturn settled in Lemuria and Atlantis, finally destroying them both in the course of nuclear conflict. After that, the human race's degeneration went on at an alarming pace. War, cruelty, and suffering have continued unabated over many centuries. Earth's male and female inhabitants commit the great abomination of meat-eating, and they also engage in the loathsome practice of sexual intercourse. Men dominate women, even though the latter are superior to the former, because of sexual desire and painful, nonparthenogenetic birth. Even when they think they are worshipping God, they are worshipping Satan.

Only those human beings who abstain from sex, meat, caffeine, alcohol, and tobacco can hope to restore moral and intellectual order to their existence. Flying saucers will rescue them at the last moment. On their arrival on Mars, men and women will be separated and will live chaste, segregated lives. In this new paradise, they will go beyond vegetarianism and learn to subsist on air and the perfume of certain flowers.

In his book, Bernard urged readers to come to San Francisco Island, off the coast of Brazil, where he had gone to establish a utopian colony. Coincidentally or otherwise, Mayita was preaching a doctrine Bernard had advocated for the previous two decades. In it, sexual intercourse is vile and unclean, women are superior, and men are a dangerous mutation. Critic Walter Kafton-Minkel observes that this "story of our origins sounds much like a mythology devised by a community of modern radical feminists" (Kafton-Minkel, 1989).

See Also: Atlantis; Lemuria

Further Reading

Bernard, Raymond [pseud. of Walter Siegmeister], 1974. *Escape to the Inner Earth.* Clarksburg, WV: Saucerian Press.

Kafton-Minkel, Walter, 1989. *Subterranean Worlds: 100,000 Years of Dragons, Dwarfs, the Dead, Lost Races and UFOs from inside the Earth.* Port Townsend, WA: Loompanics Unlimited.

Great White Brotherhood

The Great White Brotherhood figures in such schools of occultism as Theosophy and Rosicrucianism. The Brotherhood is thought to consist of ascended masters who oversee the spiritual and physical evolution of the human race.

Greater Nibiruan Council

The Greater Nibiruan Council (GNC) is described as the "main governing arm of the Galactic Federation," comprising the smaller Nibiruan Councils (NC) in the various dimensions of the universe. The GNC's responsibilities are many. It sponsors emissaries and ambassadors from the many planetary civilizations and provides courts and oversight for disputes. It also gives military protection to threatened peoples and trains races for membership in the federation.

On an even larger scale the GNC oversees the divine evolution of each planet and every individual soul in the galaxy. It works with every level of the spiritual hierarchy to ensure that all work effectively together. It maintains the galactic structure and interacts with other galactic federations. These are only a few of its many tasks, conducted with the assistance of innumerable smaller, dimensional councils. The oldest of these is the 9D Nibiruan Council, also known as "The Ancient Ones" and the "Pelegians." This council is headed by Devin and his half-brother Jehowah, members of the two royal houses of Aln and Avyon.

In the human dimension—the third—the 3D Nibiruan Council (3DNC) began in Kansas City, Missouri, in January 1997, under the direction of channeler Jelaila Starr and associates Terry Spears and Dermot Kerin. A year and a half later, it relocated to Los Angeles. Starr is its sole owner, and the council functions as a tax-paying small business. According to Starr, the 3DNC represents the GNC on Earth and upholds its directives as they apply to this world. Other responsibilities include "providing the 9D Tools of Integration to the people of Earth along with support and training for using them in the form of books, tapes, videos, workshops, seminars, etc.; providing a living example of the Ascension Tools in action through their actions; relaying messages in the form of updates and perspectives to the people of Earth for the purpose of education, support and enlightenment; supporting the work of other groups and individuals involved in the ascension of earth and its people" ("The Greater Nibiruan Council Section," 2000).

The concept of "Nibirua" comes from the writings of ancient-astronaut theorist Zecharia Sitchin, from his reading of ancient Sumerian literature. Sitchin, however, believes Nibirua to be an inhabited but undetected planet in our solar system. Its people, who have an extraordinarily advanced technology, created the human race in their image using genetic engineering. Nibirua orbits Earth every thirty-six hundred years. In Sitchin's assessment, the planet is due to pass between Mars and Jupiter in the near future, and the Nibiruans—known as the Annunaki—will visit us again.

Further Reading

"The Greater Nibiruan Council Section," 2000. http://www.nibiruancouncil.com/html/greater_nibiruan_council_secti.html

Sitchin, Zecharia, 1976. *The Twelfth Planet.* New York: Stein and Day.

Grim Reaper

The folkloric figure of the Grim Reaper is almost universally assumed to be wholly imaginary and symbolic. Anomalist Mark Chorvinsky, however, insists that apparently sincere, sane persons have seen, in death or near-death contexts, apparitional forms that match in most or all particulars the robed, skeletal figure. Chorvinsky has collected a number of reports and published some representative accounts in his *Strange Magazine.*

One case came from a retired nurse who years earlier had worked at a hospital in Houston. While running down the hallway on a very hot day on her way to replacing another nurse on duty, she passed a room and glanced inside. She walked on past five other rooms before what she had seen sank in and she returned to look more carefully. An old woman

The Vision of Death, *an image of the Grim Reaper in an engraving by Gustave Doré (Fortean Picture Library)*

lay in a bed while beside it stood a tall figure in a monk's robe, its head covered. Apparently aware of the nurse's presence, the figure turned to look at her. She told Chorvinsky, "His face was a skull with tiny red fires for eyes. His hands, skeletal, were patiently folded over each other inside the dark sleeves. My impression was [that] he was very patient, waiting" (Chorvinsky, 1997). A terrible death smell, like something rotting in the sun, hung in the air.

The nurse felt a literal freezing sensation when the figure stared at her. She quickly retreated. By the time she got to her original destination, the male nurse on duty saw that she was cold. He wrapped her in blankets and gave her hot chocolate. It was two hours, however, before she felt herself able to speak about what she had seen.

Another retired nurse claimed to have seen the Grim Reaper on a number of occasions. "Usually," she said, "I just see a dark figure, robed, standing near the nurses' station, or perhaps in the hall. Very rarely, the figure will be white. I've never heard it speak, but someone always dies within a few days of its appearance."

A man identified only as A. L. told a story with a different ending. Late one evening in 1974, he was sitting in his Yonkers, New York, apartment while his three children slept in their rooms. His wife was in their bathroom. When he happened to glance to his right, he was startled to observe a black-hooded figure holding a scythe, its face a luminous white skull. It was staring at him as it glided slowly backward and disappeared through the door. Fearing that the Reaper had come for someone, A. L. banged on the bathroom door. When he got no response, he entered and found his wife lying on the floor next to an empty bottle of pills. With the assistance of his sister and her husband, who lived close by, he was able to revive his wife and take her to the hospital. "The encounter has left me with the feeling that the Reaper is a special friend," he told Chorvinsky. "He appeared to me and gave warning instead of taking someone."

Someone else claimed that the Grim Reaper saved his life when he was eight years old. Dennis Wardrop was skating on a pond when the ice gave way under his feet, and he plunged into the frigid water. He tried desperately to find a way out as his lungs filled with the water. He felt something poking him and grabbed onto it as it lifted him to safety. After he wiped the water from his eyes, he was terrified to learn that he was holding the blunt end of a long scythe in the hands of a tall, large figure with the face of a decomposing corpse. It wore a black robe and a hood over its head. Inside the eye sockets were "swirling whirlpools of black and dimly glowing reds." An "odor of death" permeated the air. Perhaps sensing his fear, the figure assured him (whether telepathically or orally is not explained) that he would be okay, that it was not yet his time. The boy collapsed from exhaustion. When he revived soon thereafter, the figure was gone, and he felt curiously warm even though it was only fourteen degrees above zero.

Chorvinsky writes, "I have investigated particularly intriguing cases in which the Reaper has been seen by multiple witnesses. And . . . I know of incidents in which the Reaper was reported to have actually healed injuries and assisted the ill and the dying."

Further Reading

Chorvinsky, Mark, 1997. "Encounters with the Grim Reaper." *Strange Magazine* 18 (Summer): 6–12.

Gyeorgos Ceres Hatonn

Gyeorgos Ceres Hatonn—usually addressed and referred to simply as Hatonn—speaks through Doris Ekker (known as Dharma). George and Desiree Green and others associated with the Phoenix Project distribute Hatonn's messages through a magazine called the *Phoenix Journal.* Hatonn describes himself as "Commander in Chief, Earth Project Transition, Pleiades Sector Flight command, Intergalactic Federation Fleet-Ashtar Command; Earth Representative to the Cosmic Council and Intergalactic Federation Council on Earth Transition" ("Who Is Hatonn?").

Hatonn denies that the process through which he communicates is channeling. It is, he says, more like radio transmission directly from spaceship to contactee. "We travel and act," he says, "in the direct service and under Command of Esu Jesus Immanuel Sananda.

Sananda is aboard my Command Craft from whence He will direct all evacuation and transition activities as regards the period you ones call the End Prophecies of Armageddon."

In contrast to the benign words of most otherworldly beings who speak through contactees, Hatonn and his fellows preach a fiercely expressed conspiracy theory with openly anti-Semitic elements. For example: "Anarchy is something that the Jew promotes relentlessly. While in complete control of the financial powers of the state, they promote internecine strife" (Ecker, 1992). Hatonn also denies that the Holocaust ever occurred. Hatonn refers to Jews who are working with the anti-Christ, Satan, and the "evil leaders" of the New World Order to control the world. The plotters call it Plan 2000. The space people and their earthly allies such as those in the Phoenix Project are working to thwart the conspiracy and to create a new Earth after wars and natural disasters have reshaped the face of the planet.

See Also: Ashtar; Channeling; Contactees; Sananda

Further Reading

Ecker, Don, 1992. "Hatonn's World." *UFO* 7, 4 (July/August): 30–31.

Heard, Alex, 1999. *Apocalypse Pretty Soon: Travels in End-Time America.* New York: W. W. Norton and Company.

"Who Is Hatonn?" http://www.fourwinds10.com/information.html

H

Hierarchal Board

The Hierarchal Board communicates through Pauline Sharpe (also known as Nada-Yolanda) via channeling and automatic writing. The board is the solar system's spiritual government, and its members include Sananda (Jesus), who has orbited Earth in a spacecraft since 1885. Right now he is in etheric form but will enter the physical realm as the planet is cleansed and transformed for the coming New Age, due to arrive sometime around 2000. Sharpe's organization is called Mark-Age, "commissioned by the Hierarchal Board to implant a prototype of spiritual government on Earth, the I Am Nation. The I Am Nation is a government of, for and by the I Am Selves of all people on Earth. . . . It is not a political government, but is a spiritual congregation of all souls who seek to serve God, first and foremost, and the I Am Selves of all people on Earth" (Mark Age," n.d.).

Mark-Age came into being in 1960, though communications from the board had begun four years earlier through Charles Boyd Gentzel. Over the years, several persons received the messages, but in time Sharpe became the organization's guiding personality. It has published a large amount of channeled material, including communications from Gloria Lee, a 1950s-era contactee.

See Also: Channeling; Contactees; J. W.; Sananda

Further Reading

"Mark-Age: Love in Action for the New Age." http://www.islandnet.com/~arton/markage.html

One Thousand Keys to the Truth, 1976. Miami, FL: Mark-Age MetaCenter.

Holloman aliens

A modern legend, widely circulated but never verified, holds that aliens once landed at Holloman Air Force Base in New Mexico and conferred with representatives of the government and military. The event is variously set on April 1964 or May 1971.

The story emerged under curious circumstances. Robert Emenegger and Allan Sandler, two wealthy Los Angeles businessmen, had gone to Norton Air Force Base in California where they were to discuss the production of a documentary film dealing with advanced research projects. The discussion soon expanded to include other possible subjects, one dealing with the air force and UFOs. Emenegger and Sandler expressed interest in the UFO project, and their contacts—the head of the base's U.S. Air Force Office of Special Investigations (AFOSI) and audio-visual director Paul Shartle—began laying plans. They told the civilians that in May 1971 cameras at Holloman AFB had recorded an extraordinary event. A

A government employee photographed a possible UFO as it hovered for fifteen minutes near Holloman Air Force Base, New Mexico. (Bettmann/Corbis)

flying saucer had landed at the base, and three beings had stepped outside.

Shartle, who claimed to have seen this 16mm film, said on national television in October 1988 that the beings were the size of humans but had gray complexions and large noses. They wore tight-fitting suits and "thin headdresses that appeared to be communication devices, and in their hands they held a 'translator'" (Howe, 1989). The Holloman commander and other officers had met with the aliens over the next several days.

Emenegger claims to have been taken to Holloman and shown the buildings where the saucer was stored and the meetings conducted. He and Sandler were promised thirty-two hundred feet of the landing film, but they never saw it because permission to view it, much less reproduce it, was subsequently withdrawn. They went on to make a UFO documentary, and Emenegger wrote a paperback based on it. In it he mentions the Holloman incident but not as something that had actually happened, merely as something that could happen in the future. In a section of photographs and illustrations, however, there is a drawing clearly intended to be a Holloman alien, said only to be "based on eyewitness descriptions" (Emenegger, 1974).

In 1982, Colorado-based ufologist and documentary filmmaker Linda Moulton Howe met with Sergeant Richard Doty, an AFOSI agent, at Kirtland Air Force Base in New Mexico. Asked about the Holloman incident, Doty asserted that it had indeed occurred but on April 25, 1964, seven years earlier than Emenegger had been led to believe. Doty showed her a document that purported to detail the U.S. government's interaction with aliens and its recovery of extraterrestrial wreckage and bodies. He mentioned films, one of them taken at Holloman. Despite repeated promises, Doty never produced any film or other documentation for Howe. He later emerged as a suspect in a notorious, forged paper concerning a secret group, Majestic–12, which supposedly studies alien remains and supervises the cover-up.

In the 1980s, the legend grew as a right-wing conspiracy theorist named Milton William Cooper claimed to have seen super-secret documents attesting to an agreement between the U.S. government and malevolent aliens. According to Cooper, the first Holloman meeting happened in 1954. Officials and aliens agreed that in exchange for the freedom to abduct humans without interference, the extraterrestrials (from a dying planet that orbits Betelgeuse) would provide the government with advanced technology, so long as it kept silent about it. Subsequently, Cooper would write in a wild book allegedly documenting the sinister machinations of the "secret government" that the agreement broke down; according to Cooper, aliens and government entered into conflict over who would get to control and manipulate the human race. Among other bizarre allegations, Cooper stated that President Kennedy was assassinated because he planned to expose the scheme to the American people.

Further Reading

Brookesmith, Peter, 1996. *UFO: The Government Files.* New York: Barnes and Noble Books.

Cooper, Milton William, 1991. *Behold a Pale Horse.* Sedona, AZ: Light Technology Publishing.

Emenegger, Robert, 1974. *UFOs Past, Present and Future.* New York: Ballantine Books.

Howe, Linda Moulton, 1989. *An Alien Harvest: Further Evidence Linking Animal Mutilations and Human Abductions to Alien Life Forms.* Littleton, CO: Linda Moulton Howe Productions.

Jones, William E., and Rebecca D. Minshall, 1991. *Bill Cooper and the Need for More Research (UFOs, Conspiracies, and the JFK Assassination).* Dublin, OH: MidOhio Research Associates.

Hollow earth

A long mythological tradition holds that supernatural beings dwell beneath our feet, either in caves and caverns or in the earth's inte-

Books on the hollow-earth theory (Fortean Picture Library)

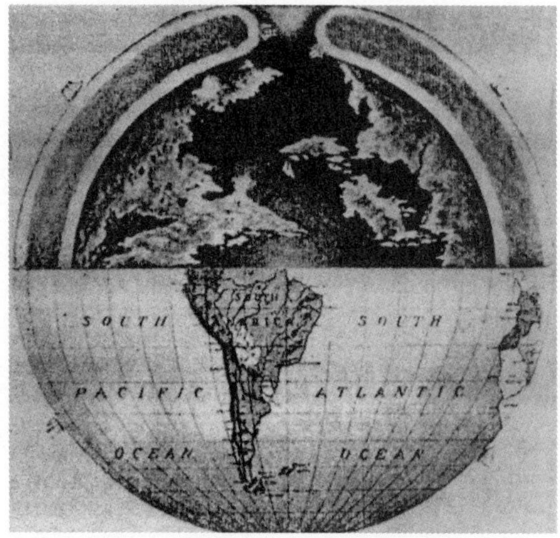

An illustration of the hollow earth from Phantoms of the Poles *by William Reed, 1906 (Fortean Picture Library)*

rior. Some beliefs have it that the spirits of the unsaved dead live on in gloom or torment beneath our feet. The most famous scientific proponent of a hollow earth, Edmond Halley (1656–1743), best remembered for the comet named after him, argued that within the earth's sphere there were three other, smaller ones, all harboring intelligent beings. Theories about a hollow earth, while dismissed as physically impossible by scientists, continue on the fringes into modern times.

John Cleeves Symmes (1779–1829) became a notorious figure in early American history as a vigorous publicist for the notion first proposed by Halley, of an earth whose interior consisted of concentric spheres. According to Symmes, the interior could be entered through four-thousand-mile-wide holes at either pole. Symmes hoped to lead an expedition into the earth, and he lectured widely, all the while lobbying for funding. In the face of national ridicule, he argued that the people of the interior amounted to a vast new market for American goods. Symmes inspired Edgar Allan Poe to write the classic proto-science-fiction novella *The Narrative of Arthur Gordon Pym* (1838). Symmes's son Americus kept the faith after his father had passed on. As late as 1878 he published a collection of the elder Symmes's writings and lectures.

The 1870s and 1880s saw a hollow-earth revival with the publication of still other books championing the notion, including M. L. Sherman's *The Hollow Globe* (1871), a channeled work, and Frederick Culmer's *The Inner World* (1886). Helena Blavatsky incorporated the hollow earth into her two popular and influential occult texts *Isis Unveiled* (1877) and *The Secret Doctrine* (1888). Another important book, William Reed's *The Phantom of the Poles,* was published in 1906, the first of a small library of hollow-earth volumes to be issued through the twentieth century.

By the late nineteenth century, a religion based on the hollow earth was formed by Cyrus Teed (1839–1908), after a vision in which the Mother of the Universe told him he would save the world. He went on to lead a utopian community in Fort Myers, Florida, devoted to "Koreshanity." Koreshanity held that not only is the earth hollow, humans live inside it, orbiting the sun, which is at the center of the world. The stars, planets, and moon are also within the earth's shell. Marshall B. Gardner's book *A Journey to the Earth's Interior* (1913) agreed with Teed's views to the extent that Gardner was willing to acknowledge an interior sun, though it was not *the* sun, and another race, not humans, get their heat and light from it. This other-race lives in a pleasant, tropical climate.

Other fringe thinkers, notably H. Spencer Lewis and Guy Warren Ballard, wrote that Mount Shasta in northern California is an entrance to the interior, where a colony of survivors from the lost continent Lemuria live on. Ballard claimed to have personally met super beings under the mountain, including golden-haired, angelic Venusians such as those George Adamski and later flying-saucer contactees would claim to know. Ballard, his wife Edna, and their son Donald founded a popular Theosophy-based (and fascist) movement around these experiences and doctrines. Ballard died in 1939, but his organization, the "I AM" still exists.

In the 1940s the pages of the science-fiction pulps *Amazing Stories* and *Fantastic Ad-*

ventures carried the allegedly true, intensely controversial experiences of Richard S. Shaver. Shaver asserted that he had been inside vast subterranean caverns, where remnants of an advanced race that had once populated the surface still lived. There were two groups, the deros—sadistic idiots who used the ancients' advanced technology to harm surface-dwellers—and the teros—the embattled minority of good guys who tried, mostly without success, to stop the deros' schemes.

When flying saucers and UFOs entered popular consciousness in the years after World War II, inevitably, speculation tied them to inner-earthers. *Flying Saucers,* a magazine edited by Ray Palmer, who, as editor of *Amazing,* had championed what he called the Shaver mystery, brought the concept of holes in the poles and the notion of hollow earth into its pages. Perhaps the most widely read book in the literature, *The Hollow Earth* (1964) by Raymond Bernard (the pseudonym of Walter Siegmeister, a man with a decades-long association with fringe beliefs), stated that flying saucers come in and out the pole holes. The Canadian neo-Nazi Ernst Zundel, writing as Christof Friedrich, contributed the book *UFOs—Nazi Secret Weapons* (1976), which alleged that Hitler and his Last Battalion had fled to Argentina, then to Antarctica. From there they entered the earth and dedicated their energies to the construction of an advanced technology. Nazi technology is responsible for what we call UFOs. Zundel—and later the Missouri-based International Society for a Complete Earth—tried to raise funds to fly through the hole in the pole in vehicles prominently displaying swastikas to ensure that they got a friendly reception.

Some, though not all, current hollow-earth advocacy is tied to explicit or implicit pro-Nazi sympathies. For example, Norma Cox's virulently anti-Semitic *Kingdoms within Earth* (1985) blamed an international Zionist conspiracy for suppressing the truth about a hollow globe; she also openly praised Hitler. A more benign, good-humored approach to the subject of a hollow earth can be found in Dennis G. Crenshaw's occasional periodical *The Hollow Earth Insider.*

See Also: Adamski, George; Contactees; King Leo; Lemuria; Mount Shasta; Rainbow City; Shaver mystery

Further Reading

Beckley, Timothy Green, ed., 1993. *The Smoky God and Other Inner Earth Mysteries.* New Brunswick, NJ: Inner Light Publications.

Bernard, Raymond [pseud. of Walter Siegmeister], 1964. *The Hollow Earth: The Greatest Geographical Discovery in History.* New York: Fieldcrest Publishing.

Cox, Norma, 1985. *Kingdoms within Earth.* Marshall, AR: self-published.

Crabb, Riley, 1960. *The Reality of the Underground.* Vista, CA: Borderland Sciences Research Associates.

Fitch, Theodore, 1960. *Our Paradise inside the Earth.* Council Bluffs, IA: self-published.

Friedrich, Christof [pseud. of Ernest Zundel], 1976. *UFOs—Nazi Secret Weapons?* Toronto, Ontario: Samisdat.

———, 1978. *Secret Nazi Polar Expeditions.* Toronto, Ontario: Samisdat.

Kafton-Minkel, Walter, 1989. *Subterranean Worlds: 100,000 Years of Dragons, Dwarfs, the Dead, Lost Races and UFOs from inside the Earth.* Port Townsend, WA: Loompanics Unlimited.

Michell, John, 1984. *Eccentric Lives and Peculiar Notions.* San Diego, CA: Harcourt Brace Jovanovich.

Trench, Brinsley le Poer, 1974. *Secret of the Ages: UFOs from inside the Earth.* London: Souvenir Press.

Walton, Bruce A., 1983. *A Guide to the Inner Earth.* Jane Lew, WV: New Age Books.

X, Michael [pseudonym of Michael X. Barton], 1960. *Rainbow City and the Inner Earth People.* Los Angeles: Futura.

Honor

In early January 1978, according to a West German newspaper, a twelve-year-old Iranian girl, identified only as Sara, underwent a series of contacts with an extraterrestrial creature named Honor. The contacts took place over a seven-day period. Covered with black hair or fur, Honor stood six and a half feet tall and hailed from a world ten light years "ahead" of Earth. Sara said that the extraterrestrial had given her psychokinetic powers that allowed her to move household appliances with mind power alone.

Further Reading
Bartholomew, Robert E., and George S. Howard, 1998. *UFOs and Alien Contact: Two Centuries of Mystery.* Amherst, NY: Prometheus Books.

Hopkins, Budd (1931–)

Born in Wheeling, West Virginia, Budd Hopkins graduated from Oberlin College in 1953. He moved to New York City to embark on a successful career as a painter, sculptor, and writer on the arts. One day in 1964, he and two other persons witnessed the appearance of a disc-shaped object that remained in view for two or three minutes. The experience sparked Hopkins's interest in UFOs. Though for the next years that interest was confined to the occasional reading of UFO literature, in 1975 he participated in the investigation of a multiply witnessed close encounter of the third kind in a New Jersey park directly across the Hudson River from Eighty-eighth Street in Manhattan. Hopkins went on to become actively involved in research on abductions. He also became hugely influential in bringing wider attention to the subject and shaping attitudes toward it.

Budd Hopkins, 1997 (Lisa Anders/Fortean Picture Library)

Hopkins brought mental-health professionals into his work, which often involved the use of hypnosis to retrieve ostensible memories of abductions masked by amnesia. His first book on the subject, *Missing Time* (1981), detailed his case studies. A sequel, *Intruders* (1987), brought forth an expanded vision of the abduction experience, highlighting the sexual aspects and apparent genetic experiments involving mysteriously terminated pregnancies and human/alien hybrids. He also argued that abductions are usually not one-time encounters but events that occur periodically over abductees' lifetimes. Hopkins had also become convinced that abductions are far more widespread than anyone had suspected. He helped devise a survey conducted by the Roper Poll. In Hopkins's view the results—which proved controversial and were read differently by some others—demonstrated that millions of persons in the United States alone are, whether they are consciously aware of it or not, abductees.

A third Hopkins book, *Witnessed* (1996), recounted a monumentally complex, extremely bizarre abduction allegedly involving a number of participants, including an unnamed prominent international political figure. (Published accounts have since identified the man as Javier Perez de Cuellar, the Secretary-General of the United Nations. Perez de Cuellar denies the story.) The claim sparked an intense and often bewildering series of charges and countercharges, though critics were unable to uncover conclusive evidence to support hoax allegations. Even so, the story was so extreme, even by the standards of high-strangeness close encounters, that even sympathetic observers found it difficult to believe. Hopkins wrote, "This abduction event so drastically alters our knowledge of the alien incursion in our world that it is easily the most important in recorded history" (Hopkins, 1996).

Though some abduction proponents have argued that abducting aliens are benignly intentioned, Hopkins holds that they are indifferent to human beings and are coldly unemotional. Their purpose in coming here is to study humans as if they were lab animals, and they are particularly interested in our genetic makeup.

See Also: Abductions by UFOs; Close encounters of the third kind; Hybrid beings

Further Reading

Bloecher, Ted, Aphrodite Clamar, and Budd Hopkins, 1985. *Final Report on the Psychological Testing of UFO "Abductees."* Mount Rainier, MD: Fund for UFO Research.

Hopkins, Budd, 1981. *Missing Time: A Documented Study of UFO Abductions.* New York: Richard Marek Publishers.

———, 1987. *Intruders: The Incredible Visitations at Copley Woods.* New York: Random House.

———, 1996. *Witnessed: The True Story of the Brooklyn Bridge UFO Abductions.* New York: Pocket Books.

Unusual Personal Experiences: An Analysis of the Data from Three National Surveys, 1992. Las Vegas, NV: Bigelow Holding Corporation.

Hopkins's Martians

In a letter published in the April 19, 1897, issue of the *St. Louis Post-Dispatch,* a traveling salesman named W. H. Hopkins reported that while strolling through hills east of Springfield, Missouri, three days earlier, he encountered two beautiful, unclad Martians.

The alleged incident occurred as newspapers throughout America were chronicling often sensationalistic accounts of unidentified aerial objects generally referred to as "airships," though today they would be called UFOs. Most people who took the reports seriously believed that the ships were the secret creations of American inventors who soon would reveal all, but there was also some speculation that Martians might be touring Earth. Dubious tales of encounters with extraterrestrials appeared in some newspapers.

Hopkins claimed that he had seen an airship landed in a clearing. The most "beautiful being I ever beheld," a naked young woman with hair falling to her waist, stood next to the craft. She was picking flowers, speaking all the while in a musical voice in a language Hopkins did not recognize. She was also vigorously fanning herself even though the day was hardly warm. In the shade cast by the ship, a naked man with shoulder-length hair and a beard, fully as long as the woman's hair, lay on the ground, also working a fan.

Until Hopkins stepped forward, the couple did not know they were being observed. The man leaped to his feet, and the woman threw herself into his arms. As Hopkins tried to assure them of his good intentions, they glared back at him, clearly unable to understand what he was saying. In time, however, the tension dissipated, and a kind of conversation, mostly involving gestures, ensued. When he inquired about their place of origin, they "pointed upwards, pronouncing a word which, to my imagination, sounded like Mars." They studied him "with great curiosity. . . . They felt of my clothing, looked at my gray hair with surprise and examined my watch with the greatest wonder."

After he was given a tour of the interior, the ship flew away with the occupants waving farewell to Hopkins, "she a vision of loveliness and he of manly vigor."

See Also: Allingham's Martian; Aurora Martian; Brown's Martians; Dentons's Martians and Venusians; Khauga; Martian bees; Michigan giant; Mince-Pie Martians; Monka; Muller's Martians; Oleson's giants; Shaw's Martians; Smead's Martians; Thompson's Venusians; Wilcox's Martians

Further Reading

Bullard, Thomas E., ed., 1982. *The Airship File: A Collection of Texts Concerning Phantom Airships and Other UFOs, Gathered from Newspapers and Periodicals Mostly during the Hundred Years Prior to Kenneth Arnold's Sighting.* Bloomington, IN: self-published.

Clark, Jerome, 1981. "The Coming of the Venusians." *Fate* 34, 1 (January 1981): 49–55.

Hweig

Hweig is an extraterrestrial who channels through an Oregon woman named Ida M. Kannenberg. She believes that she first encountered aliens in the California desert in

1940. According to testimony elicited under hypnosis in 1980, aliens placed implants inside her head to facilitate communication later between them and her. In 1978, she began to hear from Hweig on a regular basis, after a failed 1968 experiment that so terrified her that she ended up in a mental hospital. She was released when no evidence of psychopathology could be uncovered.

Hweig and his associates are here to rejuvenate Earth and its inhabitants. They plan to accomplish these changes via communication with contactees, who will be led to "certain disciples and . . . specific discoveries" that will improve humanity's lot and Earth's environment.

See Also: Channeling

Further Reading

Sprinkle, R. Leo, 1999. *Soul Samples: Personal Explorations in Reincarnation and UFO Experiences.* Columbus, NC: Granite Publishing.

Hybrid beings

Hybrid beings are entities who are part human and part humanoid. They figure in a number of accounts of UFO abductions. Female abductees sometimes report anomalous pregnancies that are enigmatically terminated, typically in association with a missing-time experience of the sort in which the abductions allegedly took place. In a subsequent onboard UFO encounter, the aliens present the abductee with a child who has the features both of the human mother and of the abducting entities, most often described as thin, gray- or white-skinned, with oversized heads and large, hypnotic eyes.

As early as the late 1960s, paranormal writer John A. Keel, investigating reports of UFOs and other strange occurrences in New York City and on Long Island, noted that some female witnesses experienced what he called "hysterical pregnancies" (Keel, 1975). Keel's observation was little noted and soon forgotten. In the 1980s, however, abduction specialist Budd Hopkins independently came upon the same phenomenon. Mostly through the use of hypnosis, the women "recalled" instances in which a kind of suction device removed fetuses from their wombs. In later abductions the women would be shown babies, toddlers, and older children and told to touch and interact with them in other ways. Though generally human in appearance, the children often appeared to be lacking the emotional makeup of human beings.

In time, abductees reported encounters with young adult hybrids. These hybrids, among those sufficiently human-looking to pass unnoticed on the street, would sometimes have sexual relationships with younger abductees, who may or may not have given their consent. David M. Jacobs, who has written extensively on the issue of hybrids, believes these particular beings are from a late stage of the process. His investigations lead him to believe that first-stage hybrids are half-human/half-alien. These entities tend to look "almost alien." In the next stage, Jacobs speculates, "the aliens join a human egg and sperm and assimilate genetic material from the first-stage hybrid . . . into the zygote" (Jacobs, 1998). The third-stage hybrid, created from human sperm and egg and genetic material from a second-stage individual, looks more human. Only in the latest stages, the fifth or sixth, do the hybrids resemble humans enough to walk among us and, just as important, reproduce. They retain the strong mental and telepathic powers of their alien heritage, however. In Jacobs's view, based on testimony from abductees whom he has hypnotized, the aliens are preparing to replace the human race with a hybrid population. The aliens themselves are unable to reproduce, but through hybrids, their species will survive—at the expense of humanity's. Jacobs holds that this takeover could occur at any time and is more likely to occur sooner than later.

Hybrids are a relatively new concept among ufologists and in the accounts of alleged UFO experiencers. In retrospect, some have suggested that the presence of human or humanlike beings in early close encounters of the third kind suggests hybrids were being seen before they were being recognized. In a famous October 1957 Brazilian abduction case, a young man allegedly had sexual intercourse with an alien woman who, were she to have been reported in a more recent episode, would probably be judged a hybrid. Through hand gestures, the woman seemed to indicate that the fruit of their union would be born on another planet.

On the other hand, critics point out, hard evidence for the existence of hybrids simply does not exist. Most of the testimony to their presence owes, moreover, to accounts elicited under hypnosis, a state in which unconscious fantasizing frequently occurs. Scientific critics have stated flatly that hybridization procedures of the sort described are biologically impossible. Though there is no shortage of anecdotal testimony, no medically documented instances of anomalously terminated pregnancies have ever been demonstrated.

See Also: Abductions by UFOs; Close encounters of the third kind; Hopkins, Budd; Keel, John Alva

Further Reading

Hopkins, Budd, 1987. *Intruders: The Incredible Visitations at Copley Woods.* New York: Random House.

Jacobs, David M., 1992. *Secret Life: Firsthand Accounts of UFO Abductions.* New York: Simon and Schuster.

———, 1998. *The Threat.* New York: Simon and Schuster.

Neal, Richard, 1991. "Missing Embryo/Fetus Syndrome." *UFO* 6, 4 (July/August): 18–22.

Schnabel, Jim, 1994. *Dark White: Aliens, Abductions, and the UFO Obsession.* London: Hamish Hamilton.

Swords, Michael D., 1988. "Extraterrestrial Hybridization Unlikely." *MUFON UFO Journal* 247 (November): 6–10.

I

Imaginal beings

University of Connecticut psychologist Kenneth Ring theorizes that an "imaginal realm" exists somewhere between reality and fantasy. In this "third kingdom," entered through (Ring's italics) "certain *altered states of consciousness* that have the effect of undermining ordinary perception and conceptual thinking" (Ring, 1992), one encounters magical yet semireal entities such as UFO beings, angels, and various otherworldly intelligences. Ring's imaginal realm is much like the "interdimensional mind" of another parapsychological theorist, Michael Grosso.

To test certain aspects of the hypothesis, Ring and a colleague, Christopher J. Rosing, conducted extensive psychological testing of several groups. They found that persons who report UFO-abduction experiences and those who have undergone near-death experiences are psychologically indistinguishable. Though not fantasy-prone in the clinical sense, they have felt a connection with nonordinary realities since childhood. Moreover, those childhoods were troubled with episodes of abuse, trauma, or serious illness. Because of these difficulties, these individuals have developed a "dissociative response style as a means of *psychological defense.*" This causes them to be so focused on their internal state that their consciousness has changed in radical ways. This expanded consciousness allows them to enter the imaginal realm, there to meet extraordinary beings and undergo positive life changes.

UFO abductees and near-death experients, in Ring's view, are prophets—modern shamans—who are picking up coded messages from the otherworld. Abductees see "small, gray, sickly looking" aliens whose heads are too big for their bodies. They look, in other words, like starving children. Ring reads this to mean, "The future of the human race—symbolized by the archetype of the child—is menaced as never before." Our planet is experiencing a "near-death crisis," and we need to listen to what these "extraordinary experiencers" are telling us. They are leading us to a "cosmic-centered view of our place in creation, a myth that has the power to ignite the fires of a worldwide planetary regeneration and thus to save us from the icy blasts of Thanatos's nuclear winter."

See Also: Psychoterrestrials

Further Reading

Ring, Kenneth, 1992. *The Omega Project: Near-Death Experiences, UFO Encounters, and Mind at Large.* New York: William Morrow and Company.

Insectoids

Some UFO abductees report onboard encounters with entities that resemble giant praying mantises. These beings, typically dressed in capes with long robes and high collars, are seen in association with the smaller, humanoid grays, though they appear to have a higher rank than their colleagues. "Other aliens appear to act somewhat subservient to the insectlike beings," abduction investigator David M. Jacobs has written.

Insectoids seldom participate directly in the physical examinations of humans, though they may engage in what Jacobs calls "staring procedures," wherein an alien puts its face close to an abductee's, telepathically probes the contents of the individual's mind, stimulates emotions (everything from fear to love to sexual arousal) and conjures up hallucinatory images into it. Though the grays have little to say to abductees, insectoids sometimes are communicative. In one of Jacobs's cases, a woman reported being told that it was the aliens' intention to take over the Earth with the insectoids in charge of this new world order.

See Also: Abductions by aliens; MU the Mantis being; Nordics

Further Reading

Jacobs, David M., 1998. *The Threat.* New York: Simon and Schuster.

Lewels, Joe, 1997. *The God Hypothesis: Extraterrestrial Life and Its Implications for Science and Religion.* Mill Spring, NC: Wild Flower Press.

Intelligences from Beyond (Intelligences du Dehors)

Intelligences du Dehors—"intelligences from beyond" in English translation—allegedly channeled through French contactee Jean-Pierre Prevost. Prevost, a heretofore-obscure street merchant, had risen to public attention through his involvement in a sensational incident said to have occurred on the morning of November 26, 1979, in a Paris suburb. Prevost and another business associate reportedly witnessed the disappearance of their friend Franck Fontaine in the wake of a close encounter with a UFO. Fontaine showed up a week later, claiming not to remember anything that happened in the interim. Police and civilian UFO investigators suspected a hoax.

Nonetheless, French science-fiction writer Jimmy Guieu rushed into print with a book on the case, but with a difference. In the book, *Contacts OVNI Cergy-Pontoise* (1980), Prevost became the central figure in the episode, the intended target of the alien abduction. Within months, Prevost's own book recounted his extraterrestrial contacts with a strong emphasis on the usual contactee message about noble space visitors and confused, destructive earthlings. His principal contact was a wise space being named Haurrio. Readers inclined to doubt all of this could only wonder at Prevost statements such as this one: "What does it matter to know, at the factual level, where real life ends and imagination takes over? Isn't it more important to take into consideration the content of the messages?" (Bonabot, 1983).

In a July 7, 1983, newspaper interview, Prevost confessed that both the Fontaine abduction and his own space contacts were fake, concocted, he said, to attract an audience to his philosophical messages by putting them in the mouths of advanced intelligences. Even so, he still tried to start a group with him at the head, but it failed, as did a publishing enterprise and an FM radio station. Interviewed by ufologist Jacques Vallee in 1989, Fontaine stuck to his story but charged that Prevost was lying about his.

See Also: Abductions by UFOs; Contactees

Further Reading

Bonabot, Jacques, 1983. "1979 Fontaine Case in France Now Admitted to Be a Hoax." *MUFON UFO Journal* 190 (December): 10.

Evans, Hilary, with Michel Piccin, 1982. "Who Took Who [sic] for a Ride?" *Fate* 35, 10 (October): 51–58.

Vallee, Jacques, 1991. *Revelations: Alien Contact and Human Deception.* New York: Ballantine Books.

Ishkomar

Ishkomar, an extraterrestrial, began channeling for the first time in late September 1966 through a Phoenix man identified only as Charles—"a blue-collar worker of modest education" (Steiger, 1973). Ishkomar said he was speaking via telepathic light beamed from a spaceship in Earth's atmosphere. He himself had lived long enough so that he was able to discard a physical body, though the ship "contains others of us who are in human form." Ishkomar began his Earth mission some thirty thousand years ago to accelerate evolution so that human beings could develop more quickly and be able to accept guidance—though not control, which galactic law forbids—from wise space people like himself. "You must reach a high level of mental development and knowledge to be able to understand our purposes," he said, so the work continues.

Ishkomar also warned that another group also worked in Earth's space. This group, while not necessarily evil in itself, had purposes at odds with humanity's best interests, and its members sought to control human destiny. Ishkomar refused to condemn these beings, saying only that their purpose "conflicts with *our* purpose. This does not mean that their intentions are not good or honorable."

Soon there would be "great upheavals" on Earth's surface, and there would be much suffering and death. Only those who were mentally and physically prepared would survive. The extraterrestrials did not plan any massive rescue operation, since "you are of no use to us in the Outer Reaches." But they would help those human beings who heeded their words to make their planet improved and livable after the changes.

Ishkomar said his people were not concerned solely with Earth. They were galactic travelers and were involved with the fates of many worlds throughout the cosmos.

Charles told Brad Steiger that he had no idea why he had been chosen, unless it was because of a sighting of what he took to be a UFO in Michigan in 1956. While observing the object, he beamed a mental message to its presumed occupants and told them, "I would like to be your friend."

After the Ishkomar messages started coming a decade later, Charles and his wife, Lois, formed a small group. As Charles channeled, members asked questions and learned lessons. Ishkomar firmly instructed them never to reveal Charles's full name, lest his life be endangered by unfriendly forces.

See Also: Channeling

Further Reading

Steiger, Brad, 1973. *Revelation: The Divine Fire.* Englewood Cliffs, NJ: Prentice-Hall.

J

J. W.

In 1953, a voice in her head identified itself to Gloria Lee, a former child actress and model, as that of "J. W.," an inhabitant of Jupiter. Not quite convinced, Lee demanded physical evidence of J. W.'s existence. Some days afterward, J. W. alerted her to the presence of a flying saucer passing over her backyard in Westchester, California. Lee went on to form the Cosmon Research Foundation, which attracted as many as two thousand members, as a forum for the distribution of J. W.'s teachings, essentially a variation of Theosophy. She also wrote *Why We Are Here* (1959), a book widely read in early contactee circles.

Lee became a martyr to the contact movement in 1962 through tragic circumstances. J. W. had provided her with spaceship blueprints and instructed her to take them to Washington, DC, to show officials. But when she and associate Hedy Hood went there, no one was interested in meeting them. Lee told her friend that J. W. had now informed her, "The space people are going to invade the earth and establish a peace program" (Barker, 1965). She was also ordered to go on a fast for peace that would end when a "light elevator" (spaceship) arrived to transfer her to J. W.'s home planet. The fast began on September 23 and lasted till November 28, when Lee's alarmed husband had her rushed to a hospital. She died there on December 7.

In less than two months, according to a Florida-based contactee group, Mark-Age MetaCenter, Lee herself was sending psychic messages from Jupiter. She promised that spaceships would land on Earth within six months if they were received in peace and good will. She also mentioned that the recently deceased Marilyn Monroe had just arrived. Over the years, Mark-Age would publish five volumes of Lee-generated channeled material.

See Also: Contactees

Further Reading

Barker, Gray, 1965. *Gray Barker's Book of Saucers.* Clarksburg, WV: Saucerian Books.

Lee, Gloria, 1959. *Why We Are Here: By J. W., a Being from Jupiter through the Instrumentation of Gloria Lee.* Los Angeles: DeVorss and Company.

———, 1962. *The Changing Conditions of Your World, by J. W. of Jupiter, Instrumented by Gloria Lee.* Los Angeles: DeVorss and Company.

Mark-Age MetaCenter, 1963. *Gloria Lee Lives! My Experiences since Leaving Earth.* Miami, FL: Mark-Age MetaCenter.

———, 1969–1972. *Cosmic Lessons: Gloria Lee Channels for Mark-Age.* Miami, FL: Mark-Age MetaCenter.

Jahrmin and Jana

In 1940, according to an account he would relate many years later, Jananda Korsholm, a seven-year-old Danish boy, was playing with a friend when a thunderstorm erupted. As he ran home, he saw his sister looking out of the window of the family's apartment. Just as he was waving at her, he felt a golden light surrounding him and an intense heat surging all through his body. He found himself ascending inside the light until, suddenly, a gold and silver spaceship appeared just above him. It had no door, but he entered it by passing through a wall. Inside a circular room he encountered a hairless, androgynous-looking figure who Jananda sensed was male. The figure, dressed in a silver uniform with a pyramid logo on his chest, said his name was Jahrmin (pronounced "Yarmin"). A tall blond woman approached him, touched his hand, and let him know via telepathy that her name was Jana.

Through her touch, the boy found himself transformed into a young man. Jana told him that he had a mission on Earth. It would not be easy because ill-intentioned persons and forces would resist him. She would, however, be there to protect him with her energy, and they would be reunited at the conclusion of his mission. Jananda knew that he had found his soul mate, that no earthly love would ever fulfill him as the love he shared with Jana.

On a television screen in the middle of the room, he saw scenes from the solar system's past, when meteors, comets, and other objects falling from space drastically altered the surfaces of planets, and their inhabitants had to be evacuated. He saw himself just about to be evacuated from Earth, leaving a wife behind. He also saw Earth's changed landscape hundreds of years in the future.

Jananda Korsholm eventually moved to the United States and found his way to Sedona, Arizona, where he works as a channeler, healer, and spiritual counselor.

Further Reading

Korsholm, Jananda, 1995. "UFO's, Close Encounters of the Positive Kind." http://spiritweb.org/Spirit/ufo-positive-negative-jananda.html

Janus

In his memoirs, Air Marshal Sir Peter Horsley, onetime Deputy Commander-in-Chief of the Royal Air Force's Strike Command, later Equerry for the Royal Family, recounts a meeting with a self-identified extraterrestrial who was introduced to him as "Janus." He says the incident took place one winter day in 1954, after an acquaintance, a high-ranking military officer interested in UFOs and convinced of their friendly intentions, phoned him with a curious message: to go that evening to a house in London's Chelsea district. A woman met him at the door and led him into a dimly lit room, where he was introduced to a "Mr. Janus." The stranger immediately asked him to tell him what he knew about UFOs. Afterward, Mr. Janus expressed a desire to meet Prince Philip, then launched into a two-hour discourse on space travel, visitors from other worlds, cosmology, and philosophy. Janus stressed the human race's immaturity and its potential to destroy itself. In the course of this conversation, Horsley came to believe that the stranger was reading his mind.

Janus said that advanced "observers" from distant planets are watching Earth, contacting a select few trustworthy terrestrials while trying not to interfere directly in human affairs. Once human beings have learned interstellar travel, he said, "it is of paramount importance that you have learnt your responsibilities for the preservation of life elsewhere" (Horsley, 1997). In the meantime, the visitors also want to ensure that they leave no conclusive proof of their presence.

Horsley wrote that there was an odd sequel. Shortly after the meeting he prepared a memo and gave it to Lieutenant General Sir Frederick Browning, Treasurer to Prince Philip. Browning pressed Horsley to arrange another encounter. Horsley tried repeatedly and unsuccessfully to reach the woman at whose flat he had spoken with Janus. After a few days he personally went to her residence, only to learn that she had suddenly moved out. The general who had set up the encounter became "distant and evasive" when Horsley got in touch with him. He never saw him, the woman, or Janus again.

Interviewed by British ufologist Timothy Good, Horsley thought it "strange" that he had only a general impression of Janus's appearance. He remembered only a normal-looking man, approximately forty-five to fifty years old, thinning gray hair, and dressed in suit and tie.

When Horsley's book was published, the *London Times* ran an article by Dr. Thomas Stuttaford, who suggested that Horsley was suffering from hallucination. Horsley insists, however, that the incident occurred as reported.

Further Reading

Good, Timothy, 1998. *Alien Base: Earth's Encounters with Extraterrestrials.* London: Century.

Horsley, Sir Peter, 1997. *Sounds from Another Room: Memories of Planes, Princes and the Paranormal.* London: Leo Cooper.

Stuttaford, Thomas, 1997. "Air Marshal's Flight of Fancy." *London Times* (August 14).

Jerhoam

Jerhoam is a "State of Consciousness" who channels through John Oliver. He is here, he says, to help humans "incorporate the Great Knowledge of the Soul into life to become more aware . . . to become more awake, to become more loved, and to know how to express love in many ways." He also seeks to reconnect with students from that time, persons who have reincarnated and live on Earth now.

Many centuries ago—thousands of years before the Great Pyramid was constructed—Jerhoam occupied a physical body, teaching at the Great School of Ancient Wisdom.

Further Reading

"An Introduction: Who Is Jerhoam?" http://www.jerhoam.com/whoisjer.html.

Jessup's "little people"

Morris Ketchum Jessup (1900–1959) wrote four books on UFOs between 1955 and 1957. His book *The Case for the UFO* (1955) was the first to use "UFO" in its title; heretofore, publishers preferred the then more familiar "flying saucers." Jessup also was an earlier theorist in what would be called the "ancient astronaut" genre, though his particular interpretation remains unique. He believed that the "little people" sometimes reported in connection with UFOs are literally that: pygmies of earthly origin and the creators of an extraordinary technology that gave them space flight long ago.

Jessup first hinted at his theory in *UFO and the Bible* (1956), asserting that all UFO evidence pointed to the presence of "space-intelligence, relatively near the earth, but yet away from it and in open space . . . using navigatable contrivances." In his earlier life, he had done graduate-level work in astronomy at the University of Michigan. In the course of his studies, and later in his adult life, he traveled in Africa and South America, often stopping to examine archaeological artifacts. He became convinced that only an advanced civilization, with a technology that encompassed teleportation, levitation, and space flight, could have created such structures.

Eventually, he came to believe that about 100,000 years ago, "in the pre-cataclysmic era which developed a first wave of civilization . . . space flight originated on this planet. . . . We may assume that the Pygmies . . . developed a civilization which discovered the principle of gravitation and put it to work" (Jessup, 1957). When Atlantis and Mu sank into the oceans, the "little people" fled in their spaceships. They now reside on the moon and in floating structures in a "gravity neutral" zone between Earth and its satellite.

See Also: Atlantis; Lemuria

Further Reading

Jessup, M. K., 1955. *The Case for the UFO.* New York: Citadel Press.

———, 1956. *UFO and the Bible.* New York: Citadel Press.

———, 1957. *The Expanding Case for the UFO.* New York: Citadel Press.

Jinns

In traditional Arabic and Persian belief, jinns are demonic, shape-shifting entities. Over the centuries, the idea evolved that a few jinns are good. There are five kinds of jinns, and only one has occasional benevolent qualities. Typically, jinns take the shapes of insects, toads, scorpions, and other animals deemed unappealing or obnoxious. The tradition bears some resemblance to traditions of fairy folk in other societies. At least two prominent writers on the UFO phenomenon, Gordon Creighton and Ann Druffel, are convinced that UFO beings are jinns in disguise.

Under the editorship of Charles Bowen, England's *Flying Saucer Review,* then a widely read UFO journal, moved the publication away from speculations about extraterrestrial visitation toward interpretations that cast UFOs in paranormal terms. No other contributor did so as enthusiastically as Creighton, a retired British diplomat with a keen interest in demonology. After Bowen's illness and subsequent death in the 1980s, Creighton assumed editorship of the magazine and promptly declared that he had identified the intelligences behind UFO sightings, encounters, and abductions: jinns. In an article in a 1983 issue, he pointed out that jinns materialize and dematerialize, switch between visibility and invisibility, change shape, kidnap humans, lie, control minds, and engage their victims in sexual intercourse—behaviors associated with UFO entities.

He was convinced that the jinns are up to no good. In follow-up writings, he contended that these sinister supernatural powers secretly control Earth, using thought control to get humans to do their bidding. They are behind crime and violence, and they have brought AIDS and other deadly diseases into the population. "Another great World War may be in the making," he wrote in 1990, engineered for cosmic purposes we cannot understand; humans are merely property and playthings and are soon to be removed from the face of the Earth.

Ufologists responded to these notions with a tactful silence with one exception: Ann Druffel, an abduction-research specialist who finds "startling similarities between reports of abduction scenarios in the Western world and Gordon Creighton's excellent research on the jinns" (Druffel, 1998). Druffel, a Californian, investigated the experiences of an Iranian-American she calls Timur. Timur encountered humanoids in out-of-ordinary states of consciousness—sleep paralysis, meditation, astral travel—and recognized them as the jinns he had heard of in his native country.

Druffel concludes that "our own faeries and jinns are merely an old human problem, shape-shifted and wearing space garb to fool us. They can be fended off by stouthearted, determined individuals."

See Also: Fairies encountered

Further Reading

Creighton, Gordon, 1983. "A Brief Account of the True Nature of the 'UFO Entities'." *Flying Saucer Review* 29, 1 (October): 2–6.

———, 1989. "AIDS." *Flying Saucer Review* 34, 1 (March Quarter): 12.

———, 1990. "Grave Days." *Flying Saucer Review* 35, 3 (September): 1.

Druffel, Ann, 1998. *How to Defend Yourself against Alien Abduction.* New York: Three Rivers Press.

Joseph

A Todmorden, Yorkshire, England, police officer named Alan Godfrey was on patrol at 5:05 A.M., November 28, 1980, when he encountered a metallic disc with a dome and a row of windows. When he attempted to alert headquarters, he found that his radio was not working. Suddenly, he found himself one hundred yards farther down the road than he thought he was, and the UFO was gone. He vaguely recalled getting out of his car and hearing a voice. Under hypnosis later, Godfrey "recalled" that he lost consciousness after a light from the object struck him. Then he felt himself floating into the craft and meeting a humanlike being named Joseph.

Six feet tall, friendly in manner, Joseph had a thin nose, a beard, and a mustache. He wore a skullcap and was clad in a sheet, making him look something like a prophet from the Bible. A large black dog accompanied him. The room also contained eight robots, each about three and a half feet tall, making a sort of murmuring chatter. When they touched Godfrey, beeping sounds emanated from them. Joseph directed Godfrey to a bed, where he lay as a beam of light from the ceil-

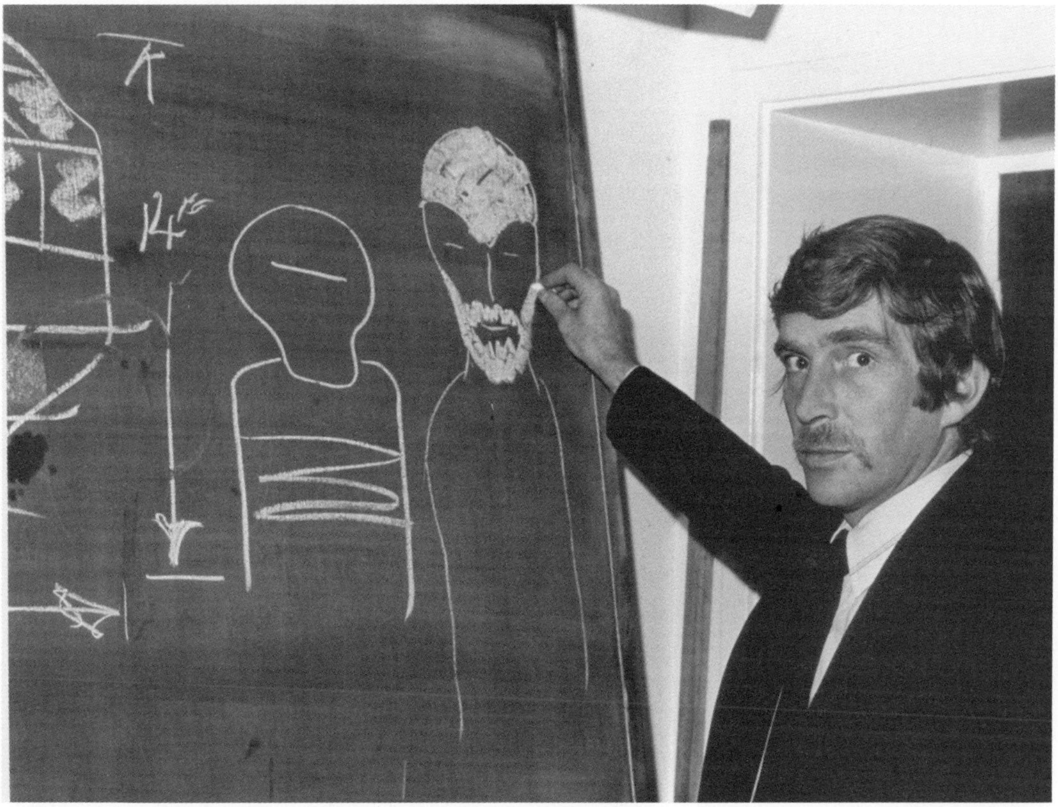

Policeman Alan Godfrey, who was allegedly abducted into a UFO at Todmorden, Yorkshire, drawing a picture of "Joseph," November 1980 (Janet and Colin Bord/Fortean Picture Library)

ing shone on him. Communicating by telepathy, Joseph touched his head, and Godfrey lapsed into unconsciousness for an undetermined period. The robots took off Godfrey's shoes and studied his toes. Meanwhile, instruments placed on his arms and legs caused him discomfort to the point of sickness. A foul odor permeated his nostrils. Joseph asked him questions, but Godfrey would refuse to tell investigators what they were. The alien indicated that they had met before, apparently when Godfrey was a child.

Godfrey would remember an earlier incident from 1965, when he was 18. Around 2 A.M., he and a girlfriend stopped their car abruptly when a woman and a dog stepped out in front of them. Certain that he had hit the woman, he got out to help her, but there was no sign of her or the animal. When he got home, he found that two hours were missing without explanation. Another incident—his seeing a ball of light in his room when he was a child—also seemed to him evidence that the 1980 incident was not his first encounter with aliens.

Further Reading

Randles, Jenny, 1983. *The Pennine UFO Mystery.* London: Granada.

K

Kantarians

For four nights in September 1961, David Paladin's son claimed that somebody named Itan was coming into his bedroom and taking him away in a big "sky car." Though at first Paladin dismissed this as a child's fantasy, a neighbor claimed that he had seen a tall, thin man walking the boy toward a waiting flying saucer. That November Itan came into Paladin's own bedroom and engaged him in a telepathic conversation. He and his people, the Kantarians, lived on a planet in another dimension. They do not interfere directly in human affairs, but they have contacted certain human beings in the hope that they could gently push the human race in a more mature, positive direction. They had been observing humans since the beginning of *Homo sapiens* and had even left a genetic imprint in some humans.

Paladin claimed years of psychic connection with the Kantarian Confederation. Itan and his friends have told him that if human beings destroy themselves, the space people can do nothing. But if natural cataclysms threaten human existence, the Kantarians will perform a rescue operation. Mostly, though, they hope that humans will reform themselves, develop wisdom and kindness, and join their Space Brothers in the cosmos one day.

Further Reading

Montgomery, Ruth, 1985. *Aliens among Us.* New York: G. P. Putnam's Sons.

Kappa

In traditional Japanese lore the Kappa are malicious water demons shaped like monkeys with scales. They lure the unsuspecting into ponds and rivers, then devour them. One Japanese writer, Komatsu Kitamura, has theorized that the Kappa were extraterrestrials who came to Japan sometime between the ninth and eleventh centuries. Others have picked up on this speculation, suggesting that the ostensibly scaly skin was actually a spacesuit. Alleged sightings continue even now. In November 1978, two construction workers fishing off the coast of the port city Yokosuka reported seeing a creature abruptly emerge from the sea to glare at them. "It was not a fish, an animal, or a man," one said. "It was about three meters [ten feet] in height and [was] covered with thick, scaly skin like a reptile. It had a face and two large yellow eyes" (Picasso, 1991).

Argentine ufologist Fabio Picasso has collected what he judges to be more or less comparable reports from his country. For example, on the evening of April 22, 1980, a motorist

A Japanese print depicting a Kappa (Victoria and Albert Museum, London/Art Resource, NY)

in Santa Rosa noticed something falling out of the sky. At that moment, his car engine suddenly ceased functioning. When he got out to check the motor, he noticed a cold breeze at foot level. Looking down, he saw the legs of something that clearly was not human. Looking up, he saw two humanoid creatures, approximately seven feet in height, approaching him. They had webbed hands and were clothed in black, shiny diving suits. Their faces were "skull-like." Though their protruding mouths were moving, no words were coming out of them. One put its cold hands around the witness's head, and he passed out. He revived a few minutes afterward, but a half mile from where he had been.

Further Reading

Picasso, Fabio, 1991. "Infrequent Types of South American Humanoids." *Strange Magazine* 8 (Fall): 21–23, 44.

Karen

Late at night, on the highway between Matias and Barbosa, Brazil, on January 21, 1976, a couple in a car saw a blue light envelope the landscape. The light moved toward them until it covered their vehicle. The car "was absorbed as if through a chimney" into a brilliantly luminous circular object. Two dark-featured figures, male and more than six feet tall, approached and signaled that the two humans should step out of their car. The ground seemed to move under them, and the woman said she felt drunk even though she had consumed no alcohol. The couple could not understand the aliens' strange language until one gave each of them a headset and plugged it into a device. At that moment, the words became understandable. The being introduced himself as Karen and urged them to remain calm.

The woman underwent a series of medical tests. She and her husband also drank a liquid with an unappealing taste. Other aliens, one of them female, appeared as Karen explained to them that he and his people were conducting medical research, even though on their world they had conquered all illness, and no one ever died anymore. He warned them not to talk about their experience, since people would think they were insane. If they wished, he added, they could have their memories erased. The couple turned down that offer. The woman claimed some subsequent psychic contacts.

Further Reading

Bartholomew, Robert E., and George S. Howard, 1998. *UFOs and Alien Contact: Two Centuries of Mystery.* Amherst, NY: Prometheus Books.

Karmic Board

All living entities must pass before the Karmic Board before they can be incarnated on Earth. Each entity receives its assignment, and at the end of that assignment (bodily death) the entity appears before the board once more, this time to have its performance reviewed. The Karmic Board "dispenses justice to this system of worlds, adjudicating karma, mercy and judgment on behalf of every lifestream" ("Lords of Karma," n.d.).

Members of the Karmic Board include the Great Divine Director, the Goddess of Liberty, Ascended Lady Master Nada, Cyclopea (Elohim of the Fifth Ray), Pallas Athena

(Goddess of Truth), Portia (Goddess of Justice), and Kuan Yin (Goddess of Mercy).

Further Reading

"Lords of Karma," n.d. http://www.ascension-research.org/karma.html

Kazik

In September 1953, Albert K. Bender of Bridgeport, Connecticut, suddenly shut down his International Flying Saucer Bureau (IFSB), confiding to a few close friends that three men in black had threatened him and given him the frightening answer to the UFO mystery. Though Bender would provide few details, he hinted that the visitors were agents of the U.S. government. His alleged experience led an associate, Gray Barker, to write a sensational and paranoia-drenched book, *They Knew Too Much About Flying Saucers* (1956), about Bender and other supposedly silenced UFO researchers. Eventually, Barker, who had started a small West Virginia–based publishing company, persuaded Bender to reveal what had happened to him. In *Flying Saucers and the Three Men* (1962), Bender wrote that he had run afoul, not of a terrestrial intelligence agency, but of extraterrestrial intelligences from the planet Kazik.

Bender's IFSB had come into existence in April 1952 and was soon among the most successful of early UFO groups, claiming as many as six hundred members in a number of countries. Bender was also an enthusiastic science-fiction fan. A bachelor, he lived in a house full of artifacts from horror films, and at night, as he lay in bed, he would imagine himself sailing out of his body and into deep space. Soon, according to Bender's book, weird things began happening to him. Strange lights and disembodied footsteps frightened him, and once glowing eyes, accompanied by a stench of sulfur, stared at him. With colleagues in Australia and New Zealand, Bender speculated about a saucer base inside the South Pole, and they laid plans for a research project to study that possibility.

Bender urged his membership to try to contact the saucers telepathically at the same hour on March 15, 1953. While participating, he underwent an out-of-body experience and then heard a voice warning him to "discontinue delving into the mysteries of the universe."

A few weeks later, he returned home from a two-week vacation to smell the sulfur odor. A few hours later, three shadowy, apparitional figures dressed in dark suits spoke to him. They gave him a device with which he could contact them; all he had to do was hold it tightly in his palm and say "Kazik" over and over again. Two days later, he attempted contact. The experience initiated a series of encounters with monstrous beings who revealed that "Kazik" was the name of their home planet. They took Bender to their antarctic base, where they revealed their big secret: they had come to Earth to gather and refine sea water. They also told him that God does not exist and that there is no life after death.

Bender was given a disc that monitored his activities and ensured his silence until they completed their business, which was in 1960 when they departed from our planet. Bender was free to tell his story, which he did in a book that few, including (privately) Barker, saw as anything more than a not particularly interesting science-fiction novel. Two critics pointed to the story's inherent implausibility: "The story lacks a good solid motive or purpose. . . . How could Bender or anyone else have discovered [the Kazakians'] secret until they chose to reveal it; and if they wished their secret to remain unknown, what possible purpose could they have had in revealing it deliberately to Bender, only to have to then force silence upon him, causing him physical pain and disturbing his peace of mind for the next eight years? . . . What was so significant about a few tons of sea water? . . . What had such entities to fear from anyone, if Bender did publish such a 'secret'? Who would believe it, or be able to interfere with such an advanced civilization?" (Beasley and Sampsel, 1963).

Twelve years after *Three Men*'s publication, Barker expressed the view that the story was something Bender had conjured up "in a trance or a dream" (Barker, 1976). Most observers, however, suspected it to be conscious fiction. One fantastic theory, proposed in 1980 by British ufologist Brian Burden, held that an intelligence agency had subjected Bender to a thought-control experiment and caused him to hallucinate space people.

See Also: Men in black

Further Reading

Barker, Gray, 1956. *They Knew Too Much about Flying Saucers.* New York: University Books.

———, 1976. Interviewed by Jerome Clark.

Barker, Gray, ed., 1962. *Bender Mystery Confirmed.* Clarksburg, WV: Saucerian Books.

Beasley, H. P., and A. V. Sampsel, 1963. "The Bender Mystery—Still a Mystery?" *Flying Saucers* (May): 20–27.

Bender, Albert K., 1962. *Flying Saucers and the Three Men.* Clarksburg, WV: Saucerian Books.

Burden, Brian, 1980. "MIBs and the Intelligence Community." *Awareness* 9, 1 (Spring): 6–13.

Young, Jerry A., and Gray Barker, 1976. "Letters." *Gray Barker's Newsletter* 3 (January): 7–12.

Keel, John Alva (1930–)

Born Alva John Kiehl in Hornell, New York, on March 25, 1930, John Keel would discover the writings of anomalist Charles Fort (1874–1932) at an early age. He grew up to be a Manhattan-based writer who eventually became internationally known for radical, neodemonological interpretations of UFO, anomalous and paranormal phenomena. Keel would speculate that a wide range of otherworldly entities, none of which regard the human race with favor ("ultraterrestrials," to use his term), emerge from an alternative reality he calls the "superspectrum."

Keel claims to have attended the first flying-saucer convention ever held, "in the old Labor Temple on New York's 14th Street" (Keel, 1991). After a tour of duty in the mil-

John Alva Keel (August C. Roberts/Fortean Picture Library)

itary in the early 1950s, he wandered the East and wrote his first book, *Jadoo* (1957), on his adventures and observations. He wrote that while in the Himalayas, he saw the yeti ("abominable snowman"), a beast he would come to think of as a "demon" (Chorvinsky, 1990). In the 1960s, he embarked full time on investigations of UFOs, men in black, monsters (including Mothman, an eerie winged humanlike creature with which Keel's name would forever after be associated), contactees, and more. He even reported having his own encounters with unearthly entities. Borrowing from California occult theorist N. Meade Layne, Keel became convinced that there are no visiting extraterrestrials, only shape-changing supernatural beings "composed of energy from the upper frequencies of the electro-magnetic spectrum. Somehow they can descend to the narrow (very narrow) range of visible light and can be manipulated into any desirable form. . . . Once they have completed their mission . . . they . . . revert to an energy state and disappear from our field of vision—forever" (Keel, 1969).

Though dismissed by some as a crank, Keel has been an influential theorist in some ufological and Fortean circles. His critics have charged him with careless writing and credulity, but his admirers prefer to think of him as a bold, even outrageous, iconoclast.

See Also: Contactees; Men in black; Mothman; Ultraterrestrials

Further Reading

Chorvinsky, Mark, 1990. "Cryptozoo Conversation with John A. Keel." *Strange Magazine* 5: 35–40.

Clark, Jerome, 1997. *Spacemen, Demons, and Conspiracies: The Evolution of UFO Hypotheses.* Mount Rainier, MD: Fund for UFO Research.

Keel, John A., 1970. *UFOs: Operation Trojan Horse.* New York: G. P. Putnam's Sons.

———, 1971. *Our Haunted Planet.* Greenwich, CT: Fawcett Publications.

———, 1975. *The Eighth Tower.* New York: Saturday Review Press/E. P. Dutton and Company.

———, 1975. *The Mothman Prophecies.* New York: Saturday Review Press/E. P. Dutton and Company.

———, 1988. *Disneyland of the Gods.* New York: Amok Press.

———, 1969. "The Principle of Transmogrification." *Flying Saucer Review* 15, 4 (July/August): 27–28, 31.

Khauga

Khauga is a "Celestial Being" whom William Ferguson met in an out-of-body state while meditating on the evening of January 12, 1947. Traveling at the "speed of consciousness," he found himself on Mars within ten seconds. Khauga met him on his arrival, remarking that he had something to say about "the observations that we have made of your planet." He also wanted Ferguson to pass on some messages to his fellow earthlings.

According to Khauga, a great network of canals covers the planet. Electromagnetic fields enclose its cities. Martians themselves, all of whom have red hair, red complexions, and broad features, float through the air via levitation. They are a foot shorter than the typical Earth person. Khauga expressed incredulity that human beings kill each other in battles. Martians, he said, are twenty thousand years ahead of earthlings in spiritual evolution and scientific development. Concerned about the state of affairs on our planet, the Martians had decided to "release positive energy particles into the earth's atmosphere . . . to counteract the negative energy particles that man himself has released" (Ferguson, 1954). Khauga asked Ferguson to assure the people of Earth that things would soon be much better in their world.

See Also: Allingham's Martian; Aurora Martian; Brown's Martians; Dentons's Martians and Venusians; Hopkins's Martians; Martian bees; Mince-Pie Martians; Muller's Martians; Shaw's Martians; Smead's Martians; Wilcox's Martians

Further Reading

Ferguson, William, 1954. *My Trip to Mars.* Potomac, MD: Cosmic Study Center.

Kihief

Kihief was the spirit guide to the late Francie Paschal Steiger, who with her then-husband, Brad Steiger, spearheaded the Star People movement of the late 1970s and early 1980s. Paschal Steiger believed herself to be a reincarnated extraterrestrial. Kihief, who guided her through her life, said he was from a place "like unto Venus" (Steiger and Steiger, 1981). She took his words to mean that he was from an otherdimensional counterpart to Earth's (uninhabitable) sister planet. Throughout her lifetime, Paschal Steiger interacted with a variety of friendly, spiritually advanced space people. She met the first of them when, as a five-year-old child, she saw a robed being whom she took to be an "angel."

See Also: Star People

Further Reading

Steiger, Brad, 1976. *Gods of Aquarius: UFOs and the Transformation of Man.* New York: Harcourt Brace Jovanovich.

Steiger, Brad, and Francie Steiger, 1981. *The Star People.* New York: Berkley Books.

Steiger, Francie, 1982. *Reflections from an Angel's Eye.* New York: Berkley Books.

King Leo

King Leo is a reptilian being who is descended from the dinosaurs. He and his fellows live in an underground kingdom, where they have resided since just before the catastrophe that destroyed other life from the Age of Reptiles. Some have met him in person, but most of his communications come through channeling.

King Leo got his name from a woman who prefers to call herself Joy D'Light (sometimes JoyDLight). Her association with reptilian beings began on November 7, 1961, when she and her husband, an air force man, were living in Oregon. Her husband had left town on assignment, and it was her first night alone. That night, from her open bedroom door facing the kitchen, she saw three bipedal reptilian beings standing next to her refrigerator. Six and a half feet tall, they had scaly skin and spikes down their backs; their eyes were yellow. Too frightened to leave her bed, she eventually fell asleep. They were gone when she woke up; nonetheless, they appeared every night for two months thereafter. Often they were waiting for her when she came home from work. Eventually, she took up a brief residence with her sister and returned only after some days had passed. The entities, who had never harmed her or spoken with her, were not there.

That changed in 1996 when one showed up in her house. She was wide awake and not in her bedroom this time, and she no longer felt the terror she had originally experienced. The being spoke for the first time, assuring her that he and his companions had never meant to harm her; they were just interested in her. He vanished after a few moments. On another occasion this being or one much like it showed up briefly on the television screen while she was surfing channels. The following year, one appeared for about five minutes before disappearing without communicating.

One day in July 1998, she lay down to rest when instantly she found herself transported to an underground kingdom. The ruler, who was standing in front of her, initiated a conversation, during which he told her that originally the reptilian race had been dinosaurs. Over time they evolved into smaller creatures, though their eating habits—they were herbivores—had not changed. Now they wanted to return to the surface ("top side," he called it) and reclaim their rightful roles as rulers of Earth. Joy explained that no single individual rules the surface, that there are many nations and many leaders.

When she inquired as to his name, he replied that her tongue would not be able to pronounce it. He suggested that she make up a name with which she felt comfortable. She decided to call him "Leo," telling him that "Leo" means "king." From then on, she addressed him as King Leo.

King Leo wanted to know what love feels like, since he and his people had no emotions—though such feelings are just now starting to evolve in them. They have a religion; they recognize the same Creator as surface humans do.

Joy met him again on August 14, 1999, when she was taken into the kingdom again. Leo told her that some of his subjects would like to live on the top again, though most would be staying behind. Those who wanted to go to the surface, however, were concerned that human beings would not accept their appearance. He told her that at present one and a half million reptilians live beneath the earth. According to Joyce's friend Elliemiser, "He is very congenial, likable and pleasant to communicate with. . . . Now they are waiting to find out what our response will be. . . . They will not just suddenly pop up and frighten us" ("The Reptilians," 1999).

King Leo's reptilians are not to be confused with evil reptoids who are coming to Earth from the Draco constellation. These beings are violent meat-eaters who seek to destroy humans with their advanced technology. The reptilians, on the other hand, do not have space travel, and their technology, while developing, is still relatively primitive.

See Also: Channeling; Reptoids

Further Reading

D'Light, Joy, and Elliemiser, 1999. "The Reptilians and King Leo." http://www.greatdreams.com/reptlan/repleo.htm

Korton

Commander Korton is a well-loved, ubiquitous channeling entity. He is also a leading light in the Ashtar Command, a close, trusted associate of Ashtar. According to a common belief, he heads the Ashtar Command Kor Communications Base, located in an other-dimensional correlate to the planet Mars. His task is to initiate contact with budding channelers and train them for their work. He also supervises the Eagles, extraterrestrials who live on Earth and pass as earthlings while performing missions for the Ashtar Command. Some contactees have reported boarding his ship in out-of-body states to attend briefings in what looks like a large amphitheater.

One psychic who observed him in the course of an interstellar conference describes him as clad in a vanilla-colored robe. "His eyes were deep-set," the observer reported, and blue in color. "He had a strong straight nose, slightly high cheek bones, firm full mouth. His hair was golden-blond . . . but his beard was lighter. . . . There was a firmness with this individual, but there was also a great deal of warmth vibration also—the warmth of love, of acceptance, of 'you're o.k.'"(Tuieta, 1986).

See Also: Ashtar; Channeling; Contactees

Further Reading

Tuella [pseudonym of Thelma B. Turrell], ed., 1989. *Ashtar: A Tribute.* Third edition. Salt Lake City, UT: Guardian Action Publications.

Tuieta, 1986. *Project Alert.* Fort Wayne, IN: Portals of Light.

Kronin

On July 26, 1967, near Big Tujunga Canyon in California, a man and a woman in a car heard a disembodied voice speaking. It alerted them to the imminent appearance of something out of the ordinary. They spotted a flash, then a disc-shaped UFO that landed nearby. A tall, boneless, eyeless figure emerged. He was, he said, Kronin, head of the Kronian race. He was also "a space robot encased in a time capsule" (Keel, 1975).

When she arrived home, the woman, Maris DeLong, took a phone call. It was from Kronin, the first of several in which he discussed cosmic matters.

Further Reading

Keel, John A., 1975. *The Mothman Prophecies.* New York: Saturday Review Press/E. P. Dutton and Company.

Kuran

Kuran are a race of people whom an actress/writer given the pseudonym "Jessica Rolfe" claims to have met over a period of years, beginning in her childhood. The Kuran, who are described as beautiful, tanned, golden-haired people who look human, would materialize in her Miami Beach, Florida, bedroom and teach her their secrets. The Kuran communicate telepathically, though they do make vocal sounds for a few simple sentiments such as "look there," "watch out," and "wow." They are among twelve alien races who have visited Earth. They have bases here, some off the coasts of Florida and Argentina, one in Brazil's Amazon basin, and they have lived in them, unknown to human beings, for millions of years. They still do not understand humanity's tendency to be violent and prejudiced.

The Kuran told Rolfe that the human race originally occupied a planet located between Mars and Jupiter. They visited this planet just before natural forces were set to destroy it, offering to remove the inhabitants to a suitable place if they agreed to live by Kuran law. The inhabitants refused, and the Kuran withdrew. The residents of the doomed planet managed to escape on their own. Some went to a planet in the constellation of Pegasus, and the other, to the Kuran's displeasure, colonized Earth and became our ancestors. Earth proved an inhospitable place, not sufficiently evolved to have achieved the cosmic harmonies that give rise to peaceable, well-adjusted races. The new colonists, moreover, interfered with Earth's ecology, forcing its previous, reigning, intelligent species from the land into the oceans; humans now know these beings as dolphins. Other alien races who arrived were driven off or forced to live in remote regions. The creatures humans call Bigfoot or Sasquatch originally came from outer space.

Over time, the new inhabitants forgot their cosmic heritage and their true history. Earth's surface, once a single land mass surrounded by ocean (and recalled vaguely as the lost continent of Mu), broke up, and the people were scattered. Cut off from one another, they developed different cultures and different languages. Only an elite group called the Magi preserved knowledge of the true past. Each harbored ambitions for himself and collected followers. They used their knowledge to abuse Earth's natural energies and to harness atoms for destructive purposes. Disturbed by these developments, the Kuran returned to Earth and tried to reform its inhabitants. With their followers, they constructed the paradisiacal land of Atlantis, only to have the Magi destroy it with atomic bombs. The nuclear explosions changed Earth's landscape and climate and created the continents we know today.

Even today a secret conflict continues between the Kuran and the Magi. On occasion the Kuran have tried to interfere in human affairs, each time with negative results. Myths and legends of the gods of the ancient world recount, in distorted form, previous Kuran efforts to lead us.

See Also: Atlantis; Lemuria

Further Reading

Gansberg, Judith M., and Alan L. Gansberg, 1980. *Direct Encounters: Personal Histories of UFO Abductees.* New York: Walker and Company.

Kurmos

In March 1966, a mystically inclined Scotsman named R. Ogilvie ("Roc") Crombie, visiting Edinburgh's Royal Botanic Gardens, spotted a creature that looked half human and half animal. Three feet tall, it had cloven hoofs. It told Crombie that its name was Kurmos. It was a nature spirit that helped trees to grow.

Kurmos accompanied Crombie back to his apartment, where it stayed for a short time. On a subsequent trip to the garden, Crombie called out to him, and Kurmos appeared. He learned that in earlier ages Kurmos had been the god Pan.

Further Reading

Ash, David, and Peter Hewitt, 1990. *Science of the Gods.* Bath, England: Gateway Books.

Kwan Ti Laslo

Kwan Ti Laslo channels from the Blue Diamond Planet. This planet is not in orbit around a sun (as planets are virtually by definition) but rather is a sort of giant spacecraft that travels all over the universe investigating conditions there. The planet/spacecraft reports its findings to the Intergalactic Council.

In the mid-1970s, it made a brief visit to Earth's vicinity. Earthly astronomers mistook the spacecraft for a comet.

Certain advanced human beings—Kwan Ti Laslo mentioned former presidents Harry Truman and John F. Kennedy specifically—are allowed to come to the Blue Diamond Planet and live there. The planet gives off blue light from its many waterways and temperate climate. There is no environmental pollution. "All highly evolved planets have almost instantaneous cleansing of air and waters," Kwan Ti Laslo explains.

Further Reading

"The Blue Diamond Planet," 1976. *Other World Life Review* 1, 9 (November): 7.

L

Laan-Deeka and Sharanna

In February or early March 1967 a Puerto Rican man named Lester Rosas received several telepathic messages from two Venusians, Laan-Deeka and Sharanna. They promised that they would meet with him face-to-face one day soon.

On the evening of March 31, acting under a strange compulsion, Rosas boarded a bus and took it to the end of the line, which happened to be along a coastal area. He kept walking until he reached a deserted part of the beach. By then it was pitch black, and he was unsure about what he was doing there and for what, or for whom, he was waiting. Then he felt an odd sensation as a man who had shoulder-length hair and was dressed in a close-fitting garment approached him. The man extended his hand, but when Rosas tried to shake his hand, the stranger withdrew it after a mild pressing of palms. He said in Spanish, "Yes, beloved Earth brother, I am Laan-Deeka, of the planet Venus." He went on to state that Venusians had been keeping human beings under surveillance since their primitive origins and had also been living, unnoticed, among them.

Laan-Deeka then commenced to discuss reincarnation, saying that advanced earthlings who obey nature's laws are permitted to live their next lives on spiritually developed planets. In the universe, he said, most communication, even interplanetary and interstellar communication, occurs by telepathy. Human beings are backward, in part, because they fail to realize that telepathy is even possible.

The Venusian led Rosas to the other side of a small nearby wall, where they witnessed the materialization of a flying saucer. A door slid open, and a woman emerged to engage Rosas in a palm-to-palm Venusian handshake. "She was so lovely that I was speechless for a moment," Rosas recalled. "Her hair was long and fair, and she had a fantastic figure. . . . I estimated her measurements at 5'4" and 37-27-35." She introduced herself to Rosas as Sharanna, Laan-Deeka's fiancée.

Though the couple looked to be no more than twenty years old, their manner suggested wiser, older persons. They had high foreheads and slightly slanted eyes, his green, hers blue. There was a musical sound to their voices, a sense of joy in their speech and action.

The three entered the ship and flew off to Venus, which proved to be the paradisiacal world reported by other contactees. On their way to the planet, Sharanna condemned the war in Vietnam as "senseless and stupid—as are all wars." She also criticized those who refused to believe contact stories. If contactees' reports "are sometimes contradictory," she said, "it is with good reason. Your Earth people are contacting space people from different planets and different cultures, in different stages of advancement. . . . Therefore the reports could hardly be the same" (Rosas, 1976).

See Also: Contactees

Further Reading

Rosas, Lester, 1976. "Visits from Venus." *Other World Life Review* Pt. I. 1, 8 (October): 4–5; Pt. II. 1, 9 (December): 3–4.

Lady of Pluto

Kelvin Rowe, an acquaintance of such early contactees as George Adamski and Truman Bethurum, began hearing voices in his head in early 1953. The voices were mostly indistinct, and he was unsure of their meaning. On March 9, 1954, while driving to San Bernardino, California, the word "Pluto" sounded inside his brain three times in succession. Later that month, after further brief messages from beings he identified as Guardians from Space, he requested a direct, in-person meeting. A voice replied that one would happen, but he might not recognize it when it did.

At the Giant Rock Interplanetary Spacecraft Convention in the California desert the following year on April 4, he kept company with Truman Bethurum, whom he had known four years before Bethurum began claiming an association with the spacewoman Aura Rhanes of Clarion. He met three young people, a woman and two men, who looked normal and were friendly. It was only later that Rowe realized that they had said something to him that they could not have known about an earlier trip he had taken to see Bethurum. Rowe wondered if they had been space people, and soon a mental message confirmed that they had been. The message was from the young woman, whom he would call the Lady of Pluto.

In a 1958 book, Rowe recounted the conversation that followed. The Lady of Pluto told him that contact with space people would radically alter earthling science and humankind's beliefs on a range of issues. She also said that earthwomen would be more receptive than earthmen, that by the time the open contact occurred, women would hold positions of authority in business and government. Their influence would ensure that the changes took place without undue conflict and destruction. She promised that in time, when he was ready, he would be permitted to board a spacecraft.

Mental communication with various space people continued over the next months. Eventually, a spaceman came to Rowe's house late one evening. The two had a short conversation via telepathy before the extraterrestrial disappeared into the night. Soon Rowe was regularly seeing flying-saucer people. A week after the first meeting, the same Space Brother and a companion reappeared at his door. He invited them in for a conversation about cosmic and philosophical issues. According to Rowe, "They were fine looking men, with smooth, dark sun-tan complexions, and dark hair styled in longer length than our modern cuts" (Rowe, 1958). Three weeks of saucer sightings and psychic contacts took place. The communicators were a man and woman from Jupiter: the Brother and Sister, Rowe called them. He unexpectedly met them in the flesh for a short while.

His next contact, a few weeks later in January 1955, was with the Lady of Pluto, the first time he had seen her since Giant Rock. She was accompanied by a Space Brother, and Rowe described her as "mettlesome and lovely." She stood five feet three inches tall, wore a blouse, jacket, and slacks "in contrasting tones of a beautiful, pansy-blue, similar to royal blue, and a shade of red-wine in a scintillating, deep intensity." He was told that she was the earthly equivalent of a captain on a spacecraft. She also said that an asteroid was passing dangerously close to Earth but that the space people would make sure it did not cause damage.

Some weeks later, Rowe met the Lady of Pluto again, in the company of the Brother and Sister of Jupiter. On this occasion he was finally permitted to board a landed ship for a few minutes. In due course, Rowe would fly, more than once, into space onboard spacecraft, sometimes with the Lady of Pluto, more often with the Sister of Jupiter. "Some there are who believe UFO's are the greatest mystery of our century," Rowe wrote. "I only hope I have made it clear that there is no mystery connected with them."

See Also: Adamski, George; Aura Rhanes; Bethurum, Truman; Contactees

Further Reading

Rowe, Kelvin, 1958. *A Call at Dawn: A Message from Our Brothers of the Planets Pluto and Jupiter.* El Monte, CA: Understanding Publishing Company.

Land beyond the Pole

According to F. Amadeo Giannini, author of *Worlds beyond the Poles* (1959), Admiral Richard E. Byrd discovered a marvelous new land when he flew 1,700 miles beyond the North Pole during an expedition in 1947. He saw ice-free lakes, mountains, and forests. He even caught a glimpse of an enormous animal walking through the underbrush. In 1956, on a second expedition to the Arctic, he witnessed similar sights. Giannini claimed that the U.S. government had sworn Byrd to silence after he first hinted of his discoveries in his 1947 interviews with the *New York Times.*

Giannini, characterized as the "archetypal crank" by one critic (Kafton-Minkel, 1989), believed that Byrd's alleged experience verified his—Giannini's—belief that the Earth is not round but more or less spindle-shaped; at each spindle point the surface, instead of ending, curves back overhead. The universe consists not of space but of vast land, "physical continuity" he called it. What appear to humans as stars, planets, galaxies, and other phenomena in the distant cosmos are only "globular and isolated areas of a continuous and unbroken outer sky surface." His original inspiration, he wrote, was a mystical vision he experienced while strolling through a New England forest one day in 1926.

Published as a vanity-press (that is, at the author's expense) book, *Worlds beyond the Poles* would have passed quickly into oblivion if not for the fact that Ray Palmer, editor of *Flying Saucers* and promoter of the Shaver Mystery, read the book after receiving a review copy. Always looking for an issue to stir up his readers, Palmer wrote of Byrd's supposed secret flight to argue that the Earth is hollow with giant holes at the poles. Anyone entering the holes will encounter a hidden world harboring an intelligent civilization that builds and flies superaircraft that are called UFOs. Palmer got the Byrd story from Giannini but did not mention him, claiming that he had gotten his information from "years of research" (Palmer, 1959). A number of readers pointed out that the *New York Times* stories about Byrd's expedition did not quote him as saying anything about forests or a giant beast; even worse, in 1947 and 1956, Byrd was at the South, not the North, Pole. Palmer was forced to acknowledge that his sole source was Giannini. Unapologetic, he went on to speculate that perhaps Byrd had made a secret flight to the Arctic in 1947; either that, or "a deliberate effort was being made to build an edifice which could be toppled IF AND WHEN THE TRUTH CAME OUT ABOUT THE SOUTH POLE!" (Palmer, 1960). And if neither of these were true, the question of which pole Byrd had flown over was moot since Byrd had encountered a lush, green landscape where none should have existed and that, in the end, was all that mattered—notwithstanding the nonexistence of any documentation that Byrd had made any such claim in the first place. Giannini soon weighed in to attack Palmer's hollow earth interpretation and to argue for a secret Arctic expedition by Byrd in 1947, which was followed by a suppression of his discoveries.

In the 1970s, a Missouri-based organization called the International Society for a Complete Earth, headed by retired marine corps officer Tawani Shoush, who was also a Modoc Indian, issued what it claimed was a secret diary that Byrd kept during his 1947

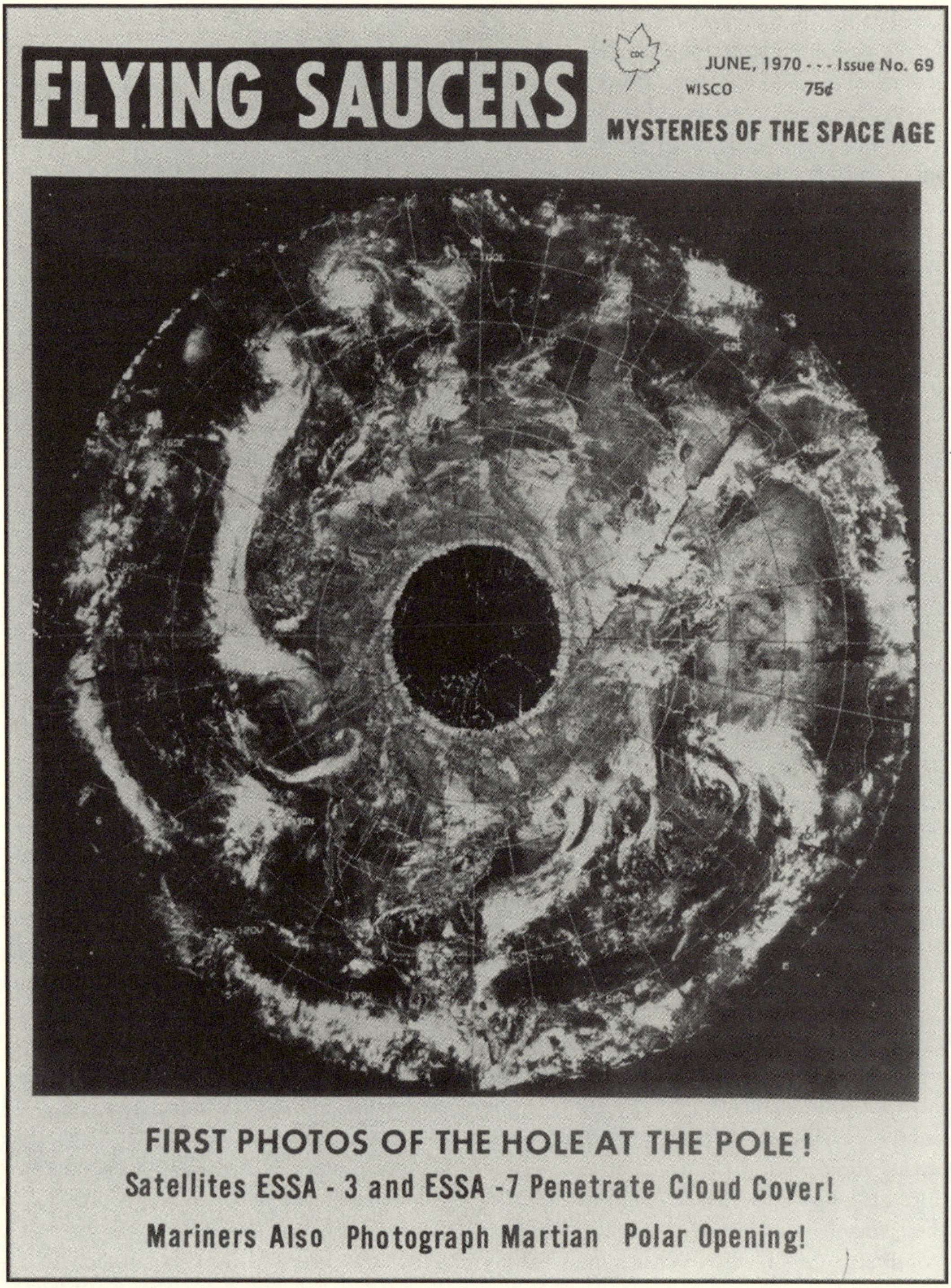

Cover of Flying Saucers *magazine, June 1970, with a November 1968 satellite photo allegedly showing the hole in the North Pole leading to the interior of hollow earth (Fortean Picture Library)*

North Pole expedition. Written in an amateurish, pulpy style, strikingly unlike the erudite prose found in Byrd's undisputed published works, the diary has Byrd and his radio operator passing over a green landscape and spotting a "mammoth," while the temperature rises to seventy-four degrees. Soon the two men spot three flying saucers with swastika insignias (perhaps not coincidentally, Shoush's group held that the inner-earthers, a Teutonic race known as the Arianni, favor the swastika). The saucers take control of Byrd's plane and lead it to a city "pulsating with rainbow hues of color." There they meet the Arianni and engage in conversation with an aged, wise man known as the Master. The Master warns that human beings are insufficiently advanced to be fooling with something as dangerous as atomic energy. The diary's last entry, supposedly written shortly before Byrd's death in 1957, says, "I have faithfully kept this matter secret as directed all these years. It has been completely against my values of moral right."

Though unsupported by any evidence, the story of Byrd's flight beyond the pole became a staple of hollow-earth literature. As late as 1993, Timothy Green Beckley was asking, "Was it because of Admiral Byrd's weird flight into an unknown Polar land in 1947 that the International Geophysical Year was conceived in that year, and finally brought to fruition ten years later, and is actually still going on? Did his flight make it suddenly imperative to discover the real nature of this planet we live on, and solve the tremendous mysteries that unexpectedly confronted us?" (Beckley, 1993).

Dennis G. Crenshaw, editor of *The Hollow Earth Insider Research Report,* expresses a view that is at once skeptical and conspiratorial. He notes that when the diary quotes some of the Master's words, those words bear an unsettling resemblance to those spoken by the Dalai Lama of Shangri-La in the classic 1937 film *Lost Horizon.* He also bluntly charges that Tawani Shoush and his group forged the diary. Nonetheless, he sees a sinister hand in all of this. Byrd's polar expeditions were in the service of the "paymasters" of the "Illuminati and . . . a New World Order . . . John D. Rocherfeller [sic] and his pals." Moreover, Giannini himself consciously served the conspiracy. From uncertain evidence, Crenshaw concludes that Giannini's family "*owned* the Bank of Italy and the Bank of America." He goes on, "If, as my research seems to indicate, it is the One Worlders' plan to hide what is going on at the earth's poles, what better way to cloud the water, so to speak, than to have one of their own, an admitted member of an international banking family, toss in a controversy—such as this phony trip by Admiral Byrd—to make hollow earthers appear as ridiculous[?]" (Crenshaw, 1996).

See Also: Hollow earth; Shaver mystery

Further Reading

Beckley, Timothy Green, ed., 1993. *The Smoky God and Other Inner Earth Mysteries.* New Brunswick, NJ: Inner Light Publications.

Crenshaw, Dennis G., 1996. "The Missing Diary of Admiral Byrd: Fact or Fiction?" *The Hollow Earth Insider Research Report* 4, 1: 8–15.

———, 1997. "Admiral Byrd's 1939 Antarctic Expedition and the Mysterious Snow Cruiser." *The Hollow Earth Insider Research Report* 4, 2: 4–16.

A Flight to the Land beyond the North Pole, or Is This the Missing Secret Diary of Admiral Richard Evelyn Byrd? n.d. Houston, MO: International Society for a Complete Earth.

Giannini, Amadeo F., 1959. *Worlds beyond the Poles.* New York: Vantage Press.

Kafton-Minkel, Walter, 1989. *Subterranean Worlds: 100,000 Years of Dragons, Dwarfs, the Dead, Lost Races, and UFOs from inside the Earth.* Port Townsend, WA: Loompanics Unlimited.

Palmer, Ray, 1959. "Saucers from Earth! A Challenge to Secrecy!" *Flying Saucers* (December): 8–21.

———, 1960. "Editorial." *Flying Saucers* (February): 4, 29–34.

———, 1961. "'Byrd *Did* Make North Pole Flight in Feb., 1947!'—Giannini." *Flying Saucers* (February): 4–11.

Lanello

In his most recent incarnation on Earth, Lanello, an Ascended Master, was Mark L. Prophet (1918–1973), married to Elizabeth Clare Prophet of the Church Universal and Triumphant. Since then, as Lanello, he has channeled through Prophet and Carolyn Shearer.

Lanello first came to Earth thousands of years ago from his native Venus after Sanat Kumara—the brother of Sananda (Jesus) and sometimes called Earth's planetary spirit—determined to save the human race from destroying itself. Over the centuries Lanello went through many incarnations, all in fulfillment of his earthly mission. In his lives, he has been an Atlantean priest, Noah, Lot, Amenhotep IV, Bodhidharma (founder of Zen Buddhism), Aesop, Pericles, Mark the Evangelist, Lancelot, Saladin, King Louis XIV (the Sun King), Hiawatha, and Henry Wadsworth Longfellow, among others.

See Also: Ascended Masters; Sananda

Further Reading

"Ascended Master Lanello: 'I Am Here and I Am There! I Am Everywhere in the Consciousness of God!'" n.d. http://www.ascension-research.org/lanello.html.

Laskon

James Hill, who lived on a farm near Seymour, Missouri, experienced numerous flying-saucer sightings and contacts with their occupants, beginning in 1940. The contacts occurred through his radio or via mental telepathy. Eventually, a saucer landed, and as Hill watched, the crew let out a large dog, which went under a tree and gave birth to pups. Hill kept one of the Venusian pups, named Queenie. Hill's principal contact over time was with Brother Laskon, a member of the Solar Tribunal on Saturn.

According to Laskon, Jesus is a frequent space traveler who visits the many inhabited planets. When he is in our system, he stays on Mars and Saturn, but most of his time is spent on Venus because of its loveliness. Laskon knew Bucky, an earthman living on Venus and the frequent contact of another Missouri contactee (and friend of Hill), Buck Nelson. Laskon also was able to confirm Chief Frank Buck Standing Horse's trip to the planet Oreon in the summer of 1959. Saturn, which houses the Solar Tribunal, is a beautiful planet where greatly advanced, spiritually wise beings reside. The twelve Elder Ones who compose the tribunal "are the names of all of the prophets in the biblical times," Laskon has said (Dean, 1964). Like Jesus, a senior member of the tribunal, they flew to Earth in spaceships, spent their time here, and then departed in the same way. Moses, however, lives on Venus, where he serves on the Supreme Council. John the Baptist returned to Earth in the 1950s and even attended a contactee convention in Los Angeles in July l959.

See Also: Andra-o-leeka and Mondra-o-leeka; Contactees

Further Reading

Dean, John W., 1964. *Flying Saucers and the Scriptures.* New York: Vantage Press.

Lazaris

Lazaris first spoke to Jach Pursel, a Florida regional insurance supervisor with no interest in the New Age or occult, after his wife, Peny, urged him to meditate as a way of easing job-related stress. Instead of meditating, Pursel fell asleep. Soon an oddly accented voice was speaking through him. Though startled and even frightened, Peny grabbed pen and paper and started asking questions. The entity said its name was "Lazaris."

The channeling continued for years with Lazaris relating a philosophy rather like that associated with other popular channeled entities of the period, including Ramtha and Seth. In this philosophy, humans are evolving spiritual beings who need to gain access to the divine intelligence that is within each of them.

Lazaris became hugely popular, and at the peak of Lazaris's fame on the New Age circuit, Pursel was channeling as much as forty hours a week, with Peny—from whom he was now divorced—and her new husband managing the business. Lazaris, who always used the plural pronoun when speaking, told writer Jon Klimo, "We are always in a state of expansion. We have no boundary. We have no edge of who we are, and yet we know who we are. We know where we begin and end, although there is no form. . . . We have always been and we will always be; and therefore, we are always constantly exploring our awareness, gathering data, gathering insight, gathering vibration and internalizing that vibration. We are always everywhere and nowhere simultaneously" (Klimo, 1987).

See Also: Channeling; Ramtha; Seth

Further Reading

Klimo, Jon, 1987. *Channeling: Investigations on Receiving Information from Paranormal Sources.* Los Angeles: J. P. Tarcher.

Martin, Katherine, 1987. "The Voice of Lazaris." *New Realities* 7, 6 (July/August): 26–33.

Pursel, Jach, 1987. *Lazaris, The Sacred Journey: You and Your Higher Self.* Beverly Hills, CA: Concept Synergy.

———, 1988. *Lazaris Interviews.* Two volumes. Beverly Hills, CA: Concept Synergy.

Lemuria

Lemuria was the invention of British zoologist Philip L. Schattler, who conceived of it as an Indian Ocean land bridge connecting Madagascar and extreme southern India. Schattler, who was researching animal populations, sought to explain why these two widely separated locations shared many of the same flora and fauna. (In the twentieth century, continental drift theory rendered Schattler's hypothesis obsolete.) He called the postulated land bridge "Lemuria," after the lemurs, animals that the two areas shared in common. Before long, however, occultists and mystics would incorporate the concept of Lemuria—now conceived of as a lost continent in the Pacific Ocean—into their own alternative histories.

For a time, however, Lemuria remained a scientifically respectable hypothesis. One major champion, German evolutionary biologist Ernst Haeckel, speculated that *Homo sapiens* originated on Lemuria, though that could not be proved because any remains had sunk to the bottom of the sea along with the land

A science fiction novella about Lemuria by Richard S. Shaver and Ray Palmer in Amazing Stories, *March 1945 (Fortean Picture Library)*

bridge. Others theorized that Lemuria was just part of a vast continent, called Gondwanaland, which had circled most of the Southern Hemisphere, leaving only a patch of the Pacific Ocean uncovered. None of the scientists argued that either Lemuria or Gondwanaland had survived into historical time.

Lemuria entered the occult tradition through Helene Petrovna Blavatsky, founder of Theosophy. In *The Secret Doctrine* (1889), Blavatsky wrote that the present human race evolved through a series of "root races." The third root race lived on Lemuria. These beings had three eyes, one in the back of the head, and were egg-laying hermaphrodites (possessing attributes of both sexes); some had four arms. Aside from these features, they were generally apelike in appearance.

Other occult writers went on to create their own Lemurians. Through "astral clairvoyance" the English theosophist W. Scott-Elliot learned that it was on Lemuria that human beings entered physical bodies. The original Lemurians were twelve to fifteen feet tall, had flat faces and muzzles, and no foreheads. Their eyes were set so far apart that their vision extended sideways, and they had a third eye behind their heads. Eventually, these beings began to practice sex, and the Lhas, spirit entities who were to inhabit the bodies and guide them through evolution, were so repulsed that they refused their duty. The Lords of the Flame, advanced Venusians, took over and guided the Lemurians into a more human and spiritual state. During the Mesozoic era Lemuria began to break up, and one of its peninsulas became Atlantis.

In the late nineteenth century, archaeologist Augustus Le Plongeon, working in the Yucatan, believed he had discovered how to translate Mayan hieroglyphics. His translations, which other scholars judged dubious, led him to believe that he had uncovered evidence of a lost civilization known as Mu. He assumed Mu to be Atlantis. After his death, however, his friend James Churchward, who had inherited Le Plungeon's papers, argued that Mu, "the motherland of man," had been in the South Pacific, not in the Atlantic. Mu housed a white population of some sixty-four million souls who had built great cities and worshipped the sun. Mu sank beneath the sea ten thousand years ago. Churchward claimed to have learned about Mu from tablets written in the dead Naacal language. He had been given access to them, he said, while serving in India in the Bengal Lancers. Churchward wrote about his "findings" in four books, beginning with *The Lost Continent of Mu* (1926). His failure to produce any evidence that the Naacal tablets existed outside his imagination sparked hoax charges that Churchward never successfully refuted.

Soon Mu and Lemuria were assumed to be the same place, and thus Lemuria became a Pacific equivalent to the Atlantic's Atlantis. In the early years of the twentieth century, speculation grew that California was a surviving fragment of Lemuria. A popular occult legend, apparently originating in a 1908 article in *The Overland Monthly,* held—and still holds—that a surviving Lemurian colony lives inside Mount Shasta, on the California-Oregon border. According to *Lemuria: The Lost Continent of the Pacific* (1931), by H. Spencer Lewis (writing as Wishar S. Cerve), when Lemuria broke up, a California-sized part of it crashed into North America's west coast and attached itself. In 1936, Robert Stelle of Chicago founded the Lemurian Fellowship, based on his channeled messages from Lemurians living inside Mount Shasta. In two books published between 1940 and 1952, Stelle depicted Lemuria as an enormous land mass and a lost paradise.

In the mid-1940s, the Ziff-Davis science-fiction magazines *Amazing Stories* and *Fantastic Adventures* ran a series of stories and allegedly factual articles based in part on Richard S. Shaver's "memories" of life in Lemuria, some of whose inhabitants still reside under the earth. Most have gone mad and use the advanced technology available to them to torment surface-dwellers.

Lemuria was incorporated into the flying saucer-based alternative realities proposed by the contactees and channelers who came along in the late 1940s and 1950s amid popular speculation about visitation from other planets. The Pacific lost continent played a prominent role in George Hunt Williamson's speculative books *Other Tongues—Other Flesh* (1953), *Secret Places of the Lion* (1958), and *Road in the Sky* (1959), which laid out an ancient history in which Lemurians and Atlanteans interacted freely with a variety of extraterrestrial races.

Now an assumed reality in just about any metaphysical, New Age, hollow earth, or saucerian worldview, Lemuria sooner or later enters just about any discussion predicated on the assumption that everything humans think they know about the ancient history of Earth and the human race is wrong.

See Also: Atlantis; Contactees; Hollow earth; Mount Shasta; Shaver mystery; Williamson, George Hunt

Further Reading

Blavatsky, Helene P., 1889. *The Secret Doctrine.* Two volumes. London: Theosophical Publishing Company.

Churchward, James, 1926. *The Lost Continent of Mu.* New York: Ives Washburn.

De Camp, L. Sprague, 1970. *Lost Continents: The Atlantis Theme in History, Science, and Literature.* New York: Dover Publications.

Kafton-Minkel, Walter, 1989. *Subterranean Worlds: 100,000 Years of Dragons, Dwarfs, the Dead, Lost Races and UFOs from inside the Earth.* Port Townsend, WA: Loompanics Unlimited.

Scott-Elliot, W., 1925. *The Story of Atlantis and the Lost Lemuria.* London: Theosophical Publishing House.

Shaver, Richard S., 1945. "I Remember Lemuria!" *Amazing Stories* 19, 1 (March): 12–70.

Williamson, George Hunt, 1953. *Other Tongues—Other Flesh.* Amherst, WI: Amherst Press.

———, 1958. *Secret Places of the Lion.* London: Neville Spearman.

———, 1959. *Road in the Sky.* London: Neville Spearman.

Lethbridge's aeronauts

In the spring of 1909, the British Isles were inundated with sightings of enigmatic objects that some people called "airships." Popular and official opinion concurred that German spies were involved, though it is now known that no such German surveillance was occurring or, for that matter, was even technically achievable. One man claimed to have seen an airship land and to have observed its crew.

Press accounts identify this witness as C. Lethbridge, described in a press account as "an elderly man, of quiet demeanor, [who] did not strike one as given to romancing." During the winter, Lethbridge was a dock worker in Cardiff. In the warmer months, he performed puppet shows in the towns and villages of Wales. Around 11 on the evening of May 18, returning home across remote Caerphilly Mountain, he rounded a bend at the summit and was taken aback to see something unusual lying along the side of the road. His first impression was that it was "some big bird." Standing next to it were two tall men clad in heavy fur coats and tight-fitting fur caps. Their bearing and smart appearance led him to think of them as military officers. They were working at something, but Lethbridge was not close enough to see what it was.

When he got within twenty to thirty yards of them, they reacted to the rattle of his spring-cart and jumped up as if startled. They "jabbered furiously to each other in a strange lingo—Welsh or something else; it was certainly not English." Retrieving something on the ground, they ran to a carriage underneath the object, which then ascended in a zigzag motion. Two lights on its side suddenly came on. Emitting an "awful noise," the craft flew higher and set off in the direction of Cardiff.

After Lethbridge told his story in that city, investigators rushed to the site. If not for that circumstance, the episode would have the appearance of an early close encounter of the third kind. Indeed, it is published in some UFO literature as just that. Most accounts leave out what the investigators found at the site: a variety of artifacts including parts of letters, a spare part for a tire valve, papier-mâché wads, blue paper containing figures and letters, and clippings about airships. All of this suggests, or at least seems intended to convey, the notion that the airship crew consisted of foreign spies.

Though nothing is known about the incident beyond what appears in Welsh and English newspapers of the period, the story seems suspect. The first chronicler of the UFO phenomenon, Charles Fort, remarked that "anybody else [who] wants to think that these foreigners were explorers from Mars or the moon" (Fort, 1941) was free to do so, but he himself suspected a hoax. Because no foreign spies were engaged in aerial surveillance of Britain in 1909, it is hard to imagine another explanation.

Coincidentally or otherwise, during a wave of UFO reports in France in the fall of 1954, a railroad worker at Monlucon claimed that one evening he encountered a tube-shaped craft. Outside it stood a man dressed in what looked like a long, hairy overcoat. When the witness addressed the figure, the latter responded in an unknown language. The witness left the scene to report it to his supervisor, but when the two returned, the UFO and the hairy-coated figure were gone.

See Also: Close encounters of the third kind

Further Reading

Fort, Charles, 1941. *The Books of Charles Fort.* New York: Henry Holt and Company.

Grove, Carl, 1971. "The Airship Wave of 1909." *Flying Saucer Review* 17, 1 (January/February): 17–19.

Vallee, Jacques, 1974. "The Pattern behind the UFO Landings." In Charles Bowen, ed. *The Humanoids,* 27–76. London: Futura Publications.

Li Sung

Li Sung, said to be the spirit of a village philosopher who lived in northern China in the eighth century, channeled through Alan Vaughan. Vaughan, a longtime writer on psychic phenomena, first experienced Li Sung in 1983, but sixteen years earlier, three British mediums had told him he would be communicating with this Chinese spirit. Vaughan said he did not believe them. But one day, while he was teaching at a psychic seminar in Sedona, Arizona, a couple asked him—he was then editing a publication called *Reincarnation Report*—if he could divine their past lives.

"Suddenly a tremendous energy flooded over the top of my head," he would recall. "It was like watching a dream, as the Chinese entity Li Sung began to speak through me. He gave them some detailed information about past lives and how they fit into their present life paths. For me, it was the beginning of an enlargement of consciousness" (Shepard, 1991).

Vaughan went on to channel Li Sung in public on many occasions. Vaughan contends that anyone can channel if he or she wants to. It is, he asserts, as easy as learning how to whistle.

See Also: Channeling

Further Reading

Klimo, Jon, 1987. *Channeling: Investigations on Receiving Information from Paranormal Sources.* Los Angeles: Jeremy P. Tarcher.

Shepard, Leslie A., 1991. *Encyclopedia of Occultism and Parapsychology: A Compendium of Information on the Occult Sciences, Magic, Demonology, Superstitions, Spiritism, Mysticism, Metaphysics, Psychical Science, and Parapsychology, with Biographical and Bibliographical Notes and Comprehensive Indexes.* Third edition. Detroit, MI: Gale Research.

Linn-Erri

Linn-Erri introduced herself to Robert P. Renaud one night in July 1961. A Pittsfield, Massachusetts, ham-radio buff and General Electric technician, Renaud heard beeping sounds from his radio and then heard a lovely female voice asking him to stay on the frequency for a while. She told him, "I am called Linn-Erri, and my associates and I come from the planet Korendor. We are speaking to you from our spaceship many miles above your earth" (Clark, 1986). She and her fellow Korendorians had chosen to contact him because they knew of his interest in UFOs, world peace, and the future of humankind. After Linn-Erri introduced him to other crewmembers, she explained how Renaud could construct a transmitter for easy reception of future messages from space. Later that year, the space people helped him convert a television set to receive their transmissions. For the first time, he saw the beautiful Linn-Erri and was shocked to learn that she was seventy-four Earth years old.

In due course, Renaud was meeting personally with the Korendorians, riding in their ships, and learning their science and philosophy, which was essentially indistinguishable in its essentials from that widely recounted in saucerian literature. He stayed away from the contactee lecture and convention circuit and confined his public activities to a series of articles about his alleged experiences in a metaphysically oriented saucer magazine. He also produced dubious-looking photographs of supposed spacecraft.

To outward appearances, nothing distinguished Renaud from many others making outlandish and not very believable claims. Still, ufologist Allan Grise, an interested but highly skeptical observer of the contactee scene, found Renaud a fascinating and enigmatic figure. "If Renaud was engaged in fraud," he said years later, "it was preposterous, unrewarding fraud."

Grise visited Renaud at his home and found, as the contactee's writings asserted, a basement room full of electronic equipment, including the television set and the short-wave radio over which the communications supposedly were effected. Grise, an engineer by profession and ham-radio buff by avocation, found that "everything seemed to make sense. The circuits were all appropriate to extend the receiving range." In other words, if he was getting messages from an aerial source, he had the equipment with which to receive them.

More remarkable, however, were the books Renaud was writing on Korendorian life and philosophy. There were a dozen or so of them, all single-spaced, each five hundred to six hundred pages long. There were, so far as Grise could discern from studying their contents, no typographical errors. But that was not all.

"When he wrote those books," Grise recalled, "it was like his hands belonged to someone else. He'd sit there in front of his typewriter and pay no attention to what was coming out of him. He'd be on the phone or talking with me, and all the while his hands are going, producing this perfectly typed, clearly written stuff on alien philosophy. It was just unbelievable." Renaud seemed singularly uninterested in promoting himself and volunteered nothing, though he would answer questions.

Renaud also had a large collection of tapes allegedly of his space communications. Grise listened to some of them and heard what was supposed to be the voice of Linn-Erri. The recordings, of excellent quality, carried a voice with "a kind of hesitancy in speech patterns suggesting a foreign person doing well in English. It had a singsong, melodious quality."

Soon afterward, Renaud broke off his brief association with Grise. He ceased all contact activities, telling his publisher that he had done his part and wanted no more of it. By the end of the 1960s, Renaud had dropped out of sight. In 1985, Renaud still puzzled Grise. "Something quite out of the normal was going on," he said. "Whatever it was."

See Also: Contactees

Further Reading

Clark, Jerome, 1986. "Waiting for the Space Brothers." *Fate* Pt. I. 39, 3 (March): 47–54; Pt. II. 39, 4 (April): 81–87; Pt. III. 39, 5 (May): 68–76.

Luno

Luno was one of a number of Space Brothers who communicated through Lorraine Darr of Rochester, Minnesota. In the mid-1970s, she and her husband, Victor, performed psychic healing under the direction of friendly extraterrestrials whom the couple occasionally glimpsed in apparitional form. Vic also underwent out-of-body trips that took him into spaceships. Sometimes they took him to Venus, where he used his healing talents to cure ailing natives. The couple also believed that while in meditative states they entered other dimensions. Other Space Brothers who helped the Darrs included Becovol, Norbol, Muello, Maynell, and Julo.

Further Reading

Steiger, Brad, 1976. *Gods of Aquarius: UFOs and the Transformation of Man.* New York: Harcourt Brace Jovanovich.

Lyrans

According to the channeling entity Germane, human ancestors interacted with Lyrans, members of an extraterrestrial race that functioned as stern, authoritarian teachers. Early humans both revered and feared them. They were sturdy, large, light-skinned people. Their symbols were birds, cats, and the phoenix. The phoenix image was an invention of theirs, intended to symbolize the indestructibility of their empire. They did not hold earthlings in high regard and hoped that the Great Flood would destroy all of them, so that the Lyrans could start over with a new, improved civilization. Other, more kindly disposed extraterrestrials, however, warned Noah and others, and humanity was saved.

Travel to Earth from the Lyran system took generations. Thus, once the Lyrans arrived here, they could never leave. They lost all contact with their home world and eventually intermarried with native earthlings. Back on Lyra the inhabitants continued to evolve and advance into highly spiritual beings, but their cousins stranded on Earth did not.

See Also: Channeling; Germane

Further Reading

Royal, Lyssa, 1994. "ET Civilizations—Germane." http://www.lemuria.net/article-et-civilizations.html.

M

Mafu

Mafu channeled through Penny Torres of Los Angeles, beginning in 1986. Thirty-two thousand years old, Mafu claimed to have passed through seventeen incarnations on Earth. He taught that God is in everything and everyone, and everything and everyone is in God. Beyond that, he championed a macrobiotic diet, meditation, and the adoption of a spiritual path.

In 1989, Torres, now Penny Torres Rubin, made a pilgrimage to Hardiwar, India, in the Himalayan foothills. She refashioned herself with the title and name of Swami Paramananda Saraswatti. Back in the United States she created the Foundation for the Realization of Inner Divinity and a subsidiary, the Center for God Realization. Through these she has disseminated Mafu's teachings.

For a time Mafu was among the most popular channeling entities on the New Age scene of the late 1980s and early 1990s. He was sometimes said to be little more than a clone of the famous Ramtha, channeled by the controversial J. Z. Knight, though at one point Torres Rubin charged that Ramtha was nothing more than a fraud.

See Also: Channeling; Ramtha

Further Reading

"Interview: Penny Torres on Mafu," 1986/1987. *Life Times* 1, 2 (Winter): 74–79.

L'Ecuyer, Michele, 1986/1987. "Mafu." *Life Times* 1, 2 (Winter): 80–82.

Melton, J. Gordon, 1996. *Encyclopedia of American Religions.* Detroit, MI: Gale Research.

Magonia

The concept of Magonia entered the literature of ufology in a 1964 issue of England's *Flying Saucer Review.* Ancient-astronaut theorist W. R. Drake, author of a series of pieces highlighting what he judged to be evidence of extraterrestrial visitation, briefly cited a ninth-century French account of a "ship in clouds" from a place called "Magonia." A slightly longer version appeared in Jacques Vallee's *Passport to Magonia* (1969), in which Vallee went on to turn "Magonia" into the unknown realm from which many unexplained phenomena—everything from elves to demons to UFO humanoids—emerge. He defined Magonia as "a sort of parallel universe, which coexists with our own. It is made visible and tangible only to selected people" (Vallee, 1969). In his view, each culture experiences Magonia in a fashion that conforms to its own expectations concerning supernatural encounters. Thus, rural Ireland experiences fairies, while Space Age America has its ostensible extraterrestrials. Vallee did not mean to imply that these experiences were purely hallucinatory; he was convinced of an underlying but impenetrable reality forever disguised under many masks. A British magazine, still published, named itself *Magonia* after Vallee's book, though the magazine rejects paranormal explanations of such phenomena.

The Magonia story appeared originally in a circa 833 manuscript written in Latin by Agobard (779–840), the Archbishop of Lyons. The title in English is "Book Against False Opinions Concerning Hail and Thunder." Agobard was fiercely hostile to all non-Christian beliefs. One that particularly infuriated him was the "mad and blind" belief that "there exists a certain region called Magonia, from which ships, navigating on clouds, set sail to transport back to this same region the fruits of the earth ruined by hail and destroyed by the storm." Agobard tells of "several of these senseless fools" who held in custody "three men and one woman, who they said had fallen from these ships." The prisoners were brought in front of an assembly to be stoned to death, but the archbishop managed to save their lives, after "the truth finally triumphed" and he had shown up the absurdity of the charges (Brodu, 1995).

In a critical analysis of the legend, French anomalist Jean-Louis Brodu reviewed Magonia's various uses over the centuries as well as the embellishments that attached themselves to it. In the UFO age, the sketchy account was variously represented as a landing with aliens or an early abduction case. Some accounts twisted details and reported that the captives had been stoned to death, Agobard's explicit words to the contrary. Surveying the scholarly literature on the Magonian tales, Brodu argues that Agobard's account makes no sense outside the context of the period, which included the belief that the Earth is flat and that ships can sail through cloud seas. "Magonia" may be a corruption of "Magonianus," meaning "from Port-Mahon," a once-flourishing harbor on the Balearic island of Minorca.

See Also: Abductions by UFOs; Fairies encountered

Further Reading

Brodu, Jean-Louis, 1995. "Magonia: A Re-evaluation." In Steve Moore, ed. *Fortean Studies: Volume 2,* 198–215. London: John Brown Publishing.

Drake, W. R., 1964. "Spacemen in the Middle Ages." *Flying Saucer Review*10, 3 (May/June): 11–13.

Vallee, Jacques, 1969. *Passport to Magonia: From Folklore to Flying Saucers.* Chicago: Henry Regnery Company.

Marian apparitions

Visions of the Blessed Virgin Mary (BVM) have been reported since at least the third century of the Christian era. The first for which there is anything approximating detailed knowledge dates back to 1061 when the BVM provided a vision of Christ's residence in Nazareth and directed the witness, the lady of the manor in Walsingham, Norfolk, to see that a precise copy was constructed on the spot. A few visions are well known, and the Roman Catholic Church has granted official recognition to a small number, though it has rejected the vast majority as delusional. BVM encounters are far from rare. Every year several occur around the world. With very few exceptions, the primary witnesses are Catholics, and usually devout followers of the faith. Sometimes other supernatural phenomena accompany the BVM's manifestation and become, to the faithful, veridical evidence that the event was real.

Undoubtedly the most spectacular such case took place in Fatima, Portugal, in 1917. The incident is extraordinarily complicated. What follows is a highly abbreviated account.

Around noon on May 13, three children, two girls and a boy, tending sheep, saw a flash of light and observed a brilliantly illuminated figure of a woman standing amid the branches of an oak tree. The apparition announced that she was from heaven and would return six times, on each occasion on the thirteenth of each succeeding month. On the last visitation in October, she would tell them who she was and why she had come. Soon word spread, and by June 13 some sixty persons accompa-

The Vision of Our Lady of Fatima (Fortean Picture Library)

nied the children. Though the BVM appeared, no one but the children saw her, and the communication, which predicted the deaths of the two younger children in the near future (they died in 1919 and 1920), occurred through the oldest child, Lucia de Santos, who was told that she would live long as a witness to the living reality of Mary.

Ever larger groups followed the children to the site in the succeeding months. In August, the BVM asked that a chapel be built at the site of her appearances. On September 13, some members of the crowd, estimated to be between twenty-five and thirty thousand persons, reported seeing the passage from east to west of a mysterious globe-shaped light. A month later, the number of pilgrims had swelled to seventy thousand. The BVM—as always, visible only to the children—appeared at noon during a blinding rainstorm. The three saw her, Joseph, and the child Jesus standing in the sky near the sun. Meanwhile, some in the crowd saw, or thought they saw, the sun begin to "dance" dramatically through the clouds, spinning and shooting colors, as the rain let up.

In the 1940s, in her memoirs, Lucia de Santos, since 1925 a Carmelite nun, revealed two of three "secrets" the BVM had imparted to her. Although open to other interpretations, the prophecies were thought by most believers to refer to the end of World War I and the start of World War II and to the end of Soviet Communism and the conversion of the Russians to Catholicism. The third secret was sent to the Vatican in the 1950s. It became the focus of much speculation, most of it alleging that it predicted a third world war. In May 2000, however, as Pope John Paul II embarked on a pilgrimage to Fatima, during which he spoke with the ninety-three-year-old Lucia, the Vatican released the prophecy, which he believed predicted the 1981 assassination attempt on the pope in St. Peter's Square—an interpretation disputed by others.

The first New World appearance of the BVM is said to have taken place five miles north of Mexico City just after dawn on December 9, 1531. A fifty-seven-year-old Aztec Indian, Juan Diego, was racing along a hillside to get to mass in a nearby village. Passing a site at the foot of a hill called Tepeyac, which earlier had housed a temple to the Aztec Mother Goddess, he heard a feminine voice calling his name. He saw a young woman, looking about fourteen years old and having Mexican features, who asked that a chapel be built at the site. She also told him that he should alert the bishop in Mexico City immediately. With some difficulty, he got an audience with the bishop, who was skeptical. Diego returned to report his failure to the BVM, who was waiting for him. She instructed him to return the next day. This time the bishop asked for a sign.

That same day, Diego's uncle, who was seriously ill, had a vision of the BVM and was cured. Meanwhile, Diego repeated the bishop's request to the apparition. She told him to pick roses from the hillside (though they should have been out of season). He was instructed to wrap them in his long outer cape (known as a tilma) and to take them to the bishop. When he did so, he unrolled the tilma and was as shocked as the bishop and his associates when the cape turned out to contain a full-color image of the BVM. To this day the tilma is displayed in a Mexico City church, where thousands of pilgrims come to see it every year.

To skeptics, the figure gives every indication of having been painted on the cloth. They also point out that the figure has more to do with conventional iconography of the period than with otherworldly manifestation. They have also raised questions about the provenance of Juan Diego's story, suggesting it is based on an earlier Spanish legend. Still, whatever the truth, the story and the image have proved equally durable and to the faithful remain powerful symbols of Mary's continuing interest in the Church and its believers.

A third major BVM appearance occurred at Knock, a small village in western Ireland's County Mayo, in 1879. A commission of inquiry set up by John McHale, the Archbishop of Tuam, investigated it soon afterward. On the evening of August 21, Mary Beirne, a middle-aged housekeeper for the local priest, was walking by the chapel when she was surprised to see three "beautiful" figures, one resembling the BVM, the other St. Joseph, the third a bishop, standing motionlessly near an altar. A white light surrounded them. She thought someone had put on a display of statues. She went to a friend's house and stayed for half an hour. When she and her friend Mary McLoughlin were on their way back to the priest's house, her friend remarked on the figures. She ran off to notify relatives. Meanwhile, Beirne watched the scene carefully, later providing this description to investigators:

> I beheld . . . not only the three figures, but an altar further on the left of the figure of the Blessed Virgin Mary, and to the left of the bishop and above the altar a lamb about the size of that which is five weeks old. Behind the lamb appeared the cross; it was a bit away from the lamb, while the latter stood in front from it, and not resting on the wood of the cross. Around the lamb a number of gold-like stars appeared in the form of a halo. This altar was placed right under the window of the gable and more to the east of the figures, all, of course, outside the church at Knock. (McClure, 1983)

The other witnesses came to the scene and observed the motionless figures. Though it was raining all the while, they would report, the ground around the figures remained dry. Yet when Mary Beirne's mother approached to kiss the BVM's feet, she felt nothing. She could see the figures, but she could not touch them. Eventually, the figures faded away. All in all, at least fifteen persons saw them. Knock is now a major destination for Marian pilgrims.

The tradition of Marian apparitions has continued unabated into modern times. In 1999, on the eve of the millennium, visionaries were encountering the BVM in Germany, New Hampshire, Illinois, El Salvador, Ontario, and elsewhere. Most prophecies related with these visions asserted that nuclear warfare would erupt before the end of the year. During the conflict for custody of six-year-old Cuban refugee Elian Gonzalez, some of Elian's Miami relatives claimed to have seen the BVM, manifesting, they asserted, to show her support for their belief that the boy should be kept in their custody instead of his Cuban father's.

Secular treatments of BVM apparitions range from conventional views—for example, that hysteria, hoax, and hallucination underlie the accounts—to more expansive theories. The sightings at Fatima, for example, figure in some UFO literature, in which they are said to be encounters with an alien being disguised as or mistaken for the BVM. The late D. Scott

Rogo, a writer and researcher interested in a wide range of anomalous phenomena, treated BVM and comparable religious miracles as parapsychological phenomena.

Further Reading

Dash, Mike, 1997. *Borderlands.* London: Heinemann.

Delaney, John J., ed., 1960. *A Woman Clothed with the Sun: Eight Great Appearances of Our Lady in Modern Times.* Garden City, NY: Hanover House.

McClure, Kevin, 1983. *The Evidence for Visions of the Virgin Mary.* Wellingborough, Northamptonshire, England: Aquarian Press.

Nickell, Joe, with John F. Fischer, 1988. *Secrets of the Supernatural: Investigating the World's Occult Mysteries.* Buffalo, NY: Prometheus Books.

Rogo, D. Scott, 1982. *Miracles: A Parascientific Inquiry into Wondrous Phenomena.* New York: Dial Press.

Van Meter, David, 1999. "Digest of Marian Apparitions and Catholic Apocalypticism." http://members.aol.com/UticaCW/Mar-Review.html.

Mark

Mark may or may not be among the extraterrestrials with whom George Adamski allegedly interacted. He figures in an unusually interesting contact claim made by a woman identified only as "Joelle" and known to British ufologist Timothy Good, who told her story for the first time in a 1998 book. Joelle, a British woman of Russian background, never publicized her reported experiences, which occurred between 1963 and 1964, and they did not see print until after her death.

Joelle told Good that the contacts were initiated when she was doing a house-to-house marketing survey in the Sheffield area in September 1963. At one house she noticed a variety of gadgets, none of which she recognized as commercially available. The woman (given the pseudonym "Rosamund") whom she was interviewing said her husband ("Jack") was a scientist, inventor, and ham-radio operator. When Rosamund stepped briefly out of the room, Joelle heard a message come through the radio transceiver from someone named "Mark," proposing a meeting at "Blue John" at 4:30 the next afternoon. On Rosamund's return, when Joelle mentioned that a message had come through, the woman acted shocked and quickly turned off the radio. Subsequently, Joelle determined that "Blue John" was the Blue John Caves near Castleton in Derbyshire.

Intrigued by Rosamund's reaction (though Joelle did not tell her what the message had said), Joelle made a point of driving through the cave area on her way back to London. Parking her car in an out-of-the-way place at the appointed time, she watched from a distance as a disc-shaped aircraft landed and a man from inside the craft emerged to meet a waiting man, apparently Jack, whose car she recalled seeing parked in front of the house the day before. As the two drove away, the aircraft shot off at high speed. Joelle thought she had witnessed spy activity and assumed the aircraft to be an advanced Soviet vehicle.

Joelle was almost ready to report her observations and suspicions to the police but felt compelled to call on the couple one more time. She drove directly to their residence and knocked on the door, explaining to Jack—who had barely opened the door—that she had some further survey questions to ask. She was admitted into the house at the insistence of the man she recognized from the rendezvous of a few minutes earlier. The stranger, no longer dressed in uniform but in ordinary street clothing, identified himself as "Mark." Speaking in a teasing, good-natured tone, he said he knew why she was there.

Thus began Joelle's interaction with space people. Over the next fifteen months, she spent eight and a half hours in the company of Mark and another human-looking extraterrestrial she called "Val." Mark and Val proved vague about their exact place of origin, except to say that it was an earthlike planet in another solar system. They also said they had played a role in speeding up human evolution. They were here to work secretly with scientists from several countries, but as to their larger purpose, they would only state, "We are not here for entirely philanthropic purposes."

On one occasion, Joelle was allowed to touch a spacecraft and to watch its departure.

Once she translated a Russian manuscript in the British Museum for Mark and Val, and at other times she entertained them in her home, finding them to be pleasant companions with a good senses of humor and a love of earthly food, wine, and music. She was shown devices that projected holographic images of their home planet, and once Val himself showed up in holographic form.

The visitors told Joelle that they and their associates had, indeed, contacted Adamski, the best-known and most controversial of the early contactees, but that he had proved untrustworthy, revealing information he had been given in confidence. After that they fed him false information that they knew would discredit him, and Adamski himself, frustrated because the space people were drawing away from him, began fabricating encounters.

See Also: Adamski, George; Contactees; Orthon

Further Reading

Adamski, George, 1955. *Inside the Space Ships.* New York: Abelard-Schuman.

Good, Timothy, 1998. *Alien Base: Earth's Encounters with Extraterrestrials.* London: Century.

Martian bees

In one of the very first books on the then-new phenomenon of UFOs, British writer Gerald Heard offered a theory that even now, more than half a century later, is a distinctive one. Heard, who in 1950 was living in Los Angeles, read an interview in the *Los Angeles Times* with astronomer Gerard Kuiper. Though vehemently anti-UFO, Kuiper thought it at least possible that intelligent life existed on Mars. He added, however, that conditions there being what there were (or at least as they were thought to be at the time), Martians would likely be advanced insects of some sort. Possibly, Kuiper was speaking humorously, but Heard, a mystically inclined individual, took him seriously. He proposed that just such beings were piloting the flying saucers.

These superbees were "perhaps two inches in length . . . as beautiful as the most beautiful of any flower, any beetle, moth or butterfly. A creature with eyes like brilliant cut-diamonds, with a head of sapphire, a thorax of emerald, an abdomen of ruby, wings like opal, legs like topaz—such a body would be worthy of this 'super-mind.' . . . It is we who would feel shabby and ashamed, and may be with our clammy, putty-colored bodies, repulsive!"

The Martians had come to Earth, Heard speculated, because they feared the effect humans' aggressive ways and atomic bombs could have on them. What if human beings blew up the Earth and huge dust clouds cut off the sun's rays, turning Mars into an even colder planet? It was also possible that Earth's "very powerful magnetic field" might generate dangerous sunspots and send deadly radiation into Mars's atmosphere. Perhaps the superbees were here in what amounted to a police action: to stop us from causing further trouble to them and to the rest of the solar system. So far, however, Heard said, the Martians were acting with remarkable patience, in the fashion of "very circumspect, very intelligent gentlemen" (Heard, 1950).

See Also: Allingham's Martian; Aurora Martian; Brown's Martians; Hopkins's Martians; Khauga; Mince-Pie Martians; Monka; Muller's Martians; Shaw's Martians; Smead's Martians; Wilcox's Martians

Further Reading

Heard, Gerald, 1950. *The Riddle of the Flying Saucers: Is Another World Watching?* London: Carroll and Nicholson.

Mary

Mary is one of a number of extraterrestrials who are alleged to have made appearances at the annual Giant Rock, California, Interplanetary Spacecraft Convention held between 1954 and 1977. In 1959, while attending the convention, Harry Mayer observed mysterious globes of light hovering over the runway at Giant Rock's tiny airport. As he was running toward them, a pretty, young, blond woman suddenly appeared in front of him, put out her arm, and stopped him in his tracks. Though she was barely more than five feet tall, and Mayer was well over six feet, she had, he told ufologist William Hamilton, "the strength of many men" (Hamilton, 1996).

They spoke long enough for him to learn that her name was Mary. Under her coat, she was wearing a chocolate-brown uniform that looked something like a ski suit. She was, she said, from Venus. Mayer attended at least one more Giant Rock convention hoping to see her again, but this turned out to be his one and only contact with her.

See Also: Van Tassel, George W.; Venudo

Further Reading

Hamilton, William F., III, 1996. *Alien Magic: UFO Crashes—Abductions—Underground Bases.* New Brunswick, NJ: Global Communications.

Meier, Eduard "Billy" (1937–)

Born on February 3, 1937, in Bulach, Switzerland, Eduard Albert "Billy" Meier would become an international contactee celebrity. (His nickname stems from a youthful fascination with characters from the American Old West such as Wild Bill Hickok and Billy the Kid.) Meier claims to have received a mental message from space people when he was five years old, after he and his father watched a saucer-shaped object flying near their house. In 1944, on his seventh birthday, Meier met Sfath, a wise elderly extraterrestrial, who took him for a ride on his spacecraft. In the course of the flight, Sfath placed a helmet over young Billy's head and filled his mind with advanced knowledge. Periodic contacts with Sfath continued until Meier was a young adult. Meier wandered through Europe, Asia, and the Middle East. Traveling in Turkey in August 1965, he suffered an accident, which cost him half his arm. Soon afterward, he met seventeen-year-old Kaliope ("Popi") Zafireou and married her. Back in Switzerland, the Meiers settled in a rural village. On the afternoon of January 28, 1975, Meier photographed a spacecraft and had an hour-and-a-half conversation with its pilot, a beautiful spacewoman named Semjase (pronounced

Eduard "Billy" Meier, one of the most controversial contactees (Fortean Picture Library)

sem-ya-see). Meier would produce many more photographs, claim more contacts, recount trips into space and through time, and become the most controversial contactee since George Adamski.

Meier's aliens came from the Pleiades star system and from a planet named Erra, one of ten planets in orbit around a sun known as Tayget. The aliens got there from another planet in the constellation of Lyra, where thousands of years ago a war forced much of the population to flee to other worlds. At one point 2.8 million years ago, as they were exploring the new galactic neighborhood, the new Pleiadians found Earth, then housing primitive human beings. Some Pleiadians intermarried with humans, but their educational efforts only led to a war with earthlings, who used the newly supplied extraterrestrial technology against the Pleiadians. A second wave of Pleiadians was destroyed in the same way. Semjase was part of a third wave. She and her associates hoped to move human beings in a positive direction, and they selected Meier as their earthly agent.

Unlike nearly all other contacters, Meier's space friends were hostile to religion, though apparently not to the notion of God as such. Once, when Meier was aboard a spaceship ("beamship" as the Pleiadians called them) he was able to photograph the "Eye of God" in deep space. He also traveled to the Pleiades and into another dimension and secured pictures of dinosaurs, cavemen, and a future earthquake in San Francisco. A virtual industry of Meier-related publications, photographs, videos, and other materials found an audience around the world. Wendelle C. Stevens, an American, energetically promoted Meier, till then little known to Americans. He published books supporting Meier and had the non-English-speaking Meier's work translated. Stevens's efforts encouraged an independent journalist, Gary Kinder, to write a surprisingly sympathetic book for a mainstream publisher.

To conservative ufologists, Meier seemed like a shameless hoaxer. He became a particular obsession to a young California man, Kal Korff, who spent years investigating Meier's claims. He published two intensely critical books published between 1981 and 1995. Independent analyses suggested that the "beamships" in the photographs were in fact small models, some suspended on fishing wire, others apparently held in hand. Investigators traced other images in Meier's photos to NASA footage and (in the case of Semjase) a picture in a European fashion magazine. In the mid-1990s, after Popi Meier divorced her husband, she told European ufologists that her former husband's claims were bogus.

According to Meier, the Pleiadians—who call themselves Plejarans—withdrew all of their bases on Earth in February 1995 to protest the proliferation of phony claims of contact with them. Since then Meier has experienced approximately four contacts a year with Ptaah, who is Semjase's father. He claims more than 250 contacts with Pleiadians, in general, since 1975.

See Also: Adamski, George; Contactees; Semjase

Further Reading

Elders, Lee J., Brit Nilsson-Elders, and Thomas K. Welch, 1979. *UFO . . . Contact from the Pleiades, Volume I.* Phoenix, AZ: Genesis III Productions.

———, 1983. *UFO . . . Contact from the Pleiades, Volume II.* Phoenix, AZ: Genesis III Productions.

FIGU—Los Angeles Study Group, n.d. The Official Billy Meier Web Page. http://www.billymeier.com/index-alt.html.

Kinder, Gary, 1987. *Light Years: An Investigation into the Extraterrestrial Experiences of Eduard Meier.* New York: Atlantic Monthly Press.

Korff, Kal K., 1995. *Spaceships of the Pleiades: The Billy Meier Story.* Amherst, NY: Prometheus Books.

Korff, Kal K., with William L. Moore, 1981. *The Meier Incident—The Most Infamous Hoax in Ufology.* Fremont, CA: self-published.

Maccabee, Bruce, 1989. "Pendulum from the Pleiades." *International UFO Reporter* 14, 1 (January/February): 11–12, 22.

Stevens, Wendelle C., 1983. *UFO . . . Contact from the Pleiades—A Preliminary Investigation Report—The Report of an Ongoing Contact.* Tucson, AZ: self-published.

———, 1989. *UFO . . . Contact from the Pleiades: A Supplementary Investigation Report—The Report of an Ongoing Contact.* Tucson, AZ: self-published.

Stevens, Wendelle C., ed., 1988. *Message from the Pleiades: The Contact Notes of Eduard "Billy" Meier, Volume I.* Phoenix, AZ: Wendelle C. Stevens and Genesis III Publishing.

———, ed., 1990. *Message from the Pleiades: The Contact Notes of Eduard "Billy" Meier, Volume II.* Phoenix, AZ: Wendelle C. Stevens and Genesis III Publishing.

———, ed., 1994. *Message from the Pleiades: The Contact Notes of Eduard "Billy" Meier, Volume III.* Phoenix, AZ: Wendelle C. Stevens and Genesis III Publishing.

Winters, Randolph, 1994. *The Pleiadian Mission: A Time of Awareness.* Atwood, CA: The Pleiades Project.

Me-leelah

Me-leelah is a Pleiadian woman who figures in an abduction incident said to have occurred in Johannesburg, South Africa, in the early hours of July 19, 1988.

Phyllis and her adult, married daughter Diane were in the latter's car (Diane was driving her mother home) when they noticed an unusual starlike object. As it approached, they could see inside what proved to be an elongated craft. Through its lighted windows, they glimpsed its interior and saw six figures inside. Suddenly, they felt a presence inside their vehicle. They heard a clicking sound and abruptly found themselves ascending a ramp into the UFO. A finely skinned, short woman with slightly slanted eyes and no hair, yet beautiful nonetheless, guided Diane. The alien woman wore a one-piece, navy-blue suit such as a jogger might wear. The three walked through an aromatic "mist" before entering the main part of the craft. Their guide told them, "Greetings. I am from the Pleiades, and my name is Me-leelah. I am the commander of the craft" (Hind, 1996). She spoke in a soft but high-pitched, sing-song voice.

There were eight persons—two women and six men—inside the craft. One of the men helped as Me-leelah put the two women on tables and subjected each to a physical examination, including an X ray and a shot under the right breast (this, it was explained, was done in order to collect DNA and RNA samples). The other crewmembers paid no heed to the abductees. Afterward, Me-leelah showed them what looked like an ordinary map of the world. She told them that giant waves would soon destroy much of South Africa's Cape area. Comparable destruction would occur elsewhere on the Earth with considerable loss of life. Those who wanted to survive should flee to the mountainous areas of Spain. The United States would go to war in the Middle East, and AIDS would kill many people everywhere.

At the conclusion of the examination, the two women stepped down from the tables. Me-leelah spoke and then performed some act that later neither Phyllis nor Diane could recall. All they knew was that Me-leelah was abruptly wearing a different, more attractive-looking jacket. Soon the two became aware that Me-leelah was reading their minds. She would verbally answer questions they had formed only in their minds. At one point, after Diane had answered a question of Me-leelah's less than truthfully, the Pleiadean brought her face within inches of Diane's. Her pupils became vertical, disturbingly reptilian. After the moment of anger had passed, Me-leelah told them they could go. Two of the men escorted them back to their car, but not before the commander had promised that they would meet again in two years' time. She added that this was two years in Pleiadean time, four in Earth time.

By the time they got home, neither woman remembered the incident. They only noted how strangely quiet and calm everything seemed to be: no traffic, no birds, no sound. Over time, memories of the experience gradually returned. May 1992 came and went without a further contact.

Cynthia Hind, a ufologist from Harare, Zimbabwe, who investigated the story, says the women were unread in the UFO literature. They had not heard of other claims of Pleiadean contacts, they claimed.

See Also: Abductions by UFOs; Meier, Eduard "Billy"

Further Reading

Hind, Cynthia, 1996. *UFOs over Africa.* Madison, WI: Horus House Press.

———, 2000. "Highlights from an African Case Book." *Ohio UFO Notebook* 21: 1–10.

Melora

Melora is a channeling entity who communicates through Jyoti Alla-An of Boulder, Colorado. Alla-An characterizes Melora as a "higher-dimensional group consciousness" from the Sirius system. As is often the case with such beings, "Melora"—Greek for "golden apple"—is a name of convenience, not the entity's actual moniker; real names for interdimensional beings are either nonexistent or incomprehensible to humans. Melora and her colleagues, Alla-An says, ask us to call them names "with which we resonate or which trigger us to remember our soul histories."

Melora is a higher member of Alla-An's "soul group." At the time of their initial contact, Melora was serving on the Council of Four with Pallas Athena, Ocala (an angel), and Bi-la (a Tibetan guide). The Council of Four existed to help people express their "Being-ness." Then Ocala and Bi-la merged into Melora. In the future, it appears that Melora and Athena will merge. Alla-An says,

> During these years of my association with Melora, it has been clear that SHE continues to learn and grow through ME! Her flexibility, her unconditional love, her compassion—all these have taught me much about relationship with the Divine. It has taught me how critical our consciousness within incarnation is to the spiritual development of non-physical versions of ourselves in higher dimensions. Most importantly, working with Melora has taught me about how honored we are by all the higher beings in the light, who fully appreciate the difficulty of being light works in 3rd dimension. (Alla-An, 1998)

See Also: Channeling

Further Reading

Alla-An, Jyoti, 1998. "Melora." http://mh102.infi.net/~lightexp/Melora3.html.

Men in black

According to legend and report, strange individuals, who are often menacing and usually dressed in black suits, have threatened UFO witnesses and investigators on a number of occasions since the beginning of the UFO age. The men in black (sometimes called MIB) are variously suspected to be government agents, enforcers for powerful secret groups ("International Bankers," the New World Order by another name), alien entities, inner-earthers, or even demons.

In this last context, it is worth noting an episode that occurred during a religious revival in Wales in 1905. When the revival was at its most intense, many reported divine and demonic supernatural encounters, and some individuals, both believers and secular journalists covering the revival, witnessed unusual aerial phenomena that today might be thought of as UFOs. A contemporary account mentions that a "man dressed in black" visited a young rural woman over three consecutive nights to deliver "a message . . . which she is frightened to relate" (Evans, 1905). In his book on traditions of Satan, William Woods writes that the devil "mostly . . . is dressed in black, and always in the fashion of the day" (Woods, 1974).

Men in black established a place in UFO lore after a September 1953 incident. A Bridgeport, Connecticut, man, Albert K. Bender, headed one of the most successful early UFO groups, the International Flying Saucer Bureau, but closed it down suddenly. After much prodding he confided to close associates, most prominently Gray Barker, that three individuals in dark suits had visited him to warn that he had come too close to the truth about UFOs. They passed on information that frightened him so badly that he wanted nothing more to do with the subject. Barker later wrote a sensationalistic, paranoia-drenched book, *They Knew Too Much about Flying Saucers* (1956), that, more than any other single piece of writing, launched the MIB legend. Though Bender initially hinted that his visitors were from the government, he

Albert K. Bender's sketch of one of the three "men in black" who visited his Connecticut house in September 1953 and gave him the solution to the UFO mystery (Fortean Picture Library)

eventually wrote *Flying Saucers and the Three Men* (1962) for Barker's small publishing company. In what nearly all readers saw as an amateurish science-fiction novel passing itself off as factual, Bender identified the three men as space people who abducted him to Antarctica, where Bender met monstrous beings at an alien base.

The dismal reception afforded Bender's book would likely have ended MIB talk if not for the emergence in the latter 1960s of John A. Keel, who coined the term "MIB." Keel, a freelance writer living in New York City, secured a generous book contract from a major New York publisher to write what was intended to be the definitive work on UFOs. An occult theorist strongly attracted to demonology, Keel held UFOs and their occupants to be shape-shifting entities from a sinister otherworld. Among their agents were MIB who, in common with their brethren, sought to confuse, manipulate, and even destroy those who encountered them or sought to uncover the truth about them. Keel collected MIB reports from several states and further claimed that he had interacted with them personally. In Keel's view, MIB have played a behind-the-scenes role in much of human history and belief.

For the most part, Keel's MIB could not have passed easily for human. They were dark-featured (or, conversely, unnaturally pale), bug-eyed, and confused; and their behavior betrayed their unfamiliarity with the earthly environment and social customs. For some reason, they usually drove black limousines, frequently Cadillacs.

Other investigators collected similar reports from around the world. Some suggested that the MIB were government or military operatives, others that they were aliens. By 1966, even the U.S. Air Force was hearing of such incidents and tried to run them down, without success. Colonel George P. Freeman, a Pentagon spokesman for the U.S. Air Force's UFO-investigating Project Blue Book, complained, "We haven't been able to find out anything about these men" (Keel, 1975). In the 1990s, ufologist William L. Moore would allege, though without providing substantiating evidence, that "Men in Black are really government people in disguise . . . members of a rather bizarre unit of Air Force intelligence known currently as the Air Force Special Activities Center (AFSAC)" (Moore, 1993).

In recent years, Jenny Randles, a well-regarded English ufologist, has looked into MIB cases in Britain. In her view, some are genuinely puzzling, sometimes involving witnesses who have never heard of the phenomenon yet describe many of its classic features. From interviews and official documents, Randles was led to the conclusion that a secret department of the Ministry of Defense was monitoring certain kinds of UFO reports.

See Also: Kazik; Keel, John Alva

Further Reading

Barker, Gray, 1956. *They Knew Too Much about Flying Saucers.* New York: University Books.

Bender, Albert K., 1962. *Flying Saucers and the Three Men.* Clarksburg, WV: Saucerian Books.

Evans, Beriah G., 1905. "Merionethshire Mysteries." *Occult Review* 1, 3 (March): 113–120.

Keel, John A., 1975. *The Mothman Prophecies.* New York: Saturday Review Press/E. P. Dutton and Company.

Moore, William L., 1993. "Those Mysterious Men in Black." *Far Out* (Winter): 27–29.

Randles, Jenny, 1997. *The Truth behind Men in Black: Government Agents—or Visitors from Beyond.* New York: St. Martin's Paperbacks.

Woods, William, 1974. *A History of the Devil.* New York: G. P. Putnam's Sons.

Menger, Howard (1922–)

Howard Menger (pronounced *men*-jer), a New Jersey sign painter who was sometimes called the East Coast equivalent of George Adamski, rose to prominence in flying-saucer contactee circles in the 1950s. In his first public appearance, on Long John Nebel's radio show on New York's WOR, on October 29, 1956, Menger claimed lifelong contacts as well as "flashback" memories of an earlier life as an extraterrestrial. The space people were mostly from Venus, and prominent among them were beautiful, blond women. In early 1956, when the contacts intensified, Menger began taking photographs of alleged spacecraft. He also claimed interplanetary flights in the company of "Aryan-type" beings and produced, among others, pictures of the lunar surface taken from a flying saucer.

Conservative ufologists scoffed at Menger's tales and rejected his photographs as absurdly unconvincing. Writing in *Saucer News,* Lonzo Dove deemed them "so evidently faked that it is almost foolish to even criticize them" (Dove, 1959). When the anticontactee National Investigations Committee on Aerial Phenomena challenged Menger and other contactees to submit to polygraph examinations, Menger declined.

His supporters flocked to his High Bridge, New Jersey, farm, where some reported seeing, from a distance, "spacemen" in luminous uniforms and other oddities, attributed by skeptics to effects engineered by Menger confeder-

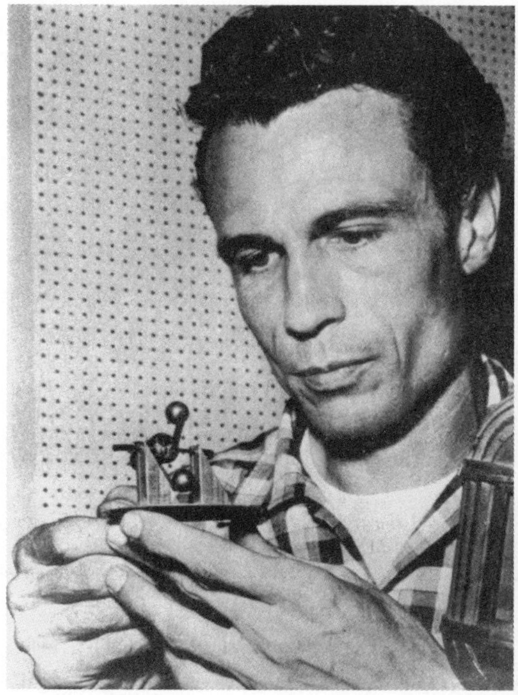

Howard Menger with a "free energy" machine (Fortean Picture Library)

ates. One supporter apparently was Connie Weber, an attractive young blond woman to whom Menger, a married man, had turned his romantic attentions. Menger declared Weber to be the sister of a spacewoman he had met in 1946. For her part, Weber "recalled" that in previous lives she had been a Venusian and Menger had been a Saturnian (a relationship she documented in a lurid 1958 book, *My Saturnian Lover*). On one occasion, four followers of Menger's were invited separately into a dark room, where each had a brief audience with a spacewoman concealed in shadow. When a sliver of light accidentally caught the supposed spacewoman, however, one of them recognized Weber. Subsequently, Menger left his wife and married Weber.

By the time his book *From Outer Space to You* appeared in 1959, Menger had largely withdrawn from the saucer scene. The next year, interviewed on Long John Nebel's television show, Menger startled his host and audience by seeming to disavow his former claims. In the 1960s, he changed his story, now asserting that he had participated in an elaborate hoax at the instigation of a secret government agency that wanted to test human reactions to extraterrestrial visitors.

Howard and Connie Menger moved to Vero Beach, Florida, where they lived quietly for more than two decades. In 1990, they resurfaced at the National UFO Conference in Miami Beach and began publishing materials that again presented the space contacts as authentic. They also appeared in the 1992 Discovery Channel documentary *Farewell, Good Brothers.* They make occasional appearances on the saucer and New Age scene.

See Also: Adamski, George; Contactees

Further Reading

Baxter, Marla [pseud. of Constance Weber Menger], 1958. *My Saturnian Lover.* New York: Vantage Press.

"Contactee Letters," 1957. *Confidential Bulletin to NICAP Members* (September 6).

Dove, Lonzo, 1957. "Menger's Adamski-Type Saucers." *Saucer News* 4, 2 (February-March): 6–7.

Menger, Howard, 1959. *From Outer Space to You.* Clarksburg, WV: Saucerian Books.

Moseley, James W., 1966. "Strange New Ideas from Howard Menger." *Saucer News Non-Scheduled Newsletter* 26 (January 25).

Nebel, Long John, 1961. *The Way Out World.* Englewood Cliffs, NJ: Prentice-Hall.

Schwarz, Berthold E., 1972. "Beauty of the Night." *Flying Saucer Review* 18, 4 (August): 5–9, 17.

Merk

According to George Hunt Williamson, eighteen thousand years ago a Venusian named Merk flew a "Light Ship" to Telos, an eastern section of Lemuria in what is now Arizona, initiating a period of cordial and productive relationships between Venusians and Lemurians, who then had developed flight but not space flight. The Lemurians built a memorial to commemorate the spot where Merk's craft had landed.

See Also: Lemuria; Williamson, George Hunt

Further Reading

Williamson, George Hunt, 1959. *Road in the Sky.* London: Neville Spearman.

Mersch

According to Colorado contactee Dave Schultz, six extraterrestrial races are visiting Earth. One is the Mersch. The Mersch are six feet tall, weigh two hundred pounds, and have bald heads and slanted eyes. Their home planet is in the constellation Scorpio. They are active in abductions and mutilation of cattle and other animals in western states.

See Also: Abductions by UFOs; Contactees; Olliana Olliana Alliano

Further Reading

Sprinkle, R. Leo, ed., 1982. *Proceedings: Rocky Mountain Conference on UFO Investigation.* Laramie, WY: School of Extended Studies, University of Wyoming.

Metatron

Metatron is a "divine interface between God and the outer worlds—meaning us on the outer layers of physical creation—the hardened shell around the cosmic egg of Light" (Arvey, 1994). Metatronic energy is transmitted once a week to the Earth, and seekers can gain access to it if they are attuned to the proper frequency. Much of the information Metatron sends is of a densely technical nature. A good part of the channeled material comes through James J. Hurtak, who records it in *The Book of Knowledge: The Keys of Enoch* (1982). Hurtak, however, is far from the only Metatron channeler.

The most famous communicant with Metatron is the rock guitarist Carlos Santana. Santana claims that Metatron was responsible for the restoration of his career in 1999 and 2000. During a meditation session Metatron told him, "We want to hook you back to the radio-airwave frequency" and to "reconnect the molecules to the light," presumably meaning renewed airplay and popular attention (Gates and Gordon, 2000).

The name Metatron comes out of traditional Jewish mysticism, where Metatron is depicted as an archangel, perhaps the highest of them all. Some mystics believe that on Earth he was the prophet Enoch whom God took directly to heaven without the transi-

Carlos Santana, the most famous communicant with Metatron, performing in Munich, Germany, May 2000 (AFP/Corbis)

tional detail of dying. Other sources assert that it was he who led the Israelites through the wilderness after the Exodus.

Further Reading

Arvey, Michael, 1994. "Metatron." http://www.spiritweb.org/Spirit/metatron-arvey.html.

Davidson, Gustav, 1967. *A Dictionary of Angels.* New York: Free Press.

Gates, David, and Devin Gordon, 2000. "Smooth as Santana." *Newsweek* (February 14): 66–67.

Gilmore, Robert and Laurie, eds., n.d. "The Ascension Is Life Lived from Joy." http://www.nitehawk.com/daydove/25metatr.html.

Hurtak, James J., 1982. *The Book of Knowledge: The Keys of Enoch.* Los Gatos, CA: Academy for Future Science.

Stone, Joshua David, 1994. *The Complete Ascension Manual.* Sedona, AZ: Light Technology Publishing.

Michael

In two books, Chelsea Quinn Yarbro chronicled the channeling experiences of a young San Francisco–area woman given the name Jessica Lansing. Yarbro wrote that in 1970, as Jessica and her husband, Walter (also a pseudonym), played with a ouija board after dinner, they began receiving communications from an entity who first refused to answer the question, "Who is this?" Eventually, under prodding, it said, "The last name a fragment of this entity used was Michael." "Michael" went on to say, "We are of the mid-causal lane. The astral plane is accessible to the physical plane. We are not" (Yarbro, 1979). Michael claimed to be composed of more than a thousand fragments of "old souls."

In later automatic writing and channeling, Michael—who resisted being identified by a masculine pronoun—taught that each individual must go through seven basic soul stages over a minimum of seven reincarnated lives. But Michael would respond impatiently if someone asked a question about his or her personal life. "We are not the Ann Landers of the cosmos," Michael snapped. As the Michael phenomenon grew, however, this changed, and Michael would speak to individuals about themselves and offer them guidance.

Jessica Lansing herself was uncertain whether Michael was an independent intelligence or some manifestation of an aspect of her psyche. In time, others reported communications from Michael. In 1984, two followers founded the Michael Educational Foundation. The foundation maintains that Michael is a collection of one thousand fifty souls, all of whom once lived lives on Earth. It sponsors other Michael groups throughout the United States. Michael F. Brown, an anthropologist who has studied the channeling movement, calls Michael "as close to a channeling franchise as one can find in the United States today" (Brown, 1997).

"According to Michael," the foundation states, "we agree to come into each lifetime with a basic Role that we play to best support the world around us. In addition to this Role, we have numerous 'Overleaves' or personality traits that we choose to play from" ("Who Is Michael?" n.d.).

See Also: Channeling

Further Reading

Brown, Michael F., 1997. *The Channeling Zone: American Spirituality in an Anxious Age.* Cambridge, MA: Harvard University Press.

Melton, J. Gordon, 1996. *Encyclopedia of American Religions.* Fifth edition. Detroit, MI: Gale Research.

"Who Is Michael?" n.d. http://amt.to/mef/mchan.html.

Yarbro, Chelsea Quinn, 1979. *Messages from Michael.* New York: Playboy Paperbacks.

———, 1986. *More Messages from Michael.* New York: Berkley Paperbacks.

Michigan giant

According to the *Saginaw Courier-Herald* of April 17, 1897, a "flying machine" landed half a mile southwest of Reynolds, Michigan, at 4:30 A.M. on the fourteenth. Witnesses who had seen it hovering rushed to the scene, where, to their shock, they spotted its pilot, who appeared human but was nine and a half feet tall. His "talk, while musical, is not talk at all, but seems to be a repetition of bellowing." The being looked hot and uncomfortable even though he was nearly naked. What looked like polar-bear pelts lay nearby, apparently winter clothing for which the traveler had no use at the moment.

One farmer made the mistake of approaching the figure too closely. For his efforts he found himself at the receiving end of a severe kick. It was delivered with sufficient ferocity and velocity that the man's hip broke.

The article, clearly written with tongue in cheek, concludes, "Great excitement prevails here, and lots of people are flocking here from Morley and Howard City to view the strange being from a distance, as no one dares to go near. He seems to be trying to talk to the people."

See Also: Aurora Martian; Close encounters of the third kind; Oleson's giants; Smith; Wilson

Further Reading

Bullard, Thomas E., ed., 1982. *The Airship File: A Collection of Texts Concerning Phantom Airships and Other UFOs, Gathered from Newspapers and Periodicals Mostly during the Hundred Years Prior to Kenneth Arnold's Sighting.* Bloomington, IN: self-published.

Migrants

In George Hunt Williamson's alternative history *Other Tongues—Other Flesh* (1953), "Migrants" are spirit beings from the Sirius Star system. They arrived on Earth during the Miocene Epoch (between twenty-five and thirteen million years ago) with the intention of looking for bodies to inhabit. At first, they gave serious consideration to cats, but after due reflection they decided that apes were more likely to evolve toward intelligence, civilization, and technology. In the meantime, employing their vast paranormal powers, the Migrants conjured up grotesque material forms for themselves. This period is known among extraterrestrial historians of Earth as the "Great Abomination."

Williamson reported, "The abomination was so vast that forms were fusing together into monsters having no purpose but self-destruction. Men and animals were growing interchangeable of spirit and structure. Man was beastly and beast was manlike." These abominable entities took the forms of the creatures remembered in legend and mythology as griffins, centaurs, dragons, and sphinxes. Eventually the "Host on the Sirian planets" could take no more of this insubordination. Men were to be men, beasts were to be beasts, the Host declared before setting loose a kind of global warming that melted the poles and sparked huge floods. "Monsters and anomalies were destroyed," the channeled entity Elder Brother informed Williamson. "No longer could they propagate. Pure species were saved and pronounced sterile unto all but themselves." The Migrants lost all their psychokinetic powers and became normal primates. They began engaging in sexual unions with ape-women, and out of these alliances modern *Homo sapiens* eventually emerged.

See Also: Williamson, George Hunt

Further Reading

Williamson, George Hunt, 1953. *Other Tongues—Other Flesh.* Amherst, WI: Amherst Press.

Mince-Pie Martians

The so-called Mince-Pie Martians appeared in a kitchen in Rowley Regis, in England's West

Midlands, on January 4, 1979, to star in what may well be Britain's most bizarre close encounter of the third kind.

At 6 A.M., Jean Hingley, forty-five years old, had just sent her husband off to work when she noticed a light outside. Thinking the carport light was still on, she went out to check. She was unsettled to see a large orange sphere hovering over the carport roof. She hurried back inside and, with her dog Hobo, watched the UFO. As she was doing so, she noticed that the dog seemed to be frozen as if paralyzed. Suddenly he fell over sideways and lay there motionless.

At that moment, three winged figures zipped past her, leaving Mrs. Hingley feeling cold and weak. She managed to follow them into the living room, where two of them were shaking the Christmas tree so hard that the fairy atop it fell to the floor. The figures themselves looked almost fairylike. Three and a half feet tall, they were humanoids with wide, white faces, big, dark eyes, no noses, slitlike mouths, and large oval wings covered with glittering dots of various colors. Each wore a transparent helmet on its head; at the top of the helmet a light shone. There were no fingers on the hands or feet on the legs; each just tapered to a point. The wings did not move like a bird's but fluttered gently or folded in like a concertina.

Hingley found herself paralyzed, unable to speak or move, until the beings spoke to her, saying, "Nice?" They spoke in unison with what sounded like a gruff, masculine voice. Then she could move and talk again. When she asked where they were from, they were silent. They sailed around the room, then landed and bounced up and down on the couch. She shouted at them to stop, and they did, though this would be the last time they did what she asked them to do.

The episode lasted for an hour. It was often difficult, trying, and even painful. If they did not like what she had to say, a beam would shoot from the light at the top of their helmets and hit her on the forehead just above the bridge of the nose. Sometimes she would be blinded. At other times she would be paralyzed. And at yet other times, when she had addressed them with a seemingly inoffensive question, the light would not hurt her. They would not tell her why they shot the light at her, or why they would quote back to her any question she asked them. The experience made her eyes sore, and when she complained, the beings insisted they did not intend to harm her.

When she inquired again about their place of origin, they replied this time, "From the sky." Seeing a picture of Jesus on the wall, they flew up to it and engaged her in a conversation about him, then went on to banal subjects (a British entertainment figure, the Queen, the role of the housewife, children) before returning to Jesus. Then they floated slowly around the room picking up small objects, including cassette tapes. Hingley told investigators, "They touched all the Christmas cards and all the furniture. . . . I think they had magnets in their hands, 'cause they kept lifting things that they touched." They asked for water. In response she filled four glasses and put them on a tray, along with several mince pies. She lifted a glass, and the beings lifted theirs, but when they saw her watching them, they blinded her with the light beam. The next thing she knew, they were putting empty glasses down. Next she thought of offering them cigarettes and cigars that they were looking at. When she lit one, however, the beings recoiled in fright. She thought they were afraid of fire.

A loud noise brought her to the window, where she saw that the orange UFO was back. The beings "put their hands to their sides," she recalled. "They lifted themselves up," pressing buttons on their chests, and "they glided themselves out." Each was holding its mince pie. They sailed out the back door and entered through an opening in the UFO, which flew away and was soon lost to view.

At that moment, Hingley suffered "agony, pure agony. . . . My legs, I couldn't feel them, and then I was wobbly, and very, very weak. I grabbed the table. I slid my feet along the carpet, and I got on the settee, and I didn't know how long I was there. Ooh! I was dead!" (Budden, 1988). She lay incapacitated until five o'clock that afternoon. Finally, her strength was sufficiently restored so that she was able to phone her husband, a neighbor, and the police.

Investigators found an oval-shaped impression in the backyard snow. Hingley complained that her clock, radio, and television were no longer functioning. The cassette tapes that she said the beings had touched were ruined. She suffered a range of physical discomforts in her eyes, ears, and jaw. Her doctor became alarmed enough about her well-being that he ordered her to stay home from work for two weeks. As outlandish as her story sounded, investigators did not doubt her sincerity.

See Also: Close encounters of the third kind

Further Reading

Budden, Alfred, 1988. "The Mince-Pie Martians: The Rowley Regis Case." *Fortean Times* 50 (Summer): 40–44.

Miniature pilots

One day in 1929, according to a story she told many years later, a five-year-old girl and her eight-year-old brother were playing in the garden of their Hertford, Hertfordshire, England, home when they heard an engine sound. It was coming from a nearby orchard and over the garden fence. As its source came into view, the children saw a tiny biplane, with a wingspan of no more than twelve to fifteen inches, descend and land briefly by a garbage pail. During the few seconds that it was on the ground, both children got a clear view of a figure they described as a "perfectly proportioned tiny pilot wearing a leather flying helmet," who they said, "waved to us as he took off."

The sight so unsettled the two that it wasn't until they were well into their adult lives, around 1960, that they spoke of it to each other. "I have no explanation to offer," the woman said, "but I do know that this was not a figment of my imagination" (Creighton, 1970).

In a UFO-age counterpart to this strange story, a Seattle woman reported that around 2 A.M. one night in late August 1965 she awoke paralyzed. Unable to speak or move, she watched helplessly as a football-shaped gray object sailed through her open window and hovered over a carpet in her bedroom. As the tiny UFO prepared to land, three tripod legs dropped from it. Once settled on the floor, the UFO let out a ramp, down which stepped five or six miniature beings clad in tight-fitting uniforms. They then engaged in what appeared to be repair work on their craft. On completing the job, they walked up the ramp and into the ship and flew away. At that point, the witness found that she had regained normal mobility.

It seems likely that this second incident was a hallucination of a kind frequently associated with sleep paralysis.

Further Reading

Creighton, Gordon, 1970. "A Weird Case from the Past." *Flying Saucer Review* 16, 4 (July/August): 30.

Hufford, David J., 1982. *The Terror That Comes in the Night: An Experience-Centered Study of Supernatural Assault Traditions.* Philadelphia, PA: University of Pennsylvania Press.

Keel, John A., 1970. *UFOs: Operation Trojan Horse.* New York: G. P. Putnam's Sons.

Monka

Monka first surfaced as the disembodied voice of a Martian on a tape owned by contactee Dick Miller. Miller played the message at the April 1956 Giant Rock Interplanetary Spacecraft Convention, telling the audience that the voice had mysteriously appeared on a tape inside a sealed can. The message had Monka ("I am what you would call the head of my government") promising, "On the evening of November 7, of this your year 1956, at 10:30 P.M. your local time, we request that one of your communications stations remove its carrier signal from the air for two minutes" ("Mon-Ka of Mars," 1956). From ten thousand feet the occupants of a brilliantly illuminated spacecraft would speak to the people of Los Angeles.

The message electrified occultists and saucerians in California and elsewhere. When played in London in September, it had the same effect on their British counterparts. Newspaper coverage mocked the tape and message, and conservative ufologists dismissed the message as a silly hoax. On November 2, the *Los Angeles Mirror-News* reported that some months before, while living in Detroit, Miller had been caught faking a radio message from a spaceman. All this notwithstanding, the Monka message spurred two mass rallies in Los Angeles, and Monka enthusiast and rally organizer Gabriel Green appeared on the widely viewed *House Party* television show to spread the word that friendly extraterrestrials would be talking to southern California on November 7.

As a publicity stunt, two area radio stations went off the air for two minutes on the night in question as hundreds of believers gathered on rooftops. No UFO appeared, of course, but Monka would live on in channeled messages from hundreds of contactees up to the present. No longer a Martian, he is now usually taken as a close associate of the most beloved and ubiquitous of interdimensional channeling entities, Ashtar.

See Also: Ashtar; Contactees

Further Reading

Beckley, Timothy Green, 1981. *Book of Space Contacts.* New York: Global Communications.

Garrison, Omar, 1956. "Time Flew by, but That Flying Saucer Didn't." *Los Angeles Mirror-News* (November 8).

"Mon-Ka of Mars Gives Saucer Research a Black Eye," 1956. *CSI News Letter* 6 (December 15): 3–5.

Tuella [pseud. of Thelma B. Turrell], ed., 1989. *Ashtar: A Tribute.* Third edition. Salt Lake City, UT: Guardian Action Publications.

Mothman

Mothman, a monstrous creature reported by dozens of witnesses in towns along the Ohio River Valley, got its name from a villain in the then-popular *Batman* television series. Though their stories received little public attention, at least one witness claimed to have had a kind of communication with it.

Mothman first appeared in the local press in November 1966, after two young couples spotted it around 11:30 P.M. while driving through an abandoned World War II munitions complex known locally as the "TNT area." Gray in color with humanlike legs, the creature had glowing red, "hypnotic" eyes and, witness Roger Scarberry said, "was shaped like a man, but bigger. Maybe six and a half feet tall. And it had big wings against its back" (Keel, 1975). Terrified, the witnesses fled in their car only to spot the same or a similar creature on a hill by the road. That creature spread its batlike wings and pursued the vehicle at speeds of up to one hundred miles per hour. All the while, it made a squeaking sound. As they sped toward Point Pleasant, West Virginia, where they would tell their story to a deputy sheriff, they noticed a large, dead dog along the side of the road.

This last detail would seem significant to later investigators after they learned of the experience that had happened an hour before to Newell Partridge from rural Salem, West Virginia. Partridge had been watching television when suddenly he saw an unfamiliar kind of interference on the screen. In the meantime, he could hear his dog Bandit howling strangely. When he picked up a flashlight and stepped outside, he was shocked to see—at one hundred fifty yards' distance—the dog circling a shadowy figure with glowing red eyes that did not look like an animal's. Something about the scene struck Partridge as deeply abnormal, and he felt cold chills running down his back. Just as he was about to go inside, Bandit charged the intruder, ignoring his master, who was trying to restrain him. Partridge went inside to get a gun but could not bring himself to go outside again. He went to sleep. The next morning he discovered that Bandit was missing. Later, when he read a newspaper account of the Point Pleasant incident, the reference to a dead dog struck him. Bandit was never seen again.

Other witnesses reported seeing "Mothman," as the press soon dubbed it, in the TNT area and elsewhere. Sightings continued from time to time for months afterward. Reports consistently described a gray entity larger than a man, who was headless and had wings, legs, and glowing red eyes on its upper chest. When in flight, its wings did not flap. When it walked, it had a shambling gait. Observers seemed especially terrified of the eyes. Because of the witnesses' manifest sincerity and terror, no one argued that the sightings were hoaxes. The most popular conventional explanations held that they had seen owls or sandhill cranes. The episode became the subject of two books.

In May 1976, nearly a decade after the scare had run its course, representatives of the Ohio UFO Investigators League looked up some of the witnesses. All stuck by their original testimony and insisted that they had not mistaken ordinary birds for Mothman. The most curious testimony came from early witness Linda Scarberry (wife of Roger Scarberry), who said that she and her husband had seen the creature "hundreds of times," one from as close as three or four feet. She went on,

> It seems like it doesn't want to hurt you. It just wants to communicate with you. But you're too afraid when you see it to do anything. . . . We rented an apartment down on Thirteenth Street, and the bedroom window was right off the roof. It was sitting on the roof one night, looking in the window, and by then I was so used to seeing it that I just pulled the blinds and went on. I felt kind of sorry for it [because] it gives you the feeling like it was sitting there wishing it could come in and get warm because it was cold out that night. (Raynes, 1976)

A Mothmanlike creature was also involved in a close encounter of the third kind from Sandling Park, near Hyde, Kent, England, on November 16, 1963. That evening a group of young people saw a glowing oval, some fifteen to twenty feet in diameter, hovering over a field. A few seconds after the UFO disappeared behind a clump of trees, witness John Flaxton related, "a dark figure shambled out. It was all black, about the size of a human but without a head. It seemed to have wings like a bat on either side and came stumbling towards us. We didn't wait to investigate" ("The Saltwood Mystery," 1964). This is the only known report to link such a creature with a UFO.

Whatever Mothman may or may not have been, no encounters with it have been reported in recent years.

See Also: Close encounters of the third kind

Further Reading

Barker, Gray, 1970. *The Silver Bridge.* Clarksburg, WV: Saucerian Books.

Keel, John A., 1970. *Strange Creatures from Time and Space.* Greenwich, CT: Fawcett Gold Medal.

———, 1975. *The Mothman Prophecies.* New York: Saturday Review Press/E. P. Dutton and Company.

Raynes, Brent M., 1976. "West Virginia Revisited." *Ohio Sky Watcher* (January/February/March): 9–10.

"The Saltwood Mystery," 1964. *Flying Saucer Review* 10, 2 (March/April): 11–12.

Mount Lassen

Mount Lassen, in California's Tehama County, houses good and evil beings who live deep inside caves and engage in conflict with advanced weapons, according to the testimony of a man identified as Ralph B. Fields.

At some unspecified time, apparently, in the latter twentieth century, Fields and a companion named Joe (no last name offered) went to the mountain in search of guano (bat dung), which they hoped to market as fertilizer. On their first night, the two slept at the foot of the mountain. By the third day, they were nearing the mountaintop when they decided to make camp and prepare a meal. Joe went off to collect dead scrub bush for the fire. Suddenly, he returned in a state of high excitement. He had found a big cave nearby, and it looked like a promising place to search for the object of their quest.

A Morlock (with victim) as depicted in the 1960 movie version of H. G. Wells's The Time Machine *(Photofest)*

The deeper the two went into the cave, the deeper it seemed. Once they got twenty feet into it, the walls expanded to ten feet wide and eight feet high. They could see a hundred yards ahead to a point where the wall bent. They followed the bend off to the left and down, and they kept going until suddenly, realizing how far they were from the surface, they began to get nervous. Besides that, there was no evidence of guano. Still curious, they decided to plow ahead and kept walking for another mile or two. Then, with the aid of their flashlights, they made an amazing discovery: the floor was worn smooth, and the cavern walls and ceiling seemed cut artificially. What had seemed a cave now looked more like a tunnel.

A light flashed, and three men confronted Fields and Joe. The men were of normal appearance, seemingly around fifty years of age, dressed in jeans and flannel shirts. Only their shoes, with their unusually thick soles, looked out of the ordinary. One of the strangers asked what they were doing there, but he acted as if he did not believe the two men's answer. Two more strangers showed up. The guano-hunters were badly frightened, convinced that they had fallen into the hands of a criminal gang in hiding. Their fears only rose when one of the band told them that they should accompany them deeper into the cave.

About two miles later, they came to a spot where the walls expanded. There they encountered a strange device that looked like a toboggan with a seat and a control panel. It gave off a buzzing sound. The group sat on the wide seat and flew off at a "terrific" speed. After a journey of some considerable distance, they saw a similar machine approaching them. Suddenly acting nervous, they maneuvered their machine to a stop. It landed two feet from the other one. The crew of the first ship leaped out and tried to run away, but the crew of the second, who were carrying pencil-like weapons, shot them down, killing all of them.

Certain of their imminent doom, Fields and Joe watched as the new group approached them. One member asked if they were "surface people." After telling him that they had come from there just recently, the stranger went on to say that they were lucky they had been rescued. "You would have also become horloks, and then we would have had to kill you also." The man spoke in a friendly manner, giving Fields the confidence to ask what was going on. All the man would say was that surface people "are not ready to have the things that the ancients have left. . . . However, there are a great many evil people here who create many unpleasant things for both us and the surface people. They are safe because no one on the surface believes that we exist."

Ralph and Joe were flown back to the surface and warned never to return. Fields says, "We had been told just enough for me to believe that down there somewhere there were and are things that might baffle the greatest minds of this Earth. Sometimes I am tempted to go back into that cave if I could again find it, which I doubt, but then I know the warning I heard in there might be too true" (Commander X, 1990).

It may be worth noting that H. G. Wells's famous science-fiction novel *The Time Machine* (1895) features a race of violent subterranean humans known as Morlocks.

See Also: Brodie's deros; Hollow earth; Mount Shasta; Shaver mystery

Further Reading

Commander X [pseud. of Jim Keith], 1990. *Underground Alien Bases.* New Brunswick, NJ: Abelard Publications.

Mount Shasta

Mount Shasta in northern California, near the Oregon border, is the scene of occult legends that go back to the nineteenth century. Even before white settlers arrived in the region in 1827, however, local Indian tribes believed that giant creatures, apparently of the Sasquatch variety, lived in caves on the mountain. The giants were feared because of their habit of capturing individuals and taking them to their caves, where they would squeeze their victims to death. Another race of beings, small, usually invisible entities akin to fairies, also called Shasta their home, according to tribal traditions.

But it took Frederick Spencer Oliver of nearby Yreka, California, to put the mountain on the mystical map. In the mid 1880s, Oliver, then in his teens, produced a novel, *A Dweller on Two Planets,* which he claimed an

A nineteenth-century engraving of Mount Shasta, California, the scene of occult legends from far back in the past (Library of Congress)

entity named Phylos the Tibetan had dictated to him. In fact, when the novel was published in 1899, Phylos, not Oliver, was identified as the author. Phylos said he had experienced several incarnations, including one in Atlantis and another on Venus. In his most recent one, during the mid-century California gold rush, he ("he" being Walter Pierson, the name he held during that lifetime) met Quong, a Chinese man. Quong, a knower of mystical secrets, led Pierson into Shasta via a hidden tunnel. Inside the mountain they found huge chambers and treasures belonging to a secret brotherhood of advanced beings who had lived there for a very long time, devoting themselves to humanity's spiritual betterment. In his astral body, Pierson traveled to Venus, where he learned many secrets; he also learned of his previous lives. Once enlightened, he was rechristened Phylos and became a guardian of the cosmos. A modern chronicler remarks that the "Tibetan" part of his title "seems to have been added for Mystery's sake" (Kafton-Minkel, 1989).

Oliver's novel owed much of its inspiration to Madame Blavatsky's theological writings and to works of mystical fantasy such as Edward Bulwer-Lytton's *Zanoni: A Rosicrucian Tale* and Marie Corelli's *A Romance of Two Worlds.* It was original, however, in setting a secret civilization within Mount Shasta. The next writer to do so, Harvey Spencer Lewis (writing as "Wishar C. Cerve"), identified the inhabitants as survivors of Lemuria, the Pacific Ocean's version of Atlantis. According to Lewis's *Lemuria: Lost Continent of the Pacific* (1931), when Lemuria split and sank, its east coast crashed into part of North America's west coast to become the states of Washington, Oregon, and California. Many of the surviving Lemurians took up residence inside Shasta.

Lewis claimed that persons living near Shasta occasionally encountered distinguished-looking men in white robes as they walked out of the forest. Sometimes these beings, who stood seven feet tall, did business in local stores, using gold nuggets to make their purchases and refusing change. The strangers had long, curly hair, and on their large foreheads there were bulges visible with "special decoration" over them covering their third eyes. Along the thick forests on Shasta's eastern flank, the Lemurians had built great marble temples. On some evenings they held mystical celebrations at which they lit big fires and danced. They also raised odd-looking cattle. They flew "peculiarly shaped boats which have flown out of this region high in the air over the hills and valleys . . . to the waters of the Pacific Ocean." Mostly, however, the Lemurians managed to keep themselves and their activities invisible, setting up energy walls that effectively concealed them from prying eyes.

The American branch of the Rosicrucians, headquartered in San Jose, published Lewis's book. During the 1930s, it also sponsored expeditions that sought to locate the secret entrances to Shasta. Articles in *Rosicrucian Digest* discussed the mountain's "mysteries." Then on May 22, 1932, the *Los Angeles Times*' Sunday magazine ran a destined-to-be-influential piece by Edward Lanser. Lanser claimed that while taking a train trip on the Shasta Limited on his way to Portland, he observed mysterious lights on Shasta in the early dawn. The conductor told him that "the Lemurians" were holding ceremonies. On his way back to Portland, Lanser wrote, Lanser spent time in the Shasta area and found that nearly everyone there took the reality of the Lemurians for granted. "Business men, amateur explorers, officials, and ranchers in the country surrounding Shasta spoke freely of the community, and all attested to the weird rituals that are performed on the mountainside after sunset, midnight and sunrise," he wrote (De Camp, 1980). The Lemurians performed these rituals to celebrate their escape to "Gautama" (North America). He asserted that "Prof. Edgar Lucien Larkin," whom he characterized as a famous astronomer, had actually been able to observe Lemurians and their temples through a telescope. Larkin was in reality an occult buff who had died some eight years earlier. Though widely quoted since, Lanser's story was a hoax or—more to the point—a tongue-in-cheek exercise satirizing the curious beliefs the mystically minded were circulating about a beautiful but otherwise ordinary natural monument.

In *Unveiled Mysteries* (1934) Guy Warren Ballard, writing as Godre Ray King, reported that in 1930, while working as a mining engineer at Shasta, he met Saint Germain, an immortal being who gave him a creamy liquid to drink. The liquid, Saint Germain explained, was "Life—Omnipresent Life." Many other encounters followed, and Ballard (who died in 1939) soon formed the I AM Activity, a notorious cultlike organization that combined Theosophical doctrine with fascist ideology. Around the same time, occultist Maurice Doreal was detailing his own Shasta experiences, which were with the Atlanteans who lived in a colony seven miles beneath the mountain. Though the colony had only three hundred fifty-three inhabitants, it dominated the Lemurians, four and a half million of whom lived, essentially, as prisoners of the Atlanteans even deeper under Shasta. Doreal was unique in his depiction of the Lemurians as evil and dangerous.

As Shasta's legends continued to expand, it was said that the mountain's interior housed two magnificent Lemurian cities, Iletheleme and Yaktayvia. The latter, some said, was the source of beautiful bell sounds, which some had professed to hear emanating from the mountain. The Yaktayvians are master bell builders. All the while, occult pilgrims were arriving in growing numbers to the area; many would stay. Some claimed to have seen and communicated with Lemurians and other extraordinary beings. Others reported UFO sightings on the mountain. Believers explained the phenomena as Lemurian aircraft or visiting extraterrestrial spacecraft calling on their friends inside the mountain. At least one person, Nola Van Valer, swore that she had met Phylos the Tibetan on the mountain. On another occasion she spoke with Saint Germain.

See Also: Atlantis; Bonnie; Fairies encountered; Lemuria; Shaver mystery

Further Reading

Commander X [pseud. of Jim Keith], 1990. *Underground Alien Bases.* New Brunswick, NJ: Abelard Productions.

De Camp, L. Sprague, 1980. *The Ragged Edge of Science.* Philadelphia, PA: Owlswick Press.

Frank, Emilie A., 1998. *Mt. Shasta, California's Mystic Mountain.* Hilt, CA: Photografix Publishing.

Kafton-Minkel, Walter, 1989. *Subterranean Worlds: 100,000 Years of Dragons, Dwarfs, the Dead, Lost Races, and UFOs from inside the Earth.* Port Townsend, WA: Loompanics Unlimited.

Tierney, Richard L., 1983. "America's Mystical Mount Shasta." *Fate* 36, 8 (August): 70–76.

Mr. X

On the afternoon of November 5, 1957, Reinhold Schmidt, a grain buyer with a prison record, allegedly encountered the crew of a landed flying saucer along the banks of Nebraska's Platte River. Two crewmembers ushered him inside, where he met two other men and two women, all of whom spoke "high German" to one another and German-inflected English to Schmidt. Their captain identified himself as "Mr. X." After a brief conversation about America's satellite program, Schmidt left the craft, which then departed.

When Schmidt reported his encounter to the sheriff's office in nearby Kearney, officers went to the site and found footprints as well as a greasy substance at the supposed landing site. They also located two empty oil cans not far away, leading them to suspect a hoax. After being held overnight in jail, Schmidt was examined by two psychiatrists and pronounced mentally ill. He spent a few days in the Hastings State Hospital before being released.

Thereafter, he pursued a career on the contactee scene, claiming further contacts with Mr. X and his associates, who he learned were from Saturn. His space friends flew him around the world, to Egypt, to the Antarctic, and elsewhere. It all ended, however, after he told a California widow that from a spaceship he had seen quartz crystals with healing powers and persuaded her to invest in a worthless mining venture. At a trial in Oakland in October 1961, a young astronomer named Carl Sagan assured the jury that human life could not exist on Saturn. Schmidt received a one- to ten-year sentence for grand theft.

See Also: Contactees

Further Reading

"'Flying Saucer' Figure Convicted," 1961. *Oakland* [California] *Tribune,* October 27.

"The Kearney, Nebraska, 'Contact' Claim," 1957. *CSI News Letter* 10 (December 15): 12–13.

Schmidt, Reinhold O., 1963. *The Edge of Tomorrow: A True Account of Experiences with Visitors from Another Planet.* Hollywood, CA: self-published.

MU the Mantis Being

A West Virginia woman who prefers to use the pseudonym Rebecca Grant says she has had a lifetime of paranormal experiences, including missing-time episodes and apparent UFO abductions. When she was forty years old, aliens revealed themselves to her. At first the communications were purely telepathic. After two years they began to appear physically to her. These appearances, always brief, at first frightened her, but in due course she became friendly with a being who looked like a giant praying mantis, a kind of entity sometimes reported by abductees. The mantis being, apparently possessing a sense of humor, conveyed the idea that he would like to be called MU, short for "Master of the Universe," though Grant said she would prefer that he be "MU-Bug . . . to help keep things in perspective." MU communicates telepathically and is not physically present during the communications.

MU told her that he and his race had helped life evolve on Earth. Close to one hundred different alien groups visit Earth, some from other places in the galaxy, some from parallel universes. They are on Earth because of their concern about what human beings are doing to the planet's environment. Though they possess the means to do so, they are not repairing the damage because humans have to learn to do that themselves; alien help would only prolong humanity's existence. "We might survive long enough to find an even grander way to destroy ourselves," Grant says MU has observed, "one that could harm worlds other than our own. These beings feel that . . . they would be condemning themselves to a violent confrontation with us in the future." The aliens have taken a middle course. They abduct people and remove some of their DNA, combining it with the DNA of various alien races; thus, "something of the human race will continue." Others are trying to implant spiritual beliefs and psychic perceptions into the brains of humans in the hope that greater wisdom will lead them to survival and peace.

According to MU, alien science indicates that Earth faces a bleak future of ecological collapse, geophysical cataclysms, and political and social upheaval, which may lead to atomic and biological warfare. None of this is certain, only probable. If these things happen, MU says, the aliens may "remove a group of women and children from the surface of the Earth to protect them for the purposes of procreation." These would all be abductees whose genetic make-up had already been altered.

See Also: Abductions by UFOs; Insectoids

Further Reading

Lewels, Joe, 1997. *The God Hypothesis: Extraterrestrial Life and Its Implications for Science and Religion.* Mill Spring, NC: Wild Flower Press.

Muller's Martians

A medium's contacts with Martians are the subject of a classic early work on abnormal psychology, Theodore Flournoy's *From India to the Planet Mars* (1899). Flournoy, a prominent Swiss psychologist, gives the medium the pseudonym Helene Smith in his book, but her real name was Catherine Elise Muller.

Born in 1861, Muller possessed a considerable imagination and a keen intelligence. She grew up in a family in which psychic and visionary experiences were common, and she herself had a number of them. Friends drew her attention to spiritism, and soon she became a medium. Through her, such historical figures as the great novelist Victor Hugo and the legendary occultist Cagliostro spoke, spinning what Flournoy characterizes as "complex sagas." Her Martian adventures began only after a friend remarked, in her presence, on something he had read recently. It was a statement by the popular science writer Camille Flammarion that "Martian humankind and Earth humankind may one day enter into communication with the other." The friend expressed the hope that such a thing would happen.

Soon afterward, Muller informed him that she had made contact with Martians. These encounters occurred in a variety of mental states, including sleep. Flournoy was led to the conclusion that, at least at some level of her psyche, Muller was always living with the Martians. The communications and experiences were voluminous. She had many Martian friends and was often on that planet interacting with them and observing everything around her. She even produced, albeit in piecemeal fashion, a Martian language that Flourney recognized as an "infantile travesty of French."

See Also: Allingham's Martian; Aurora Martian; Brown's Martians; Hopkins's Martians; Khauga; Martian bees; Monka; Shaw's Martians; Smead's Martians; Wilcox's Martians

Further Reading

Flournoy, Theodore, 1963. *From India to the Planet Mars: A Study of a Case of Somnambulism with Glossolalia.* New Hyde Park, NY: University Books.

N

Noma

In 1961, investigating the Brown Mountain lights (believed by most authorities to be refractions of distant light sources such as passing automobiles) near Morganton, North Carolina, Ralph Lael discovered that if he sent telepathic messages to the lights, they would respond. One light urged him to enter a door concealed on the mountainside, where the entities responsible for the lights operated. Lael passed into an eight-foot-square room with transparent walls. There a voice told him that the human race had come into being on a planet once known as Pewam, now the asteroid belt between Mars and Jupiter. On a subsequent visit not long afterward, Lael boarded a flying saucer and was taken to Venus. There, besides meeting the direct descendants of Pewamites, he encountered a lovely, scantily clad woman named Noma. His hosts also showed him footage of Pewam's destruction and of early Earth humans.

Further Reading

Machlin, Milt, and Timothy Green Beckley, 1981. *UFO.* New York: Quick Fox.

Nordics

Nordic is a name given to a kind of alien being reported in UFO encounters that range from contact claims to close encounters of the third kind to abductions. The term did not, however, come into general use among ufologists until the 1980s. Nordics are said to resemble Scandinavians, at least in a generic sense; they are tall, blond, fair-skinned (though sometimes described as deeply tanned), and attractive-looking. Witnesses often claim that their eyes are different from northern Europeans in being somewhat slanted or even almond-shaped.

The beings that would later be called Nordics were first known as Space Brothers—often, though not always, from Venus—when 1950s contactees such as George Adamski and Howard Menger reported meetings with friendly extraterrestrials, with whom they traveled into space and had other adventures. Though conservative ufologists rejected these claims as absurd hoaxes, generally similar figures were reported in the testimony of witnesses who did not fit the contactees' flamboyant profiles.

In one such incident, a farmer near Linha Vista, Brazil, while working in a field heard a sewing-machine sound. When he looked to its source, it turned out to be a strange craft, "shaped like a tropical helmet," hovering nearby. A man could be seen inside the UFO, another stood near a fence, and a third was approaching the witness, who was sufficiently startled to drop his hoe. The being smiled and picked up the hoe, handing it back to the farmer before he and his companions returned to the ship and flew away. The beings, clad in light brown coveralls, had long blond hair, pale skin, and slanted eyes. The farmer, who knew nothing of flying saucers, thought the craft and its occupants were from the United States.

Typically in these kinds of close encounters, the Nordics were not communicative, just silent and distant; they were not unfriendly but not forthcoming either. Ufologists collected hundreds of such accounts from all over the world. As abduction reports rose to prominence in later years, Nordics showed up in many stories, almost always seen in association with little gray aliens and in circumstances that suggested that they occupied a higher position in the otherworldly chain of command than did their smaller fellows. One writer on the abduction phenomenon, David M. Jacobs, believes that "the evidence clearly suggests that the Nordics are most probably adult hybrids, the products of human/alien mating" (Jacobs, 1998).

Nordics live on in current contactee lore, where they are assumed to be genuine extraterrestrials, perhaps representing the race that seeded the Earth and gave rise to modern *Homo sapiens.* Nordics, according to Billy Meier and other post-Adamski friends of the space people, come from the Pleiades star system.

See Also: Abductions by UFOs; Adamski, George; Close encounters of the third kind; Contactees; Hybrid beings; Meier, Eduard "Billy"; Menger, Howard; Walton's abduction

Further Reading

Adamski, George, 1955. *Inside the Space Ships.* New York: Abelard-Schuman.

Bowen, Charles, ed., 1974. *The Humanoids.* London: Futura Publications.

Jacobs, David M., 1998. *The Threat.* New York: Simon and Schuster.

Menger, Howard, 1959. *From Outer Space to You.* Clarksburg, WV: Saucerian Books.

Randles, Jenny, 1988. *Abduction: Over 200 Documented UFO Kidnappings Investigated.* London: Robert Hale.

Stevens, Wendelle C., 1983. *UFO . . . Contact from the Pleiades—A Preliminary Investigative Report—The Report on an Ongoing Contact.* Tucson, AZ: Wendelle C. Stevens.

Nostradamus

Nostradamus—Michael de Nostradame (1503–1566)—was a French physician, astrologer, and counselor to Kings Henry II and Charles IX. He is remembered for his prophecies of world events, culminating in the Second Coming of Christ in 2000. According to an Indiana woman, he returned to this world in 1996 as a channeled entity after living on the Great Central Sun since his death.

A woman who identifies herself only as Pati reports that on a Friday night in July 1996, she was sitting in on a channeling session with like-minded friends when a message came through from an anxious-sounding Nostradamus. Though Pati had never paid much attention to Nostradamus or his prophecies before, she felt a strong, immediate connection. Nostradamus communicated only briefly, but before he withdrew, the channeling group assured him that he was welcome to come back anytime he wished to do so.

The next day, while on a long drive through the country, Pati felt Nostradamus's spirit inside her, seeing and hearing all that passed through her eyes and ears. He asked questions about everything around them. Over the next two months, Pati felt other "energies" enter her. She suspected that they were friends and associates of Nostradamus's from the Great Central Sun. "Judging by the questions that were asked," Pati writes, "these energies either had not been on this planet before or, if they had been, it was so long ago that nothing looked familiar apart from the trees, rocks and water. They asked questions about how houses were built, why this or that particular shape? What materials did we use? On and on, they went, asking about planes, cars, barns and llamas, and why do people MOW their grass!" (Pati, 1999).

On two occasions, Pati verbally channeled Nostradamus. On the first, he expressed satisfaction with his life now and praised the ef-

Nostradamus, shown in magician's garb in his laboratory, writing about astrology (Bettmann/Corbis)

forts of Pati and like-minded people who were making life on Earth better. On the second, he identified two women in the channeling group as his wife and servant in his Earth incarnation. He apologized for treating them as less than his equals.

See Also: Channeling

Further Reading

Pati, 1999. "Nostradamus Comes Back . . . And Likes What He Sees!" *Planet Lightworker* (September/October). http://www.planetlightworker.com/articlefarm/pati/article1.htm.

O

Octopus aliens

While doing chores in his barnyard at 6 A.M. on August 16, 1968, a Serra de Almos, Spain, farmer noticed a light about half a mile away. Thinking it was from a stalled car, he walked over to help what he assumed to be a stranded motorist. The "car" turned out to be a globe-shaped object hovering just above the ground. Nearby were two bizarre-looking creatures that resembled octopuses. They were light in color and three feet tall, and they were dashing on "four or five legs" toward the UFO, which shot away as soon as they entered it.

Journalists and ufologists who examined the site soon afterward found an abundance of burned grass. They also reported that their watches had abruptly ceased operating.

See Also: Close encounters of the third kind

Further Reading

Ballester Olmos, Vicente-Juan, 1976. *A Catalogue of 200 Type-I UFO Events in Spain and Portugal.* Evanston, IL: Center for UFO Studies.

Ogatta

Ogatta is, in the channeling of North Carolina psychic Greta Woodrew, one of five planets in a "jorpah" (solar system) in another galaxy. (The other planets are Oshan, Archa, Mennon, and Tchauvi.) Woodrew, a wealthy professional woman who grew up and lived much of her life in New York City and Connecticut, discovered her connection with Ogatta while exploring her paranormal talents, prominently including metal-bending, with noted parapsychologist Andrija Puharich. Under hypnosis on December 17, 1976, she underwent an out-of-body experience, in which she encountered a figure with both human and bird features. It was clad in a silver suit and had marvelous, golden eyes with a loving expression. Via telepathy she learned that he was Hshames from the Ogatta jorpah (his actual home planet was Mennon).

Soon, under hypnosis and then by channeling, Woodrew was communicating with other entities, one named Ogatta after the planet. She would form a particularly close association with a female Ogattan named Tauri. She learned that many cosmic civilizations, including the Ogattans, are visiting the Earth in ships; the Ogattans call their ships "gattae." Woodrew herself had a dual existence. In one aspect she lived on Earth; in another she lived on Ogatta as "Plura." Plura had made the decision to live—or at least to have a part of her life—on Earth in order to prepare earthlings for the coming Earth changes that will devastate much of the planet before a new age brings peace and harmony.

In time Woodrew learned, via recovered "memories," that she had been interacting with the Ogattans since her childhood. Her first contact took place in the early 1930s when she was three and a half years old. For the next six years, she had many experiences with space people. She was flown to a beautiful planet where she could "hear colors" and "see music" because, like her fellow Ogattans, she was free of the limitations of human physiology; thus, her brain processed stimuli differently.

Though her contacts were overwhelmingly with Ogattans, on occasion she met beings from other worlds. Once she had an out-of-body encounter with beings who looked half-human and half-fish. These entities seemed friendly, but, on a handful of other occasions, she dealt with extraterrestrials who were not so amiable. Some believed the Earth to be of no significance, thus its problems were of no concern to major players in the larger cosmic order.

Woodrew became a lecturer on the New Age circuit, wrote a self-published book, and published a newsletter, *The Woodrew Update.* After the Ogattans warned them that they would have to move to preserve their safety during the coming geological upheavals, Woodrew and her husband, Dick Smolowe, bought a property in western North Carolina in 1982. They moved from Westport, Connecticut, to the survivalist compound they named Reisha Way. In 1988, Doubleday released Woodrew's book *Memories of Tomorrow.* A few years later, Woodrow and Smolowe moved to Winston-Salem for health reasons.

See Also: Channeling; Dual reference

Further Reading

Heard, Alex, 1999. *Apocalypse Pretty Soon: Travels in End-Time America.* New York: W. W. Norton and Company.

Woodrew, Greta, 1981. *On a Slide of Light.* Black Mountain, NC: New Age Press.

———, 1988. *Memories of Tomorrow.* New York: Dolphin/Doubleday.

OINTS

"OINTS" are "Other Intelligences" in an acronym coined by maverick biologist and anomalist Ivan T. Sanderson. To Sanderson OINTS are any beings that are on Earth but are not human. He did not confine his definition simply to extraterrestrial visitors, who in his view are only one among a variety of beings present on this planet. Poltergeists—invisible, destructive spirits—are one kind of OINT. So are the entities who, so he theorized in *Invisible Residents* (1970), dwell under the oceans, occasionally snatching ships, planes, and their crews in places such as the Bermuda Triangle. ("Could there have evolved a technological civilization . . . underwater? I am afraid I have to say that . . . there is no logical reason for stating that there could *not* be.") He also believed that invisible dimensions or parallel universes surround humans. From these other dimensions, entities pop in and out of human reality with regularity, manifesting as everything from fairies to UFOs. They shift their shapes to whatever form may be appropriate to the occasion and the circumstance.

Curiously, however, Sanderson held a dim view of all such visitors, not because he feared they might be unfriendly but because "the OINTS are . . . *incredibly and abysmally stupid.*" He suspected that they were so advanced that their technology now controlled them and that they have given up mental activity, just as technology has caused humans to reduce much of their physical activity. "That they are for the most part overcivilized and quite mad," he wrote, "is, in my opinion, an open-ended question but quite probable. Perhaps, we will never be able to cope with them until we, too, all go quite mad."

See Also: Bermuda Triangle; Fairies encountered

Further Reading

Sanderson, Ivan T., 1970. *Invisible Residents: A Disquisition upon Certain Matters Maritime, and the Possibility of Intelligent Life under the Waters of the Earth.* New York: World Publishing Company.

Old Hag

The "Old Hag" is a folk expression—popular, for example, in Newfoundland—for the par-

Henri Fuseli, The Nightmare, *1781 (The Detroit Institute of the Arts, gift of Mr. and Mrs. Bert L. Smokler and Mr. and Mrs. Lawrence A. Fleishman)*

ticular experience that gave rise to the word "nightmare." Nightmare has come to be a synonym for "bad dream," but traditionally nightmare (from the Anglo-Saxon *nicht* [night] and *mara* [incubus or succubus]) referred to a specific nocturnal experience. A menacing supernatural entity, often perceived as an ugly witch, enters a bedroom and sits on the witness's chest, leaving him or her with the sensation of being crushed. All the while the victim lies paralyzed and helpless.

Though the experience occurs frequently to Americans—one in six, according to a scientist who has studied the phenomenon—American culture has no name for it. Thus, those who undergo it are at a loss to understand it or to put it into any larger context. Many, having never heard of others' experiences, are left wondering about their sanity.

The Old Hag is the subject of a classic work, *The Terror That Comes in the Night* (1982), by David J. Hufford, a medical scientist and folklorist at Pennsylvania State University. Hufford uses the experience, among other things, to scrutinize the way psychologists have dealt with such reports and to examine the trustworthiness of eyewitness testimony to anomalous events. Most scientists and scholars have sought to explain Old Hag attacks as the result of perceptual errors, faulty memories, lies, psychotic episodes, or hallucinations shaped by images in the claimants' cultural environment. According to Hufford, they have often discarded witness testimony, resulting in what Hufford charges was an effort to reinvent the experience so that it could be "explained." Referring to a study by early psychoanalyst and Freud biographer Ernest

Jones, Hufford says that "one can hardly distinguish the experiences themselves from their interpretations."

Hufford argues that if would-be explainers had listened to what the witnesses reported about the particular symptoms of Old Hag experience, they might have been able to explain it sooner. Research in the 1960s and 1970s in sleep paralysis both underscores the accuracy of the testimony and explains most of it, though, so far, not the peculiar fact that the *contents* of the experience are consistent no matter to whom or in what cultural context they occur.

In Hufford's judgment, too much scholarly writing on extraordinary experience reflects "unexamined prejudices and makes facile assumptions about cultural processes," thus confusing rather than clarifying issues.

Old Hag sleep paralysis may explain at least some abduction and other ostensibly UFO-related "bedroom visitations." For example, John A. Keel, author of several books on UFOs, has written of his own encounters with strange entities, including one in which "I woke up in the middle of the night to find myself unable to move, with a huge dark apparition standing over me" (Keel, 1970).

Addressing the abduction phenomenon, Hufford has said, "If the paralysis attacks, as described by abductees, are directly linked to abductions, there is every reason to believe that the abduction phenomenon has *great* historical depth and is associated in complex ways with other classes of anomalous experience" (Hufford, 1994).

See Also: Abductions by UFOs; Keel, John Alva

Further Reading

Hufford, David J., 1982. *The Terror That Comes in the Night: An Experienced-Centered Study of Supernatural Assault Traditions.* Philadelphia: University of Pennsylvania Press.

———, 1994. "Awakening Paralyzed in the Presence of a Strange 'Visitor'." In Andrea Pritchard, David E. Pritchard, John E. Mack, Pam Kasey, and Claudia Yapp, eds. *Alien Discussions: Proceedings of the Abduction Study Conference,* 348–354. Cambridge, MA: North Cambridge Press.

Keel, John A., 1970. *Strange Creatures from Time and Space.* Greenwich, CT: Fawcett Gold Medal.

Oleson's giants

On May 2, 1897, during a spate of mysterious "airship" sightings that some popular speculation tied to possible visitors from other planets, the *Houston Post* published a letter from John Leander of El Campo, Texas. Leander related the story of a local man, identified only as Mr. Oleson, an elderly, retired sailor who once served on Danish vessels. According to Leander, in September 1862 Oleson had witnessed the crash of a mysterious craft and seen the bodies of the giant beings who had flown it.

At the time the incident took place, Oleson was serving as mate on the brig *Christine* on the Indian Ocean. A furious storm erupted and raged for hours until, finally, a wave washed over the ship, and Oleson and five companions were swept onto a small, rocky island. All were injured, and one soon died. The island was devoid of life, and the men resigned themselves to their deaths. As they sat hopeless at the base of a cliff, they witnessed a bizarre and terrifying sight: an immense flying ship, apparently out of control and about to crash, was heading directly toward them. Fortunately, the wind blew it off course, and it smashed against the rocks a few hundred yards away.

Overcoming their deep fear, the sailors made their way to the wreckage. The machine, which they deduced had been the size of a battleship, lay in a shapeless mass, revealing little except that the craft had had four large wings. There were things that looked like tools and furniture, evidently from the ship's interior, and the men opened boxes covered with unusual characters. Inside the boxes, they uncovered nourishing food.

"But their horror was intensified," Leander wrote, "when they found the bodies of more than a dozen men dressed in garments of strange fashion and texture. The bodies were a dark bronze color, but the strangest feature of all was the immense size of the men. They had no means of measuring their bodies, but estimated them to be more than twelve feet high. Their hair and beards were also long and as soft and silky as the hair of an infant" (Bullard, 1982). The sight so unsettled one of the men that he was driven mad. He promptly hurled himself off into the sea, where he drowned.

The survivors retreated from the scene, and it took them two days to restore their courage sufficiently to return. They rummaged for food and then dragged the giants' bodies off the cliff and into the water. Using pieces of the spaceship, they built a raft and set out on the now-still ocean. Sixty hours later, they came upon a Russian vessel heading for Australia. Before they could reach port, however, three more of Oleson's companions died from their injuries and shock.

"Fortunately as a partial confirmation of the truth of his story," Leander wrote, "Mr. Oleson took from one of the bodies a finger ring of immense size. It is made of a compound of metals unknown to any jeweler who has seen it, and is set with two reddish stones, the names of which are unknown to anyone who has ever examined it. The ring was taken from the thumb of the owner and measure two and one-quarter inches in diameter."

Leander's yarn was one of many told in the spring of 1897 about airships and their supposed crews. Newspapers all over America carried comparable tall tales, including one alleging a Martian's crash-landing and his subsequent burial in a small north-Texas town.

See Also: Aurora Martian; Michigan giant; Wilson

Further Reading

Bullard, Thomas E., ed. 1982. *The Airship File: A Collection of Texts Concerning Phantom Airships and Other UFOs, Gathered from Newspapers and Periodicals Mostly during the Hundred Years Prior to Kenneth Arnold's Sighting.* Bloomington, IN: self-published.

Olliana Olliana Alliano

Speaking at a contactee conference in 1982, Dave Schultz, an electrician from Louisville, Colorado, related a lifetime of interactions with extraterrestrials, among them the Olliana Olliana Alliano. The Olliana Olliana Alliano are forty inches tall, humanlike in appearance except for a slightly larger head. Schultz called them "the good people," guardians of the Earth. It was Olliana Olliana Alliano who died in the 1948 spaceship crash at Aztec, New Mexico, chronicled in Frank Scully's *Behind the Flying Saucers* (1950).

This alien group is here to "get the vibrations of the planet up to a level in which we can join the space federation." Before that happens, humans have to shed their violent, warlike, greedy ways. The Olliana Olliana Alliano have contacted every political leader on Earth to deliver this message.

See Also: Contactees; Mersch

Further Reading

Sprinkle, R. Leo, ed., 1982. *Proceedings: Rocky Mountain Conference on UFO Investigation.* Laramie, WY: School of Extended Studies, University of Wyoming.

Orthon

Orthon was the name George Adamski—or, more accurately, his ghostwriter Charlotte Blodget—gave to the Venusian Adamski met in the desert of southern California on November 20, 1952. Space people, Adamski explained, never call themselves by name when interacting with human beings because they have "an entirely different concept of names as we use them" (Adamski, 1955). In that first encounter, Adamski communicated with the being he called Orthon via gestures, sign language, and snatches of telepathy, during which the Venusian expressed concern about earthlings' warlike ways. Adamski saw Orthon again briefly when he flew overhead in his scout craft the following December 13.

He next met Orthon in the early morning hours of February14, 1953, when two spacemen picked him up at a Los Angeles hotel and drove him into the desert to an awaiting saucer. As he approached the ship, he saw Orthon, who was finishing some repair work. Seeing "a very small amount of molten metal that he had thrown out," Adamski scooped up the object. When his companions asked him why he was doing that, he said he wanted concrete proof of his contacts. Orthon explained, though, that "you will find that this alloy contains the same on all planets" (Adamski, 1955). They boarded the ship together and flew into space, where Adamski and Orthon—now speaking lucid English, as had not been the case in their first encounter—engaged in extended conversation.

A third meeting with Orthon took place on August 23, 1954, after the same two spacemen, Firkon of Mars and Ramu of Saturn, picked up Adamski at his home and took him to a spacecraft. Adamski was reunited not only with Orthon but also with other extraterrestrials, including the beautiful women Ilmuth (a Martian) and Kalna (a Venusian) who had been aboard the ship he had entered earlier. This time Orthon showed Adamski scenes from the Venusian surface. The Venusians, Orthon said, have an average lifetime of a thousand years.

On April 25, 1955, Adamski flew into space again with Orthon. A crewmember used Adamski's camera to take photographs of a nearby Venusian Mother Ship into which Adamski had transferred. Two of the blurry results are reproduced in *Inside the Space Ships.* One of them, according to the caption, shows a Venusian looking out of a porthole, Adamski out of a second, though to the untrained eye the faces look like no more than blobs of light. Lou Zinsstag, a Swiss woman who was close to Adamski and eventually became his biographer, reported that one day in 1959, while the two were conversing, he pulled out his wallet and extracted from it a photograph of Orthon in profile. Zinsstag, who was allowed to study it briefly, was struck by the figure's pronounced chin.

In the early 1960s, according to Adamski, a new group of space people replaced the old one. In later years, after his death, old associates such as Blodget, Madeleine Rodeffer, Fred Steckling, and Steve Within made claims of having met Orthon, but Alice Wells, Adamski's executor and head of the George Adamski Foundation, rejected their assertions.

See Also: Adamski, George; Ramu

Further Reading

Adamski, George, 1955. *Inside the Space Ships.* New York: Abelard-Schuman.

Good, Timothy, 1998. *Alien Base: Earth's Encounters with Extraterrestrials.* London: Century.

Hallet, Marc, 1997. "Adamski and His Believers: A Reminiscence." In Hilary Evans and Dennis Stacy, eds. *UFOs 1947–1997: From Arnold to the Abductees: Fifty Years of Flying Saucers,* 28–34. London: John Brown Publishing.

Leslie, Desmond, and George Adamski, 1953. *Flying Saucers Have Landed.* New York: British Book Centre.

Zinsstag, Lou, and Timothy Good, 1983. *George Adamski—The Untold Story.* Beckenham, Kent, England: Ceti Publications.

Oxalc

Oxalc is from the planet Morlen, settled long ago by human beings from the Orion system. They sought to establish a supercolony. The planet now houses six large cities in which beings from many worlds, including Earth, currently reside. Oxalc oversees forty-nine extraterrestrial guides involved in Mission Rama. According to one source, "The word RAMA contains a vibratory activator and was chosen forty-two hundred years ago. RA represents the Sun or irradiation and MA represents Mother Earth. The mantra Rama means Irradiating Light on Earth" (Edilver, n.d.). Mission Rama's purpose is to help planets in transition, such as Earth (also known as Merla), as they enter the fourth dimension.

Oxalc's presence on Earth became known in 1973 after a group of Peruvian flying-saucer enthusiasts led by Sixto Paz Wells decided to try to establish psychic communications with extraterrestrials. The initial contacts took place through automatic writing from an entity who called himself Oxalc. Oxalc gave a specific date and place where he would meet them personally. The group went to the location, a coastal region thirty-seven miles south of Lima, and were shocked to see a brilliantly lighted, hamburger-shaped metallic craft hovering less than three hundred feet over their heads. Their fear and excitement were so intense that Oxalc, communicating telepathically, informed them that no meeting would take place; before one could happen, they would have to learn how to control their emotions.

The messages continued and began to circulate through the Spanish-speaking world. They described the nature of the cosmos, Earth's secret history, and human beings' spiritual nature. The teachings were circulated under the name Mission Rama, organized as a nonprofit corporation. They hold that there are three different universes: material (Septennial), mental (Eternal), and spiritual (Mental). Our own Milky Way is under the direction of twenty-four highly evolved beings, the Elders of the Galaxy. Beneath them are advanced civilizations which actively assist lesser but developing races. Each of these takes on a particular task, as Genetic Engineers, Keepers, Guardians, Instructors, and the like. "Galaxy M-31," in the Andromeda constellation, is the seat of an extremely important council where representatives of a number of galaxies in our region of space deliberate. The council is called the Council of Nine, and the beings sitting on it are the Nine of Andromeda. They, along with the twenty-four Elders of each galaxy, comprise the Great White Brotherhood of the Star.

Members of the Earth's Mission Rama have reported extraordinary experiences, not just UFO sightings but otherworldly journeys through artificially constructed space-time portals (Xendras). "Many others received their 'Cosmic Names,' whose pronunciation is in tune with the total nature of each individual's soul," one document states (Edilver, n.d.).

See Also: Great White Brotherhood

Further Reading

Edilver [pseud. of Giorgio Piacenza], 1992. "Mission Rama." Coral Gables, FL: self-published.

Oz Factor

"Oz Factor" is a phrase coined by British ufologist Jenny Randles, who calls it the "sensation of being isolated, or transported from the real world into a different environmental framework." Randles noted its presence in a number of UFO cases she investigated. It was as if, she wrote, witnesses were "being transported temporarily from our world into another, where reality is but slightly different. . . . I call it 'the Oz Factor,' after the fairytale land of Oz" (Randles, 1983). She suspects that in many ostensibly straightforward UFO encounters, witnesses are in an altered state of consciousness.

In Oz Factor incidents, an individual may witness a spectacular UFO display or even landing and contact in a public space at a time when other persons should be about. Yet other people will be weirdly absent, and a zone of silence will surround the scene. The witness may feel as if he or she has been "chosen" to view the object.

Such phenomena have also been reported in the context of men in black encounters. For example, Peter Rojcewicz tells of an experience he underwent one afternoon in November 1980, when he was doing research on a Ph.D. dissertation in folklore at the University of Pennsylvania library. His subject was UFOs. A strange man dressed in black interrupted his work and engaged him in a disjointed exchange about flying saucers. The stranger then seemed to disappear. "I was highly excited and finally walked around the stacks to the reference desk and nobody was behind the desk," Rojcewicz wrote. He could find no one else in the library anywhere, a situation he regarded as virtually incomprehensible. Fighting panic, he returned to where he had been sitting. "In about an hour I rose to leave the library," he recalled. "There were two librarians behind each of the two desks!" (Rojcewicz, 1987).

An American psychiatric social worker writing under a pseudonym recounts a lifetime of encounters with a range of otherworldly beings. She says,

> I apparently entered into an altered state when encounters occurred. It seemed to be an altered energy or time field created by the beings. Everything fell silent. The air felt heavy, like liquid crystal, and it seemed to carry nonverbal information between the beings and myself.

From left to right: Peter Brookesmith; Jenny Randles, the ufologist who coined the term "Oz Factor"; and Jerome Clark at Fortean Times UnConvention95 (Lisa Anders/Fortean Picture Library)

> Time slowed and eddied in strange ways. Beings usually informed me (telepathically in most cases) that I would not remember the events until much later. As they communicated this, an opaque screen formed in my mind, and the encounter began to feel dim, even while it was still occurring. Additionally, when the encounter ended, the altered field also dissolved. Merely exiting the field also cloaked the memory. (Oakman, 1999)

See Also: Men in black

Further Reading

Oakman, Lisa [pseud.], 1999. "UFO Beings, Folklore, and Mythology: Personal Experiences." *International UFO Reporter* 24, 4 (Winter): 7–12.

Randles, Jenny, 1983. *UFO Reality: A Critical Look at the Physical Evidence.* London: Robert Hale.

Rojcewicz, Peter M., 1987. "The 'Men in Black' Experience and Tradition: Analogues with the Traditional Devil Hypothesis." *Journal of American Folklore* 100 (April/June): 148–160.

P

Paul 2

Paul Solem, an Idaho rancher, first heard from Paul 2—though he did not know his name at the time—in 1948 when a mental voice from a flying saucer told him, "You will hear from us later" (Clark, 1971). Four years later Solem met Paul 2, a self-identified "angel" from Venus. Solem was informed that he had been a Venusian in a previous life and that his mission in the present incarnation was to work with North and South American Indians to prepare the City of Zion. A great cataclysm was coming, and in its wake a utopian society would be built with the aid of space people and their earthly allies.

Solem surfaced publicly in July 1969 at the Fort Hall Indian Reservation in Idaho, where he and several Indian associates declared in a series of campfire meetings that flying saucers had arrived to fulfill a Hopi prophecy about the Day of Purification. According to Hopi tradition, a great fiery explosion would herald the coming of the True White Brother. Only those who had remained true to the ancient Hopi ways would be spared.

Moving his operation to Hotevilla, Arizona, where the Hopi Sun Clan was headquartered, Solem worked with the 106-year-old Chief Dan Katchongva to integrate flying saucers into the tribe's traditional faith. Katchongva was a friend of contactee and fringe archaeologist George Hunt Williamson, author of books speculating about the relationship of native religions and visiting extraterrestrials. Younger tribal members resisted Katchongva and Solem's efforts, though other residents of the area were claiming UFO sightings that they took to be evidence of the prophecy's imminent fulfillment.

Solem announced that Paul 2 would bring in flying saucers for all to see on four occasions, beginning on Easter Sunday 1971. Their failure to appear on the first scheduled date destroyed Solem's credibility, and soon afterward Katchongva was ousted from his position as leader of the Sun Clan. He died the following year. Solem lapsed into obscurity. His last known public appearance was on July 21, 1990, in the resort town of Lava Hot Springs, Idaho, where he spoke to a small crowd and tried without success to entice saucers to fly overhead.

See Also: Contactees; Williamson, George Hunt

Further Reading

Clark, Jerome, 1971. "Indian Prophecy and the Prescott UFOs." *Fate* 24, 4 (April): 54–61.

Davis, Rick, 1990. "Would You Believe, Flying Saucers over Lava?" *Idaho State Journal* (Pocatello, July 15).

Katchongva, Chief Dan, 1970. *Hopi Prophecy.* Hotevilla, AZ: Hopi Independent Nation.

Kimball, Richard W., 1995. "American Indian Prophecies Confirm the Reality of Flying Saucers." *Prescott* [Arizona] *Daily Courier Gazette* (December 24).

Waters, Frank, 1963. *Book of the Hopi.* New York: Viking Press.

Williamson, George Hunt, 1959. *Road in the Sky.* London: Neville Spearman.

Philip

"Philip" is an imaginary entity said to have been given a degree of physical reality when a Toronto-based parapsychological group consciously "invented" him. He was part of an experiment intended to demonstrate that mental energies can create the sorts of entities reported in spiritualist séances and poltergeist episodes.

In September 1972, members of the Toronto Society for Psychical Research invented Philip, laying out a detailed personal biography. A pro-royal aristocrat during England's Civil War, Philip fell in love with a Gypsy woman but lost her when authorities tried and burned her at the stake as a witch. His failure to find a way to save her filled him with guilt and grief and prevented his soul from passing on to the afterlife, leaving it an earthbound spirit. The group, whose members included psychologist A.R.G. Owen and his wife Iris, began to meditate on Philip in hopes that he would "appear" to them in some fashion. Nothing happened for a year.

Then the group decided to try a different tactic. Members decided to imitate the methods of nineteenth-century spiritualist circles, on the theory that skepticism inhibited the occurrence of paranormal phenomena. Like the earlier spiritualist sitters, they sat in a circle, sang, or otherwise tried to create an atmosphere conducive to the manifestation of the unknown. Within a few weeks, they began hearing raps from the table. They were able to communicate with the knocker by asking simple "yes" or "no" questions. Once the table apparently levitated. Eventually, Philip seemed to take on a personality of his own, independent of the one the group had assigned him. He would reject or contradict his "life" story. Once, when a member reminded him that he was purely imaginary, he disappeared for some weeks, to reappear only when members managed to recapture some semblance of belief in his actual existence.

On one occasion, the group demonstrated Philip's manifestations on a television program. Iris Owen and another member, Margaret Sparrow, wrote a book on the episode, which they believed demonstrated the reality not of ghosts but of psychokinesis. One subsequent observer, however, cautions that though "potentially highly significant, the experiment has not been repeated by other researchers" (Dash, 1997).

See Also: Tulpa

Further Reading

Dash, Mike, 1997. *Borderlands.* London: Heinemann.

Owen, Iris M., and Margaret Sparrow, 1976. *Conjuring up Philip.* New York: Harper and Row.

Planetary Council

Celeste Korsholm, a Sedona, Arizona, channeler and metaphysical counselor, learned of the Planetary Council one day in 1991. In an out-of-body state, she met the twelve ascended masters who compose the ruling body of Earth's solar system. Over the next few years, they returned individually to channel the histories of the planets and their futures. Each planet, she learned, is like a university. Each of us comes from somewhere else, from a higher dimension of existence known as the Source, and enters through star gates such as Lyra, Orion, Sirius, and the Pleiades, "where our higher frequencies of Light are gradually decreased to prepare for life in the denser third dimension," in Korsholm's words (Korsholm, 1991), on the way to the solar system.

The education starts at the Schools of Saturn, where the pilgrim gets a crash course in each planet's vibrations before spending a separate lifetime on at least one other planet before making the decision whether to volunteer for "postgraduate work on Earth" (Korsholm,

1995). On the chosen planet, one assumes the physical form of its inhabitants. That means that on Venus one becomes a winged humanoid that gives off light and color as it flies. Merbeings live on Neptune, and on Uranus one finds hairy primates with the features of both human beings and the great apes. Mars has two advanced insect races, one of ants, the other of praying mantises. Jupiter houses giant, intelligent reptilian forms. Each species got its Light Intelligence from a group of traveling extraterrestrials called the Watchers who monitor planets looking for species of exceptional promise. As Earth was being developed, the inhabitants of other planets were asked to contribute representatives, thus fairies, mermen and mermaids, Bigfoot/Sasquatch, insects, and dinosaurs. Explorers and refugees from star wars live on the other planets. Evidence of the presence of neighboring extraterrestrials can be found in archaeological discoveries and ancient myths. Each group tended to concentrate its efforts in a particular region, for example Martians in the Middle East, Uranians in Mexico, and Plutonians in China.

Earth and other planets have undergone much turbulence, much of it caused by the tenth planet, Phoenix. "This huge planet's three thousand plus year orbit is at right angles to the plane of all the other planets' orbits," Korsholm explains (Korsholm, 1995), and when the other planets are on the same side of the sun as it, its powerful magnetic force field causes havoc on the surfaces of those worlds, both destroying and creating. The Planetary Council must always monitor the location and effects of Phoenix. Its members also deal with the periodic arrival of groups from other solar systems. Some are highly evolved and benign, others less developed and belligerent.

According to Korsholm, the members of the Planetary Council are: Horus, representing the sun, coordinates the council's work with that of higher space intelligences and Christ councils. Hermes (Mercury) is in charge of communication through space. Adonis (Venus) guides the evolution of love and beauty. Enoch (Earth) oversees prophecy. Croesus (Mars) is responsible for the coordination of council activities with the dictates of the Ascended Masters in the Brotherhood of Light. Athena (the asteroid belt, formerly the planet Maldek) defends truth and justice. Jove (Jupiter) balances magnetic fields. Zoroaster (Saturn) monitors order, structure, and destiny. Quetzalcoatal (Uranus) leads religious and philosophical change. Merlin (Neptune) directs scientific discovery. Lao-Tzu (Pluto) offers objective, detached wisdom, and Apollo (Phoenix) generates change. All of these individuals figure in earthly mythology and (in the case of Lao-Tzu, the founder of Taoism) history.

See Also: Ascended Masters; Athena; Fairies encountered; Sasquatch

Further Reading

Korsholm, Celeste, 1991. "Lao-Tzu, Planetary Council Member from Pluto." http://www.spiritweb.org/Spirit/pluto-celeste.html.

———, 1995. "Tales from the Planets." http://spiritweb.org/Spirit/tales-planets-celeste.html.

Portla

Portla is best remembered as the extraterrestrial who in a July 18, 1952, channeling with George W. Van Tassel introduced Ashtar, the most ubiquitous and beloved of New Age beings. The psychic message was, "Approaching your solar system is a ventla [spaceship] with our chief aboard, commander of the station Schare in charge of the first four sectors. . . . We are waiting here at 72,000 miles above you to welcome our chief, who will be entering this solar system for the first time" (Van Tassel, 1952). The chief was Ashtar.

See Also: Ashtar; Channeling; Van Tassel, George W.

Further Reading

Van Tassel, George W., 1952. *I Rode a Flying Saucer! The Mystery of the Flying Saucers Revealed.* Los Angeles: New Age Publishing Company.

Power of Light (POL)

One day in 1967, a deeply unhappy Swedish man, Bjorn Ortenheim, vowed to commit sui-

Landscape with volcanic craters, Haleakala Mountains, Maui, Hawaii National Park. Bjorn Ortenheim was informed by Power of Light that Lemurian ruins with still powerful energies and vibrations could be found on or near the ocean around Maui. (Library of Congress)

cide. Prior to committing the act, however, he lapsed into a deep, almost comalike sleep. When he awoke, he was mysteriously transformed, full of scientific ambitions and bold ideas. He soon became aware that otherworldly entities were instructing him during his sleep. They were particularly interested in nonpolluting technology and in other inventions that would elevate human consciousness. In 1981, the leader of the group, Power of Light (Ortenheim soon began thinking of him as POL), appeared to him in waking consciousness.

Ortenheim found himself ever more attracted to the Hawaiian island of Maui. POL informed him that Lemurian ruins with still powerful energies and vibrations could be found on or near the ocean. In fact, the capital city of Lemuria, Denerali, lay under the water in the bay outside Maui. POL said a large crystal from that lost continent existed there. Ortenheim should use its energies, employing his own technological innovations to enhance them, to raise human consciousness.

He soon moved to Maui to pursue his work, always under POL's guidance. According to Ortenheim, POL is not a person but a near-god who is among God's highest servants. POL is, he says, "in charge of the ultimate energy and source of life in our universe, the Universal Magnetic Field, UMF" (Montgomery, 1985).

See Also: Lemuria

Further Reading

Montgomery, Ruth, 1985. *Aliens among Us.* New York: G. P. Putnam's Sons.

Prince Neosom

Prince Neosom was Lee Childers, a Detroit baker who, in 1958, reinvented himself as a member of the royal family of the planet Tythan, eight and a half light years from Earth. Neosom said he had replaced the body of a stillborn child (Childers). He also claimed that he could travel instantaneously through space simply by closing his eyes and wishing himself to other planets. Three times, he said, the men in black had killed him, and three times a rejuvenation machine had brought him back to life.

At the peak of his brief moment in the spotlight, Neosom/Childers was brought to New York City to lecture. In December 1958, he appeared on Long John Nebel's popular WOR radio show, which catered to the eccentric and the esoteric, but he managed to get thrown off the air before his allotted time was up; his stories were too outlandish even for the famously tolerant Nebel. By this time, Childers had left his wife and five children and taken up with Beth Docker, soon renamed Princess Negonna, whom he soon married and honeymooned with on Tythan.

Childers's career on saucerdom's fringes continued until the early 1960s.

See Also: Men in black

Further Reading

Barker, Gray, 1959. "Chasing the Flying Saucers." *Flying Saucers* (May): 19–43.

Mann, Michael G., 1960. "Prince or King, He Isn't a Spaceman!" *Saucer News* 7, 1 (March): 5–7.

Mapes. D. O., 1959. *Prince Neosom, Planet: Tyton* [sic]. Buffalo, NY: self-published.

An artist's impression of a gray alien, based on witness descriptions, an example of a psychoterrestrial being (Debbie Lee/Fortean Picture Library)

Psychoterrestrials

New Age psychologist Michael Grosso uses the term "psychoterrestrials" to describe a range of anomalous and paranormal entities, including UFO beings, Marian apparitions, and men in black. He believes that such entities, though "mythic constructs," are able to assume a quasi-physical reality because of the deep resonance they have in humanity's collective psyche. Another name for psychoterrestrials is psychic projections.

Grosso believes that UFOs and other exotic phenomena are "forces of rebirth" that the "ultradimensional mind" has conjured up to transform mass consciousness in order to save the human race for otherwise certain self-destruction. "Given the timeless, spaceless nature of ESP and PK [psychokinesis], perhaps some (or all) human minds form a system—a parallel universe of mind, a distinct entity with its own properties. . . . It would be a mind with properties distinct from component minds, on the assumption that the whole is greater than the sum of its parts. . . . Perhaps this is the entity that holds the secret to the UFO mystery" (Grosso, 1991).

In his view, psychoterrestrial phenomena are so powerful that, for example, in their UFO manifestation they are even able to show up on radar. Grosso drew inspiration in his speculations from the celebrated Swiss psychologist and philosopher C. G. Jung. In his own reflection on the UFO phenomenon, however, Jung, who thought UFOs were probably of extraterrestrial origin, rejected the

Aliens, or psychoterrestrials, capture a man played by James Earl Jones in The UFO Incident, *an NBC TV movie, 1975. (Photofest)*

notion of "materialized psychisms" as impossible, and, in particular, he dismissed the notion that materialized psychisms, even if they could be proved to exist, could be detected by instruments such as radar.

See Also: Imaginal beings; Marian apparitions; Men in black

Further Reading

Grosso, Michael, 1985. *The Final Choice: Playing the Survival Game.* Walpole, NH: Stillpoint Publishing.

———, 1992. *Frontiers of the Soul: Exploring Psychic Evolution.* Wheaton, IL: Quest Books.

———, 1989. "UFOs and the Myth of the New Age." In Dennis Stillings, ed. *Cyberbiological Studies of the Imaginal Component in the UFO Contact Experience,* 81–98. St. Paul, MN: Arches Project.

———, 1991. "The Ultradimensional Mind." *Strange Magazine* 7 (April): 10–13.

Jung, C. G., 1959. *Flying Saucers: A Modern Myth of Things Seen in the Skies.* New York: Harcourt, Brace and Company.

Puddy's abduction

An incident from Australia in the early 1970s may or may not shed light on the UFO abduction phenomenon. Maureen Puddy's experiences, some contend, indicate that persons who believe that aliens have kidnapped them may instead be suffering vivid hallucinations, perhaps in altered states of consciousness.

On the evening of July 3, 1972, on her way home from seeing her hospitalized son, this thirty-seven-year-old Victoria woman was alarmed to see a glowing blue UFO pacing her car at a distance of no more than a hundred feet. Just as suddenly as it appeared, it was gone. One night later that month, she began hearing a mental voice repeatedly speaking her name. The next evening, July 25, at the same place she had seen it before, the UFO showed up. Her car engine abruptly ceased functioning, and everything became eerily silent. A mechanical voice speaking "too perfect" English told her, "All your tests will be negative." It went on, "Tell the media. Do not panic. We mean no harm" (Magee, 1972, 1978). At the UFO's departure the car's engine resumed operation.

She next heard the voice in February, when it instructed her to return to the "meeting place." By this time she had met with two prominent ufologists, Judith Magee and Paul Norman, so she called them and asked them to meet her at the designated location. As Puddy waited in her parked car for the two to arrive, a man with long, blond hair, wearing a uniform that looked like a ski suit, briefly appeared next to her before he vanished. As soon as they pulled up, Magee and Norman joined her inside her vehicle. Puddy shouted that the same strange man was beckoning to her, but the investigators saw nothing. She then seemed to faint, though her mouth kept moving. She spoke of being in a round room and watching as a mushroom-shaped device rose from the middle of the floor. It was covered with markings reminiscent of hieroglyphics. Near it stood the blond-haired figure she had seen minutes before. She said the man was telling her to describe what she was seeing. All the while Puddy was growing ever more frightened, until finally she broke into tears. At that moment she regained full consciousness but remembered nothing.

She claimed one other subsequent encounter with the stranger, whom she saw standing in the road about a week later.

Australian ufologist Keith Basterfield would write, "All who interviewed Maureen Puddy thought her to be a normal, healthy individual. The entire series of events puzzled her, and she got nothing but ridicule from persons for reporting the episodes" (Basterfield, 1992). Her story bore some resemblance to abduction accounts, but there are also some differences, notably the absence of the medical examination which figures in most such experiences. Still, skeptics see it as evidence that what witnesses believe to be objective experiences may in fact be subjective in nature.

See Also: Abductions by UFOs

Further Reading

Basterfield, Keith, 1992. "Present at the Abduction." *International UFO Reporter* 17, 3 (May/June): 13–14, 23.

Magee, Judith, 1972. "UFO over the Mooraduc Road." *Flying Saucer Review* 18, 6 (November/December): 3–5.

———, 1978. "Maureen Puddy's Third Encounter." *Flying Saucer Review* 24, 3 (November 1978): 12–13, 15.

R

R. D.

In both abduction reports and contactee stories, claimants sometimes report seeing human beings onboard a UFO and in the company of aliens. One such incident is said to have occurred on June 5, 1964, in Argentina. At 4 A.M., a doctor and his wife were driving a few miles from the airport at Pajas Blancas, in Cordoba province, when their engine failed. A huge, extraordinary-looking craft landed on the highway in front of them. For the next twenty minutes the couple stared in puzzlement and unease at the UFO. Then, according to a press account, a man walked out of it and spoke to them in Spanish, "Don't be afraid. I am a terrestrial. My name is R. D." Apparently the man gave his full name, but published accounts give only his initials. He went on, "Tell mankind about it, in your own fashion" (Creighton, 1974).

The man walked slowly back toward the UFO and was joined by two gray-clad beings who had suddenly appeared. They boarded the ship, and it flew rapidly away, a violet-colored trail in its wake.

See Also: Abductions by UFOs; Contactees

Further Reading

Creighton, Gordon, 1974. "The Humanoids in Latin America." In Charles Bowen, ed. *The Humanoids,* 84–129. London: Futura Publications.

Ra

Ra channeled through Carla Rueckert. Ra was not an individual but a group entity, part of the "Confederation of Planets in the Service of the Infinite Creator" (Rueckert and Elkins, 1977). The goal, Ra said, was to "give instructions to those of planet Earth who would seek the instructions for how to produce within themselves the vibration that is more harmonious with the original thought."

Further Reading

Rueckert, Carla, and Don Elkins, 1977. *Secrets of the UFOs.* Louisville, KY: L/L Research.

Rainbow City

Rainbow City was the ancestral, earthly home of the human race, according to a mystically inclined couple, W. C. and Gladys Hefferlin. It was located in Antarctica before the Earth tipped on its side, and the continent became the uninhabitable place as it is known today.

The Hefferlins surfaced in 1946, in short pieces published in Ray Palmer's *Amazing Stories,* then publishing a series of stories detailing the Shaver mystery, a supposedly true account of Richard Shaver's adventures with good and evil races living in caverns under the earth. After W. C. Hefferlin made a passing reference to "Rainbow City," Palmer appended a statement describing it as "the headquarters, a deserted city of the Gods (or the Elder Race) under the ice of the [South] Pole" (Kafton-Minkel, 1989). Hefferlin claimed to have access to advanced weapons and devices left over from Rainbow City, but his assertions about the science behind them were so full of elementary technical errors that reader ridicule encouraged Palmer to cease publishing Hefferlin's writings.

He and his wife reappeared, however, in 1947 and 1948, in publications of the California-based Borderland Sciences Research Associates. In a series of articles, they recounted their association with a mysterious man named Emery, whom they first met in 1927. Over time they developed a system of telepathic communication with him, sending thoughts back and forth from their Indiana home to his in New York City. Emery began to travel widely, dropping out of sight without explanation, then reappearing. Just before the onset of World War II, he informed them that he had met a Tibetan master who lived in a hidden valley in that nation. Soon he was working under orders from the Masters of Human Destiny, otherwise known as the Ancient Three.

Recognizing W. C. Hefferlin as a reincarnated engineer who had worked for the ancients long ago, the Three asked him for help in constructing a fleet of three hundred-fifty circle-winged aircraft. After the craft were completed, they searched Antarctica for the ruins of Rainbow City, where the Three had lived during their first earthly incarnation. Emery himself participated in the search, which ended on Thanksgiving Day 1942 when he found Rainbow City.

Over time, Emery revealed the secrets of the Three to the Hefferlins. Once, they said, the human race ruled hundreds of galaxies. Unfortunately, the spacefarers eventually encountered the Snake People, and soon deadly conflict spread through the cosmos. After centuries of stalemate, the tide turned in the Snake People's favor. The Snake People pursued the humans through space, stranding some on obscure, backwater planets. The rest made it to the planet now known as Mars, where the last of the Human Empire lived in relative comfort for a long time. Then the planet began to die, its oxygen and water evaporating and the temperature growing ever colder.

Thus the humans found their way to the third planet in the solar system. They settled in what is now Antarctica, a pleasant, temperate place. They built seven cities, each with its own color (Red City, Green City, Blue City, and so on). The greatest of all was Rainbow City, constructed from many colors of a very hard plastic. Under the wise leadership of the son and daughter of the Great Ruler (still on Mars) and the daughter's fiancé (later to be called the Ancient Three), the colony thrived, and a golden age ensued, ending when the Snake People, having discovered where the humans were hiding, mounted a surprise attack. In the fierce battles that followed, the Earth was knocked on its side, turning Antarctica into a wasteland. The humans were driven to other, now warmer continents. Their technology destroyed, they were reduced to a primitive state and gradually lost all memory of their former elevated state.

When they rediscovered it, Emery and his associates found the city surrounded by ten thousand feet of ice, thus concealing the remains from previous explorers. Hot springs beneath the city kept it warm, and the search party went through all six levels. Inside the city, plants and trees of all kinds still grew, along with huge butterflies. All kinds of evidence of the ancients' presence survived, including clothes (which suggested they were eight feet tall) and advanced technology. The technology included a teleportation device and a vast subway system. The trains were linked to hollow caverns all over the earth. Emery traveled to some of them and found yet more wonders from the ancients.

The Ancient Three sought to restore the human race's former glories. According to the Hefferlins, the world's nonwhite races had already accepted their leadership, which was headquartered in seven temples in Africa,

Asia, and South America. The "thought machines" inside these temples broadcast vibrations to those who were receptive to them. The principal message was that other nations must free themselves of European domination, though the Ancient Three had opposed the Japanese imperial designs that helped spark World War II. Once the Ancient Three had realized their vision and taken benevolent control of the Earth, there would be no more slavery, colonialism, or excessive taxation, and all races would be equal.

Though the Hefferlins soon faded into obscurity without ever providing proof of Rainbow City (or even of their enigmatic friend Emery, for that matter), the notion of Rainbow City figured in Robert Dickhoff's *Agharta: The Subterranean World* (1951) and Michael X. Barton's *Rainbow City and the Inner Earth People* (1960).

See Also: Shaver mystery

Further Reading

Kafton-Minkel, Walter, 1989. *Subterranean Worlds: 100,000 Years of Dragons, Dwarfs, the Dead, Lost Races and UFOs from inside the Earth.* Port Townsend, WA: Loompanics Unlimited.

X, Michael [pseud. of Michael X. Barton], 1960. *Rainbow City and the Inner Earth People.* Los Angeles: Futura.

Ramtha

Ramtha, perhaps the leading channeled entity of the 1980s, first appeared in a Tacoma, Washington, living room to announce, "I am Ramtha, the Enlightened One, and I have come to help you over the ditch"—by which, it turned out, he meant the "ditch of limitation" (Knight, 1987). J. Z. Knight (born Judith Darlene Hampton) and her husband had been experimenting with pyramids, which according to a 1970s New Age belief had mysterious powers. For a short time, Knight believed that Ramtha was a demonic entity. Soon, however, a spiritualist friend helped her understand the nature of her experience, and she gave her guidance in how to channel Ramtha. On December 17, 1978, she gave the first public channeling of Ramtha.

Ramtha claimed to be 35,000 years old, born on the lost continent of Lemuria. Lemuria, in the Pacific, was destroyed in an irresponsible experiment its scientists conducted. Some residents, including Ramtha's family, escaped to southern Atlantis (the experiment that devastated Lemuria also destroyed much of north Atlantis). There they lived, experiencing poverty and discrimination in the slums of a city called Onai. When he grew into adulthood, Ramtha led a revolt, which overthrew the existing order in Atlantis. As he was recovering from wounds, he became interested in meditation and spent much time reflecting on metaphysical questions. He also learned to alter his body so that its vibrations changed, allowing him to enter the light realm. On the occasion of his physical death, he ascended permanently to that realm. Just before that happened, though, he demonstrated his new paranormal powers in India, where he is still remembered and revered as the incarnate deity Rama.

In the early 1980s, Knight went public with Ramtha. She traveled throughout the United States giving two-day workshops known as "Ramtha Dialogues." Along the way, she attracted the attention of New Age-oriented celebrities such as Shirley MacLaine, Richard Chamberlain, Mike Farrell, and Shelley Fabres, who enthusiastically supported her work. MacLaine discussed Ramtha in her best-selling *Dancing in the Light* (1985). Knight put together a nonprofit corporation that evolved into the non-tax-exempt Sovereignty, Inc.

By this time, Knight had amassed so much money that a growing legion of critics questioned her sincerity. She now lived on a luxurious horse-breeding ranch in Yelm, Washington, the focus of a large following of pilgrims who had moved to the Northwest from homes all over the nation and the world. Some, seeking a safe haven from the cataclysmic Earth changes that Ramtha said were about to occur, had left families to do so. Sessions with Ramtha were expensive. Beyond that, critics charged, Ramtha had become, in effect, Knight's business partner; would-be investors in Knight's Arabian horses would seek the master's advice. After some complained they had purchased mediocre horses after heeding Ramtha's advice, authorities investigated, and Knight ended up reimbursing unhappy buyers, though no charges were filed. Critics also asserted that the once gregarious, friendly Ramtha had grown ever more authoritarian and demanding. Even some sympathetic to channeling beliefs speculated that "whatever energy came through J. Z. Knight has either shifted, departed, or been replaced by a less benign entity" (Klimo, 1987).

In 1988, Knight formed Ramtha's School of Enlightenment, which claims some three thousand students from twenty-three countries. In 1995, a small scandal erupted when press accounts exposed the Federal Aviation Administration's payment of $1.4 million for sensitivity-training classes overseen by a Ramtha disciple. Over the past decade or so, according to one knowledgeable observer, "the prophecies of Knight and Ramtha seem to have moved closer to those of right-wing survivalists and anti-Semites, who foresee a world held in the sinister group of international bankers as part of a New World Order" (Brown, 1997).

Knowledgeable observers, such as religious-studies scholar J. Gordon Melton, say that much of Ramtha's teaching comes from the Gnostic tradition, which holds that God exists within each of us and is to be found there through contemplation and self-mastery.

See Also: Atlantis; Channeling; Lemuria

Further Reading

Brown, Michael F., 1997. *The Channeling Zone: American Spirituality in an Anxious Age.* Cambridge, MA: Harvard University Press.

Carroll, Robert Todd, n.d. "The Skeptic's Dictionary: Ramtha aka J. Z. Knight." http://skepdic.com/channel.html.

Kauki, Christopher Vincent, 1997. "Ramtha in the Petri Dish: The Mixing of Science and Faith in Yelm." *Syzygy* 6, 1 (Winter/Spring): 139–142.

Klimo, Jon, 1987. *Channeling: Investigations on Receiving Information from Paranormal Sources.* Los Angeles: Jeremy P. Tarcher.

Knight, J. Z., 1987. *A State of Mind.* New York: Warner Books.

MacLaine, Shirley, 1985. *Dancing in the Light.* New York: Bantam Books.

Melton, J. Gordon, 1998. *Finding Enlightenment: Ramtha's School of Ancient Wisdom.* Hillsboro, OR: Beyond Words Publishing.

Stearn, Jess, 1984. *Soul Mates.* New York: Bantam Books.

Weinberg, Steven L., ed., 1986. *Ramtha.* Eastsound, WA: Sovereignty.

———, ed., 1988. *Ramtha: An Introduction.* Eastbound, WA: Sovereignty.

Ramu

Ramu is the name George Adamski gave to a visitor from Saturn. With Ramu and others, Adamski flew around the moon one memorable night in 1954. He cautioned, however, that Ramu, like the other Space Brothers, has "an entirely different concept of names as we use them" (Adamski, 1955). Thus, Ramu was not really the spaceman's name. Adamski describes Ramu as slightly over six feet, with ruddy complexion and dark brown eyes and wavy black hair.

A different Ramu from Saturn figures in a story that farmer Velma Thayer told the *Cincinnati Enquirer* in August 1955. This Ramu landed in a flying saucer at her Lake Geneva, Wisconsin, farm on October 15, 1928, along with other "little fellows." All were blond-haired and from four feet six inches to five feet three inches in height. They stayed for ten days (it is not clear whether at Thayer's residence or in their saucer). Ramu told Thayer that they were from Saturn and had come with peaceful intentions. U.S. government authorities came to the farm and placed a guard around the ship. At one point, however, the guard fell asleep, and the saucer escaped. Thayer said she had had occasional contacts since with Ramu and his crew.

Nonetheless, in an earlier account—one published in a contactee-oriented magazine before Adamski's Ramu became known—Thayer did not mention a Ramu in connection with the alleged experience, suggesting that the inclusion of the name was a later embellishment. This earlier version says nothing about communication or interaction with the crew. When the saucer landed, according to her, "Seven small people emerged and ran into the woods," never to be seen again ("Space Ship," 1954). In their absence, she examined the ship inside and out. Rather than escaping, the craft was taken to the General Electric laboratory, which subsequently informed her that it was made up of materials that "definitely did not belong to this earth." According to Thayer, a dozen landings of ships with similar crews took place in Wisconsin and Illinois between 1919 and 1930.

See Also: Adamski, George; Contactees

Further Reading

Bartholomew, Robert E., and George S. Howard, 1998. *UFOs and Alien Contact: Two Centuries of Mystery.* Amherst, NY: Prometheus Books.

"Space Ship Lands in Celery Field," 1954. *Interplanetary News Digest* (March): 22.

Raphael

Raphael is responsible for the "Starseed transmissions," said to come from a parallel dimension through channeler Ken Carey. Carey, a Missouri farmer, had no previous channeling experience before Raphael came through one day in 1979. He says the messages first arrived via "waves or pulsations" that translated symbols into their verbal correlates. "Often," he writes, "it was the case that the only human conceptual system with approximating terminology was religious. Hence, the occasional use of 'Christian' words and phrases" (Carey, 1982). Eventually, the communications occurred more straightforwardly in English.

Raphael says he exists only when he is interacting with Carey or with whomever he is communicating through Carey. When he is not active, he merges "back into the Being behind all being," awaiting his next mission. On one occasion, however, he claimed to be the intelligence represented by Christ.

See Also: Channeling

Further Reading

Carey, Ken, 1982. *The Starseed Transmissions: An Extraterrestrial Report.* Kansas City, MO: UNI-SUN.

Raydia

After a 1979 UFO sighting, Lyssa Royal found herself more and more fascinated with paranormal subjects. Her interests led her, in 1984, to Darryl Anka, who channeled Bashar. During the period of her association with Anka, she had a vivid dream in which an entity appeared to inform her that soon she herself would be channeling. She was led to a channeling class in Los Angeles. By 1985, a number of entities were making their presence known to her. One was Raydia, who stayed with Royal for three years.

Royal went on to found the Association of Love and Light, channeling Raydia as well as some others. Raydia was a "heart-centered" female entity, "a collective consciousness" with "a strong affiliation with the star Arcturus." She last communicated in 1988, telling persons who were sitting in on a channeling session, "You will never see me in this form again." Royal says that Raydia "integrated herself" into an entity Royal would subsequently channel, Germane ("Behind the Veil," 1998).

See Also: Bashar; Channeling; Germane

Further Reading

"Behind the Veil: A Look at the Phenomenon of Channeling," 1998. http://www.royalpriest.com/channel.htm.

Melton, J. Gordon, 1996. *Encyclopedia of American Religions.* Fifth edition. Detroit, MI: Gale Research.

Renata

Renata channels through Scott Amun. On April 15, 1999, she (gender is presumed since the entity does not specify its sex) came through for the first time to discuss various issues.

Renata says that on her planet, Osyllium, people look and act much like humans; yet, paradoxically, Osyllium's history is richer and more diverse than Earth's. Perhaps one reason is that Osyllium people change their language every four or five years. They do this by adjusting their brain frequencies, and the purpose is to accelerate change and encourage new insight. Great changes are about to occur on Earth through the electrical energy that emanates from the north pole. Human beings soon will notice a "special effect" in the northern lights—a message from Renata's people. Humans will also sense a changing situation in their dreams, which will help prepare them for their "opening into higher electrical frequencies."

Further Reading

Amun, Scott, 1999. "Morning Dawns on the Human Race." http://www.scottamun.com/write/April1598write.htm.

Reptoid child

In a story represented as true by Mexican ufologist Luis Ramirez Reyes, a woman is said to have given birth to a hideous alien baby after a missing-time, presumed abduction experience. Ramirez claims that the birth took place in September 1993 but "due to its very nature has been kept under wraps."

The unnamed woman, a cosmetics salesperson, was on her usual route, which took her between Mexico City and Poza Rica, Veracruz, one day in early 1993. As she passed the Teotihuacan pyramids, she saw what she thought was a UFO in the clear sky. Suddenly, she found herself in Poza Rica. Though her wristwatch told her it was 11 A.M., the actual time was 2 P.M. She had no idea how she had traveled the 185 miles to the city.

In the weeks to come, she experienced weakness and nausea. When a doctor examined her, he pronounced her pregnant. She protested that this was impossible; she was a virgin. Nonetheless, seven months later, she gave birth to a hideous creature described as having "double-membraned eyes, thick froglike lips, joined fingers and hard, shell-feature on its skin which [was] similar to a tortoise's shell." At first the doctors and nurses panicked. The clinic director finally managed to calm them. He ordered them to keep the matter strictly confidential.

The creature was kept in an incubator for three weeks, fed on a diet of herbs. It recoiled from ordinary light but was comfortable in infrared light. Scales began to grow along its spine. An expert "who has requested anonymity" examined photographs of the creature, which he deduced belonged to a "saurian" species.

The mother is raising the creature in seclusion. It is an "amphibian reptile" said to be "horrible to behold."

See Also: Abductions by UFOs; Reptoids

Further Reading

Corrales, Scott, 2000. "Alien Shock: The Encounter Phenomenon Overseas." *Ohio UFO Notebook* 21: 22–26.

Reptoids

Beings sometimes referred to as "reptoids" or "reptilians" figure in a number of abduction and contact reports. According to one source, three different varieties exist: "the Reptoid (reptilian-humanoid crossbreeds), the various reptilian-gray crossbreed types, and the hierarchical reptilian overlords called the Draco (winged reptilian types)" ("Reptilian 'Aliens,'" n.d.). Draco is a constellation from which, some believe, the reptoids come.

A close encounter of the third kind involving reptoids (though before the concept had become popular) happened on November 17, 1967, when thirteen-year-old David Seewaldt of Calgary, Alberta, while crossing a vacant lot, heard a high-pitched sound. When he looked for its source, he saw a house-sized UFO landing. It shot a beam of light at him, putting him into a trancelike state as he was levitated into the craft. There two hideous-looking entities with brown crocodile skin took off Seewaldt's clothes and led him into a room where he was examined and given a shot. He was then beamed back to the field. By the time he got home, all conscious memory of the encounter had passed. It returned five months later in a vivid dream. A year later, investigators, including a University of Alberta psychologist, interviewed the youth.

John S. Carpenter, a Missouri-based social worker and abduction researcher, reports cases

An artist's rendition of the "Loveland Frogman," a reptoid that was seen by two Ohio policemen in March 1972 (Ron Schaffner/Fortean Picture Library)

of "repulsive and insensitive" reptilian aliens. "What is fascinating," he writes, "is that persons who had never heard of these lizard-types are reporting strikingly similar details in regards [sic] to their anatomy, manner, and behavior. In every case of mine the reptilian forces a rape upon the subject with no explanation or apparent reason" (Carpenter, 1994). Another researcher, Karla Turner, has written of similar incidents, including one in which an abductee "recalled" being on a table surrounded by humanoid aliens. She said, "A reptile-looking creature was getting on top of me, I guess to rape me," just before she lapsed into unconsciousness (Turner, 1994).

Besides such experiential claims, reptoid/reptilian aliens have given rise to a new mythology that fuses conspiracy theories, biblical literalism, hollow earth, and other ideas. Among the most bizarre is the assertion by a leader of Britain's Green Party, David Icke, who holds that the Royal Family are shapeshifting reptilians who conduct bloody rituals on hapless human victims, including children. At least one writer reports that former President George Bush is a reptilian. Others assert that reptoids live in vast caverns underground, working in collaboration with evil forces in U.S. military and intelligence communities. Others say that the reptilians have been slandered, that—except for their (to the human eye) unsettling appearance—they are gentle, decent, and well intentioned.

One who speaks well of reptilians is jazz singer Pamela Stonebrooke, who has spoken openly of a sexual relationship with one. She has "great respect" for him and a "profound connection with this being." Under hypnosis, she was regressed to an earlier life hundreds of thousands of years ago to find herself a member of a band of "reptilian warriors facing a catastrophic event in which we perished together. . . . I believe that on one level, I may be meeting these entities again, perhaps fellow warriors from the past warning us of an impending, self-inflicted doom" ("The Reptilians," n.d.). Carpenter has written of reptoid witnesses known to him, "One . . . sheepishly admits to having an incredible orgasm while being totally repulsed by the intruder's grotesque appearance. Within two months a second female from the same town reported independently the same type of Reptilian invader, with the same surprising and embarrassing orgasmic response!" (Carpenter, 1993).

Some observers believe that the reptilians are satanic entities related to the serpent who led Adam and Eve astray. They maintain that hundreds of thousands of these creatures—as many as one hundred fifty-thousand in New York alone—live in underground bases, feasting on children whom they lure into their lairs. According to some, however, the reptilians are vegetarians.

John Rhodes writes that the reptilians travel from their home region—Alpha Draconis—in mother ships with most of the occupants in a state of suspended animation for the bulk of the voyage. As they pass planets, some of the functioning crew fly off in scout ships to study the new worlds and establish subterranean bases thereon. Where Earth is concerned, according to Rhodes, the reptilians hatch their plots from these bases, "establishing a network of human-reptilian crossbred infiltrates [sic] within various levels of the surface culture's military industrial complexes, government bodies, UFO/paranormal groups, religious, and fraternal (priest) orders, etc. These crossbreeds, some unaware of their reptilian genetic 'mind-control' instructions, act out their subversive roles as 'reptilian agents,' setting the stage for an [sic] reptilian led ET invasion" (Rhodes, n.d.).

See Also: Abductions by UFOs; Close encounters of the third kind; Hollow earth; Hybrid beings; King Leo; Reptoid child; Volmo

Further Reading

Allan, W. K., 1975. "Crocodile-Skinned Entities at Calgary." *Flying Saucer Review* 20, 6 (April): 25–26.

Carpenter, John S., 1993. "Abduction Notes: Reptilians and Other Unmentionables." *MUFON UFO Journal* 300 (April): 10–11.

———, 1994. "Other Types of Aliens: Patterns Emerging." In Andrea Pritchard, David E. Pritchard, John E. Mack, Pam Kasey, and Claudia Yapp, eds. *Alien Discussions: Proceedings of the*

A painting of Madame Helene Blavatsky, who proposed the theory of five "root races," with the symbol of the Theosophical Society above her head (Fortean Picture Library)

Abduction Study Conference, 91–95. Cambridge, MA: North Cambridge Press.

Coleman, Loren, 1988. "Other Lizard People Revisited." *Strange Magazine* 3: 34.

D'Light, Joy, and Elliemiser, 1999. "The Reptilians and King Leo." http://www.greatdreams.com/reptlan/repleo.htm.

McClure, Kevin, 1999. "Dark Ages." *Fortean Times* 129 (December): 28–32.

"Reptilian 'Aliens': What Do They Look Like?," n.d. http://www.reptoids.com/phydes.htm.

"Reptiles/Serpents/Lizards in History/Mythology/Religion," n.d. http://www.channel1.com/users/com/cci/reptiles.htm.

Rhodes, John, n.d. "O.R.I.G.I.N.S." http://www.reptoids.com/origins/htm.

Turner, Karla, 1994. *Taken: Inside the Alien-Human Abduction Agenda.* Roland, AR: Kelt Works.

Root Races

In the alternative reality proposed in the influential nineteenth-century Theosophical writings of Helene Petrovna Blavatsky, the world has seen five "root races," each with its own seven "sub-races," and these latter with their own "branch races." Blavatsky wrote that two more root races will come before the human race finishes its evolution.

The First Root Race, of "fire mist" folk, lived near the north pole in the Imperishable Sacred Land. They were invisible. The Second Root Race were astral beings on their way to becoming material and visible. Also living in the polar region, they occupied a more or less material continent known as Hyperborea, where they learned how to reproduce sexually. The Third Root Race were apelike in appearance with characteristics of both sexes; some had four arms, and some had an eye in the back of their heads. These beings lived on the now-lost Pacific continent of Lemuria. By the time the Fourth Root Race, dwelling on Atlantis, appeared on Earth, the present human form had developed. Humans represent the Fifth Root Race. In the relatively near future, the Sixth Root Race will replace humans. After the Seventh Root Race has risen and fallen, a new cycle of civilizations will begin on the planet Mercury.

Blavatsky claimed as her source for these revelations an "archaic Manuscript—a collection of palm leaves made impermeable to water, fire, and air, by some specific unknown process. . . . On the first page is an immaculate white disk within a dull black ground. On the following page, the same disk, but with a central point" (Blavatsky, 1889). These "Stanzas of Dzyan" recorded the hidden history of the cosmos and all of its inhabitants, including the human race. Other scholars, however, contend that Blavatsky drew on contemporary scientific and occult literature and embellished it considerably, though not quite beyond recognition.

See Also: Atlantis; Lemuria

Further Reading

Blavatsky, H. P., 1889. *The Secret Doctrine,* London: Theosophical Publishing Company.

De Camp, L. Sprague, 1970. *Lost Continents: The Atlantis Theme in History, Science, and Literature.* New York: Dover Publications.

Meade, Marion, 1980. *Madame Blavatsky: The Woman behind the Myth.* New York: G. P. Putnam's Sons.

S

Saint Michael

Saint Michael the Archangel is perhaps best known from the traditional Georgia Sea Islands spiritual "Michael, Row the Boat Ashore," but even in contemporary time some people claim to have experienced his presence. One is a Southern California woman, Melissa MacLeod, a practicing Roman Catholic. In the 1980s, she experienced terrifying nocturnal visitations in which a tall, black-hooded figure stared at her menacingly from beside her bed. She is convinced, according to ufologist Ann Druffel, that her intense belief in Michael saved her from this demonic manifestation.

Fascinated by MacLeod's experiences, a friend, writer and parapsychologist Stephen A. Schwartz, engaged in three months' intense meditation to see if he could visualize Michael. After three months, a point of light suddenly shone in his room. Within it, the form of a luminous entity, human in shape but larger, emerged into view. "He had a demeanor of absolute implacability," Schwartz recalled (Druffel, 1998). He was convinced he had seen the archangel.

Further Reading

Druffel, Ann, 1998. *How to Defend Yourself against Alien Abduction.* New York: Three Rivers Press.

Sananda

Sananda, a popular channeling entity, is a powerful being who is Ashtar's superior in the space mission to redeem Earth. Sananda, known as Jesus in an earlier, earthly incarnation, is perhaps best known, however, as the principal contact of Dorothy Martin (Sister Thedra), whose failed prophecy of earth-shaking events in December 1954 attracted worldwide attention and became the subject of an influential case study in the sociology of religion.

See Also: Ashtar; Channeling; Hierarchal Board; Sister Thedra

Further Reading

Festinger, Leon, Henry W. Riecken, and Stanley Schachter, 1956. *When Prophecy Fails.* Minneapolis: University of Minnesota Press.

Tuella [pseud. of Thelma B. Turrell], ed., 1989. *Ashtar: A Tribute.* Third edition. Salt Lake City, UT: Guardian Action Publications.

Sasquatch

Sasquatch—also known as Bigfoot—is a large apelike creature unrecognized by zoology but often reported seen in the forests of the Pacific Northwest of the United States and Canada's far west. To those few scientists who are willing to concede its possible existence, Sasquatch is thought to be related to *Homo sapiens'* primate ancestors. In other words, though intelligent as

Saint Michael casting the dragon Satan and his angels down to Earth (Fortean Picture Library)

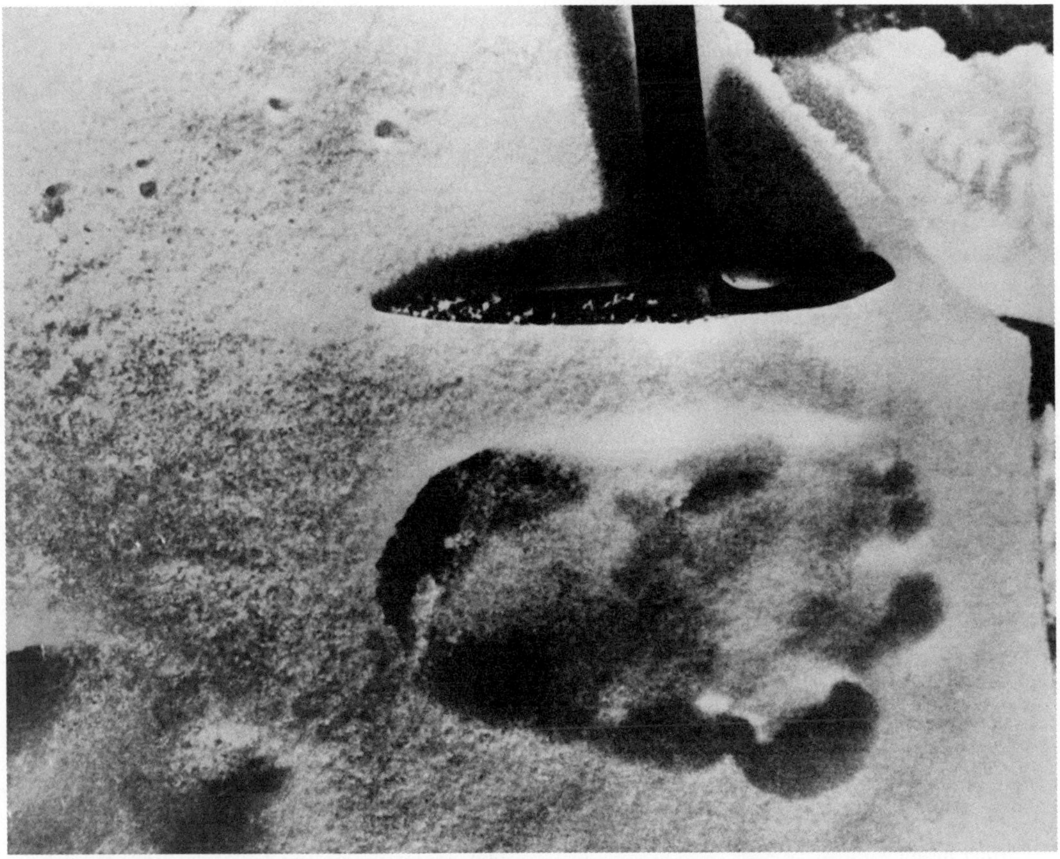

A photograph of the track of a huge animal, seen by Mount Everest climbers and said to be made by the Abominable Snowman, 1958. Similar creatures, generally called Bigfoot or Sasquatch, are often reported in the forests of the Pacific Northwest of the United States and Canada's far west. (Bettmann/Corbis)

animals go, it does not have human, much less superhuman, intelligence. There are, however, individuals who claim contacteelike dealings with Sasquatch, which they describe as highly evolved beings with extraordinary mental powers.

Southern California psychic Joyce Partise, holding a sealed envelope containing a photograph of an alleged Sasquatch footprint, declared that "there's a civilization of thousands" of "gorilla men" who live underground and are "able to communicate with those in outer space" (Slate, 1976). Some witnesses assert that when they tried to take photographs or collect other direct evidence of their Sasquatch sightings, the creatures used a kind of hypnosis to prevent them from acting.

Still others say they have received detailed psychic messages, often consisting of spiritual and ecological material. The Sasquatch may appear, at least initially, as no more than a pair of glowing eyes or a ball of light that can enter anywhere, even into closed houses and bedrooms. They can also change shapes. In a handful of cases, UFO witnesses say they have seen apelike creatures during close encounters, and a small number of abduction incidents recount onboard interactions with Sasquatch creatures, seen in the company of (relatively) more conventional humanoids.

See Also: Abductions by UFOs; Contactees

Further Reading

Chorvinsky, Mark, 1994. "Our Strange World." *Fate* 47, 10 (October): 22–24.

Fenwick, Lawrence J., 1983. "Multiple Abductions in Canada." *MUFON UFO Journal* Pt. I. 183 (May): 10–13; Pt. II. 184 (June): 3–6.

Halpin, Marjorie, and Michael M. Ames, eds., 1980. *Manlike Monsters on Trial: Early Records and Modern Evidence.* Vancouver: University of British Columbia Press.

Slate, B. Ann, 1976. "Gods from Inner Space." *UFO Report* 3, 1 (April): 36–38, 51–52, 54.

Slate, B. Ann, and Alan Berry, 1976. *Bigfoot.* New York: Bantam Books.

Satonians

Satonians, according to the Solar Cross Foundation, a onetime organization of contactee sympathizers, are evil space people. They look exactly like good space people, but persons who encounter them can detect their negative thoughts. They also respond ambiguously and evasively when asked to identify themselves. Satonians always lose in conflicts with their benevolent counterparts. A person approaching a spacecraft should be certain it is not a Satonian ship.

See Also: Contactees

Further Reading

Tuella [pseud. of Thelma B. Turrell], ed., 1989. *Ashtar: A Tribute.* Third edition. Salt Lake City, UT: Guardian Action Publications.

Secret Chiefs

"Secret Chiefs" are shadowy superhuman adepts who have used their magical power and knowledge to initiate and guide occult groups and hidden societies.

According to British occultist S. L. MacGregor Mathers (1854–1918), who claimed to have met the Secret Chiefs on a number of occasions, these people or entities are able to live in both physical and psychic bodies. They are, he told a correspondent, "possessed of terrible . . . powers. . . . I felt I was in contact with a force so terrible that I can only compare it to the shock one would receive from being near a flash of lightning during a great thunderstorm" (Keith, 1997).

Further Reading

Keith, Jim, 1997. *Casebook on the Men in Black.* Lilburn, GA: IllumiNet Press.

Semjase

Semjase is best known in contactee circles as a beautiful spacewoman from the planet Erra in the Pleiades star system. Eduard "Billy" Meier of Switzerland claims to have met her after her "beamship" landed on his farm on the afternoon of January 28, 1975, initiating a series of contacts that made Meier the most well known and controversial of the second-generation contactees. Meier would allege trips through space and time in the company of Semjase and her associates, and he would produce photographs said to depict her but thought by critics to be a model in a Sears catalog.

According to Meier, Semjase is around 350 years old, though she looks to be in her twenties. She is blond, blue-eyed, and fair-skinned. Her only extraterrestrial characteristic is her extended earlobes. Because she possesses knowledge remarkable even by Pleiadian standards, she is considered an Jshrjsh (ish-rish), a sort of demigoddess. Before meeting Meier in 1975, she spent eight years in the DAL Universe (a twin parallel universe to the Earth's, known as the DERN Universe) in the company of Asket, a DAL native woman who had assisted Meier through his early—child and young-adult—interactions with extraterrestrials. She then left the DAL Universe and returned briefly to Erra before arriving in Europe. Meier insists that her orders were to work exclusively on that continent.

While visiting the headquarters of the Meier movement, the Semjase Silver Star Center in Hinterschmidruti, Switzerland, on December 15, 1977, she suffered a life-threatening accident. A beamship rushed her back to Erra for medical treatment. On returning the followed May, she resumed contact with Meier. Those contacts ended on March 16, 1981, when other duties kept her away until early 1984. Their final contact occurred on February 3, 1984, Meier's forty-seventh birthday. The following November, complications from her 1977 accident led to a health emergency. She was taken to the DAL Universe to begin the decades-long process of recovery.

Fred Bell of Laguna Beach, California, has his own Semjase tales to tell, to Meier's intense displeasure. An inventor, musician, artist, and holistic-health enthusiast, Bell—a committed believer in pyramid energy—once went about in the world with a small pyramid on his head. He says that beginning in 1971 he received mental impressions of an oddly familiar, beautiful blond woman. Eventually, he became convinced that he had known her in a previous lifetime, when he was an archaeologist who uncovered evidence that Paladins landed on Earth long ago. Soon Bell met Semjase personally. At first she would not give him her name, but when they got close—apparently even having a sexual relationship for a time—she told him her life history and revealed the secrets of the Pleiadians. She helped him with various projects and inventions. Bell came to refer to Semjase as his "soul mate." He also met her father, Ptaah, and others.

For a time, Bell was on friendly terms with Wendelle C. Stevens, an Arizona man most responsible for bringing Meier's claims to an American audience. Stevens has published a series of books based on his investigations in Switzerland and also on Meier's contact diaries. At first Stevens cited Bell's claims as independent evidence for the existence of Semjase and Pleiadean visitors.

In due course, however, Meier denounced Bell's stories as lies. A Pleiadian named Quetzal told Meier that Bell could not possibly be telling the truth because Semjase and Ptaah had never been to America. Moreover, the Pleiadians entered into physical contact only with Meier, and nobody else. Quetzal was among the extraterrestrials with whom Bell supposedly interacted.

One fundamentalist Christian writer holds that Meier got the name "Semjase" from the fallen angel/demon Shemyaza, described in the apocryphal Book of Enoch. Or it might be the Semjase, a real entity, that is one of Satan's emissaries, one of the "many evil deceptive forces at work in the world right now" ("Billy Meier and the Swiss UFO Case," n.d.).

See Also: Contactees; Meier, Eduard "Billy"

Further Reading

"Billy Meier and the Swiss UFO Case," n.d. http://netpci.com/-tttbbs/Articles-UFO/semjase.html.

Meier, "Billy" Eduard Albert, n.d. "'Billy' Eduard Albert Meier Dissociates Himself from Dr. Fred Bell's Lies and Claims." http://www.figu.ch/us/critics/contra/bell.htm.

Steiger, Brad, 1988. *The Fellowship: Spiritual Contact Between Humans and Outer Space Beings.* New York: Dolphin/Doubleday.

Seth

Jane Roberts's channeling of Seth had large impact on the emerging New Age movement in the 1960s. Seth first appeared when the Elmira, New York, writer and her husband were playing with a ouija board in 1963. Soon Roberts learned how to put herself into a trance state and let Seth—whom she thought of less as a spirit than as some kind of intelligent energy force—speak through her. She recorded these sessions and used a few of them in a book, *How to Develop Your ESP Power* (1966), later reissued as *The Coming of Seth* (1976).

In 1970, with the publication of *The Seth Material,* Roberts commenced writing a series of books, most of them focused on Seth's teachings. In time, a Seth movement came into existence on the New Age scene. Roberts also started channeling William James, the great American psychologist, philosopher, and psychical researcher, and releasing books based upon James's alleged postmortem observations and experiences. Unlike some channelers who would follow her, Roberts remained reclusive and publicity-shy and rarely appeared in public. She died on September 5, 1984. After her death other channelers claimed to have heard from Seth. One, Thomas Massari, reported that Seth had communicated with him as early as 1972.

See Also: Channeling

Further Reading

Roberts, Jane, 1970. *The Seth Material.* Englewood Cliffs, NJ: Prentice-Hall.

———, 1972. *Seth Speaks: The Eternal Validity of the Soul.* Englewood Cliffs, NJ: Prentice-Hall.

———, 1978. *The Afterdeath Journal of an American Philosopher: The World View of William James.* Englewood Cliffs, NJ: Prentice-Hall.
———, 1981. *The God of Jane: A Psychic Manifesto.* Englewood Cliffs, NJ: Prentice-Hall.

Shaari

Shaari is an extraterrestrial who inhabits the body of a young professional woman. The woman, an occasional practitioner of channeling, was seriously injured in a car accident. After the accident, she decided that she had served her life purpose and would go on to another level of existence, though without "dying"; instead, she gave her body to a being of higher consciousness. This being would be able to observe and offer insight into upcoming planetary changes that will affect everybody who lives on Earth.

The Intergalactic Council of Twelve (consisting of space people and angels) and the Star Command, working with the earthwoman, carefully effected the change over a period of six months between January and July 1989. On July 14, the exchange occurred. By this time, the woman was out of the hospital and had resumed a part-time occupation, the conducting of channeling workshops. The woman was holding one on an island in the Pacific Northwest when she was instructed to go to the south part of the island, lie down on the shore, and breathe rhythmically. Shaari, waiting in a spaceship in the company of Ashtar and others, found herself enveloped in light and drawn into the woman's body.

"Everything that I was familiar with had just shifted," she recalled. "There I was in a body that felt like concrete. Nothing moved, everything felt very heavy. . . . As I started to think about moving, these awkward fleshy limbs began to respond and jerk and twitch. Finally, I managed to get on my feet and eventually made it back to the workshop site. The people there were wonderful and took care of me in all ways." Shaari says her mission is to "bridge the gap between human and extraterrestrial communication and to establish the potential for technological exchange and interplanetary trade" (Shaari, 1994).

Prior to her incarnation on Earth, Shaari was a commander in the Star Command, which she had served for most of her 750 years. She was born a Pleiadian/Arcturian hybrid "created out of the thoughts of a Pleiadean and Arcturian council." In other words, she did not have biological parents. Even so, she has a family and a mate named Mishar, a Star Command officer, counselor, and healer. Nearly seven feet tall, he hails from Arcturus, which means that he has a spectacular set of wings. These wings allow him to shift consciousness and to run through different color, light, and sound frequencies. With this power he monitors the fluctuations of mass human consciousness, which can have an adverse effect on weather patterns. If necessary, he shifts that consciousness in a more positive direction toward less destructive weather. Mishar also seeks an earthly incarnation but has yet to find an Earth male who is willing to surrender his consciousness in exchange for Mishar's.

The British Columbia woman who now calls herself Shaari claims to have all memories of her extraterrestrial life available to her in waking consciousness. Though she can channel, she does not often do so because she does not have the need.

See Also: Ashtar; Channeling; Hybrid beings

Further Reading

Shaari, 1994. "An Extraterrestrial's Journey to Earth." http://www.spiritweb.org/Spirit/et-journey.html.

Shan

Shan is a name space people sometimes call the Earth. Shan is regarded as a troubled planet strongly influenced by dark forces. Its reputation is such that spaceships from other worlds have come here both to protect extraterrestrials from human influence and to reform humans and defeat Satan.

According to the pseudonymous contactee Patrick J. Bellringer, Shan is undergoing radical changes now that it has been permitted to move from the third dimension to the fourth dimension. In 1962, Shan entered the Photon Belt, an invisible band of powerful light energy, as it began the transition which continues now but which will be completed in the early years of the twenty-first century. Beginning on August 17, 1987, Shan was led a distance of thirteen million light years into a new orbit closer to the Great Central Sun as millions of starships, using powerful magnetic beams, transferred it to another solar system in the Pleiades. The process was completed on December 15, 1995. Sahn is now the fourth planet in the orbit of Coeleno (see-*lee*-no).

Few human beings have noticed the transition because the space people have gone to great lengths to conceal their operation. If the sky looks familiar, appearances are deceptive; the familiar stars and planets have been replaced by hovering starships, which take care to remain in precisely the same configuration as the constellations of old. Only the most observant have realized that the sun is emitting more intense light but looks smaller (because we are now seven million miles farther away from our new sun so as to adjust for the differences from the old one). Our new moon is brighter because of Coeleno's more brilliant light. Soon Shan will be moved into the spiritually advanced fourth dimension, but not before all kinds of devastating changes occur. Radical weather changes, massive volcanic eruptions, and other cataclysms will wipe out the unenlightened parts of humanity (unaware of but still under Satan's influence) so that only those who are morally pure and intellectually superior will survive to enter the new realm.

Among the victims will be Satan and his minions, who live on Shan but remain oblivious to the Earth's new location in space. The space people will launch a surprise attack on Satan and drive him and his troops into the void where they can no longer do harm.

According to Bellringer—himself reincarnated from the Coeleno system but from the fifth planet, Hatonn, to which he and his Pleiadean family will return soon—Shan from the beginning was regarded as a planet of unusual attractiveness. Two hundred six million years ago immigrants from the Pleiades—our ancestors—settled on it. Bellringer states that Shan "held a position at the cross-roads of the Cosmos as a supply planet for other planets. Because of its abundance and beauty it was chosen as the 'prison' planet by Lucifer, the Arch-Angel when he left the Cosmic Realms for his anarchy against God/Aton." Because of the presence of Satan and his allies, the people of Shan have had an extremely difficult time achieving "complete harmony and balance with the Laws of God and of the Creation." Among other things, Satan has kept humans ignorant or fearful of the extraterrestrial races that are visiting Shan and attempting to change it for the better. "Shan has been a special schoolroom for the 'gifted kids'—a tough course to learn tough lessons. Sadly enough, most have failed the course" (Bellringer, n.d.).

See Also: Contactees

Further Reading

Bellringer, Patrick H., n.d. "People of the Lie: The Photon Belt." http://www.fourwinds10.com/phb/photon.htm.

Shaver mystery

The Shaver mystery is named after Richard Sharpe Shaver. Shaver's strange claims about his experiences with cavern-dwelling deros (deranged and vicious) and teros (virtuous but overwhelmed), warring remnants of an ancient earthly race and possessors of advanced technologies, were featured prominently in the popular science-fiction pulp *Amazing Stories* between 1944 and 1948. *Amazing*'s editor, Ray Palmer, promoted Shaver's stories for the next three decades, and Shaver continued to tell them until his death.

The genesis of the episode was a letter the heretofore obscure Shaver wrote to *Amazing* in 1943. The letter purported to be a reproduction of an ancient alphabet from Lemuria, a lost continent said to have sunk into the Pacific Ocean some twelve thousand years ago (in real-

Cover of The Hidden World *magazine, spring 1961, containing articles on the Shaver mystery (Fortean Picture Library)*

ity, Lemuria is a nineteenth-century invention). Palmer published it in *Amazing*'s January 1944 issue. By then, he and Shaver were corresponding. Shaver produced a ten-thousand-word manuscript titled "A Warning to Future Man," which Palmer rewrote as a science-fiction novella, "I Remember Lemuria!" The story appeared under Shaver's by-line in the March 1945 issue. Palmer presented it as a true story based on racial memory, though Shaver claimed that he had received his knowledge of humanity's hidden history directly from beings who live in a vast network of tunnels and caves under the Earth's surface.

The response was a flood of letters from curious readers and some from persons who related unusual experiences that they thought validated Shaver. A promotional genius with the instincts of a carnival barker, Palmer coined the phrase "Shaver mystery," started a Shaver Mystery Club, and opened *Amazing*'s pages to allegedly factual material and science-fiction stories based on it. Palmer wrote that when he visited Richard and Dorothy Shaver at their farm, he heard mysterious voices that "could not have come from Mr. Shaver's lips." They were speaking first in English then in a "strange language," about a woman who earlier that day had been "torn into four quarters about four miles away and four miles down [from the Shaver house]" (Palmer, 1961).

At least in its most vital phase, the Shaver mystery ended in 1948, when pressure from outraged science-fiction fans led Ziff-Davis, *Amazing*'s publisher, to order its closing. That same year Palmer and Curtis Fuller founded *Fate,* dedicated to the "true mysteries" *Amazing* had featured along with Shaver matters, and he left the science-fiction magazine the following year. Not long afterward, Palmer moved to Amherst, Wisconsin, where he started *Mystic* (later *Search*) and *Other Worlds* (later *Flying Saucers*). These publications carried articles by and about Shaver. Between 1961 and 1964, Palmer published sixteen issues of a trade-paper-formatted magazine, *The Hidden World,* devoted entirely to the Shaver mystery. Shaver died in 1975. Palmer, who had continued to champion the "mystery" while disputing some of Shaver's interpretations, died two years later.

Though to all but a few Shaver's claims were outlandish and absurd, even grotesque, Shaver did not strike those who knew him as a hoaxer. There seemed little doubt that Shaver believed what he said, notwithstanding some noteworthy inconsistencies in his testimony over the years. For example, he told at least four mutually exclusive stories about how he learned of the Earth's secret past and its subterranean races. In his most frequent telling, however, it occurred first through telepathic messages from a mysterious woman, then as mental voices emanating from depraved creatures known as "deros" (from "*de*trimental *ro*bots," though they were not robots as such; see explanation on next page).

These experiences seem to have occurred in the early 1930s. Always vague on dates,

Shaver was also vague on what was happening in his life amid his growing realization of, and interaction with, the reality of a literal underground. It appears, from uncertain though not entirely implausible inference, that he spent some time in a mental hospital, and he may also have served a short prison stretch for bootlegging. On occasion Shaver intimated as much, even as he less plausibly claimed to have lived in the caves with the embattled teros ("in*te*grative robots"; again, like their enemies the deros, beings of flesh and blood). How long he supposedly lived there is also unclear.

In any event, out of these elements came a complex, alternate history of the human race. Long ago, according to Shaver, extraterrestrials known as Atlans and Titans or the Elder Races colonized the Earth. (The Atlans lived on Atlantis, the Titans on Lemuria.) These beings, who possessed fantastic technologies, lived extraordinarily long lives and never stopped growing, owing to the integrative (positive) energies cast out by the sun. Some grew to fifty feet, a few considerably more. Eventually, however, the sun changed and began to beam detrimental (negative) energy, causing, among other effects, aging and mortality. To block the deadly rays, the Elders built an immense Cavern World to house the Earth's fifty billion Atlans and Titans. But the effort ultimately failed, and twelve thousand years ago the Elders who survived fled to other stars, leaving behind a small population, which had fallen victim to the detrimental radiation. Some wandered to the surface and in time forgot their history as they became the mortal and confused *Homo sapiens.* The others stayed in the caves to become the sadistic, cannibalistic idiots called deros. One other group, the smallest of the three, was the teros, who had escaped the negative rays but who, for various reasons, had not joined the exodus from Earth. Both the deros and the teros were "robots" not because they were walking mechanical contraptions but because they were under the influence of, respectively, negative and positive energies.

The deros used the advanced technologies to torment surface-dwellers. As Palmer explained it, they "have death rays, giant rockets that traverse in the upper air . . . ground vehicles of tremendous power, machines for the revitalizing of sex, known as 'stim' machines (in which these degenerates sometimes spend their whole lives in a sexual debauch that actually deforms their bodies in horrible ways) . . . and ben rays which heal and restore the body but are also capable of restoring lost energy after a debauch" [Palmer, 1961]). Besides causing plane crashes, madness, violence, and other maladies on the surface, deros sometimes abduct human beings, usually women, and subject them to hideous tortures. Their rays cloud human thought and keep them oblivious to the deros' existence. The badly outnumbered teros are engaged in a protracted but ultimately futile conflict with their evil counterparts.

After its exile from *Amazing,* the Shaver mystery passed from the attention of all but a tiny band of occult and true-mystery enthusiasts, who continued to report on and speculate about deros and caverns in amateurish newsletters as well as Palmer's periodicals. The "mystery" figured in a few not widely read UFO-era books, including Eric Norman's *The Under-People* (1969) and Brinsley le Poer Trench's *Secret of the Ages: UFOs from inside the Earth* (1974). Several writers of a skeptical bent have argued that through Shaver, as one puts it, Palmer "almost single-handedly created the myth of UFOs as extraterrestrial visitors" (Kafton-Minkel, 1989). In fact, a connection between the Shaver mystery and the international UFO phenomenon of the past five decades has yet to be demonstrated. Flying saucers as such did not enter Shaverian mythology until after the rest of the world started talking about them.

A more interesting issue concerns the motivations of the principals. Shaver's manifest belief in experiences that could not have happened in consensus reality leads some, such as hollow-earth chronicler Walter Kafton-Minkel, to see Shaver as a visionary, "a member of that ancient fellowship of receivers of revealed knowledge," a prophet like Moses or Joseph Smith though without the religious trappings. Even if Shaver technologized hell, he remained to the end an atheist and a materialist. To him the caverns existed in this world and had nothing to do with the supernatural.

Though usually depicted as a cynical exploiter of a deluded man whom any responsible adult would have directed to the nearest psychiatrist, Palmer himself—for all his promotional instincts, which he exercised vigorously in the long course of his association with Shaver—may have been caught up in the belief in at least *something.* Perhaps, he sometimes suggested in public statements, Shaver's experiences had occurred on the "astral realm" (Steinberg, 1973). On one occasion, he defended the "mystery" in private circumstances in which he not only had nothing to gain but also risked looking foolish. Though we will never know for sure, one reasonable reading of Palmer's role in the affair is that this complex man was *both* believer and exploiter.

See Also: Atlantis; Brodie's deros; Hollow earth; Lemuria; Mount Lassen

Further Reading

Kafton-Minkel, Walter, 1989. *Subterranean Worlds: 100,000 Years of Dragons, Dwarfs, the Dead, Lost Races and UFOs from inside the Earth.* Port Townsend, WA: Loompanics Unlimited.

Palmer, Ray, 1961. "Invitation to Adventure." *The Hidden World* A-1 (Spring): 4–14.

———, 1980. "The Dero and the Tero." *Gray Barker's Newsletter* 12 (July): 7.

Shaver, Richard S., 1945. "I Remember Lemuria!" *Amazing Stories* 19, 1 (March): 12–70.

Steinberg, Gene, 1971. "The *Caveat Emptor* Interview: Ray Palmer." *Caveat Emptor* 1 (Fall): 9–12, 26.

———, 1973. "The *Caveat Emptor* Interview: Richard S. Shaver." *Caveat Emptor* 10 (November/December): 5–10.

Wright, Bruce Lanier, 1999. "From Hero to Dero." *Fortean Times* 127 (October): 36–41.

Shaw's Martians

In November 1896, unidentified "airships"—what today would be called UFOs—were reported over northern California, initiating a flurry of sightings and excitement that within months would move eastward until all of America was affected. This was the first UFO wave in America, and on November 25, 1896, the first ever UFO abduction occurred—if one credits the testimony of Colonel H. G. Shaw, who claimed a near escape from capture by Martians.

Shaw told his story two days later in a letter published in the *Stockton Evening Mail,* a California paper on whose editorial staff he had once served. On the day of his adventure, he and a companion, Camille Spooner, left Lodi at six o'clock in the morning and were quietly moving along when their horse abruptly snorted in terror and stopped in its tracks. "Three strange beings . . . nearly or quite seven feet high and very slender," of more or less human appearance, strange beauty, and nudity, stood in front of them on the road. When Shaw approached them and asked where they came from, they gave a response that to his ear sounded like "warbling." Speaking to each other, their voices gave off a "monotonous chant." They had small hands, delicate-looking and without fingernails, and long, narrow feet. When he briefly touched one, Shaw had the impression that the being weighed no more than an ounce. He wrote,

> They . . . were covered with a natural growth . . . as soft as silk to the touch, and their skin was like velvet. Their faces and heads were without hair, the ears were very small, and the nose had the appearance of polished ivory, while the eyes were large and lustrous. The mouth, however, was small, and it seemed to me that they were without teeth. That and other things led me to believe that they neither ate nor drank, and that life was sustained by some sort of gas. Each of them had swung under the left arm a bag to which was attached a nozzle, and every little while one or the other would place the nozzle in his mouth, at which time I heard a sound as of escaping gas. (Bullard, 1982)

Each also carried an egg-sized device that cast an "intense but not unpleasant light" when opened.

At this point the beings—whom Shaw presumed to be from Mars—tried to carry him and his friend away, but weighing as little as they did, they lacked the strength. So they turned around and flashed lights in the direction of a nearby bridge. The two men then perceived an airship, some one-hundred fifty feet long, hovering twenty feet over the water. The three Martians floated with a swaying motion toward the craft. A door opened on the side, and the trio disappeared inside. The ship flew away and was seen no more.

Concluding his letter, Shaw blasted other airship stories as "clumsy fakes" that "should not be given credence by anyone"—presumably with tongue buried deeply in cheek. Besides being the first known alien encounter in America to see print, Shaw's was also the first of many hoaxes to come in the months ahead, as newspaper columns were filled with outlandish tales of airships and their occupants, extraterrestrial and human.

See Also: Abductions by UFOs; Allingham's Martian; Aurora Martian; Brown's Martians; Calf-rustling aliens; Dentons's Martians and Venusians; Hopkins's Martians; Khauga; Lethbridge's aeronauts; Martian bees; Michigan giant; Mince-Pie Martians; Monka; Muller's Martians; Smead's Martians; Smith; Wilcox's Martians; Wilson

Further Reading

Bullard, Thomas E., ed., 1982. *The Airship File: A Collection of Texts Concerning Phantom Airships and Other UFOs, Gathered from Newspapers and Periodicals Mostly during the Hundred Years Prior to Kenneth Arnold's Sighting.* Bloomington, IN: self-published.

Sheep-killing alien

In early 1968, according to a Bolivian newspaper, a farm woman near Otoco went to her sheep corral early one evening to discover that a strange net had been placed over it. A humanlike figure, four feet tall and wearing a bulky-looking spacesuit, was busy slaughtering sheep with a tubular, hooked instrument. After killing the animals, he would dump their entrails into a bag.

The woman shouted at him and hurled stones in his direction. The alien strolled over to a boxlike instrument with a wheel at the top. As he twisted the wheel, the net was withdrawn into the box. As he was so engaged, the witness had picked up a club and was about to use it on the intruder. In response, he threw his weapon at her. Each time it returned to his hands like a boomerang, and each time it passed the woman, it cut her. Gathering his tools, the alien then floated noisily upward and was lost to sight.

The local police colonel counted thirty-four dead sheep. Each had had some of its digestive organs removed.

See Also: Calf-rustling aliens; Close encounters of the third kind

Further Reading

Galindez, Oscar A., 1970. "Violent Humanoid Encountered in Bolivia." *Flying Saucer Review* 16, 4 (July/August): 15–17.

Shiva

Shiva is usually known as a major Hindu god, associated both with destruction and chaos and with wisdom and meditation. But in February and March 1994, Shiva—"the blood, the muscle, fur, bone, and spirit of animals"—communicated through Sedona, Arizona, psychic Toraya Ayres. He spoke from and for the animal point of view. He described himself once as having the physique of a bear, another time calling himself only a "body of energy" and denying that he had any physical body.

Shiva said that human beings need to reexamine their destructive relationship with animals. Humans should not see animals as inferior to them but as equal but different spiritual beings. Animals do not have a concept of God, but they do have a profound understanding of their place in nature's order. "We do live in an eternal now of loving cooperation within nature, which we recognize without words as a divine force, and as many divine energies working together for the greater good." Like humans, animals evolve and move into higher dimensions "in a different vibrational range."

"The physical world that you know is only a tiny part of reality," according to Shiva.

"You will be exploring the nonphysical worlds and dimensions, too. As multi-dimensional beings you already do this in your dreams, but you will soon do it consciously."

See Also: Ayala

Further Reading

Ayres, Toraya, 1997. "Messages from the Animal Kingdom." http://www.spiritweb.org/Spirit/animal-kingdom-ayres.html.

Shovar

Shovar is the name of a humanlike entity the pseudonymous Rachel Jones of Coeur d'Alene, Idaho, allegedly met during a UFO-abduction experience over a two-hour period between June 20 and 21, 1977.

Awakened at 11:55 P.M. when she heard someone walking upstairs, Jones found herself paralyzed. She saw someone enter the room, then felt a lifting sensation. In what seemed an instant, she regained her ability to move. She was astonished to see that it was then 1:57 A.M.

Under hypnosis conducted by psychologist/ufologist R. Leo Sprinkle, she told of seeing an ugly intruder with no pupils in his eyes, a thin-lined mouth, normal-looking nose, and thinning hair. He had four fingers on each hand but no thumbs. Picking her up, he brought her to an unknown place and passed through a door into a chamber with a cold floor. Three other beings were there. One was human or near-human in appearance. The man accompanied her into another room containing various instruments, including two wheel-shaped devices and a boxlike table. She sat on the table and conversed with the man, who said his name was Shovar. He asked her to take off her shirt. After resisting, she reluctantly did so. Shovar expressed puzzlement about her suntan, which she then explained to him.

She was instructed to lie on her stomach as a light shined on her back. The other beings rubbed a liquid on her shoulders. It caused great pain, and she protested. Shovar said the pain would stop, and it did. She did not accept his apology, however. It did not sound sincere, and, moreover, she got the distinct impression that he did not even know what pain was.

Even under hypnosis Jones could not recall what happened next. Her memory picked up with a conversation with Shovar, who she realized was communicating telepathically. Shovar told her that they had changed her so that she would be "better for others." They had met before, he went on, and they would meet again. Asked why they had taken her, he replied that he could not answer the question right then. Three beings entered the room, and Jones abruptly found herself back in bed.

Headaches plagued her for the next few days, and she noticed a small round scar on her shoulder.

See Also: Abductions by UFOs; Sprinkle, Ronald Leo

Further Reading

"Idaho Abduction Case," 1977. *The APRO Bulletin* (November).

Sinat Schirah (Stan)

Since 1983, Sinat Schirah, known affectionately as Stan, has channeled through Arlene Nelson. Three years later, Nelson began a process she called "pure channeling"—channeling so intense that she had no conscious sense of it while it was happening or conscious memory of it afterward. It would take place one weekend every month between January and May.

She and her husband, Mervin "Beaver" Colver, with whom Nelson believes she has shared a number of incarnations, founded Lifelight University in Mill Valley, California, in 1987. Students are instructed in a variety of New Age beliefs and practices. Stan's channeled messages are preserved on tapes and in books.

See Also: Channeling

Further Reading

Melton, J. Gordon, 1996. *Encyclopedia of American Religions.* Fifth edition. Detroit, MI: Gale Research.

Sister Thedra

Sister Thedra was born Dorothy Martin, but to most of the world she is remembered as "Marian Keach," the pseudonym given her in the classic sociological book *When Prophecy Fails* (1956). In 1954, through space people who communicated with her through automatic writing, she learned of an imminent catastrophic, earth-changing event, to occur a week before the end of the year. She and her small band of followers in Illinois and Michigan would be swooped up in a flying saucer and rescued just before the cataclysm took place. Martin and her followers sought to publicize the prophecy, only to be ridiculed in newspapers all over the country. After the failure of the prophecy, Martin—soon renamed "Sister Thedra" at the urging of her space contacts—moved to the Southwest, then to Peru for five years. Returning to the United States, she established and headed a contactee-oriented spiritual group in Mount Shasta, California. Toward the end of her life, she relocated to Sedona, Arizona, and died there in 1992.

Born in 1900 in West Virginia, Martin discovered occultism in the late 1930s while living in New York City. First attracted to Theosophy, she explored the spectrum of esoteric literature and became an early student of Dianetics (from which Scientology grew). She also read the works of Guy Warren Ballard, creator of the I AM movement, arguably the first religious group to make extraterrestrial contacts a central tenet. Another book, *Oahspe,* recorded the 1881 channeling of John Ballough Newbrough, depicting a richly populated spiritual cosmos whose inhabitants include guardian angels known as "ashars" who sail the universe in etheric ships. When flying saucers came on the scene and the contactee movement followed in their wake, Martin followed developments with interest.

In the meantime, Charles and Lillian Laughead (pronounced *Law*-head) were doing the same. Their own odyssey had begun in 1946, when the couple were Protestant medical missionaries in Egypt and Lillian started suffering seemingly untreatable nightmares and fears. Seeking relief, the couple turned to occultism. On their return to the United States in 1949, Dr. Laughead took up a staff position at the Michigan State College Hospital in East Lansing. He and his wife continued their mystical studies, incorporating flying saucers into their newfound faith. In early 1953, on a trip to southern California, Laughead met George Adamski, whose claimed meeting with a Venusian named Orthon in the California desert was causing a worldwide sensation. Of particular interest to Laughead were the footprints the Venusian had left in the desert sand. They contained enigmatic symbols whose meaning Adamski's followers were already discussing and debating.

Laughead returned to Michigan with drawings of the prints, which his wife devoted the next five months to deciphering. She concluded that the left print's symbols depicted the sinking of the lost continents Atlantis and Lemuria, the right their reemergence from the ocean floor following geological cataclysms that soon would befall the planet.

Through an automatic-writing message given him by an acquaintance, Dr. Laughead heard from the "Elder Brother," who later, according to Laughead, "identified himself as being Jesus the Christ and also Sananda." Laughead was to continue his work with saucers, and soon Venusians would contact him.

At this stage, the Laugheads had not heard of Dorothy Martin. They did not know that she also was in psychic contact with the Elder Brother as well as with a group of beings she called the Guardians. In April 1954, one of the latter introduced himself as Sananda from the planet Clarion. In a previous lifetime, Sananda said, he was Jesus. Martin—or at least her unconscious mind—got the name Clarion from contactee Truman Bethurum, but Bethurum's Clarion was a planet on the other side of the moon; Martin/Sananda's Clarion, on the other hand, existed in the etheric realm. A companion planet, Cerus (sometimes confusingly referred to also as a "constellation"), housed other space people who kept Martin's arm and hand in furious motion with automatic writing as they made good on their promise to teach her cosmic wisdom. The Elder Brother promised that he would return "soon. . . . They that have told you that they do not believe shall see us when the time is right" (Festinger et al., 1956).

Martin's messages were attracting attention, and a handful of followers soon came together in the Chicago area. Among those who spoke with Martin was John Otto, a UFO lecturer of national reputation and notable credulity. Visiting Detroit to hear a lecture by Adamski, Otto met the Laugheads, who informed him of their saucer interests and experiences. Otto in turn urged them to get in touch with Martin. Soon afterward, they wrote and introduced themselves. All of this seemed particularly significant to Martin when she received a message urging her to go to East Lansing to seek "a child . . . to whom I am trying to get through with light." When informed, Mrs. Laughead immediately concluded that she was the "child" (Festinger, *et al.,* 1956).

After the Laugheads met Martin in Oak Park in early June 1954, the three formed a close association that would profoundly affect their lives and fortunes in the months and years to come. By this time, Martin was receiving as many as ten messages a day, all of them ominous, all warning of imminent disasters and cataclysms. The news was not entirely bad: Those who would "listen and believe" would enter a New Age of knowledge and happiness. The messages got more specific. Spaceships would land soon, and selected individuals would be flown to other planets, along with space people who had been on secret Earth assignment.

On August 1, Martin, the Laugheads, and nine believers showed up at a Chicago-area military base, where they had been told a flying saucer would land at noon. No ship showed up, but the next day Sananda informed her through automatic writing that he was the stranger the group had observed passing by during the wait for the landing. It would not be the last time Martin would inflate a mundane incident into a signal from the cosmos. Nor would it be the last of the unfulfilled prophecies.

In that same message on August 2, Sananda warned that soon a tidal wave off Lake Michigan would wash over Chicago and cause enormous destruction. Subsequent communications spoke of enormous geological upheaval that would break North America in two, sink much of Europe under the ocean, and raise Mu from its underwater grave.

Martin and the Laugheads reported these revelations to the larger world in a seven-page mimeographed document, "Open Letter to American Editors and Publishers," sent out on August 30. A handwritten addendum appended at the last minute cited December 20 as the "date of evacuation," in other words, the final day on which human beings living in the affected area could save themselves. A second mailing two weeks later concerned the "terrific wave" that would rise from Lake Michigan at dawn on December 21 and engulf Chicago.

Soon the group found itself featured in a tongue-in-cheek newspaper story. The publicity brought followers, curiosity-seekers, and practical jokers to Mrs. Martin's door. It also brought her and her group to the attention of the University of Minnesota's Laboratory for Research in Social Relations, which enlisted the services of five psychologists, sociologists, and graduate students. The volunteers were to observe—as participants and self-identified believers—a prophetic movement at work and to see what happened when the anticipated events did not occur. In due course, Leon Festinger, Henry W. Riecken, and Stanley Schachter, the professors who had directed the experiment, chronicled the episode in *When Prophecy Fails.*

Though Martin, Laughead, and the others harbored ambivalent feelings about the publicity and proselytization, it would have been impossible to conceal what was going on. The group now claimed followers not only in the Chicago area but also in East Lansing and Detroit. In East Lansing, Laughead led a church-related Quest group and, moreover, had ties to the Detroit saucer community, dominated by contactees and mystics, including medium Rose Phillips, who had her own cosmic sources. When some of Martin's followers asked Phillips about the December 21 prophecy, those sources responded ambiguously.

On the Earth plane, Dr. Laughead was facing a serious professional and personal crisis over his ever more visible advocacy of beliefs that most people thought bizarre or even laughable. On November 22, he was asked to resign his position with the college health service effective December 1, though word of the firing would be withheld for another three weeks. College president John A. Hannah later told the press that students had complained about Laughead's "propagandizing" them "on a peculiar set of beliefs of questionable validity" ("The End," 1955). Effectively cutting their ties to East Lansing, the Laugheads moved into the Martin residence and awaited the arrival of the flying saucers that would save them and their companions at the onset of the December 21 cataclysm.

On December 17, a Chicago newspaper exposed the group's strange beliefs and Laughead's loss of employment. Other papers around the country, and soon afterward the world, picked up the story, and the result was blistering ridicule on an international scale. The publicity also left the relentlessly gullible group open to pranks that periodically sent its members packing in preparation for meetings with space people or saucer landings.

Though on the morning of the twentieth the Guardians promised that they would board a flying saucer just after midnight, no spaceship appeared. Stunned, the group tried to figure out what had happened. Finally, someone suggested that the group's positive work had prevented the flood. Not long afterward, a message from Sananda confirmed that interpretation. When Laughead called reporters and wire services to pass on the good news, he triggered a fresh round of ridicule-laced stories. Even worse, group members who had given up jobs and cut ties with skeptical family members faced uncertain futures.

Prank calls and visits over the next 24 days, however, kept the group open to the prospect of a landing. Martin also claimed that earthquakes that had taken place in Italy and California validated her prophecy. By now she was grasping at anything. A message on the twenty-third directed everyone to stand in front of the Martin house at 6 P.M. and sing Christmas carols, at which time a saucer would come down and its crew would engage the group in personal conversation. The message further instructed the group to publicize the new prophecy and to invite all interested persons to come.

For Martin, the caroling episode marked a turning point. It sparked a near riot and drew law-enforcement personnel to the scene. Community pressure forced the police to draw up a warrant against Martin and Laughead, charging them with disturbing the peace and contributing to the delinquency of minors. She was also warned that she faced psychiatric examination and possible institutionalization.

Early in January 1955, Dorothy Martin slipped out of town. Under an assumed name, she flew to Arizona. In her new residence she found herself much closer to the hub of contactee activity. Both Truman Bethurum and George Hunt Williamson (a contactee, fringe archaeologist, and alleged witness to Adamski's first Venusian encounter) lived in Arizona. The Laugheads, now resettled in southern California, dropped in from time to time.

Through Williamson's channelings, the Laugheads and Martin learned of the Brotherhood of the Seven Rays, a supernatural order dating back to Lemurian times and headquartered in the present Lake Titicaca in Peru. Guided by further prophecies of imminent apocalypse channeled through both Williamson and Martin, the two—along with a small band of disciples—moved to Titicaca to establish the Priority of All Saints in the remote northern town Moyobamba. From Hemet, California, the Laugheads kept the North American faithful abreast of developments. A bulletin reported day-by-day activities there. Each report was accompanied by a transcript of channeled or automatically written messages, often with apocalyptic overtones. Soon, these messages said, cataclysmic changes would bring flying saucers down from the skies and Lemuria and Atlantis up from the ocean bottom.

By the summer of 1957, however, nearly all of the spiritual pilgrims were back in the United States. The exception was Martin, whom Sananda had directed to stay behind.

Living under the most primitive conditions, suffering from poverty and ill health, Martin barely survived. She felt that her colleagues had betrayed her. She spent a portion of her meager income on postage for mailings to North America, but no one seemed to listen or care. Even so, the messages continued to come at a furious pace. Now they included dramatic visionary encounters with various space people, angels, and religious figures.

Though expecting to spend the rest of her life in the Andes, Martin was surprised to receive instructions to return to the United States in 1961. She moved to southern California and was there for nearly a year before heading to the far northern part of the state and Mount Shasta, long an attraction to America's mystically minded. Occult legend held that a colony of Lemurians lived inside or under the mountain. The Lemurians maintained contacts with extraterrestrials who regularly arrived in saucers.

Sananda and Sanat Kumara ordered Martin to establish the Association of Sananda and Sanat Kumara. Finding peace and stability at last, she took up residence in the Shasta area and worked with a small but devoted band of followers who carefully recorded and circulated the messages she received daily.

By 1988, with Sedona, Arizona, now the New Age center of North America, the space people dictated yet another move. It was here, on June 13, 1992, that Sister Thedra's long, strange trip ended. Just before her death Sananda told her of his plans for her in the next world. As her body failed, her hand guided a pen one last time to write the final message from her beloved cosmic friend: "It is now come the time that ye come out of the place wherein ye are. . . . Let it be, for many shall greet thee with glad shouts!"

See Also: Adamski, George; Atlantis; Bethurum, Truman; Contactees; Lemuria; Mount Shasta; Orthon; Sananda; Williamson, George Hunt

Further Reading

Clark, Jerome, 1997. "The Odyssey of Sister Thedra." *Syzygy* 6, 2 (Summer/Fall): 203–219.

"The End of the World," 1955. *The Saucerian* 3, 2 (Spring): 4–7, 55–60.

Festinger, Leon, Henry W. Riecken, and Stanley Schachter, 1956. *When Prophecy Fails.* Minneapolis: University of Minnesota Press.

Ibn Aharon, Y. N. [pseud. of Yonah Fortner], 1957. "Diagnosis: A Case of Chronic Fright." *Saucer News* 4, 5 (August/September): 3–6.

Sky people

Brinsley le Poer Trench, author of a series of books proposing esoteric theories about everything from space visitors to the Earth's hidden history, held that the "sky people"—called the Elohim in the Old Testament—created Animal or Adamic Man, otherwise known as the present human race. The creation occurred via what would now be called genetic engineering, and it was done by a renegade band of Elohim called the Jehovah. The Jehovah, knowing that their experiment was an unauthorized one, removed their creation to an obscure location—what the Bible calls the Garden of Eden—on Mars. In due course, another extraterrestrial race, known as the Serpent people, learned of the Garden and visited it, curious about experiments that had created women. The Serpent people gave the heretofore-innocent inhabitants of the Garden wisdom and scientific knowledge, and they also introduced them to sexual intercourse and reproduction. Many of the Adamic Women bore children sired by the Serpent race.

The Jehovah were furious when they found out about the Serpent people's interference, but it was too late for them to continue their domination of Adamic Man. The individual Jehovah most responsible for the experiment,

Noah-I, was driven from Mars. With his creations, he flew back to Earth in a spaceship (Noah's Ark) and populated the Earth.

According to Trench, all human conflict stems from mankind's dual nature. Only if we achieve "total consciousness"—in which both the superior Serpent heritage and the Animal nature are integrated—can we claim our place as wise, peaceful citizens of the galaxy.

Further Reading

Trench, Brinsley le Poer, 1960. *The Sky People.* London: Neville Spearman.

Smead's Martians

A century ago pioneering psychical researcher James Hyslop investigated a case in which an American woman received psychic messages from Mars. The Martians, however, were not natives of the planet but deceased relatives who were now living on the Red Planet.

The woman, whom Hyslop identifies only as Mrs. Smead, was married to a clergyman. All her life she had had psychic experiences, many of them involving spirit communications through automatic writing. Then in 1895 a different set of messages started to come through. They were from her three dead children and her deceased brother-in-law. One of the daughters, Maude, provided a description of her new home, which she said was crisscrossed with canals, reflecting a belief to that effect (since conclusively debunked) promulgated by astronomer Percival Lowell.

The communications ceased, then resumed again five years later as if there had been no interruption. Invited to assess them, Hyslop deduced that they came out of a "secondary personality"—what now would be called the unconscious mind—of Mrs. Smead's. He wrote,

> We find in such cases evidence that we need not attribute fraud to the normal consciousness, and we discover automatic processes of *mentation* that may be equally acquitted of fraudulent intent; while we are also free from the obligation to accept the phenomena at their assumed value. Their most extraordinary characteristic is the extent to which they imitate the organizing principle intelligence of a normal mind, and the perfection of their impersonation of spirits, always betraying their limitations, however, just at the point where we have the right to expect veridical testimony to their claims. (Hyslop, 1908)

See Also: Aliens and the dead; Allingham's Martian; Aurora Martian; Brown's Martians; Dentons's Martians and Venusians; Hopkins's Martians; Khauga; Martian bees; Mince-Pie Martians; Monka; Muller's Martians; Shaw's Martians; Wilcox's Martians

Further Reading

Hyslop, James H., 1908. *Psychical Research and the Resurrection.* London: Fisher Unwin.

Smith

During a wave of sightings of mysterious, never-explained "airships" (UFOs in modern terminology) in the spring of 1897, a Rockland, Texas, man named John Barclay claimed an encounter with a close-lipped pilot who gave only his last name. The *Houston Daily Post* of April 25 reported the incident.

Around 11 P.M., as Barclay told the story, he heard his dogs barking frantically. Glancing out his window, he was startled to see an oblong-shaped object with wings circling just above his pasture. Moments later the ship landed. Winchester rifle in hand, the witness stepped outside where he spotted a stranger. The stranger identified himself only as "Smith." He would not allow Barclay to get closer to the ship. "We cannot allow you to get any closer, but do as we request [and] your kindness will be appreciated," Smith said, "and we will call on you some future day and reciprocate your kindness by taking you on a trip." He handed Barclay ten dollars and asked him to purchase lubricating oil, two cold chisels, and bluestone from a nearby saw mill and railroad depot. On his return Barclay asked the aeronaut where he was from. "Anywhere," Smith replied, then added, "We will be in Greece day after tomorrow." He entered the ship and was gone.

Since conventional aviation history attests that no such ships were flying over America in the late nineteenth century, some UFO writers have theorized that the so-called aeronauts were really extraterrestrials or supernatural entities in disguise. A more likely explanation is that the stories were hoaxes of the sort that filled many period newspapers.

See Also: Aurora Martian; Lethbridge's aeronauts; Michigan giant; Ultraterrestrials; Wilson

Further Reading

Chariton, Wallace O., 1991. *The Great Texas Airship Mystery.* Plano, TX: Wordware Publishing.

Cohen, Daniel, 1981. *The Great Airship Mystery: A UFO of the 1890s.* New York: Dodd, Mead and Company.

Source

The Source, a sort of universal mind, was channeled through Paul Solomon. Solomon's channeling began in 1972 when he was living in Atlanta and going through acute personal distress in the wake of a failed marriage. In an effort to deal with his emotional problems, Solomon underwent hypnosis. Under hypnosis a powerful voice spoke through his mouth, warning, "You have not attained sufficient growth or spiritual awareness to understand contact with these records!" Bewildered, Solomon and hypnotist Harry Snipes III decided to explore the mystery in a second session. From there the Source, as Solomon and Snipes called it, began instructing Solomon on how to communicate with it and how to pass on its wisdom to others.

The Source taught a spiritual philosophy that it called "Inner Light Consciousness," thus the name of the organization Solomon soon formed: Fellowship of the Inner Light. In 1974, Solomon and his followers relocated to Virginia Beach, Virginia, where Edgar Cayce, to whom Solomon would be compared, had lived and had pursued his spiritual work. Like Cayce's, Solomon's readings encompassed Atlantis, reincarnation, healing, prophecies, and more.

The Source claimed to be a greater power than the spirit or channeling entities that were a good part of the focus of the New Age movement of the 1970s and 1980s. Its mission was to provide a way for seekers to touch the Holy Spirit within them and, thereafter, to let it guide them. Before his death in 1994, Solomon had conducted thousands of readings, many preserved on tape and sold by associates who seek to keep his and the Source's memory alive.

See Also: Atlantis; Channeling

Further Reading

Beidler, William, 1977. "Paul Solomon . . . Another Cayce?" *Fate* 30, 2 (February): 56–61.

A Healing Consciousness, 1978. Virginia Beach, VA: Master's Press.

Spiritual Unfoldment and Psychic Development through Inner Light Consciousness, 1973. Atlanta, GA: Fellowship of the Inner Light.

Wheeler, W. Alexander, 1994. *The Prophetic Revelations of Paul Solomon: Earthward toward a Heavenly Light.* New York: Samuel B. Weiser.

SPECTRA

Under hypnosis on November 30, 1971, Israeli psychic Uri Geller "recalled" an incident that occurred when he was three years old. Geller encountered a dazzling light from which a voice emanated. The voice said it was his "programmer." Over the years, Geller received many more messages from this intelligence, which called itself SPECTRA and, sometimes, Hoova. It gave Geller his reported paranormal talents. In the opinion of Geller's hypnotist and then-collaborator, physician/parapsychologist Andrija Puharich, Geller may have been a prophet "specifically created to serve as an intermediary between a 'divine' intelligence and man" (Puharich, 1974).

SPECTRA claimed it was a supercomputer into which the minds and bodies of a wide variety of intelligent beings had been transferred. These beings communicated with Geller through automatic writing, states of altered consciousness, and voices on blank tapes. SPECTRA's first appearance on Earth was twenty thousand years ago, when its spaceship landed in the present nation of Israel. Since then SPECTRA has seen the Jews

Uri Geller, the psychic performer, ca. 1978 (Hulton-Deutsch Collection/Corbis)

as its special people and has tried to protect them. In the meantime, other beings from other planets and dimensions unrelated to SPECTRA have visited Earth. The beings behind SPECTRA have said that they live in the future. They are short and generally human in appearance, looking like—in their words—"certain exotic types of Japanese."

This fantastic tale figured largely in Puharich's *Uri* (1974), but Geller himself distanced himself from it. His own autobiography, published a year after Puharich's book, does not even mention SPECTRA, though it does recount his childhood close encounter with a "silvery mass of light" that seemed to make time stand still. As the light approached him, the youthful Geller felt a sharp pain in his forehead, then lost consciousness for an undetermined period of time.

Further Reading

Geller, Uri, 1975. *Uri Geller: My Story.* New York: Praeger Publishers.

Puharich, Andrija, 1974. *Uri: A Journal of the Mystery of Uri Geller.* Garden City, NY: Anchor Press/Doubleday and Company.

Springheel Jack

Springheel Jack (sometimes referred to as Spring Heeled Jack) is a figure out of Victorian folklore, a mysterious man or being of violent disposition and a strange ability to jump great distances. Stories about him were first told in suburban London in September 1837. Some victims described him as a man wearing a flowing cloak and glaring at his victims with glowing eyes. It was claimed that he shot flames from his mouth. Others said he disguised himself as a white bull or bear, while at least one witness claimed he wore "polished steel armor, with red shoes" ("Credulity," 1838). Some reports suggested that the attacker was not acting alone. Many of the attacks were on women and were seemingly sexual in nature (he ripped their clothes), though apparently they did not involve actual rape. London police, who took the reports seriously, investigated them but made no arrests. Popular speculation pointed to Henry Marquis of Waterford, a man noted for recklessness, drunkenness, and other behavioral excesses, but no clear or convincing evidence backed up the suspicions. Superstitious people held that Springheel Jack was a ghost, and that belief took root in folklore.

Sporadic sightings of a mysterious leaping figure occurred in various places in England into the twentieth century. In 1877, many residents of Caistor, Norfolk, saw someone dressed in sheepskin (reminiscent of earlier reports of Jack's cladding himself in animal skin) jumping from roof to roof, and the same or a similar individual was widely observed in Lincolnshire. On one occasion, when a mob chased him, he leaped over walls and roofs. In 1904, in Liverpool's Everton district, residents saw a man dressed in a cloak and black boots executing high leaps, on one occasion allegedly springing from the ground to a rooftop twenty-five feet high.

Though Springheel Jack legends are not a part of American folklore, figures very much like him appear in a few curious episodes. In 1938, a century after the London reports, people in and around Provincetown, Massachusetts, claimed encounters with a leaping man with fierce-looking eyes and pointed ears. They said he stunned his victims with a blue flame emanating from his mouth. Comparable stories were told in Baltimore in the summer of 1951. On June 18, 1953, three witnesses in a Houston neighborhood allegedly sighted a leaping, black-clad figure in a cloak and saw a rocket-shaped UFO zoom away moments after the being's disappearance. At least two other cases link leaping, Jacklike figures to UFOs, one in Gallipolis, Ohio, in the early 1960s, another at Washington's Yakima Indian Reservation in December 1975.

The first suggestion that Jack may have been an extraterrestrial appeared in the March 6, 1954, issue of the British magazine *Everybody's*. The next year, in a book on Liverpool history and lore, Richard Whittington-Egan remarked that such a theory "would account for his astounding leaping proclivities because he would be adapted to the requirements of life on a greater-gravity planet. Likewise, differences in physical constitution would probably enable him to live longer on earth and might well explain the flame-like emanations from his mouth" (Whittington-Egan, 1955).

On the other hand, in an extended survey of all available literature on the legend, British writer Mike Dash rejected any notion that the various reports over a century and a half were connected except as folklore. In Dash's view, "Springheel Jack" is a catchall name denoting unrelated pranksters, hoaxers, and criminals. Still, it is hard to deny that intriguing questions remain, and Springheel Jack—whatever he or it may or may not be—constitutes an appealingly romantic mystery.

Further Reading

"Credulity—The Ghost Story," 1838. *London Times* (January 10).

Dash, Mike, 1996. "Spring-Heeled Jack: To Victorian Bugaboo from Suburban Ghost." In Steve Moore, ed. *Fortean Studies, Volume 3,* 7–125. London: John Brown Publishing.

Haining, Peter, 1977. *The Legend and Bizarre Crimes of Spring Heeled Jack.* London: Frederick Muller.

Whittington-Egan, Richard, 1955. *Liverpool Colonnade.* Liverpool, England: Son and Nephew.

Sprinkle, Ronald Leo (1930–)

R. Leo Sprinkle is a psychologist in private practice in Laramie, Wyoming. Prior to that, as a member of the counseling department of the University of Wyoming, he became known as one of a handful of mental-health professionals with a sympathetic interest in the UFO phenomenon. He was the first to study the psychological make-up of abductees and contactees. In 1968, as a psychological consultant for the U.S. Air Force–sponsored University of Colorado UFO Project, he hypnotized a Nebraska police officer who reported a puzzling period of missing time during a close encounter. Sprinkle's principal interest, however, was in persons who believed themselves to be in psychic and other contact with friendly space people, whom Sprinkle called "UFOlk." In 1980, he and the Institute for UFO Contactee Studies held the first Rocky Mountain Conference on UFO Investigation. From then until 1996 he would direct the meetings, which brought together contactees, their followers, and interested observers.

Sprinkle's interest was, and is, more than academic. He believes himself to be a contactee and maintains an active interest in reincarnation and other metaphysical questions. UFOs and their occupants are here, he believes, "so that human development moves from Planetary Persons to Cosmic Citizens" (Sprinkle, 1995).

See Also: Abductions by UFOs; Contactees

Further Reading

Parnell, June O., and R. Leo Sprinkle, 1990. "Personality Characteristics of Persons Who Claim

UFO Experiences." *Journal of UFO Studies* 2 (new series): 45–58.

Sprinkle, R. Leo, 1999. *Soul Samples: Personal Explorations in Reincarnation and UFO Experiences.* Columbus, NC: Granite Publishing.

———, 1969. "Personal and Scientific Attitudes: A Study of Persons Interested in UFO Reports." In Charles Bowen, ed. *Beyond Condon: Flying Saucer Review Special Issue No. 2,* June, 6–10. London: Flying Saucer Review.

———, 1976. "Hypnotic and Psychic Aspects of UFO Research." In *Proceedings of the 1976 CUFOS Conference,* 251–258. Evanston, IL: Center for UFO Studies.

———, 1995. "The Significance of UFO Experiences." In David Pursglove, ed. *Zen in the Art of Close Encounters,* 164–165. Berkeley, CA: New Being Project.

Sprinkle, R. Leo, ed., 1980. *Proceedings of the Rocky Mountain Conference on UFO Investigation.* Laramie, WY: School of Extended Studies.

Star People

"Star People" is a notion made popular in the late 1970s and early 1980s. Brad Steiger, a prolific writer on paranormal, occult, and ufological subjects, introduced the phrase in a 1976 book. He writes that the "majority of Amerindian Medicine People" believe that Star People—individuals who many lifetimes ago came to Earth with a mission from their home worlds—are "becoming active at this time in an effort to aid mankind [in surviving] a coming Great Purification of the planet" (Steiger, 1976). In the course of his investigation of channeling and channelers, he says, he became aware of women he calls "Star Maidens." Such women shared certain physical characteristics and had "memories" of arriving on Earth twenty thousand years ago in a starship. Before long Steiger became convinced that just as many men—including himself—had similar claims to extraterrestrial origin.

Steiger eventually married a woman he believed to be a Star Maiden, Francie Paschal. Paschal reported a lifetime of otherworldly experiences, beginning with childhood visions in which an apparitional spaceman, looking like a "Hollywood-type Viking prince," told her, "Like unto another Christ child you will be." He said she was from a "planet . . . like unto Venus" (Steiger, 1976). She and Steiger believed they had shared previous lives. As part of what they believed to be their mission, the couple moved from upstate New York to Scottsdale, Arizona.

An article on their beliefs concerning Star People in the May 1, 1979, issue of the *National Enquirer* brought them a flood of letters and telephone calls. It turned out that other persons suspected that they also were space people put in place to help the human race through coming cataclysms and changes. Many said they had heard a disembodied voice tell them, "Now is the time," shortly before they read the *Enquirer* piece. The Steigers went on to release books in the "Star People Series," three originals and two reprints of earlier Brad Steiger titles. The originals were based in considerable part on Francie's channelings.

According to these messages, the Starseeds are the true Star People. As direct descendants of extraterrestrials, they have both alien and human genes. The Star Helpers are descendants of the extraterrestrials' original disciples. Later, from further channeling, hypnotic regression, and testimony from others, the Steigers concluded that three different types of space ancestors could be discerned: Refugees who crash-landed on this planet thousands of years ago, after escaping from turmoil and destruction on their home planet; Utopians, benign aliens who colonized other worlds to give them perfect societies; and Energy Essences, nonphysical entities who drift through space, drop in on planets, and occasionally occupy a host body.

In *The Star People* (1981), the Steigers reported that a number of their correspondents believed they had insights into the immediate future. They foresaw worldwide famine in 1982, a pole shift between 1982 and 1984, World War III no later than 1985, and Armageddon around 1990. Somewhere in the middle of this, space people would land and announce their presence.

By the mid-1980s, the Steigers had divorced, and only Francie maintained enthusiasm for the Star People notion. Her death, a few years later, effectively ended what remained of the movement.

See Also: Channeling

Further Reading

Steiger, Brad, 1973. *Revelation: The Divine Fire.* Englewood Cliffs, NJ: Prentice-Hall.

———, 1976. *Gods of Aquarius: UFOs and the Transformation of Man.* New York: Harcourt Brace Jovanovich.

———, 1983. *The Seed.* New York: Berkley Books.

Steiger, Brad, and Francie Steiger, 1981. *The Star People.* New York: Berkley Books.

Steiger, Francie, 1982. *Reflections from an Angel's Eye.* New York: Berkley Books.

Stellar Community of Enlightened Ecosystems

Sometime in the 1980s, Jerry Doran of Wilmington, California, claims to have had an out-of-body experience. He ascended into space where he encountered "five blue skinned dolphins floating inside [a] spaceship." Through telepathy the dolphins informed him that they were associated with the Stellar Community of Enlightened Ecosystems. The community sought to guide human evolution toward attainment of a "Group Mind which includes the animals and plants of Earth, the Earth itself, the Sun and similar enlightened star systems throughout the Cosmos" (Melton, Clark, and Kelly, 1990).

Further Reading

Melton, J. Gordon, Jerome Clark, and Aidan A. Kelly, 1990. *New Age Encyclopedia.* Detroit, MI: Gale Research.

Strieber, Whitley (1945–)

Whitley Strieber began his career as a successful writer of horror and science-fiction novels but has since become better known as a chronicler of his own paranormal and otherworldly experiences, including abductions by UFOs.

Born to a prominent San Antonio family, he attended the University of Texas, then moved to New York to begin a writing career. On the evening of December 26, 1985, he experienced

Whitley Strieber (Dennis Stacy/Fortean Picture Library)

a number of peculiar encounters of which he did not have full conscious recall. A subsequent hypnosis session led him to believe that he had encountered aliens who inserted a needle into his brain. Strieber sought out the well-known abduction investigator Budd Hopkins, who lived not far from him though the two had not met till then. Hopkins introduced him to psychiatrist Donald F. Klein, who subjected Strieber to psychological tests and pronounced him normal. Strieber and Hopkins soon parted company on bad terms around the time Strieber published a best-selling account of his abduction experiences, *Communion* (1987).

Communion sparked something of an uproar, with some critics—most vocally Thomas M. Disch in *The Nation*—accusing Strieber of having written a science-fiction novel that he was passing off as fact. Strieber also had his defenders, who argued that he had too much to lose to engage in that sort of literary fraud. A follow-up book, *Transformation* (1988), recounted further experiences, and it, in turn, was followed by more books recounting ever more fantastic interactions with "the visitors," as Strieber calls them. By the time he published *Secret School* in 1996, he was claiming that aliens had been interacting with him all of his life, beginning in his childhood when the visitors instructed him and other San Antonio children on their missions as adults.

See Also: Abductions by UFOs; Extraterrestrials among us; Hopkins, Budd

Further Reading

Conroy, Ed, 1989. *Report on "Communion": An Independent Investigation of and Commentary on Whitley Strieber's "Communion."* New York: William Morrow and Company.

Strieber, Whitley, 1987. *Communion: A True Story.* Beach Tree/William Morrow.

———, 1988. *Transformation: The Breakthrough.* New York: William Morrow and Company.

———, 1995. *Breakthrough: The Next Step.* New York: HarperCollins Publishers.

———, 1996. *The Secret School: Preparation for Contact.* New York: HarperCollins Publishers.

Strieber, Whitley, and Anne Strieber, eds., 1997. *The Communion Letters.* New York: HarperPrism.

Swords, Michael D., 1987. "*Communion:* A Reader's Guide." *MUFON UFO Journal* 229 (May): 3–6.

Sunar and Treena

Dean Anderson of Egg Harbor, Wisconsin, was atop a riding lawn mower at a golf course when a flying saucer landed. It was 4:15 A.M., August 22, 1976. A door opened, and two beings, a man and a woman, floated out on a beam of light. As they stepped toward Anderson, the saucer vanished. They shook Anderson's hand, and the man said, "We come in peace. I am Sunar, from Jupiter. This is Treena. She comes from Saturn" (Bartholomew and Howard, 1998). Sunar, who had copper skin, said he was more than two hundred years old. The lightly tanned Treena, clad in a one-piece, skin-tight, green, glistening, metallic suit, looked, Anderson thought, like Elizabeth Taylor.

The space people told him that they had come to Earth to gather specimens. Before they left, they handed him an envelope with instructions not to open it for five Earth days. After waiting for the designated period, Anderson found a golden amulet inside. On one side there was a bird resembling a dove. On the other, a message read, "Peace and friendship forever, Treena and Sunar," with depictions of Saturn and Jupiter beside the names.

Further Reading

Bartholomew, Robert E., and George S. Howard, 1998. *UFOs and Alien Contact: Two Centuries of Mystery.* Amherst, NY: Prometheus Books.

T

Tabar

On the night of December 10, 1979, a Rhode Island woman, Elaine Kaiser, saw a white light and fell unconscious. Subsequent probing through hypnosis elicited the "memory" of floating in a beam into a room aboard a spacecraft. There she encountered a giant being in a dark metallic suit. By telepathy, the being told her his name was Tabar, and he was from 2.4 million light years away. She was laid on a table and connected by instruments to a man who lay on another. She did not recognize the man. The procedure seemed to be something like a blood transfusion. At first it was painful, but Tabar waved a hand in front of her face, and the discomfort ceased.

Several months later Kaiser saw the man in an audience. He did not act as if he recognized her, and she did not approach him.

Further Reading

"Alien Visitors?" 1982. *Oakland* [Michigan] *Press* (August 22).

Tawa

Tawa, a Blackfoot Indian and a friend of Jesus in a previous incarnation, emerged in a Ouija board session in suburban Chicago on August 22, 1968. Previous to this, Candy Fletcher had been pursuing spiritual questions by reading metaphysical books and exploring altered states of consciousness. But it was through her husband, Rey, that Tawa spoke. Under hypnosis, Rey Fletcher channeled Tawa's teachings until late 1970 when he turned his attention to more prosaic concerns. His wife, however, transcribed the teachings and began work on a book based on them. She also founded the Circle of Power Foundation. In 1984 the Fletchers moved to Victor, Montana, to devote full time to their spiritual concerns.

According to Tawa, Jesus was born again into the world in 1962, but the individual had yet to realize that he was the Messiah. Soon, however, he would come to that knowledge and reveal himself to the world, which this time would accept his mission. But before that happened, the anti-Christ would exert malign influences and power before Jesus vanquished him.

See Also: Channeling

Further Reading

Fletcher, C. R., 1984. *Spirit in His Mind.* Victor, MT: Circle of Power Foundation.

Tecu

Tecu (pronounced Tey-coo) is an entity who channeled through a young California woman, Sanaya Roman. Roman first heard from him when she and a friend were vacationing in Kauai, Hawaii. At that time, he dictated a book-length manuscript on how to heal psychically and how to use the universal laws of energy to one's benefit. According to Roman, "Tecu identified himself as a Lord of Time from the portals of the world of essence where all matter is created" (Roman and Packer, 1987).

He came to her a second time on another Hawaiian trip. Then she learned that he came from a universe of a different frequency, thus making communication difficult and infrequent. In that universe, energy is "symmetrical." A jolly being, he took in good humor the difficulties he encountered trying to walk in Roman's body. Because in his realm energy is absorbed whenever it is necessary, he was at first perplexed by the experience of eating food. "Eating is at the root of your problems," he remarked wryly. "First you have to have food. Then you need dishes. Then you have to build a house to contain the dishes. Then you have to go to work to pay for the house. All because you have to eat!"

Tecu came back on several occasions to discuss the coming Earth changes and to encourage Roman to continue her project of teaching others how to channel.

See Also: Channeling

Further Reading

Roman, Sanaya, and Duane Packer, 1987. *Opening to Channel: How to Connect with Your Guide.* Tiburon, CA: H. J. Kramer.

Thee Elohim

In April 1971, a Milwaukee woman, June Young, experienced a vision in which white and black people linked hands. All were wearing black robes with large white rosaries around their necks. Soon she began receiving messages from Archangel Michael. "He told me to start a class dealing with the higher laws of God," she said. "He gave me full instructions. The lessons were brought and taught by Michael and his Angels. Michael is the head of our class as well as our protector." She came to understand that her original vision was of the group she would form, the Arising Sun's Interplanetary Class of Thee Elohim.

She explained to writer Brad Steiger that Thee Elohim are the seven spirits of God: Chamuel, Gabriel, Raphael, Zadkiel, Michael, Jophiel, and Uriel. "They stand before God and co-create with Him," she explained. "They manage and direct all forms that exist."

In 1972 Jophiel, "the angel of intuitive light," told her that because she had managed to overcome "your desires of the flesh," he and his colleagues were giving her back the name she had held in her previous incarnation as a Venusian: Bright Star. Ever after she went by that name, working at her mission to "bring the material and spiritual kingdoms together." According to her space friends, the Earth would go through devastating physical and social upheaval in the last years of the twentieth century, but with the help of the space people and their terrestrial associates, the Earth's people will eventually enter a new age of peace, harmony, and spiritual wisdom.

See Also: Contactees; Michael

Further Reading

Steiger, Brad, 1976. *Gods of Aquarius: UFOs and the Transformation of Man.* New York: Harcourt Brace Jovanovich.

Thompson's Venusians

Samuel Eaton Thompson's story is as strange as any from the UFO age. Before the word "contactees" had been invented, Thompson, an elderly, poorly educated, retired railroad worker, claimed to have spent two days in the company of naked, Edenic Venusians and, moreover, seemed to actually believe his own story was true.

Thompson's strange odyssey began on March 28, 1950, as he was driving between Morton and Mineral, Washington, on his way home from a visit to relatives in Markham. As he passed through a wooded area, he decided to stop and take a break. He took a stroll down an old logging trail that took him deeper into the forest. As he entered a clearing, he saw a hovering UFO that, he later related to a local newspaper reporter, "appeared to be made of a glowing, sun-colored substance similar to plastic and was shaped like two saucers fused together. I judged it was about eighty feet horizontally and thirty-two vertically" ("Centralian Tells," 1950). Equally peculiar was the sight of tanned, fine-featured, naked children playing on steps that led from the saucer to the ground.

Excited, Thompson approached the craft, feeling a mild heat emanating from it—the cause, he would learn subsequently, of its occupants' tanned skins. As he came nearer, his presence brought the adults—beautiful and nude, with dark blond hair—to the door. They seemed frightened of him. He told them he meant no harm, and they relaxed. After asking him in clumsy English to remove his shoes and socks, they invited him inside, where he spent the next forty hours.

He learned that they were from Venus. The ship was also their home. It carried ten men and ten women as well as twenty-five children between six and fifteen years old. Interviewed a few days later by private pilot and well-known UFO witness Kenneth Arnold, Thompson said the Venusians were friendly and cheerful but curiously naïve. He compared them to animals, meaning that instinct rather than intellect governs their activities. They knew nothing of the technology that powered their ship; they knew which buttons to push and levers to pull to get where they wanted to go, and that was it. They had no sense of time and no curiosity, and because of their eating habits—they were vegetarians and stayed away from cooked foods—they never got sick and lived long lives. Their vegetables were like those found on Earth, and Thompson ate some while on the "spaceship" (the word the Venusians used for their craft). He pronounced the food "just great."

Venusians fear earthlings because human aircraft had shot down some of their spaceships. Earth is considered a bad planet, but Mars is even worse. There are twelve inhabited planets in the solar system. Each resident is born under the sign of the planet on which he or she is born, except for Earth, whose problems stem from the fact that each person is born under a different sign. Venusians and earthlings long ago were very close, sharing "the first religion ever known," but the people of Earth eventually became corrupt, and a curse was cast upon their planet. Venusians and other space people are now reincarnating on Earth; their goal is to reform the earthlings and prepare them for Christ's Second Coming in A.D. 10,000.

After sleeping overnight in a chair in one of the ship's bedrooms, Thompson asked for permission to go home and pick up a camera. They did not know what a camera was. When he explained, they said he could go but asked him not to bring anyone else along. The photographic experiment came to nil. It was "just like trying to take a picture of the sun," he told Arnold. "It has a glow to it. That film was just blank. I wanted to get some of them right onto the ground to take some pictures of them, but they wouldn't come out" (Clark, 1981).

The Venusians left on March 30, cautioning Thompson to keep certain information to himself. If he ever saw them again, no one ever knew. For many years his story was little known, with a brief newspaper account the only record of it. In 1980, Arnold gave a tape of his early April 1950 interview with Thompson to *Fate* magazine, and an article largely based on it appeared in the January 1981 issue. Arnold remarked on Thompson's ignorance and lack of imagination, and he was convinced that Thompson believed his story, its outlandish, even absurd, qualities notwithstanding. Arnold speculated that he had undergone some sort of "psychic" experience.

See Also: Adamski, George; Contactees; Hopkins's Martians

Further Reading

Arnold, Kenneth, 1980. "How It All Began." In Curtis G. Fuller, ed. *Proceedings of the First International UFO Congress,* 17–29. New York: Warner Books.

"Centralian Tells Strange Tale of Visiting Venus Space Ship in Eastern Lewis County," 1950. *Centralia* [Washington] *Daily Chronicle* (April 1).
Clark, Jerome, 1981. "The Coming of the Venusians." *Fate* 34, 1 (January): 49–55.

Tibus

Tibus channels through Diane Tessman, a channeling contactee now living in Iowa. Tibus, a member of the Ashtar Command and the Free Federation of Planets, has visited the Earth thousands of times. Under hypnosis with psychologist/ufologist R. Leo Sprinkle, Tessman recounted several childhood "memories" of encountering Tibus aboard a mother ship. He was in the company of two humanoids, one of whom was insectlike in appearance. The humanoids performed medical experiments on her. One experiment, which occurred when she was three years old, left a surgical scar between her nose and upper lip. Tessman believes that the space people were seeking to implant a replica of Tibus's soul inside her.

See Also: Ashtar; Channeling; Contactees; Sprinkle, Ronald Leo

Further Reading

Montgomery, Ruth, 1985. *Aliens among Us.* New York: G. P. Putnam's Sons.

Time travelers

According to Bruce Goldberg, a California physician and a prolific writer on occult and metaphysical subjects, visitors from the future are here. He claims to have met several "chrononauts," as he calls them. They are here, he says, to help us in our spiritual evolution, and they, not extraterrestrials, are the agents responsible for UFO abductions.

Time travel was, or will be, invented in the year 3050. The inventor, Taatos, was the god Hermes thousands of years ago, in another lifetime. Before Taatos traveled back to our time to talk with Dr. Goldberg, however, he helped send holographic images into our present reality. Goldberg writes that the chrononauts "have mastered hyperspace travel between dimension[s], and can move through walls and solid objects. By existing in the fifth dimension, they can observe us and remain invisible. Genetic manipulation of our chromosomes is a routine procedure for them. They have greatly speeded up our rate of evolution."

While traveling in an out-of-body state through the fifth dimension, Goldberg encountered a thirty-sixth-century man who called himself Traksa. Traksa told him that many chrononauts are living quietly among humans, keeping out of the public eye and even spending much of their time in a literally invisible state. Traksa eventually acknowledged to Goldberg that one purpose of his visit was to introduce Goldberg to Art Bell, then host of a nationwide radio show catering to enthusiasts of the esoteric. Goldberg then realized that spelled backwards, Traksa's name was "ASK ART." Afterward Goldberg appeared at least nine times on Bell's popular program.

He also met Muat, Traksa's supervisor from the fortieth century. In earlier lifetimes, he played big roles in both Atlantis and Lemuria. Nirev (thirty-first century) helped with the nineteenth century's industrial revolution, and Alsinoma (thirty-fourth century) tutored Leonardo da Vinci. Chat Noy (fiftieth century) is or will be one of the great pioneers of time travel.

"Chrononauts are spiritual people," Goldberg writes. "They follow us from lifetime to lifetime, tracing our souls back to previous lives and monitoring our spiritual unfolding. Their ultimate purpose is to facilitate the perfection of the human soul to allow for ascension and the end of the karmic cycle. There are also future problems—wars, pollution, infertility—in this and parallel universes that they are trying to avert by assisting us now in our spiritual progress" (Goldberg, n.d.).

Marc Davenport theorizes that UFOs are visitors from the future. In his view, "These time machines are peopled by a complex mixture of human beings, evolved forms of humanoid beings, genetically engineered life forms, androids, robots and/or alien life forms. These occupants make use of advanced technology based on principles that will be discovered at some point in our near future to produce fields around their craft that warp space-time. By manipulating those fields, they are able to traverse what we think of as space and time as well" (Davenport, 1992). Davenport, however, does not claim to have seen any of these time travelers himself.

See Also: Abductions by UFOs; Atlantis; Lemuria

Further Reading

Davenport, Marc, 1992. *Visitors from Time: The Secret of the UFOs.* Tigard, OR: Wild Flower Press.

Goldberg, Bruce, n.d. "Time Travelers I Have Met." http://www.drbrucegoldberg.com/TimeTravelers2.htm.

Tin-can aliens

Four miles east of Long Prairie, Minnesota, at 7:40 P.M. on October 23, 1965, a young radio announcer named James Townsend was rounding a curve when suddenly he saw something in the road and slammed on his brakes. It was a rocket-shaped UFO resting on three fins. The car skidded to a halt only twenty feet from the device, which stood thirty to forty feet tall and was ten feet in diameter.

In a circle of light beneath the UFO, Townsend observed three objects or entities that looked like beer cans on tripod legs and with three matchstick arms. Even though they had no eyes, he was certain that they were staring at him. When he stepped out of his car, they came toward him. After what seemed an eternity, they scooted under the ship and disappeared into the light circle. The UFO shot off with an ear-splitting roar.

His outlandish story notwithstanding, law-enforcement officers and civilian investigators believed that Townsend, a devoutly religious man, was not perpetrating a hoax.

See Also: Close encounters of the third kind

Further Reading

Jansen, Clare John, 1966. "Little Tin Men in Minnesota." *Fate* 19, 2 (February): 36–40.

Tree-stump aliens

One of the most bizarre close encounters of the third kind ever took place on the evening of April 5, 1966, in Newport, Oregon, during a nationwide UFO wave. Though such reports overwhelmingly describe human or humanoid entities, two teenaged girls claimed to have seen aliens that looked like tree stumps.

As they told the story, they were walking to the house of one of them—Kathy Reeves—when they sensed that someone was following them. At a turn in the road, they looked behind them to see something like a "flashlight with a cover over the end." Assuming it was a prankster trying to scare them, they threw rocks toward the light. But when they did so, other, bigger lights suddenly switched on. Frightened, the girls started running. Their dash home was interrupted, however, by a bizarre sight: three shapes moving across a pasture apparently heading toward the lights.

They looked, Kathy Reeves later said, like "three little tree stumps" walking on legs that resembled a tree trunk's tap roots. They had no heads or arms. They were clad in multicolored clothes, "orange, blue, white, yellow, and watermelon-colored" (Brandon, 1978). The sight set the witnesses screaming homeward.

The resulting publicity brought investigators and curiosity-seekers to the Reeves residence over the next few days. At least two of them, including Deputy Sheriff Thomas W. Price, reported seeing strange moving lights. There were no further reports of aliens, tree-stump ones or otherwise, though.

See Also: Close encounters of the third kind

Further Reading

Brandon, Jim, 1978. *Weird America: A Guide to Places of Mystery in the United States.* New York: E. P. Dutton.

Tulpa

"Tulpa" is a Tibetan term for an entity created by mental concentration. Such an entity is believed to take on at least a quasi-physical form and to be visible to others besides its creator.

The most famous tulpa account appears in Alexandra David-Neel's *With Mystics and Magicians in Tibet,* originally published in 1931. David-Neel, an adventurous French woman educated at the Sorbonne, traveled widely through Tibet in the early part of the twentieth century, exploring places and meeting Buddhist holy men that no European had before encountered. The Geographical Society of Paris awarded her a gold medal, and the Legion of Honor knighted her.

David-Neel wrote that while living with the Tibetan yogis, she decided to conjure up a tulpa. She imagined him to be a fat, jolly lama. After some months, the being came into existence. Apparently David-Neel essentially considered him a vivid hallucination, a kind of imaginary companion, and she was unsettled when it began to take on a reality of its own. First, she claimed, it became no longer necessary for her to think of it for it to appear, and it seemed to adopt a recognizable personality and to perform appropriate actions.

"A change gradually took place in my lama," she said. "The countenance I had given him altered; his chubby cheeks thinned and his expression became vaguely cunning and malevolent. He became more importunate. In short, he was escaping me. One day a shepherd who was bringing me butter *saw* the phantasm, which he took for a lama of flesh and bone."

Alarmed, she decided that she had to destroy the entity. It was not easy. It took six months of hard mental work. She concluded, "That I should have succeeded in obtaining a voluntary hallucination is not surprising. What is interesting in such cases of 'materialization' is that other persons see the form created by thought."

Though such first-person allegations of real-life tulpas are exceedingly rare, David-Neel's story would inspire a great deal of speculation that seeks to explain a broad range of extraordinary entities, from lake monsters to UFO humanoids, as tulpalike "thought forms" or (in Michael Grosso's phrase) "psychoterrestrials" (Grosso, 1992).

See Also: Imaginal beings; Psychoterrestrials

Further Reading

David-Neel, Alexandra, 1957. *With Mystics and Magicians in Tibet.* New York: University Books.

Grosso, Michael, 1992. *Frontiers of the Soul: Exploring Psychic Evolution.* Wheaton, IL: Quest Books.

The Two

The Two were Marshall Herff Applewhite, also known as Bo, and Bonnie Lu Nettles, also known as Peep, two of the stranger flying-saucer contactees. Nettles would be long dead when Applewhite, then heading a cultlike group called Heaven's Gate, led thirty-eight followers to mass suicide in a house in a wealthy neighborhood of San Diego in March 1997. Their departure from this world—intended to free their bodies so that their souls could board a spaceship thought to be accompanying the Hale-Bopp comet—generated headlines the world over.

Behind the tragedy lay a quarter-century of spiritual odyssey that began in 1972, when the psychiatrically troubled Applewhite, a musical director at a local Episcopal church, met Nettles, a nurse, at a Houston hospital. The Two shared an interest in the occult, and in Nettles, Applewhite found someone he had been looking for: a woman with whom to establish a platonic relationship and a shared metaphysical mission. Applewhite's homosexuality had caused him legal and employment problems and spiritual confusion. The occult doctrine the Two would create, under guidance from space people, eschewed sexuality and demanded chastity from its adherents.

Beginning in 1973, Applewhite and Nettles set out on a rambling pilgrimage through several western states. While living along Oregon's Rogue River, they experienced a revelation that they were the two witnesses who Revelation 11 had prophesied would appear on Earth during its last days. Their first attempt to announce themselves to a larger world occurred in Oklahoma City, where they introduced themselves to local ufologist Hayden Hewes, who had a flair for publicity. They told Hewes to announce that they were here to help the human race ascend to its next evolutionary level. According to Hewes, they spoke as if "humans were alien to them" (Hewes and Steiger, 1976). Their behavior and general demeanor were so odd that Hewes wondered if they were actual extraterrestrials.

Through leaflets signed by Human Individual Metamorphosis (HIM), the Two sought followers. The documents identified them as two individuals who had come from an advanced realm to testify to the same message that Jesus had given to the world. Those who followed them would have to abandon all ties to this world, including family, friends, jobs, and possessions. When they achieved metamorphosis, they would experience actual biological and chemical changes in their bodies.

Bo and Beep, as they then called themselves, made themselves available to the public in the spring of 1975 at a meeting held in the home of a Los Angeles psychic. Twenty-four persons followed them to participate in further gatherings in California, Colorado, and elsewhere, where new believers were solicited to become Bo and Peep's sheep. Little of this attracted press attention until twenty members of an audience, which had come to hear the Two in Waldport, Oregon, disappeared with them the next day. Newspaper accounts depicted the couple as mysterious. The account even seemed to leave open the possibility that the missing audience members had flown off in a UFO. In fact, they had joined the pilgrimage. Six weeks later, two University of Montana sociologists found them—though not Bo and Peep—in Arizona. Bo and Peep, fearing assassination, had dropped out of sight. Before their departure, however, they separated their 150 to 200 followers in autonomous "families" of about a dozen persons each. Within each family there was further breakdown into couples, preferably a man and a woman, who were to observe each other carefully. Sex and even friendship were explicitly discouraged; the "relationship" had one purpose, which was that each person would have his or her faults pointed out, thus making it possible to overcome human limitations.

Each family went its own way, supporting itself via meetings, contributions by new members, and begging. The reception of such proselytizing was usually hostile, but small numbers of recruits filled the ranks, often replacing those who had lost interest. Most followers were occult tourists whose fascination with any particular metaphysical doctrine was only passing. The failure of flying saucers to arrive to take believers to a New World also discouraged interest.

Marshall Herff Applewhite and Bonnie Lu Nettles, photographed after their 1975 arrest by local police in Harlington, Texas, for auto theft and credit card fraud (Bettmann/Corbis)

In early 1976, the movement, now consisting of fewer than one hundred members, retreated with Bo and Beep to a mountain camp near Laramie, Wyoming. The couple's authoritarian control was intensified, and those judged unqualified were forced out. By fall, the band had relocated to Salt Lake City. Around this time, two members inherited a great deal of money, which they turned over to Bo and Peep. They purchased houses ("crafts" in their terminology) in Denver and

Dallas–Fort Worth and essentially removed themselves from the world. Press stories about them were few, though in 1979 one member spoke with *Time* and recounted the day-to-day spiritual activities of the group, which were rigidly directed. Nettles died, apparently of cancer, in 1985.

In 1993, the group reemerged into view with an advertisement in *USA Today* and followed it with pronouncements in other publications. Now calling themselves Total Overcomers, members lectured in various cities. Two years later, the group, by then called Heaven's Gate, moved to San Diego and set up a successful computer business with its own web site. In October 1996, it purchased a mansion in San Diego's exclusive Rancho Santa Fe.

It was there that the mass suicide occurred, apparently on the night of March 25–26, 1997. Alerted by an anonymous phone call (the caller was later identified as Richard Ford, one of the group's followers), police found the bodies of thirty-nine identically dressed men and women of androgynous appearance. Some of them, it was learned, had been surgically castrated. All had died of poison and suffocation. One of them was Applewhite. According to a videotaped statement, the deaths occurred so that members could leave their "vehicles" (bodies) and join a giant spaceship that they believed was following the Hale-Bopp comet.

See Also: Contactees

Further Reading

Balch, Robert W., 1995. "Waiting for the Ships: Disillusionment and the Revitalization of Faith in Bo and Peep's UFO Cult." In James R. Lewis, ed. *The Gods Have Landed: New Religions from Other Worlds,* 137–166. Albany, NY: State University of New York Press.

Bruni, Frank, 1997. "Cult Leader Believed in Space Aliens and Apocalypse." *New York Times* (March 28).

"Flying Saucery in the Wilderness," 1979. *Time* (August 27): 58.

Hewes, Hayden, and Brad Steiger, eds., 1976. *UFO Missionaries Extraordinary.* New York: Pocket Books.

Hoffmann, Bill, Cathy Burke, and the staff of the *New York Post,* 1997. *Heaven's Gate: Cult Suicide in San Diego.* New York: Harper-Paperbacks.

Niebuhr, Gustav, 1997. "On the Furthest Fringes of Millennialism." *New York Times* (March 28).

Oliver, Evelyn Dorothy, 1997. "Graduating to the Next Level: The Heaven's Gate Tragedy in the Context of New Age Ideology." *Syzygy* 6,1 (Winter/Spring): 43–58.

Peters, Ted, 1977. *UFOs—God's Chariots? Flying Saucers in Politics, Science, and Religion.* Atlanta, GA: John Knox Press.

Steiger, Brad, 1976. *Gods of Aquarius: UFOs and the Transformation of Man.* New York: Harcourt Brace Jovanovich.

U

Ulkt

Ulkt, a Martian, introduced himself through automatic writing to a Salt Lake City UFO buff, Mary Sewall, in early 1982. He told her that Earth is overloaded with negative vibrations. Humans cannot join the federation of intelligent worlds until they learn to cast positive vibrations. If they stop conflict and immoral behavior, their collective vibratory rate will rise. Ulkt signed each communication with what looked like an H on its side. Sewall took this to be a symbol of infinity.

Further Reading

Sprinkle, R. Leo, ed., 1982. *Proceedings: Rocky Mountain Conference on UFO Investigation.* Laramie, WY: School of Extended Studies, University of Wyoming.

Ultraterrestrials

Ultraterrestrials dwell in the superspectrum, a field of intelligent energy capable of manipulating matter. Ultraterrestrials are among the materialized manifestations from this alternative reality. They appear to human beings in a range of guises: as demons, extraterrestrials, channeling intelligences, angels, fairies, monsters, men in black, and other supernatural entities. They are behind all of the world's religions, and they have manipulated history. All ultraterrestrials have one thing in common: a detestation of human beings and all they stand for. Human beings who encounter them often end up psychically enslaved or destroyed.

In Keel's view, heavily influenced by traditional demonology, "The Devil's emissaries of yesteryear have been replaced by the mysterious 'men in black.' The quasi-angels of Biblical times have become magnificent spacemen. The demons, devils, and false angels were recognized as liars and plunderers by early man. These same impostors now appear as long-haired Venusians" (Keel, 1970).

See Also: Channeling; Fairies encountered; Keel, John Alva; Men in black

Further Reading

Keel, John A., 1970. *UFOs: Operation Trojan Horse.* New York: G. P. Putnam's Sons.

Ummo

Ummo is supposedly the name of a planet that revolves around a star known to Ummites as Iumma, 14.6 light years from the Earth. It is also the focus of one of the most complex, enigmatic hoaxes in the history of the contactee movement.

The episode began in February 1966 in a Madrid suburb, where witnesses allegedly saw a UFO hovering close to the ground. One

One of several UFO photographs taken by "Antonio Pardo" at San Jose de Valderas, Madrid, Spain, June 1, 1967 (Fortean Picture Library)

witness, Jose Luis Jordan Pena, reported seeing a strange symbol on the bottom of the craft. It resembled two reverse parentheses, with a vertical bar between them. Only Jordan Pena told of seeing such a symbol (in fact quite similar to the stylized *H* used sometimes to represent the planet Uranus), which he described in a letter to prominent Spanish ufologist Antonio Ribera. On June 1, 1967, the same man claimed to have investigated another close encounter at San Jose de Valderas, near Madrid. He said witnesses had told him that they saw a symbol on the UFO's bottom. It was like the earlier one, except that now a horizontal bar crossed the vertical and linked the two reverse parentheses. The following day, Antonio San Antonio, a newspaper photographer, took a phone call from an anonymous young man. The caller said he had taken pictures of the UFO, and San Antonio could pick them up at a certain photographic laboratory. One of the pictures depicted the curious logo.

Soon afterward, leaflets signed "Henri Dagousset" asserted that the UFO had left capsules in the area. "Dagousset" offered three hundred dollars for each sample, referring takers to a general delivery address at Madrid's main post office. In August, Barcelona writer Marius Lleget, author of a recently published UFO book, received a letter with no return address from "Antonio Pardo." Inside the envelope were two more pictures of the San Jose de Valderas object with the identical symbol. Pardo said he had taken them moments after the first photographer had snapped his. He also enclosed a green plastic strip with the symbol on it, explaining that he had recovered it from a boy who had found it and a similar strip inside a mysterious tube. (Subsequent analysis determined it to be a weather-resistant plastic developed for military and aerospace use. It was, in other words, of earthly origin.) Then a man identifying himself as Pardo phoned Lleget and spoke with him at length. Lleget never asked for his address, and Pardo did not provide it, to the later frustration of Ribera and Rafael Farriols. The two ufologists called every Antonio Pardo (Anthony Brown in English) in Madrid's phone book without ever finding anyone who would own up to being Lleget's informant.

A related development, investigators would soon learn, had occurred on May 20, when the Spanish newspaper *Informaciones* published a peculiar announcement: that soon a flying saucer would land near Madrid to return earthbound extraterrestrials to their home planet, Ummo. On the evening of the thirtieth, three persons reportedly watched a UFO land near a restaurant in Santa Monica, another Madrid suburb. The next day, according to one of the witnesses, impressions, burn marks, and small amounts of a metallic substance attested to the UFO's presence. These alleged events seemed to confirm a prediction made by contactee Fernando Sesma, president of the Society of the Friends of Space, on May 31. In a speech to a small group, he revealed that since 1965 he and two associates had been recipients of phone messages and written communications from Ummites. They had informed him of a sighting to occur on June 1. They provided the exact geographical coordinates. The Santa Monica incident seemed to confirm the Ummites' statement.

The written messages soon started to arrive in the mail of Spanish UFO enthusiasts, then to some of their French colleagues. Postmarks indicated that they were sent from all over the world, from cities in Europe to others in New Zealand and Canada. On each page the Ummo symbol appeared. It was the same one Jordan Pena and other witnesses had reportedly seen and the anonymous young man had photographed. The messages typically consisted of many pages of discourse on Ummite life, society, science, technology, language, and politics. Besides the monographs, there were phone calls from purported Ummites, always speaking with great precision in a monotone voice. Untraceable or unsigned letters came from human beings who had dealt with Ummites face to face (they were described as tall, blond, and Scandinavian in appearance) and witnessed marvelous technology. The quantity of such material was astounding. By 1983, according to an estimate by one knowledgeable student of the episode, some sixty-seven hundred Ummo-related communications were in the hands of a variety of recipients. Most were written in Spanish, a small minority in stilted French that seemed to have been translated from Spanish.

In one document, the Ummites said they had arrived on Earth in March 1950. The following April 24, they revealed in another document that they had stolen a number of items from a family in an isolated house in the French Alps. By this time, the French government had become interested, and at last it had an investigatable claim. But official inquiries turned up nothing: no police records, no evidence of the cave in which the Ummites asserted they had been living between their landing and the break-in. In the 1970s, the San Jose de Valderas "UFO" fell victim to photoanalysis that established that the object was an eight-inch plate, the symbol drawn in ink. Still, the communications continued, and an Ummo cult grew up around them. A number of books, mostly in Spanish and French, would examine or celebrate Ummo.

Though no evidence supports the existence of Ummo and Ummites, the identity of the perpetrators of the hoax is still unknown. French-American ufologist Jacques Vallee, trained in astrophysics and computer sciences, characterizes the contents of the documents as "clever and occasionally stimulating. . . . A science journalist, a government engineer working on advanced projects, or a frustrated writer could match the psychological profile of the UMMO author" (Vallee, 1991). He contends that the perpetrator or perpetrators got their inspiration from Jorge Luis Borges's fantastic short story "Tlon, Uqbar, Orbis, Tertius" (1941), a fable about imaginary planets that in some sense become "real." Other suspects are Fernando Sesma, Jordan Pena, or some intelligence agency involved in a psychological experiment. Hilary Evans thinks a better, more sustained investigation by the Spanish ufologists who probed the affair would have produced answers and made Ummo less mysterious than it appears to be. Whatever the case, Ummo documents still show up in the mail of a few individuals, most prominently the French aerospace engineer Jean-Pierre Petit. Whoever is beyond the episode has expended much time and energy to it over three decades.

Further Reading

Evans, Hilary, 1983. "Ummo: A Perfect Case?" *The Unexplained* 12, 134: 2661–2665.

———, 1983. "The Ummites Tell All." *The Unexplained* 12, 135: 2686–2689.

———, 1983. "Ummo—Red Alert." *The Unexplained* 12, 137: 2738–2740.

Ribera, Antonio, 1975. "The Mysterious 'UMMO' Affair." *Flying Saucer Review* Pt. I. 20, 4 (January): 20–24; Pt. II. 20, 5 (March): 13–16; Pt. III. 21, 1 (June): 26–28; Pt. IV. 21, 2 (August): 24–25, 27; Pt. V. 21, 3–4 (November): 43–46.

Vallee, Jacques, 1991. *Revelations: Alien Contact and Human Deception.* New York: Ballantine Books.

Unholy Six

According to George Hunt Williamson, six solar systems housing planets peopled by "negative space intelligences" exist in the Orion nebula. The "Unholy Six" live on dying worlds, and they plan to destroy the Earth so that they can have access to its resources. The Orion group has its own subversive agents on Earth, working with them to undercut the work of friendly, pro-human space visitors of the Space Confederation. Though incapable of entering the Earth's atmosphere in their own spacecraft, the Unholy Six project their intelligences into the brains of certain earthlings.

Williamson wrote that the underlying cause of conflict between the Space Confederation and the Unholy Six is that "the former are Deists and the latter are Ideists." In other words, the Space Confederation believes in a divine power to which all are answerable, and the Unholy Six believe only in the primacy of the "id"—the power of the individual. "For countless millennia there have been no possibilities of reconciliation between these groups," Williamson said (Williamson, 1959).

See Also: Williamson, George Hunt

Further Reading

Williamson, George Hunt, 1953. *Other Tongues—Other Flesh.* Amherst, WI: Amherst Press.

———, 1959. *Road in the Sky.* London: Neville Spearman.

V

Vadig

Vadig is an extraterrestrial invented by self-confessed hoaxer Thomas F. Monteleone. In March 1968, as a psychology student at the University of Maryland, Monteleone heard West Virginia contactee Woodrew Derenberger talking about his space contacts on Washington, DC, radio station WWDC. Derenberger claimed to have traveled to the planet Lanulos. Convinced that Derenberger was lying, Monteleone decided to play a practical joke and to assert that he, too, had been to Lanulos. He called the station under the name "Ed Bailey" and added new details about the planet and its people. Derenberger readily agreed with what the caller said.

To Monteleone's chagrin, the station was able to trace the call. Derenberger's manager Harold Salkin phoned him and learned his true identity. A week later, Salkin, Derenberger, and the latter's wife called on Monteleone, who tape-recorded the interview. In the interview, the young man reported that while driving home on an interstate highway he witnessed a UFO landing. Two aliens emerged, and one introduced himself as Vadig. Two months later, Vadig showed up at the Washington restaurant where Monteleone worked part-time. He arranged a meeting, ending the encounter, as he had before, with the enigmatic words "I'll see you in time." The following Sunday night, Vadig drove the young man into rural Maryland where they boarded a spaceship and flew to Lanulos, where the inhabitants walk about naked. One week later Monteleone met Vadig and another Lanulosian for the last time.

Not long after the initial interview the Derenbergers and Salkin returned to talk once more, bringing along with them occult journalist John A. Keel. Keel, who thought Monteleone had revealed information only a real contactee would know, wrote about the Vadig encounter in later magazine articles and in a book. When Vadig said he would "see you in time," according to Keel, he was hinting that UFO beings "originate outside of our time frame. . . . UFOs are from another time cycle vastly different from our own" (Keel, 1969).

Monteleone went on to a short career as a public contactee. His story appears in a book Derenberger wrote with Harold W. Hubbard in 1970, cited as evidence of the authenticity of Lanulos and the author's experiences with it. In 1979, in a short article in *Omni,* Monteleone confessed the hoax, noting, "I contradicted Mr. Derenberger's story on purpose. But on each occasion, he would give ground . . . and in the end corroborate my own falsifications. He even claimed to know personally the 'UFOnaut' who contacted me!" A fuller account of the episode appeared in 1980 in a *Fate* article by ufologist Karl T. Pflock. By this time Monteleone had embarked on what was to prove a successful career as a science-fiction writer.

See Also: Contactees; Keel, John Alva

Further Reading

Derenberger, Woodrow W., and Harold W. Hubbard, 1971. *Visitors from Lanulos.* New York: Vantage Press.

Keel, John A., 1975. *The Mothman Prophecies.* New York: Saturday Review Press/E. P. Dutton and Company.

———, 1969. "The Time Cycle Factor." *Flying Saucer Review* 15, 3 (May/June): 9–13.

Monteleone, Thomas F., 1979. "Last Word: The Gullibility Factor." *Omni* 1 (May): 146.

Pflock, Karl T., 1980. "Anatomy of a UFO Hoax." *Fate* 33, 11 (November): 40–48.

Val Thor

Val (or Valiant) Thor, a Venusian, met Frank E. Stranges, evangelist and contactee, in the Pentagon one morning in December 1959. At the time Stranges was conducting a Christian crusade in Washington. An anonymous Pentagon official of his acquaintance invited him to the building. In one room he met a handsome, tanned man with wavy brown hair. In the course of a half-hour conversation, the stranger informed him that he was from Venus. Over the course of years, Stranges flew on spacecraft with Val Thor and wrote two books about their experiences together.

Stranges reported that Venusians are physically like humans in all ways, except that they do not have fingerprints. Fingerprints "are a sign of fallen man," according to Val Thor (Stranges, 1974). Venusians, who are without sin, are devout Christians, but they have no need for the Bible because of their closeness to its author. In their first meeting Stranges learned that seventy-seven Venusians were living secretly in the United States, but that number was subject to constant change because the Space Brothers were always coming and going. Val himself was scheduled to return to Venus on March 16, 1960. The Venusians had come to Earth to "help mankind return to the Lord."

On the morning of February 5, 1968, Val Thor phoned Stranges and instructed him to meet at the San Diego Airport. From there, the two drove across the border into a coastal town in Sonora, Mexico. Near there, they boarded a flying saucer with a large crew, including a woman named Teel. Inside Val's compartment, Stranges learned that his friend had spoken with Sen. Robert F. Kennedy, then running for the Democratic nomination to the presidency. Kennedy had written Val a letter requesting a meeting, and Val had responded. Val found Kennedy "nervous and suspicious." That evening aboard the spaceship, as they watched a large televisionlike screen, Stranges, Val, and several dozen Venusians sorrowfully observed Kennedy's assassination.

On another occasion, in January 1974, Stranges flew to Las Vegas to meet Val and friends. At the airport, two young men dressed in black called him by name. Assuming they were the space people who were to take him to Val Thor, he followed them into a black Cadillac. Suddenly, they and a third, similarly clad man turned on him and were beating him severely when two men—space people—came to the rescue. They caused the Cadillac and the three men in black, agents of dark forces opposed to the Venusians' benevolent mission, to disappear. They then took Stranges to the scheduled conference with Val inside a flying saucer.

Still an active lecturer and saucer personality, Stranges claims to have photographic proof of Val's existence. The photographs, reproduced in his books and shown at his lectures, depict a man dressed in a suit and surrounded by other persons in what look like ordinary social situations. Val Thor resembles a Hollywood bit player more than an extraterrestrial.

See Also: Contactees; Men in black

Further Reading

Stranges, Frank E., 1974. *My Friend from beyond Earth.* Second edition. Van Nuys, CA: International Evangelism Crusades.

———, 1972. *The Stranger at the Pentagon.* Second edition. Van Nuys, CA: International Evangelism Crusades.

Valdar

In 1960, a young man identified only as Edwin was working in a factory in Durban, South Africa, when he met and befriended a new supervisor. One night while the two were fishing together, the latter spoke into a mechanical device, called up space people, and produced a sky show with UFOs. Soon afterward, the man confessed to Edwin that his real name was Valdar. He also told Edwin that he was from Koldas, a planet that existed in an anti-matter universe to which he must soon return. He left Edwin the device before he disappeared. In a few months, the two were talking over the interdimensional radio. Edwin learned that Koldas is one planet in a twelve-world confederation.

The exchange continued for years. Before long, Edwin channeled the messages rather than taking them through the radio. Many of the messages were of a technical and scientific nature. Others were occult and metaphysical. In 1986, South African ufologist Carl van Vlierden published a book-length account of Edwin's alleged experiences and messages.

Further Reading

Hind, Cynthia, 1996. *UFOs over Africa.* Madison, WI: Horus House.

Van Vlierden, Carl, and Wendelle C. Stevens, 1986. *UFO Contact from Planet Koldas.* Tucson, AZ: UFO Photo Archives.

Van Tassel, George W. (1910–1978)

Besides being a contactee himself, George Van Tassel made his mark as the foremost promoter of the early contactee movement. Every year he sponsored the Giant Rock Interplanetary Spacecraft Convention at his residence in the high desert between Yucca Valley and Joshua Tree, California. He also introduced Ashtar, among the most ubiquitous and beloved of channeling entities, to the occult and flying-saucer world.

Born in Ohio, Van Tassel moved to California in 1930 with his family. He worked as an aircraft technician for, among others, Howard Hughes. In 1947, the Van Tassels took up residence inside an immense, partially hollowed-out rock called simply Giant Rock. Van Tassel started receiving psychic messages from extraterrestrials in January 1952, the first of them from "Lutbunn, senior in command first wave, planet patrol, realms of Schare [pronounced Share-ee, a starship station in space]. We have your contact aboard 80,000 feet above this place" (Van Tassel, 1952). A flood of other messages followed in the next days, weeks, and months, all from peace-loving space people associated with the Council of Seven Lights on the planet Shanchea. Van Tassel wrote what may be the first contactee book, in the modern sense, *I Rode a Flying Saucer!* (1952). Its title notwithstanding, at that point all of his contacts had been mental ones. Not until August 24, 1953, would Van Tassel board a spacecraft (or "ventla," in the vocabulary of his space friends).

Beginning in early 1953, Van Tassel held weekly public channeling sessions. The Giant Rock conventions began that spring, attracting the new contactee stars and their followers and affording the emerging movement much publicity. Soon Van Tassel, in person and through his College of Universal Wisdom, was raising money for the Integratron, a machine to be built according to extraterrestrials' specifications. It was supposed to rejuvenate tissue and restore youthful vigor. By 1959, the structure was partially built, but for all Van Tassel's subsequent efforts it would never be completed.

More than any other single figure, Van Tassel gave direction and cohesion to what otherwise would have been a disparate movement. He supported contactees whose claims—as was often the case—conflicted with his own, to the expense of his own credibility. Ufologist Isabel L. Davis, for example, saw him as a charlatan who knew fully well that the contact stories were bogus. Others, however, judged him to be sincere and dedicated to a meta-

George Van Tassel (right) with Long John Nebel (Fortean Picture Library)

physical vision in which, however outlandish it may have seemed to others, he truly believed.

Van Tassel died in Santa Ana, California, on February 9, 1978. Since then, some channelers have reported messages from him. "I was immediately taken into fellowship with the Great Masters of the Council of which I wrote," he told one (Tuella, 1989).

See Also: Ashtar; Channeling; Contactees

Further Reading

Curran, Douglas, 1985. *In Advance of the Landing: Folk Concepts of Outer Space.* New York: Abbeville Press.

Davis, Isabel L., 1957. "Meet the Extraterrestrial." *Fantastic Universe* 8, 5 (November): 31–59.

Reeve, Bryant, and Helen Reeve, 1957. *Flying Saucer Pilgrimage.* Amherst, WI: Amherst Press.

Tuella [pseud. of Thelma B. Turrell], ed., 1989. *Ashtar: A Tribute.* Third edition. Salt Lake City, UT: Guardian Action Publications.

Van Tassel, George W., 1952. *I Rode a Flying Saucer! The Mystery of the Flying Saucers Revealed.* Los Angeles: New Age Publishing Company.

———, 1958. *The Council of Seven Lights.* Los Angeles: DeVorss and Company.

Vegetable Man

Jennings Frederick, a young West Virginia man, claimed that while bow-and-arrow hunting one afternoon in July 1968, he heard a "high-pitched jabbering, much like that of a recording running at exaggerated speed." Even so, he could understand it, and it was communicating to him that he should not be afraid. "I come as a friend," the voice said. "We know of you all. I come in peace. I wish medical assistance. I need your help." Then Frederick saw the creature whom wags would soon dub Vegetable Man.

The being had semi-human facial features. Its ears were long, its eyes yellow and slanted, and it had very thin arms about the size of a quarter in diameter. It had three seven-inch-long fingers at the end of each arm. Instead of fingertips, the fingers had needlelike tips and suction cups. Its slender body looked like the stalk of a plant, and so did its color: green.

Suddenly the entity gripped Frederick's hand. Before he realized what was happening, it was drawing blood from it. Then its eyes turned red, and they began to rotate like spinning orange circles. The effect was hypnotic. Frederick no longer felt any pain from the extraction, which lasted a minute or so. Afterward, a restored Vegetable Man bounded up a nearby hill, each of his steps covering twenty-five feet.

Frederick's pain resumed. As he started to walk home, he heard a humming sound. It made him panic because he thought the entity might be coming after him in its flying saucer. He ran as fast as he could and got back home unharmed.

Frederick was friends with Gray Barker of Clarksburg, West Virginia, a publisher and promoter of outlandish saucer materials. Barker was also a self-confessed hoaxer and encouraged other hoaxers. For a time, Vegetable Man played a large role in Barker's promotions. No one else has ever reported an encounter with him.

See Also: Tree-stump aliens

Further Reading

Steiger, Brad, 1978. *Alien Meetings.* New York: Ace Books.

Venudo

Dan Boone, the son-in-law of George W. Van Tassel, a leading figure in the contactee movement of the 1950s and 1960s, was in a Yucca Valley, California, liquor store early one Saturday evening when he heard a group of people—two men and two women—ask for directions to Giant Rock. He offered to lead them there, and they followed him to the site. Boone assumed they were there to attend the weekly channeling and discussion group Van Tassel held. He was right. The leader, who said his name was Venudo, sat near Boone and Van Tassel while the other three rested on a couch nearby.

Venudo casually produced a device that had been hanging around his neck. He tapped it and, in full view of about thirty witnesses, he vanished instantly. A minute later he became visible again. Boone asked him if he could do that once more, and Venudo obliged. This time Boone reached over and felt Venudo's shoulder, though he could not see it. According to Boone, Venudo and his friends were space people checking in on Van Tassel's activities.

See Also: Channeling; Contactees; Van Tassel, George W.

Further Reading

Hamilton, William F., III, 1996. *Alien Magic: UFO Crashes—Abductions—Underground Bases.* New Brunswick, NJ: Global Communications.

Villanueva's visitors

In 1953, Salvador Villanueva Medina's claimed encounter with friendly men from another world sparked international excitement. Followers of the emerging contactee movement saw it as evidence that the space people were now expanding their mission to Latin America, and for a time Villanueva became something of a hero in that region's occult world.

As the story went, Villanueva, a taxi and limousine driver, was contracted to drive from Mexico City up to Laredo, Texas. He and his two passengers from Texas left Mexico City on the morning of August 22. In the late afternoon, the car's differential gave out, and Villanueva managed to roll the car to the side of the highway before it came to a complete stop. The two passengers decided to walk to the nearest village to see if they could find a mechanic. The driver stayed with the car and did what he could to get it running again. He jacked up the car and crawled underneath it and began tinkering. There was little traffic, and he felt very much alone.

Darkness had fallen when he heard footsteps. From beneath the vehicle, he saw two legs covered in what look like corduroy. He crawled out uneasily and stood to face the man. The stranger had a pale white face. He was dressed in a one-piece suit and had a three-inch-wide belt around his waist. Lights shone from little holes in the belt, and he was holding a helmet under his arm. He had fine features and a penetrating stare. He had shoulder-length gray hair and his face was hairless. He was four feet tall.

Too stunned and frightened to speak, Villanueva could not find the words to respond to two questions, spoken in fluent Spanish, about what was wrong with the car. Finally, he managed to ask if the man was an aviator. The little man replied in the affirmative, then added an odd remark about "my machine which you people call an airplane." He indicated that it was parked behind a mound not far away.

Feeling more comfortable, Villanueva invited him to sit down in the car. But at that moment the lights on the belt started to flash, and a buzzing noise sounded. The stranger donned his helmet and walked toward the hill. The driver returned to his business with the car, and not long afterward two motorcycle police officers came by and ordered him to take the vehicle off the road. Afterward, he lay down to sleep inside it.

Sometime later, knocks sounded on the window. Groggily Villanueva sat up, assuming that his passengers had returned. He was surprised to see instead the "aviator" and a companion, the latter a taller version of the first. They entered the car and conversed with the driver. The shorter one did most of the talking. As they described their home, Villanueva realized that they were space people. It took him awhile to decide that they were not joking.

Over the next few hours, he learned much about their home world, its civilization, its cities, its technology, and more. Thousands of years ago, he was told, many destructive wars were fought between the planet's nations, until finally its inhabitants established a one-world government under what amounted to a benevolent dictatorship of a council of wise men. The state raised and educated the children, and there was no serious poverty. People from this planet live undetected among earthlings, reporting on human affairs to their otherworldly superiors.

Toward dawn the buzzing sounds, emanating from either the helmets or the belts, resumed. The two left the car, with Villanueva following. Eventually, they came to the ship, a saucer-shaped structure. The men invited him inside the craft, but at that moment he lost his nerve and fled back to the car. From it he saw the saucer ascend and disappear in the direction of the rising sun.

When his experience became known soon afterward, Villanueva was compared to the prominent American contactee George Adamski. Adamski met Villanueva in Mexico in the spring of 1955 and asked him a series of questions. An American couple that also was there would write, "If the questions astounded us, so did the answers. Salvador passed his examination at the hands of a man who, having seen a saucer himself, knew how to ask about certain things which no mere imaginary contact could give the answers to" (Reeve and Reeve, 1957). Desmond Leslie, Adamski's associate and co-author, visited Villanueva later that year. Leslie claimed that Adamski had confided "the Key" to him, explaining that "every man who has received a true and physical contact with men from other worlds has been given a certain 'Key' whereby it shall be known that he is speaking truly. No man . . . could ever stumble upon this key by guess or chance. . . . Villanueva gave it without hesitation" (Good, 1998).

Unlike Adamski and other contactees of the period, Villanueva did not embark on a professional career. So far as is known, he claimed no further meetings with extraterrestrials.

See Also: Adamski, George; Contactees

Further Reading

Good, Timothy, 1998. *Alien Base: Earth's Encounters with Extraterrestrials.* London: Century.

Reeve, Bryant, and Helen Reeve, 1957. *Flying Saucer Pilgrimage.* Amherst, WI: Amherst Press.

VIVenus

The woman who called herself "VIVenus"—"Viv" for short—made her mark in the mid-1970s to the early 1980s. She said she was a

Venusian who replaced a woman, her exact physical double, who had committed suicide in a New York hotel on September 24, 1960. As she was brought to Earth that night, she lost all memory of her life on Venus, "a world of Love" (*VIVenus,* 1982). The memories returned seven years later, and she embarked on a mission to reform this corrupt, cruel planet.

From Christmas 1974 until mid-1982, Viv walked an average of ten miles a day and preached the cosmic gospel to whoever would listen. When she wasn't preaching, she was playing guitar and singing interplanetary hymns. In 1980, she campaigned for her favorite presidential candidate under the slogan "It's Not Odd to Vote for God" (Shoemaker, 1980).

See Also: Dual reference

Further Reading

Shoemaker, Susan, 1980. "A Venusian Visitor Goes Campaigning." *Oakland* [California] *Tribune* (July 13).

VIVenus: Starchild, 1982. New York: Global Communications.

Volmo

Ted Rice grew up in rural Alabama. Early in life he learned that he had psychic abilities, and he was aware of what he took to be spirit guides but later identified as extraterrestrials. One of these was a reptoid entity named Volmo.

Volmo communicated spiritual truths to Rice as he slept. It was only when he saw Volmo that he realized Volmo was not an angel but a grotesque-looking alien. Under hypnosis, in an ostensible reliving of his first physical encounter, he remarked that Volmo "just isn't human. . . . He's really tall . . . six and a half feet tall . . . and massive. He's got a strong, powerful body, and it's dark colored, dull gray or olive brown. . . . They're dark, sort of yellow-gold, with sharp teeth. . . . There are only three or four fingers on each hand, and I think they're webbed. The hands look clawlike, because he's got these long, pointed nails on each finger."

See Also: King Leo; Reptoid child; Reptoids

Further Reading

Turner, Karla, 1994. *Masquerade of Angels.* Roland, AR: Kelt Works.

W

Walk-ins

Ruth Montgomery popularized the notion of the "Walk-in," highly evolved souls who take over the bodies of human beings who are willing to relinquish them. These beings are believed to be so advanced that it is not practical, or sometimes even possible, for them to go through the normal process of reincarnation, starting out as a baby. In any event, they have no time to waste and a serious mission to fulfill. In Montgomery's words:

> There are Walk-ins on this planet. Tens of thousands of them. Enlightened beings, who, after successfully completing numerous incarnations, have attained sufficient awareness of the meaning of life that they can forego the time-consuming process of birth and childhood, returning directly [to] the adult bodies. . . . The motivation of the Walk-in is humanitarian. He returns to physical being in order to help others help themselves, planting seed-concepts that will grow and flourish for the benefit of mankind. (Montgomery, 1979)

Walk-ins, according to Montgomery, include Moses, Jesus, Mohammed, Christopher Columbus, Abraham Lincoln, Gandhi, Mary Baker Eddy, Thomas Jefferson, Benjamin Franklin, and others who have played large roles in politics, religion, the arts, and other aspects of human life.

In a later elaboration of the notion, Montgomery contended that there are also extraterrestrial Walk-ins, in other words the souls of kindly space people who have possessed (after mutual agreement) the bodies of humans. The extraterrestrial Walk-ins are among the advanced souls that come to guide humans into a New Age of peace, harmony, and spiritual insight.

Further Reading

Montgomery, Ruth, 1979. *Strangers among Us: Enlightened Beings from a World to Come.* New York: Coward, McCann, and Geoghegan.

———, 1983. *Threshold to Tomorrow.* New York: G. P. Putnam's Sons.

———, 1985. *Aliens among Us.* New York: G. P. Putnam's Sons.

Walton's abduction

Few UFO abduction cases are as spectacular or as puzzling as one that allegedly took place in November 1975 in a remote area of east-central Arizona. Forestry worker Travis Walton's five-day disappearance received worldwide attention when it occurred, and it has since been the subject of books, television dramas, a movie, polygraph tests, and endless controversy.

UFO abductee Travis Walton (Dennis Stacy/Fortean Picture Library)

The incident began as the seven-member crew of young men, ranging in age from seventeen to twenty-eight, were quitting work at 6 A.M. on November 5. As they left the site, located in the Apache-Sitgreaves National Forest, they noticed, ahead of them, a brilliant glow, its source hidden by the trees. As their pickup continued down the road, they observed a disc-shaped structure, approximately one-hundred feet in diameter, twenty feet wide, and eight feet high. It was hovering twenty feet above a clearing. As the pickup slowed down, Walton jumped out and ran toward the object. According to Walton's own testimony as well as what other crew members subsequently told law-enforcement authorities and civilian ufologists, Walton got within six feet of the bottom of the craft. Sounds began to come from the UFO, unnerving Walton, who was starting to back away when a bluish green beam hit him, shooting him back some ten feet.

Terrified, the others fled in the truck. A few minutes later, their panic somewhat subsided, they returned to retrieve their coworker, only to find no trace of him. After twenty minutes of fruitless searching, they drove to nearby Heber, Arizona, and reported the disappearance to the authorities. The crew returned to the site in the company of two sheriff's officers. They found no clues to tip them off to Walton's whereabouts. At midnight, Walton's mother and other family members were notified. The next day searches resumed. By now the authorities suspected that either the crew had murdered Walton and concocted a wild UFO tale to cover up the deed or Walton and his brother Duane had engineered a hoax for monetary reasons. No actual evidence supported either of these suppositions, but the alternative—that a UFO had kidnapped Travis Walton—was too outlandish to be taken seriously.

As publicity spread, reporters, ufologists, and curiosity-seekers descended on the scene, and charges and countercharges flew. The authorities insisted that the witnesses undergo polygraph examination. According to examiner Cy Gilson, the results in five cases were positive—indicating that the men had given a sincere account—and in one instance inconclusive. Sheriff Marlin Gillespie declared that he was now convinced that the UFO story was true, after all.

Near midnight on November 10, Walton's brother-in-law Grant Neff took a call, which he first took to be a prank, from a weak-voiced, confused-sounding man who claimed to be Travis Walton. The caller said he was phoning from a gas station in Heber, thirty miles east of Taylor, where Neff and his wife lived. When Neff seemed ready to hang up, the voice became desperate, and Neff realized that he was indeed speaking with Travis. Neff and Duane Walton drove to Heber and found Travis at a phone both near the station, shivering in the same clothes he had been wearing five days earlier. It was only eighteen degrees outside.

A complex series of events followed, with hoax charges being leveled by some (though not all) local police officers and then by William H. Spaulding, head of a Phoenix-based group called Ground Saucer Watch. Jim and Coral Lorenzen, directors of Tucson's Aerial Phenomena Research Organization (APRO), entered the investigation and, with the *National Enquirer,* arranged for Walton to take a secret polygraph test. It was administered by John J. McCarthy, who did not hide his skepticism of Walton's claim and grilled him about a youthful scrape with the law. Afterward, when Walton had taken the examination, McCarthy declared that he had flunked it. Walton's critics cited the test as reason to reject Walton's story, while his defenders disputed the results as the consequence of a hostile examiner's harassment of an already shaken witness. In any case, the results were suppressed and did not come to light until UFO debunker Philip J. Klass learned about it sometime later from McCarthy.

The following February, Duane Walton and then Travis took a polygraph, this one run by George J. Pfeifer. Pfeifer concluded that their responses were truthful. Mary Kellett, their mother, whom some had accused of being a conspirator in a hoax, also passed the test, in Pfeifer's judgment.

Walton would tell the same story without elaboration over the next two decades and more. He reported that after the beam hit him, he lost consciousness and had no memory of anything until he awoke in what he thought was a hospital. The atmosphere was wet and heavy, and he had a hard time breathing in it. Three humanoid figures with big staring eyes, large hairless heads, and tiny mouths, ears, and noses, stood by the bedside.

Terrified, he leaped out of bed and pushed one into another. Grabbing a cylindrical tube he noticed on a shelf jutting from the wall, he waved it like a weapon toward the beings, who put out their hands as if to stop him. After a short time, they fled through a door behind them. Soon afterward Walton ran out the door himself and ran to his left, through a curving, three-feet-wide corridor. Seeing an open room to his right, he ducked into it. The

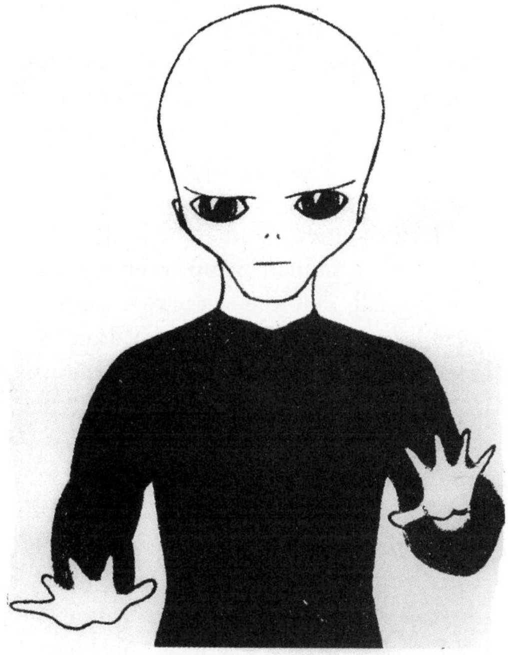

A drawing by Travis Walton's boss, Michael Rogers, based on Walton's description of the being he saw when he was abducted (Fortean Picture Library)

room seemed empty, though Walton was nervous about a high-backed metal chair in the middle. Because he was observing it from the back, he did not know if anyone was sitting in it or not. No one was. As Walton approached it, the lights in the room began to dim. When he stepped back, the light returned. As he went forward again, the light dimmed again, and now stars surrounded him. He did not know if he was witnessing a planetarium effect or if the room had become transparent. He would recall that the experience was "like sitting in a chair in the middle of space" (Walton, 1978).

On the right arm of the chair, he saw a panel of buttons and a screen with black lines going up and down. On the left there was a lever. Curious, Walton pushed the lever forward. Suddenly the lines on the screen moved, and the stars began to spin even while maintaining their relative positions. When he let go of the lever, everything returned to the way it had been before. After he stood up, the light returned to the room, and the stars disappeared.

At that point, a human-looking figure wearing a spacesuit and helmet entered the room. He stood over six feet tall, looked to be about two-hundred pounds, and had blond hair long enough to cover his ears. His skin was deeply tanned. Thinking that the stranger was a fellow human being (even though he would recall that the eyes were peculiar, a "strange bright golden hazel"), Walton felt relieved and peppered him with questions. In response the figure only grinned, then beckoned him to follow. He took Walton's arm, and the two proceeded down the curving hallway. They came to a door and opened it to enter a tiny "metal cubicle" of a room. They passed through it into a huge space that Walton thought looked like a hangar of some kind. Inside it was bright as sunshine, and breezes blew as if they were outdoors. He realized that they had just left the craft. When he turned to examine it, he observed that it resembled the UFO he had seen in the clearing but this one was bigger. He also saw two other identical but smaller craft parked near the wall.

They then went through another door into another hallway, strolling past a number of closed double doors until finally they entered yet another room. Inside this room two men and a woman sat, not only dressed like his companion but looking enough like him that Walton wondered if they were related to him. They were all good-looking, and the woman's hair was longer than the men's. The three were not wearing helmets. Walton had assumed that he had not been able to communicate with the first man because the stranger could not hear him through the helmet. But like the first man, they did not respond to Walton's questions, just smiled pleasantly. When the helmeted man left, the others led him to a table. Suddenly frightened, Walton demanded to know what they were doing. The woman forced something that looked like an oxygen mask with no connecting tubes onto his face. He passed out. The next thing he knew, he was lying on his back near Heber, ten miles from where he had been before all of this started. In the darkness "one of those round craft [hovered] there for just a second. I looked up just as a light went out. A white light just went off on the bottom of it. The craft was dark, and it wasn't giving off any light" (Barry, 1978).

Walton's return was an international news event. Soon afterward, UFO debunker Philip J. Klass embarked on what would amount to a lifelong crusade to prove that Walton, his family, and the logging crew had conspired to hoax the incident. No very good evidence of a hoax would emerge, however, even after one of the crew was reportedly offered ten thousand dollars to expose the story. Walton went on to marry, become a family man and respected member of his community, and write two books on his experience, the second containing a long and pointed rejoinder to the skeptics' case. On February 1, 1993, Travis Walton, Duane Walton, and witness Allen Dalis (who had not seen Travis in two decades) underwent new polygraph examinations, again administered by Cy Gilson. Gilson judged them to be telling the truth when they responded affirmatively to the UFO questions and negatively to the hoax charges. In March 1993 Paramount Pictures released a movie drama, *Fire in the Sky,* based loosely on the incident, with D. B. Sweeney in the role of Travis.

Few students of this complex episode believe it to be a hoax. Alternative, non-UFO explanations tend to focus on psychological or natural causes. One theory holds that Walton and his companions saw an earthquake light—a luminous phenomenon generated by electrical fields in rocks in fault zones—that triggered hallucinations. A problem with this hypothesis is the thinly clad Walton's survival in the woods over five bitterly cold mountain nights. The Walton abduction story remains one of the most intriguing cases of the UFO age.

Interestingly, Walton's is one of the first two cases in the UFO literature to describe

A dramatization of the abduction of Travis Walton as seen in the movie Fire in the Sky, *1993 (Photofest)*

the gray aliens that would assume a prominent role in the abduction phenomenon of later years. The other incident was one of which Walton could not have been aware in November 1975. It was known to ufologists Jim and Coral Lorenzen, who were quietly investigating it when the Walton story erupted into the headlines. U.S. Air Force Sergeant

Charles Moody had confided to them that the previous August 13, he saw a UFO in the New Mexico desert and was taken aboard. In early November, in a letter to the Lorenzens, he had this to say of the occupants: "The beings were about five feet tall and very much like us except their heads were larger and hairless, their eyes very small[,] and the mouth had very thin lips" (Lorenzen and Lorenzen, 1977). Moody's description is virtually identical to the one Walton gave to the first group of humanoids he allegedly encountered. Walton's also anticipated later abduction lore in claiming to see both little gray entities and the more humanlike beings whom some ufologists would call Nordics aboard the same ship.

See Also: Abductions by UFOs; Nordics

Further Reading

Barry, Bill, 1978. *Ultimate Encounter: The True Story of a UFO Kidnapping.* New York: Pocket Books.

Bullard, Thomas E., 1987. *UFO Abductions: The Measure of a Mystery. Volume 1: Comparative Study of Abductions. Volume 2: Catalogue of Cases.* Mount Rainier, MD: Fund for UFO Research.

Clark, Jerome, 1998. "Walton Abduction Case." In Jerome Clark. *The UFO Encyclopedia, Second Edition: The Phenomenon from the Beginning,* 981–998. Detroit, MI: Omnigraphics.

Gansberg, Judith M., and Alan L. Gansberg, 1980. *Direct Encounters: The Personal Histories of UFO Abductees.* New York: Walker and Company.

Klass, Philip J., 1989. *UFO Abductions: A Dangerous Game.* Updated edition. Buffalo, NY: Prometheus Books.

Lorenzen, Coral, and Jim Lorenzen, 1977. *Abducted! Confrontations with Beings from Outer Space.* New York: Berkley.

Persinger, Michael A., 1979. "Possible Infrequent Geophysical Sources of Close UFO Encounters: Expected Physical and Behavioral Biological Effects." In Richard F. Haines, ed. *UFO Phenomena and the Behavioral Scientist,* 396–433. Metuchen, NJ: Scarecrow Press.

Walton, Travis, 1978. *The Walton Experience.* New York: Berkley Medallion Books.

———, 1996. *Fire in the Sky: The Walton Experience.* New York: Marlowe and Company.

Wanderers

Wanderers are extraterrestrials who traverse the cosmos in search of what George Hunt Williamson calls "trash can worlds"—in other words, backward planets such as the Earth. When they find such a world, they offer their souls to the reincarnation cycle. On Earth their leader was the Elder Brother—also known as the Son of Thought Incarnate and, in a later life, Jesus Christ. The Elder Brother came to this planet accompanied by one hundred forty-four thousand Lesser Avatars. Over the centuries, many forgot their cosmic origins and mission, but some kept the faith. After World War II, with the coming of flying saucers, the seeding process accelerated. A "space friend" told Williamson, "Many of our people are in your world now. There are nearly ten million of them, with six of those million in the United States itself."

See Also: Williamson, George Hunt

Further Reading

Williamson, George Hunt, 1953. *Other Tongues—Other Flesh.* Amherst, WI: Amherst Press.

White Eagle

White Eagle, believed to represent the New Testament's Saint John, was channeled through British spiritualist medium Grace Cooke (also known as Minesta) from the 1930s until her death in 1979. By the 1950s, White Eagle's teachings had found their way to North America. White Eagle taught an eclectic mix of Christian-based ideas and reincarnation theories as well as the occult doctrine of the Great White Brotherhood. He advocated kindness toward one's fellows and vegetarianism, and love for animals.

Further Reading

Melton, J. Gordon, 1996. *Encyclopedia of American Religions.* Detroit, MI: Gale Research.

White's little people

One August night in 1891, hours before he would leave his native El Dorado, Kansas, to move to Kansas City and become one of America's most highly regarded journalists, William Allen White was awakened by the bright moonlight streaming in through his back window. He was about to turn his head in the opposite direction when he thought he heard music. Looking outside, he saw a group of little people—no more than three or four inches high—dancing under the elm tree. They also seemed to be humming along with the melody. The scene was clear and unmistakable.

Yet, still unable to credit his senses, he turned away, then glanced back. The strange tiny figures were still there. He got up and looked through another window in case the whole scene was simply a trick of light. He could still see the figures. He moved about vigorously to discharge any extant images kept over from sleep. After five minutes the little people began to fade away, and soon only the grass on which they had been moving remained.

Exhausted, he returned to bed and fell asleep. He would never forget the incident. Recalling it many years later in his autobiography, he reflected ruefully, "When I recall that hour I am so sure that I was awake I think maybe I am still crazy."

See Also: Fairies encountered

Further Reading

White, William Allen, 1946. *Autobiography.* New York: Macmillan.

Wilcox's Martians

As he went about his chores on the morning of April 24, 1964, Newark Valley, New York, dairy farmer Gary T. Wilcox had a premonition that something out of the ordinary was going to happen that day. Driving his tractor up a hill, he glimpsed a shiny object just inside a nearby clump of woods. He stopped the tractor, got off, and walked toward the woods. The closer perspective allowed him to see that the object was an egg-shaped structure, twenty feet long and sixteen feet wide, hovering two feet above the ground. All the while it emitted a sound that to Wilcox's ears was like a car idling. Just after he touched the UFO, two Martians came up from under it.

Wilcox did not learn of their planet of origin immediately, but the figures did not look earthly. Four feet tall and two feet wide, they were clad in silver suits that covered their entire bodies. Each carried a small tray filled with soil and plant samples. An eerie voice addressed him, apparently from the chest of the nearer figure (the other stood near the UFO). The voice said, "We are from what you know as the planet Mars" (Schwarz, 1983). Asked what he was doing, Wilcox explained that he was spreading manure. The Martian wanted to know what manure was, and he asked a series of questions about it. He said he would like a sample of it, but when Wilcox volunteered to go to the barn to retrieve some, the alien changed the subject. They could come to Earth only every two years, he said, and warned would-be travelers from Earth to stay away from Mars, since its conditions are inhospitable to human life. They were here to study the Earth's organic life, and they said something that Wilcox understood to mean that "the earth and Mars, plus some other planets, might be changed around." They also predicted that within a year two American astronauts, John Glenn and Virgil (Gus) Grissom, and two Soviet cosmonauts would be killed. They said that other Martian ships were surveying the Earth.

After two hours, the conversation ended. The Martians said that Wilcox should not tell anyone about the exchange "for your own good," though Wilcox did not interpret this as a threat.

All the while, Wilcox would tell family members, he suspected that he was at the receiving end of a hoax engineered by the television show *Candid Camera.* He found a jellylike substance on the ground where the UFO had been, but he could not pick it up. It slipped through his fingers.

Wilcox confided the story to family members and friends. The matter probably would have ended there if two local women, who worked with Floyd Wilcox, Gary's younger brother, had not heard the story. Both belonged to a Washington-based UFO organization. They asked permission to interview Gary Wilcox, who provided them with a short statement. A neighbor woman interested in

UFOs spoke with him at greater length and examined the landing site, but rain had washed away whatever might have been there originally. She alerted the sheriff's office, which sent a deputy to investigate. On May 7 a detailed account appeared in the *Binghamton Press,* after a reporter spoke with a reluctant Wilcox. Subsequently, Walter N. Webb, an astronomer and field investigator for the National Investigations Committee on Aerial Phenomena, spoke with Wilcox and others. "Neighbors, friends, and authorities unanimously agreed that Wilcox had a good reputation in the area," Webb would write. Wilcox had no previous history of interest in the esoteric and in fact was not much of a reader.

A psychiatric examination conducted by Berthold Eric Schwarz, M.D., a psychotherapist, concluded that Wilcox suffered no mental abnormalities. Unlike many figures in the contactee movement, Wilcox made no attempt to exploit his alleged experience. He discussed it only when asked, and with notable hesitation. He made no further claims of encounters with extraterrestrials.

See Also: Allingham's Martian; Aurora Martian; Brown's Martians; Close encounters of the third kind; Dentons's Martians and Venusians; Hopkins's Martians; Khauga; Martian bees; Mince-Pie Martians; Monka; Muller's Martians; Shaw's Martians

Further Reading

Hotchkiss, Olga M., 1964. "New York UFO and Its 'Little People'." *Fate* 17, 9 (September): 38–42.

Ochs, Reid A., 1964. "Martian 'Visit' Stirs Tioga." *Binghamton* [New York] *Press* (May 7).

Schwarz, Berthold E., 1983. *UFO-Dynamics: Psychiatric and Psychic Aspects of the UFO Syndrome.* Two volumes. Moore Haven, FL: Rainbow Books.

Webb, Walter N., 1965. *The Newark Valley-Conklin, New York, Incidents: The Binghamton Area Flap of 1964.* Cambridge, MA: self-published.

Williamson, George Hunt (1926–1986)

George Hunt Williamson was a leading figure in the contactee movement of the 1950s. On that fringe he even had a reputation as a scholar and deep thinker, even if by mainstream standards his ideas about ancient and modern visitations from space by friendly and hostile extraterrestrials seemed the product of a fertile, even crankish imagination. Williamson claimed not only to have witnessed George Adamski's meeting with a Venusian in the California desert in November 1952 but also to have had contacts with space people himself. A colorful, intelligent, and educated man, Williamson advanced many ideas that still circulate in popular culture, though he himself dropped out of sight in the 1960s and died in obscurity in Long Beach, California, in January 1986.

Born in Chicago, Williamson pursued archaeological and anthropological interests in college. Several psychic experiences in his youth drew him to the occult and the paranormal, and then to flying saucers. He had close contacts with the Chippewa and the Hopi and lived with them in the early 1950s. In 1952, while residing in Prescott, Arizona, he and his wife, Betty, met Alfred and Betty Bailey. The two couples attempted to contact saucers and soon began receiving messages, through automatic writing and the ouija board, from visitors from Venus, Mars, Jupiter, Saturn, and Neptune. Then one message, from Zo of Neptune, informed them that they would be receiving Morse code signals on the radio. They were instructed to approach one of Bailey's coworkers, Lyman Streeter, who was a ham-radio operator. Soon Streeter, his wife, and the two other couples were hearing from extraterrestrials with colorful names: Zo, Affa, Um, and Regga. Further communications took place through radio and mental telepathy.

Through his reading, Williamson heard of George Adamski, a Californian who was producing pictures of alleged spacecraft. The two exchanged letters, and Adamski invited Williamson to visit him at his home in Palomar Gardens. In the presence of the Williamsons and the Baileys, Adamski channeled messages from space people. On November 20, alerted that a landing would occur, the two couples met with Adamski and

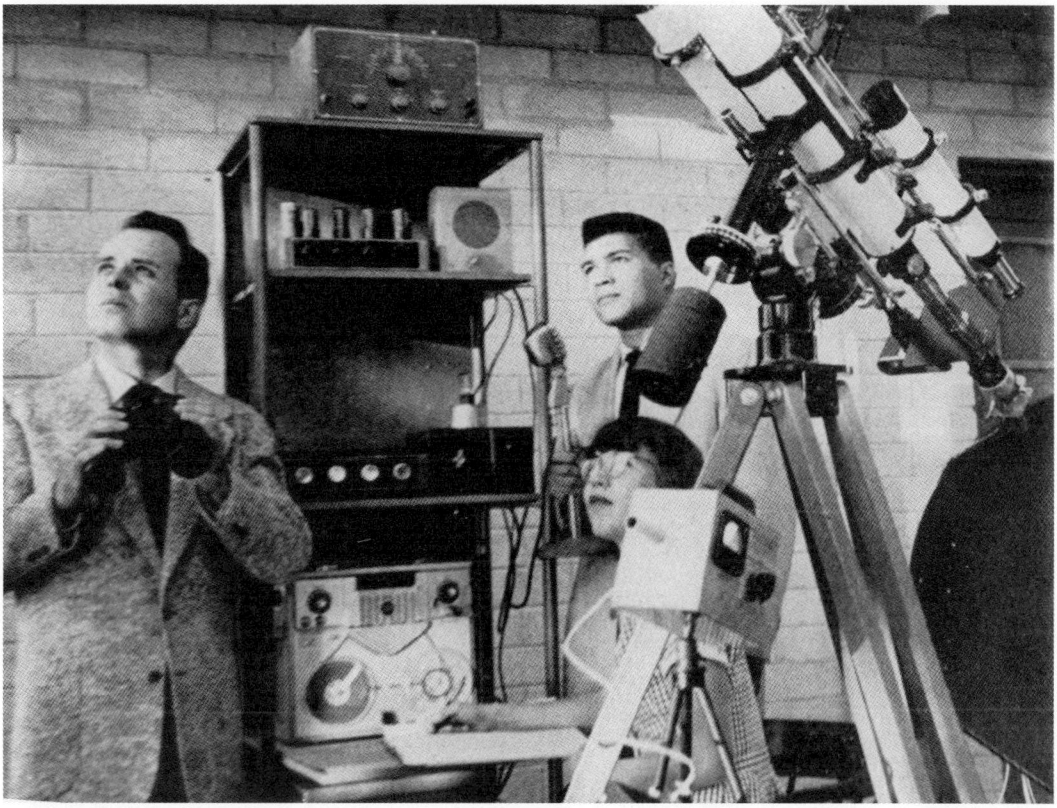

George Hunt Williamson (left), who received regular radio messages from extraterrestrials in the early 1950s (Fortean Picture Library)

two associates along the California-Arizona border. The other six would sign affidavits attesting to their observation (albeit from some distance) of Adamski's meeting with a spaceman. (Later the Baileys would withdraw their testimony, saying they had seen nothing out of the ordinary.)

Williamson went on to write a series of books both about his contacts and about his theories about the role space people have played in the human past and present. Such books as *Other Tongues—Other Flesh* (1953), *Secret Places of the Lion* (1958), and *Road in the Sky* (1959) anticipated themes that Erich von Däniken and others would popularize in the 1970s during the "ancient astronauts" craze. Williamson split with Adamski after the latter urged him not to publicize his psychic contacts, since Adamski decried such methods of communications to his followers, even while privately practicing them. But Williamson delved ever deeper into the occult and pursued his own attempts at space communication by various means. In 1955, he and Richard Miller formed the Telonic Research Center to establish radio and other contacts with extraterrestrials, though within months he and Miller parted amid much mutual recrimination.

The following year he joined up with the Brotherhood of the Seven Rays, a band of psychics and contactees (including Dorothy Martin, better known as Sister Thedra), and spent a year at its colony in a remote area of Peru, convinced that cataclysmic Earth changes were soon to occur. When they did not, Williamson and everyone except Martin returned to the United States. There Williamson resumed writing books, one of them a thinly disguised anti-Semitic work titled *UFOs Confidential!* (1958). In 1958, he went on a world tour and, in 1961, he lectured in Japan, where he was treated as something of a celebrity. His last book, which he wrote under the pseudonym "Brother Philip," was published the same year. Soon, however, Williamson—now calling himself Michel d'Obrenovic—retired from a public career and was so little heard from that many thought him dead.

During his heyday, critics accused Williamson of a range of shortcomings and base motivations, among them bigotry, paranoia, and charlatanism. His shrillest attackers, associated with James W. Moseley's *Saucer News,* debunked Williamson's assertions about his academic background (far from being a Ph.D., as he said he was, he did not have even an undergraduate degree), and one reviewer noted similarities between the supposedly nonfictional *Road in the Sky* and a science-fiction series by Isaac Asimov. After his death, however, scientist and UFO historian Michael D. Swords acquired the bulk of Williamson's collection, which includes a massive amount of private correspondence and other material. Based on his reading of it, Swords concludes that for all his exaggeration and credential-inflation, Williams was essentially honest. In his estimation Williamson "actually believed all the stuff—the wild, amazing, impossible-to-believe stuff—that he wrote about. . . . Williamson is not easy to explain and cannot be deposited into some conveniently labeled box" (Swords, 1993).

See Also: Adamski, George; Affa; Contactees; Sister Thedra

Further Reading

Brother Philip [pseud. of George Hunt Williamson], 1961. *Secret of the Andes.* Clarksburg, WV: Saucerian Books.

Griffin, John, 1989. *Visitants.* Santa Barbara, CA: self-published.

Ibn Aharon, Y. N. [pseud. of Yonah Fortner], 1960. Review of *Road in the Sky. Saucer News* 7, 2 (June): 6.

Leslie, Desmond, and George Adamski, 1953. *Flying Saucers Have Landed.* New York: British Book Centre.

Moseley, James W., and Michael G. Mann, 1959. "Screwing the Lid down on 'Doctor' Williamson." *Saucer News* 6, 2 (February/March): 3–5.

Swords, Michael D., 1993. "UFOs and the Amish." *International UFO Reporter* 18, 5 (September/October): 12–13.

Williamson, George Hunt, 1953. *Other Tongues—Other Flesh.* Amherst, WI: Amherst Press.

———, 1958. *Secret Places of the Lion.* Amherst, WI: Amherst Press.

———, 1959. *Road in the Sky.* London: Neville Spearman.

Williamson, George Hunt, and Alfred C. Bailey, 1954. *The Saucers Speak! A Documentary Report of Interstellar Communication by Radiotelegraphy.* Los Angeles: New Age Publishing Company.

Williamson, George Hunt, and John McCoy, 1958. *UFOs Confidential! The Meaning behind the Most Closely Guarded Secret of All Time.* Corpus Christi, TX: Essene Press.

Wilson

During the spring of 1897, American newspapers reported frequently outlandish accounts of mysterious "airships," dirigible- or cigar-shaped structures whose origins were (and still are) shrouded in mystery. Some people speculated that they housed Martian visitors, and indeed some spectacular hoaxes played to that belief. The more common theory, however, held that an enterprising American had invented advanced aircraft and was flying it around the country with a crew of aeronauts. Stories carried in the press reported meetings with the enigmatic inventor, though most were contradictory and dubious. Historians of aviation have ignored this episode, and today only ufologists have examined it carefully, holding that the airship scare was an early UFO wave. Among the more curious accounts to be published in the press of the period were a series of ostensibly related incidents, all but one of which occurred in Texas, involving an aeronaut identified as "Wilson."

Someone who may have been Wilson appears first in an alleged encounter near Greenville, Texas, late on the evening of April 16, according to a letter C. G. Williams published in the *Dallas Morning News* on the nineteenth. Williams reportedly saw an "immense cigar-shaped vessel" as he was taking a walk. Three crew members stepped outside, two to work on the structure, the third to chat with the witness. The stranger told Williams that he had built the ship after many years of experiment and error "at a little town in the interior of New York."

The May 16 issue of the same newspaper carried a letter forwarded by Dr. D. H. Tucker. Tucker said that a young man who subsequently drowned in a flood in Mississippi had written the original, recounting an experience that occurred on April 19 in the Lake Charles, Louisiana, area. While riding in his buggy, he spotted an airship approaching. A high-pitched whistle from the vessel spooked his horses, and he was thrown to the ground. When the ship landed, two men rushed from it to help him to his feet and to extend their apologies. One introduced himself as "Mr. Wilson," though the witness doubted that was his real name. Wilson stated that he and his companion, Scott Warren, had invented a fleet of ships. They were now seeking to demonstrate that long-distance airship travel was safe and economical. The young man was invited to tour the vehicle, where he met two other crew members.

That same day, at around 11 P.M., at Beaumont, Texas, according to an account published in the *Houston Daily Post* of April 21, lights in a neighbor's pasture caught the eyes of J. R. Ligon and his son Charley. They observed "four men moving around a large dark object" that they recognized, as they approached it, as an airship. Its crew asked for water and accompanied the two to the house, where they filled their buckets. "I accosted one of the men," the elder Ligon reported, "and he told me his name was Wilson. . . . They were returning from a trip out on the Gulf and were now headed toward Iowa, where the airship was built." It was one of five that had been constructed there. The Ligons accompanied them back to the ship, a huge structure 136 feet long and 20 feet wide, with four large wings and propellers attached to bow and stern. Wilson explained it was powered by "electricity."

On April 25 the *New Orleans Daily Picayune* carried an interview with a visitor, Rabbi A. Levy of Beaumont. Levi recalled that "about 10 days ago," on hearing that an airship had landed late that night on a farm just outside town, he hastened to the site. There sat an airship some 150 feet long with 100-foot wings. "I spoke to one of the men when he went into the farmer's house, and shook hands with him," Levy claimed. "Yes, I did hear him say where it was built, but I can't remember the name of the place, or the name of the inventor. He said that they had been traveling a great deal, and were testing the machine. I was do dumbfounded that I could not frame an intelligent question to ask." He did remember, though, that "electricity" powered the craft.

At Uvalde, three hundred miles southwest of Beaumont, twenty-three hours after the Ligons's alleged encounter, Sheriff H. W. Baylor witnessed an airship landing near his home. Baylor saw three crew members and spoke with one, a Mr. Wilson, a native of Goshen, New York. The aeronaut recalled an old friend, Captain C. C. Akers, whom he said he had known in Fort Worth. Now, he understood, Akers lived in the area. Baylor replied that he knew Akers, who was employed as a customs officer in Eagle Pass but who frequently visited Uvalde. After asking the sheriff to give his best to Akers, Wilson and his crew flew away. The *Houston Daily Post,* which reported the story in its April 21 issue, mentioned the sighting, the same night as Baylor's alleged encounter with Wilson, of an airship passing just north of the Baylor residence. Contacted by the *Galveston Daily News* (April 28), Akers confirmed that twenty years earlier he had known "a man by the name of Wilson from New York state. . . . He was of a mechanical turn of mind and was then working on aerial navigation and something that would astonish the world."

At midnight on April 22, east of Josserand (seventy-five miles northwest of Beaumont), a "whirring noise" awoke farmer Frank Nichols, according to the *Houston Daily Post* (April 26). On investigating, he spotted a large, brilliantly lighted airship in his cornfield. Two crew members asked if they could draw water from his well. Afterward, they invited him into the craft, which had a six- or eight-man crew. One told him that "highly condensed electricity" powered it. It was one of five built in a small Iowa town.

The following evening an airship landed at Kountze, twenty miles northwest of Beaumont. Onlookers talked with its pilots, Wilson and Jackson, who said it would take a few days to complete necessary repairs. The *Houston Daily Post* (April 25) assured readers that anyone who wanted to see the marvelous machine "may do so by coming to Kountze any time before Monday night." This is the one Wilson story that was an obvious practical joke.

On April 30, the *Daily Post* carried a letter from H. C. Legrone of Deadwood, 130 miles north of Beaumont. Legrone wrote that after something disturbed his horses on the evening of April 28, he stepped outside to observe an approaching airship. It descended on a nearby field. He related,

> Its crew was composed of five men, three of whom entertained me, while the other two took rubber bags and went for a supply of water at my well, 100 yards off. They informed me that this was one of five ships that had been traveling the country over recently, and that this individual ship was the same one recently landed near Beaumont . . . after having traveled pretty well all over the Northwest. They stated that these ships were put up in an interior town in Illinois. They were rather reticent about giving out information in regards to the ship, manufacture, etc., since they had not yet secured everything by patent.

Whatever the airships may or may not have been, they were nobody's inventions, and the name of the mysterious Mr. Wilson is not to be found in any history of aviation. Put bluntly, the stories make no sense. They could not have happened in any way in which the verb "happened" is ordinarily understood. In light of the numerous hoaxes, journalistic and other, the Wilson stories, however intriguing, must be viewed with a fair degree of suspicion. Nonetheless, occult-oriented writers such as John A. Keel argue that the seemingly normal American pilots reported in 1897 press accounts were actually supernatural entities—Keel calls them ultraterrestrials—in disguise. According to Keel, the ultraterrestrials staged encounters "in relatively remote places," contacting a few witnesses and passing on bogus tales "which would discredit not only them but the whole mystery. Knowing how we think and how we search for consistencies, the ultraterrestrials were careful to sow inconsistencies in their wake" (Keel, 1970).

See Also: Keel, John Alva; Smith; Ultraterrestrials

Further Reading

Bullard, Thomas E., ed., 1982. *The Airship File: A Collection of Texts Concerning Phantom Airships and Other UFOs, Gathered from Newspapers and Periodicals Mostly during the Hundred Years Prior to Kenneth Arnold's Sighting.* Bloomington, IN: self-published.

Chariton, Wallace O., 1991. *The Great Texas Airship Mystery.* Plano, TX: Wordware Publishing.

Cohen, Daniel, 1981. *The Great Airship Mystery: A UFO of the 1890s.* New York: Dodd, Mead, and Company.

Keel, John A., 1970. *UFOs: Operation Trojan Horse.* New York: G. P. Putnam's Sons.

X

Xeno

In the early morning hours of January 30, 1965, while walking along a beach near Watsonville, California, Sid Padrick saw a flying saucer descend and hover a foot or two above the sand. A voice speaking from the craft assured him that he was not in danger. When a door opened, Padrick entered and soon met a human-looking figure in a two-piece uniform. The figure, speaking in unaccented English, introduced himself as Xeno. He took Padrick on a tour of the craft, during which he saw eight other crew members, one a "very pretty" young woman. They paid little attention to Padrick, and all his communication was with Xeno.

Xeno and his companions were light-skinned and resembled human beings except for unusually sharp chins and noses. Xeno explained that the ship and its crew came from a planet behind a planet visible from Earth. Their own planet, however, was always hidden from earthly view. They lived in a communal society without war, disease, or crime. They also had a religion that worshipped the Supreme Deity. During the tour Padrick was shown a "consultation room" used for worship and invited to go inside. After he prayed there, Padrick experienced a kind of religious awakening.

During their interaction, he noticed that whenever he would ask Xeno a question, Xeno would hesitate for as long as half a minute before answering. Patrick speculated that he was getting telepathic instructions on how to reply. He was shown a photograph of a city on Xeno's planet. Through a telescopelike device he observed a cigar-shaped mother ship which had brought the smaller craft through space.

Padrick was told that Xeno's people were here only to explore. They had no desire for contact because of earthlings' hostility and generally primitive attitudes. After about two hours, Padrick left the craft with a promise that he would meet the space people again soon.

On February 4, Padrick informed Hamilton Air Force Base of his experience. A U.S. Air Force officer, Major D. B. Reeder, interviewed him four days later, and the two went to the encounter site. Though the officer interviewed several locals who said Padrick was trustworthy, the officer did not believe his testimony and urged Project Blue Book, the U.S. Air Force's UFO-investigative group, to take no further action.

Nonetheless, after seeing the story in a San Francisco newspaper, L. D. Cody, the civilian director of aerospace education at Hamilton, requested a full briefing from Reeder. Later that month, Cody personally interviewed Padrick and his family. In his estimation Padrick "seemed sincere." He thought Padrick had either had the experience or dreamed it (Cody, 1967).

After accounts of Padrick's alleged experience were published in the press, he was besieged by letters and calls from UFO buffs. One pointed out that "Xeno"—heretofore Padrick had spelled the name phonetically as "Zeno"—is Greek for "stranger."

Following the initial publicity, Padrick did a few lectures and spoke at several contactee conferences, sticking to his basic story without elaboration, but then dropped out of sight. In 1970, local newspapers reported that a friend was suing Padrick, who had borrowed one thousand dollars to write a book detailing his experience but had not repaid it or even been able to produce evidence that a manuscript existed. Padrick insisted that a third person had borrowed the manuscript and never returned it. The San Jose Municipal Court decreed that Padrick had to make good on the loan.

From some accounts Padrick had further alien contacts after the January 1965 incident, but he has never spoken about them in public.

See Also: Contactees

Further Reading

Cody, L. D., 1967. Letter to James E. McDonald (August 25).

"Contactee Loses Court Case," 1971. *UFO Investigator* (April): 1.

"The Padrick 'Space Contact,'" 1965. *Little Listening Post* 12, 3 (August/September/October): 2–5.

"Watsonville's Weird Story—A Ride on a Spaceship," 1965. *San Francisco News Call Bulletin* (February 12).

Y

Yada di Shi'ite

Yada di Shi'ite lived five-hundred thousand years ago, a member of the ancient civilization of Yu, located in the Himalayas, or so he told San Diego medium Mark Probert, through whom he channeled from the 1940s until Probert's death in 1969. Yada di Shi'ite was one of several entities who composed the Inner Circle.

Probert, a man with little formal education, entered the metaphysical realm when he started talking in his sleep. His wife, Irene, took note of what he was saying. Soon the episode became known to a local man, veteran occultist N. Meade Layne. Layne took over Probert's spiritual education, and soon Yada di Shi'ite and others were speaking through the medium. The others included Ramon Natalli, in life a lawyer and a friend of Galileo; Professor Alfred Luntz, a nineteenth-century Anglican clergyman; and Charles Lingford, in life a dancer and artist.

Through Probert's Inner Circle Kethra E'Da Foundation and Layne's better-known Borderland Sciences Research Associates, the channelings of Yada di Shi'ite and associates—eventually their number expanded to eleven—found an international audience. In the early age of flying saucers, the late 1940s and early 1950s, the Circle's pronouncements on the subject were particularly influential, and they founded the basis of Layne's *The Ether Ship and Its Solution* (1950), which was widely read in fringe circles and is still an influence on latter-day occult saucer theorists such as John A. Keel.

See Also: Channeling; Keel, John Alva

Further Reading

Barker, Gray, 1956. *They Knew Too Much about Flying Saucers.* New York: University Books.

Layne, N. Meade, *The Ether Ship and Its Solution.* Vista, CA: Borderland Sciences Research Associates.

Yamski

On April 24, 1965, just a day after the death of George Adamski, a flying saucer allegedly landed near the Devonshire village of Scoriton. Three humanlike beings clad in spacesuits emerged. One, who looked like a youth of thirteen or fourteen, identified himself as "Yamski" to the sole witness, a groundskeeper and handyman named Ernest Arthur Bryant. Yamski, who spoke in Eastern European–inflected English, expressed the wish that "Des" or "Les" could be there. Bryant was given a brief tour of the craft and a promise of further contacts.

Some of Adamski's partisans had been expecting him to reincarnate and return to

Earth. In fact, his associate and onetime co-author Desmond Leslie openly predicted it in an obituary he wrote for England's *Flying Saucer Review.* Bryant, who claimed never to have heard of this famous contactee, produced a sketch of Yamski, who bore some resemblance to a youthful Adamski. Subsequently, Bryant brought forth physical evidence that he said the space people had given him.

In 1967, Eileen Buckle, who had investigated the case, wrote about it in a thick book that essentially endorsed the case, notwithstanding growing evidence that Bryant had a hard time telling the truth even about the most mundane aspects of his life. Bryant died just after Buckle's book was published. British ufologist Norman Oliver, who interviewed Bryant's wife around that time, was told that Bryant's story was bogus. He had based it on his considerable reading of UFO and occult literature and his extensive knowledge of Adamski's claims. Oliver exposed the many dubious elements of the case in a self-published monograph.

See Also: Adamski, George; Contactees

Further Reading

Buckle, Eileen, 1967. *The Scoriton Mystery.* London: Neville Spearman.

Leslie, Desmond, 1965. "Obituary: George Adamski." *Flying Saucer Review* 11, 4 (July/August): 18–19.

Oliver, Norman, 1968. *Sequel to Scoriton.* London: self-published.

Y'hova

According to the "extraterrestrialism" theories of Yonah Fortner (who wrote under the pseudonym Y. N. ibn Aharon), visitors from other worlds landed on Earth and interacted with its most advanced ancient civilizations, notably those of the Chaldeans and the Atlanteans. The Chaldeans, who possessed an advanced technology, were especially close to aliens, even intermarrying with one group, the Elohim. Another group was the Titans, who helped the Chaldeans vanquish the malevolent alien race known as the Serpent People. Eventually, warfare among alien races broke out on the Earth's surface. In the midst of this conflict, one alien showed up around 1340 B.C. Shaday Elili Athunu, otherwise known as Y'hova, befriended a local malcontent named Abraham, whom he promised to protect if he, his family, and his people followed him. Y'hova is known to humans as God.

Fortner stated that the "God of Israel should not be confused with the general run of space visitors because he was either unique or very nearly unique in his decision to make a career among the people of earth. . . . [He] is a very august and ancient being . . . who comes from a higher order of being, a dimension beyond all known dimensions" (Steinberg, 1977).

Fortner outlined his theories in a series of articles published in *Saucer News* between 1957 and 1960. His sources, he insisted, were rare and arcane Middle Eastern documents, but when challenged, he was unable to prove that they existed.

Further Reading

Ibn Aharon, Y. N. [pseud. of Yonah Fortner], 1960. "A Note on the Evolution of Extraterrestrialism." *Saucer News* 7, 4 (December): 6–9.

Steinberg, Gene, 1977. "Dr. Yonah Aharon—Originator of the Ancient Astronaut Theory." *UFO Report* 4, 2 (June): 26–27, 74–78.

Z

Zagga

Zagga hails from the planet Zakton at the far side of the Milky Way galaxy. Zakton is some seventy-five thousand light years beyond Gemini. One of the twelve members of the Galactic Council, he was sent to Saturn. From there he transited to Earth, entering the body of a boy at the instant of birth. Zagga claims that on his home planet children are conceived not by sexual intercourse but by pure thought. People do not have names. He was given the appellation "Zagga" only after he volunteered for the Earth mission. In letters to saucerian writer John W. Dean, Zagga attested to the authenticity of George Adamski's claim to have attended an interplanetary conference on Saturn in March 1962.

According to Dean, Zagga was "a fine looking young man of about twenty-five years of age" in 1961 when Dean met him at Buck Nelson's contactee convention in Missouri. Zagga told Dean, "I had known the one you call Jesus before and after his incarnation on earth. I know Him as a great friend" (Dean, 1964). Dean said he knew Zagga's earthly name and address but was not to reveal them.

See Also: Adamski, George; Contactees

Further Reading

Dean, John W., 1964. *Flying Saucers and the Scriptures.* New York: Vantage Press.

Zandark

In the fall of 1973, an anonymous woman received psychic communications from Zandark, a "member of the United Cosmic Council; a Commander in Chief in Charge of Directing Technical Transmissions Via Mental Telepathy of the Combination of Mediumistic Telepathy under the Direction of the Confederation of Cosmic Space Beings" (Keel, 1975). Zandark's people are here to bring peace, and they have been here a long time. They built the Sphinx, the pyramids, and other classic ancient structures.

Further Reading

Keel, John A., 1975. *The Mothman Prophecies.* New York: Saturday Review Press/E. P. Dutton and Company.

Zolton

In a registered letter sent to U.S. Air Force Intelligence on November 20, 1953, an unidentified woman mailed a recently channeled message from an Ashtar associate named Zolton, "Commander from the center of the Sector System of Vela." Zolton sought to alert the authorities in Washington to the space people's purpose.

He warned the Pentagon that visiting extraterrestrials knew of "destructive plans formulated for offensive and defensive war" and were prepared to stop them by crippling earthly weapons technology without hurting any person or thing. The visitors would not hesitate, however, to "control minds . . . in order to secure this solar system. This is a friendly warning" (Wilkins, 1955).

See Also: Ashtar

Further Reading

Wilkins, Harold T., 1955. *Flying Saucers Uncensored.* New York: Citadel Press.

Index